SQL-3
Implementing the
Object-Relational Database

McGraw-Hill Enterprise Computing Series

SQL-3: Implementing the Object-Relational Database by Fortier
ISBN 0-07-022062-X

DB2 Universal Database Developer's Guide for Call-Level Interface by Sanders
ISBN 0-07-134572-8

Enterprise Java Developer's Guide by Narayan/Liu
ISBN 0-07-134673-2

Web Warehousing and Knowledge Management by Mattison
ISBN 0-07-0041103-4

ODBC 3.5 Developer's Guide by Sanders
ISBN 0-07-058087-1

Data Warehousing, Data Mining & OLAP by Berson/Smith
ISBN 0-07-006272-2

Data Stores, Data Warehousing, and the Zachman Framework by Inman
ISBN 0-07-031429-2

SQL-3
Implementing the Object-Relational Database

Dr. Paul J. Fortier

McGraw-Hill
New York • San Francisco • Washington, D.C. • Auckland • Bogotá
Caracas • Lisbon • London • Madrid • Mexico City • Milan
Montreal • New Delhi • San Juan • Singapore
Sydney • Tokyo • Toronto

McGraw-Hill

A Division of The McGraw·Hill Companies

1 2 3 4 5 6 7 8 9 0 DOC/DOC 9 0 4 3 2 1 0 9

ISBN 0-07-022062-X

The sponsoring editor for this book was Simon Yates, the editing supervisor was Alan Rose, and the production supervisor was Clare Stanley. It was set in Vendome by Multiscience Press, Inc.

Printed and bound by R. R. Donnelley & Sons Company.

 This book is printed on recycled, acid-free paper containing a minimum of 50% recycled de-inked fiber.

CONTENTS

Contents

PREFACE

The SQL relational database language is enjoying great success as a national and international standard for the definition and manipulation of relational databases. The SQL language was initially standardized by the American National Standards Institute (ANSI) in 1986 and adopted as an international standard in 1987 by the International Organization for Standardization (ISO). The SQL language has experienced a few revisions since 1986, which improved and matured the language's features. The first revision, released in 1989, provided features for referential integrity and generalized integrity constraints, as well as cleaning up some minor language deficiencies. This first revision of SQL was followed by a second, more encompassing revision in 1992, which enhanced the data manipulation, schema manipulation, and data definition features of SQL and has been referred to as SQL-2 or SQL-92.

Follow-on efforts by the SQL national and international language standards bodies focused on wide-sweeping changes to the data model, including providing object-oriented features, multimedia data types, temporal data types and manipulation, persistent stored modules, a standard call-level interface, remote data access, a computationally complete language facility, and transactional facilities. The focus of SQL-3 language development falls within the domain of the ISO database languages rapporteur group. ANSI is a member of the NCITS database language committee. This group has championed the development of the evolving SQL-3 object-relational database language.

The ANSI NCITS database language development process is an open process, oriented toward achieving a consensus on all language features. The committee operates by developing base standards documents and then issues change proposals, which alter or repair the base documents to the majority of the members' satisfaction. The database language standards process goes through many stages before an acceptable standard is realized. A new standard begins as a working draft (WD), which is refined until the committee feels it is near completion. The document then is transformed into a committee draft (CD) standard, which is released to the open world community for review and comment resolution. Once the CD is refined and corrected, it is released as a draft international standard (DIS) and ultimately an international standard (IS).

The ANSI NCITS database language committee embarked on a major revision of the relational SQL-2 database language in 1991. Efforts focused on evolving the SQL database language into a computationally complete language supporting the combined relational and object model paradigms. The resulting data model has been referred to as the extended relational data model, or the object-relational data model. This new data model and database language, referred to as SQL-3, includes features for specifying abstract data types, object identifiers, object methods, inheritance, polymorphism, encapsulation, and most other features found in object-oriented databases. This model and language, however, are not complete but are still evolving, with the expectation of a preliminary standard being released in 1999. The SQL-3 standard consists of eight parts: Part 1, SQL Framework; Part 2, SQL Foundation; Part 3, SQL CLI; Part 4, SQL PSM; Part 5, SQL Bindings; Part 6, SQL Transactions; Part 7, SQL Temporal; and Part 8, SQL Object. Many of SQL-3's language components are envisioned to become national standards beginning in the 1999 time frame with international standards following within a year after U.S. standardization.

Features of the Book

This book focuses on describing many of the essential features of the SQL-3 object-relational database model, its language specification, and semantics of use. Included in this description is an overview of the eight parts comprising the SQL-3 database language. The introduction to SQL-3's foundation introduces readers to the most sweeping changes to the SQL database language since its inception as a standard in 1986. The SQL database language has become synonymous with databases, database users, and database applications developers and will continue to be well into the next century, supported by the changes being made today. The SQL-3 database language moves the original relational model from rigid adherence to first normal form relational structuring, and relational calculus manipulations within embedded host languages, to more flexible tables with embedded row types and abstract data types—all within a computationally complete language. This book describes the essential features of the new SQL language in a manner useful to students, users, and database applications developers.

- It introduces the new object-relational language in a simple-to-understand fashion.

- It condenses the eight parts of the new SQL language into concise overviews.
- It provides a detailed presentation of the new system and envisioned extensions.
- It provides coverage of new language features beneficial to database design and data manipulation.
- It provides a presentation of extended features, such as triggers and persistent stored modules, along with their use.

This book directly covers the concept of combining the object and relational database models into a unified database model. It addresses the important market enhancement feature of persistent stored modules and call-level interface, which will allow third-party vendors to develop and supply application-specific add-ons for increased database functionality. Triggers, a new concept requested by users to enhance a database's functionality, are discussed, as is condition handling. Both these features allow applications developers to make database management systems more responsive to users' requirements.

This book is aimed at database users, database designers, database applications programmers, and database managers working in a variety of business domains, who need to understand how to get the most value out of their database system. In addition, it provides assistance to those who wish to understand the design, applications development, and use of the new SQL-3 object-relational database language. This book provides a comprehensive overview of the complexities and features of the new SQL-3 language.

ACKNOWLEDGMENTS

This book would not have been possible if not for the contributions of many individuals who were and still are involved in the development of the SQL database language standard—in particular, the ANSI NCITS database language committee members who worked on this language for seven years from the time of its inception, after SQL-92's release, up to the release of the new language during 1999. Without the insight gained from many of these individuals this book would not have been possible.

A second note of thanks goes to two graduate students, Vijay Kumar Bommireddipalli and Rahul Mutha, who contributed Chapter 13, which examines some present products and the degree to which they meet some of the new database language features.

Special thanks go to the staff of Intertext Publications, specifically Dr. Alan Rose, for support in seeing this project to completion and making the final production as painless as possible.

Finally, I wish to thank my wife Kathleen, always an inspiration and supporter, and my three children, Daniel, Brian, and Nicole, for their assistance and support during the writing and production of this book.

CHAPTER 1

Introduction

The SQL database language is experiencing great success as a national and international standard for the definition and manipulation of relational databases. SQL was initially standardized by ANSI in 1986 and adopted as a standard in 1987 by the International Organization for Standardization (ISO). The SQL database language provided features for defining relations (tables) and manipulating tables based on relational calculus and algebra concepts. SQL has experienced a few revisions since 1986, which have improved and matured the basic features. The first revision was released in 1989 and provided features for referential integrity and generalized integrity constraints. Minor language deficiencies were cleaned up as well. This first revision of SQL was followed by a second, more encompassing revision in 1992. The second revision enhanced the data manipulation, schema manipulation, and data definition features of SQL and is referred to as SQL-2.

Present efforts by the SQL national and international standards organizations—while maintaining compatibility with the existing standard SQL language—are focusing on wide-sweeping changes to the model to provide object-oriented features, multimedia data types, temporal data types, persistent stored modules, call-level interface, remote data access, a computationally complete language facility, transactional interface to X-open, and, potentially, real-time support into the SQL standard language. Extensions include abstract data types, object identifiers, inheritance, polymorphism, and the majority of features found within object data management systems—all within a relational paradigm framework.

Databases are being applied to more complex information-processing applications as the popularity of these applications has increased. Such applications typically exceed the capabilities of conventional relational database management systems. Complex applications, such as document management, digital video, graphics, specific data types, audio, images, and geographical data, do not lend themselves to be modeled and operated upon within conventional relational database systems.

Complex applications such as these drove the initial research and development of object-oriented database systems. Initially, these applications required extending the basic database system services to support storage and retrieval of nonstandard data types, such as video, graphics, and so on, but eventually they evolved into more complete models, where data storage and data processing merged. The result was object-oriented database system products integrated with object-oriented programming languages.

The needs of advanced applications dictated the move toward computationally complete database management systems and languages. Databases could not simply provide access to complex stored data alone. Applications demanded that databases provide application-specific manipulation of application-defined data types. Stored data objects need to map one to one with application data types, if database management systems were to be useful within these application domains.

To meet the demands of this large, new volume of applications, the ISO's Joint Task Committee (JTC1), Subcommittee 21 (SC21) (Figure 1.1), formed a variety of working groups aimed at addressing the demands and other issues related to information retrieval, transfer, and management. JTC1/SC21 has a number of working groups. Among the groups are Working Group 3 (WG3), Database, and the database rapporteur groups within WG3. WG3 has rapporteur groups for database languages, remote database access, SQL multimedia, information resource dictionary system, reference model of data management, conceptual schema modeling facility, and the export/import groups. The focus of SQL-3 falls within the domain of the database languages rapporteur group. Eleven countries are participating in the language development at the international level. A member of this international group is the American National Standards Institute (ANSI) X3H2 database language committee. This ANSI committee is composed of a mixture of vendors and user and academic organizations, which have voting rights. As of this writing the committee has 28 voting members and a number of others participating under nonvoting status. This group of volunteers has championed the development of the evolving SQL-3 object-relational database language.

The goal of the ISO and ANSI database standards activities is to develop a database language standard to allow database applications to run on database management systems seamlessly. However, within this context, vendors are allowed to implement extensions, and may have features that are left as implementation defined. Users and vendors, if operating within the defined and validated features of the language, will be able to move applications seamlessly from one platform or product to another.

The ANSI X3H2 database language development process is an open process, oriented toward achieving a consensus on all language features. The committee operates by developing base standards documents, and then issues change proposals that alter or repair the base documents to the majority of members' satisfaction. The standards process goes

Figure 1.1

National and
international
standards body
structure.

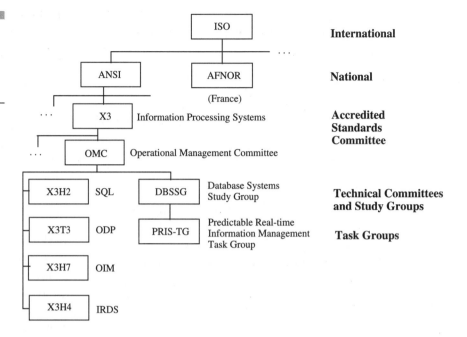

through many stages before an acceptable standard is realized. A new standard begins as a committee working draft (WD) and is refined until the standards committee feels it is near completion. The working draft is then transformed or elevated into a committee draft (CD), which is released to the world community for review and comment resolution. Once the CD is refined and corrected based on injected comments, it is released as a draft international standard (DIS) and ultimately as an international standard (IS).

The ANSI X3H2 database language committee has embarked on a major revision of the relational SQL-2 database language. In 1991, X3H2 began efforts to evolve SQL into a computationally complete language supporting the relational and object model paradigms for data management. The resulting data model is referred to as the extended relational data model, or the relational/object data model. This new data model and language, referred to as SQL-3, include constructs for specifying abstract data types, object identifiers, object methods, inheritance, polymorphism, encapsulation, and most other features associated with object-oriented databases, as well as the fundamental table of its relational predecessor. This model and language, however, have not been completed; they are still evolving, with the expectation that a preliminary standard will be released in mid to late 1999. The SQL-3 standard consists of eight parts:

1. Framework
2. Foundation
3. Call-level interface (CLI)
4. Persistent stored modules (PSM)
5. Bindings
6. Transactions
7. Temporal
8. Object

The SQL-3 committee efforts are envisioned to become national standards in the 1999–2000 time frame, and international standards within a year after U.S. standardization. Early progression into the concept development phase is anticipated by later this year on all but Part 6, SQL Transactions.

This book describes the essential features of the SQL-3 database model and its support specifications. The description includes an overview of the eight parts of SQL-3. This chapter introduces the relational object model in the context of existing database models and discusses this model's place in relation to other database language standardization activities.

Chapter 2 examines the basis for SQL-3 as it has been formulated by SQL-2. The topic is covered at a high level; readers interested in more details on the SQL-2 language can refer to the bibliography.

Chapter 3 introduces SQL-3 and its parts. The discussion is also at a high level and meant to introduce readers to the concepts of the different parts of SQL-3. This overview of SQL-3 includes an introduction to the language, a review of major features of the language's foundation, and an overview of the call-level interface, persistent stored modules, language bindings, the transactional interface, temporal data and transactions, and pure object extensions, as well as future areas of interest.

Chapter 4 starts a detailed examination of the new language features, first by introducing the relational object model from a high level and then by examining the basic database structures and supported data types. Basic features are then extended by examining the SQL-3 type system extensions compared with SQL-2. These extensions include Boolean, large binary objects, large character objects, the row type, abstract data type specification, and the constructor types. The chapter progresses to examine the abstract data type and its place and role in the new language.

Chapter 5 examines abstract data types in isolation from any other data types supported within the language. The chapter presents abstract data type specification, construction, and use.

Chapter 6 expands on the abstract data type definition, examining its use in database applications. This chapter in particular examines how the abstract data type is merged into and operated on by the fundamental relational database operations.

Abstract data types further enhance the language and are described in Chapter 7. Abstract data type subtyping, inheritance, substitutability, type checking, and abstract data type functions are addressed. Abstract data type functions have unique structures and meaning within a relational paradigm. The scope of abstract data type function operations and their binding to abstract data type instances are covered. The chapter concludes with the cast function as applied to abstract data types.

Chapter 8 addresses the need for abstract data types and advanced applications for stored operations and persistence. Databases traditionally stored data only, but with the advent of abstract data types, operations were also required to be stored. This chapter looks at how abstract data types alter the traditional relational model of table persistence through the need to persistently store abstract data types with embedded operations.

Chapter 9 introduces a new and controversial portion of the SQL-3 database model, the collection type. Collections are important to the relational object model to support efficient query processing and advanced schema structures. The chapter introduces the various collection types proposed for SQL-3 and how these types can be manipulated within SQL-3 expressions. Chapter 9 expands on the collection type by focusing specifically on SQL-3 collection type manipulation. SQL-3 collections must support the basic relational operations as well as extended abstract data type operations. To provide these features, the collection can be transformed into fundamental data structures, returned as the result of a query, and constructed through extractions from other relational object structures.

Chapter 10 introduces a second major addition to the SQL database languages, the trigger. Triggers provide the applications designers with the capability to detect and act on a variety of predefined events within the database system. Triggers can be used to signal other transactions when a data value has changed or when a transaction has completed.

Trigger definition, events, operation, and SQL statement structure are described.

Chapter 11 describes some initial aspects of the SQL-3 persistent stored module extension. This capability allows SQL users to create their own reusable modules or use other third-party vendor capabilities in building their applications. SQL-3 procedures provide full computational capabilities, alleviating the need for host languages to support database activities. Procedures can be used within client/server applications or within conventional applications.

Chapter 12 examines added language features. Concepts for statement recursion, roles, savepoints, added predicates, referential integrity rules, and transactions are presented. These additions provide features that enhance the usability and applicability of the language to a wider range of applications.

Chapter 13 describes the concepts, structure, and operations of this concept in relation to existing early releases by vendors.

Database Systems and Language Evolution

Database systems have been of interest to computer system applications developers as long as computers have been in commercial existence. Early computer systems lacked extensive data storage (primary memory as well as secondary storage), forcing them to rely heavily on externally archived information. Data storage repositories initially were simple file systems, where data needed for an application could be persistently stored for future retrieval and use. File systems offered a means to store and retrieve information using coarse semantic means. One could open a file, read a file, read a record, write a file or record, and close a file. Information had no meaning to the file system other than as an index to an entry point in a file delineating some user-defined semantics. File systems and their crude access schemes served the needs of early mainframe machines, where jobs were run in a sequence, and no sharing between jobs was explicitly required at run time.

The advent of multiuser operating systems and concurrent access to file systems spawned the need for database management systems. Multiprocessing and multiuser systems demanded that stored information in files be available for sharing. In addition, this information was not only to be shared, but also shared dynamically. Information storage, access, and retrieval—within such evolving systems—needed more controls so that information could be shared and remain correct.

One issue with new information requirements was security—how do you allow only the owner, or group of users, to access or alter a file. In line with this issue was access integrity—how to keep data intact and correct while multiple users access, modify, add, or delete information. Initially, file systems addressed this concern by adding access controls, such as locks, and access lists to file managers to allow only one user at a time to access data in a file. Though this was an admirable enhancement, it was far too crude to allow applications true sharing of online data. Files needed to be further decomposed into finer elements if higher concurrency was to be allowed. File-level locking resulted in longer waits on locks and reduced availability of data for use by other applications.

To alleviate the first problem, file systems added finer-grained definition of stored information. For example, files went from unstructured data to structured, record-oriented collections, where each record had a specific head and tail—as well as semantic meaning—to the file system organization. At first, this semantic meaning may have simply been order of occurrence in a file (a list structure). Semantics dealing with structure led to added organization by using records as definitions of stored information and a record's definition as an entry pointer into the file. Through such means, access control through locking and sharing could be brought down to the record level, or some level of structure between the file and a simple record.

It was only a matter of time before records took on further semantic meaning and were used as a means for organizing related information. For example, to define a group of students, a set of records could be defined such that each record held the information needed to define a single student. To organize the students in a way that the application can use them, a file system could allocate one region of a file for these records, or could provide a means to link related records in a chain.

This structural concept led to the first database system storage concept and access scheme, referred to as the *network database model*. The network database model organizes data as linked lists or chains of related information (Figure 1.2). Any information that has a relationship to some other piece of stored information must have a physical link to the related pieces of information. The network model was formalized into the CODASYL database standard and was immortalized by early implementations such as the IMS system. Network database systems became

Figure 1.2

Network database
model.

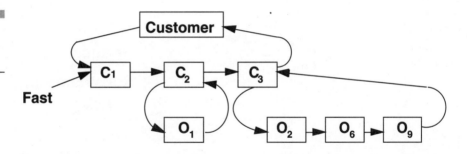

the mainstay of most information systems until the advent of the relational model in the 1970s. The network database model began to lose its luster in the late 1970s and early 1980s due to its inherent limitations. Networks of information required extensive added meta information to maintain links (pointers) to related database information. The loss of a single link in a chain could cause the database to become unusable due to the inability to access data past the lost link. Another drawback of network models and their derived databases was the complexity of the links. All data were organized as entry points into the database and as chains of chains to managed informational semantics. The complexity of information alone made these databases extremely difficult to maintain and utilize. Another detriment to this data model is encountered when you attempt to access stored information. To access data, you must enter the database at a defined database entry point and then follow stored relationship chains until either the information you want is discovered, or you encounter an end point or return point.

These and other limitations with the network database model led to the gradual demise of the model. An issue to consider briefly is the legacy this model left behind. Due to its early entry into computer-based information systems, much stored information was encoded in the network database form. It is unlikely that all this information will be rehosted within new data models, and therefore it must be understood from a legacy system's perspective. At some point in your career you will need to address an interface with or rehosting of such a repository.

What Is a Database?

Before a database management system language interface can be defined, you need to understand the basic elements of a database system.

Figure 1.3
Database
components.

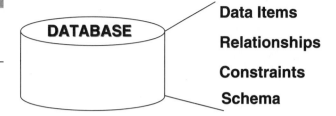

Figure 1.3
Database
components.

A database system consists of three major components: the database or data storage repository, the database management system control software, and the language interface.

The database or storage repository consists of four main elements: data items, relationships, constraints, and a schema (Figure 1.3). Real-world information is represented as data stored in binary computer formats. Data relationships represent a correspondence among data items. Database constraints are predicates that define correct and consistent database states. The database schema describes the organization of data and relationships in the database.

The database schema defines various views of the database used for assisting in database manipulation, database management, and applica-

Figure 1.4
Database schema
concept.

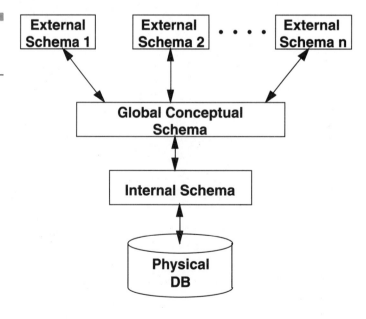

Figure 1.5

Services of a
database
management
system.

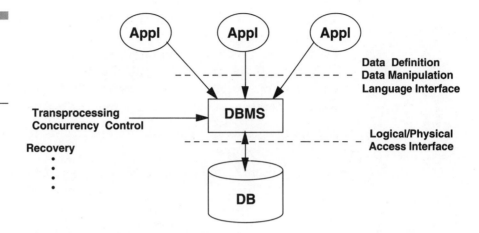

tions security. A schema separates the physical aspects of data storage from the logical aspects of data representation (Figure 1.4). The internal schema defines how data are physically organized and where in physical data storage these data reside. The conceptual schema defines the stored data structures in terms of the database data model (e.g., the relational or object model). The external schema defines views of the database for particular user(s). A database schema data model is an abstract definition of the database and provides a notation for describing data.

A database management system provides services for accessing, manipulating, and altering the database while maintaining required correctness and consistency features of the stored information (Figure 1.5).

The transaction is the unit of computational work in a database management system where consistency and correctness are defined. A transaction is required to support the *ACID* properties (atomic, consistent, isolation, durability) of transaction execution. Atomicity ensures that a transaction is treated as an all-or-nothing unit of operation. Consistency of transaction operations ensures correctness of transformation of the database from an initial consistent state to a new consistent state, where the consistency is defined by predicates on data items defined over the database. Isolation is the property of transactions defining what allowable database state is viewable. An isolated transaction sees a view of the database as if the transaction were performed alone on the database. Finally, durability is the property of transactions ensuring that once a transaction is committed, its results are permanent and cannot be removed from the database.

Features of Data in a Database

Databases are different from simple file systems and stored program data, because of the properties applied to the data and how these properties affect operations on database-controlled information. Data stored within a database are required to support the following:

1. *Sharing.* Data in a database are shared among several users and application programs.

2. *Persistence.* Data in a database exist permanently (Ullman and Widom 1997). A data item in a database exists beyond the scope of the process that created it (Zdonik 1990).

3. *Security.* Data stored within a database are protected from unauthorized disclosure, alteration, or destruction (Date 1990).

4. *Validity.* Also referred to as data *integrity* or *correctness.* Data in a database should be correct with respect to the real-world entity that they represent.

5. *Consistency.* Whenever more than one data item in a database represents related real-world values, the database-stored values should be consistent with respect to the defined relationship.

6. *Nonredundancy.* No two data items in a database should represent the same real-world entity.

7. *Independence.* The three levels in the three-schema model should be independent of each other so that changes in the schema at one level should not affect either of the other two levels. *Physical data independence* implies that the internal schema can be changed without altering the conceptual or external schema. Therefore, programs that access these data are independent of *how* and *where* these data are stored (Vasta 1985). Implying a change in the physical storage of the database should have no effect on any application programs that access those data. *Logical data independence* indicates that modifications to the conceptual schema require no change (or possibly only a redefinition of the mapping) to the external schema. Of course, if the modification involved is a deletion of a data item (at any level), then the other levels are affected, but this can be controlled (Ullman and Widom 1997).

What Is a Database Management System?

A database management system (DBMS) (Figure 1.6) is composed of a collection of software elements, which provide services for accessing, manipulating, or altering a database while maintaining the desirable features of the data as previously defined. A database management system provides functions that support application program access and manipulation of data to guarantee that the defined properties of data in the database are met. A summary of the most important components and their functions within a database management system is given in the following sections.

Figure 1.6

Database system management components.

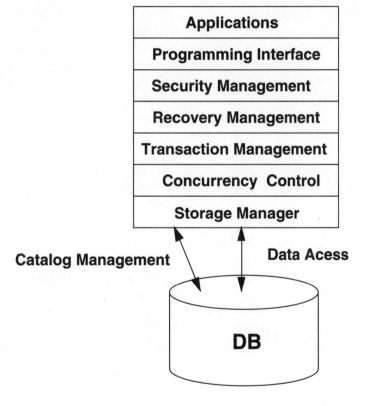

Transaction Processing

A *transaction* is a partially ordered sequence of *database operations* that represents a logical unit of work and accesses a shared database. A transaction transforms a database from one consistent state to another consistent state. Database operations fall into two categories: data access operations and transaction operations. There are three specific transaction operations:

1. *Begin* indicates that a new transaction is about to start.
2. *Commit* indicates that the transaction has terminated normally and that its effects should be made permanent.
3. *Abort* indicates that the transaction has terminated abnormally and that all of its effects should be obliterated.

Transactions are required to have the *ACID* properties. A *schedule* or *history* indicates the partial order in which the operations of one or more transactions are executed relative to each other.

Transaction processing involves applying transaction operations coming from various sources (users, application programs, etc.) to the database in such a way that the properties of the transactions are maintained. As a part of transaction processing, access to resources, such as the CPU and data items, is scheduled to meet the requirements of the transactions. The next two services, concurrency control and recovery, are closely related to transaction processing, because they help maintain the *ACID* properties of transactions (Ozsu and Valduriez 1991).

Concurrency Control

Concurrency control is the database management activity of coordinating the actions of database manipulation processes that operate concurrently, access shared data, and therefore potentially interfere with each other (Bernstein et al. 1987). The goal of a concurrency control mechanism is to allow concurrency while maintaining the consistency of the shared data. The unit of concurrency in a database system is a transaction.

Varying degrees of concurrency may be allowed or required by a database system. Most techniques follow some given *correctness criterion*, which dictates the maximum amount of concurrency allowed among transactions. The amount of concurrency is defined by the degree of interleaving among concurrent transactions and the number of transactions that run concurrently. The simplest correctness criterion is *mutual exclusion,* which requires that each transaction run from start to finish without interruption from any other transaction. This execution criterion produces *serial* schedules—that is, schedules in which all operations of a transaction are executed consecutively. Many traditional concurrency control techniques use *serializability* as their correctness criteria; these techniques produce serializable schedules. A schedule is serializable if it produces the same output and has the same effect on the database as some serial schedule of the same transactions (Bernstein et al. 1987). Other, less-restrictive correctness criteria have been suggested that carefully relax serializability in order to increase concurrency.

Recovery

The goal of recovery in a database is to ensure that aborted or failed transactions produce no adverse effects on the database or the other transactions. The two kinds of effects on an aborted transaction are effects on data and effects on other transactions. The effects on the data are any changes made to the data by the transaction. Recovery makes sure that the database is returned to a consistent state after a transaction abort. One transaction may affect another transaction if the second transaction reads data that were changed by the first transaction (Bernstein et al. 1987). The database recovery mechanism ensures that these conflicting transactions view consistent data or are aborted. Recovery is closely related to concurrency control, because the more concurrency that is allowed, the more likely it is that an aborted transaction will affect other transactions.

Security

Security refers to the protection of data against unauthorized disclosure, alteration, or destruction (Date 1990). Each individual user and application program has specific data access privileges granted to them; these privileges may be defined by the external schema. That is, each user may be given a different view of the data based on the data that he or she is allowed to access and/or change. The security system provides some means of determining what view a particular user or application program may access. Security also has the function of limiting initial access to the database through use of authorization and authentication procedures. The most common of these procedures are the login name and the password protection service, which most computer users are already familiar with.

Language Interface

The DBMS provides support for languages for definition of data and for manipulation of data. The conceptual schema is specified in a data definition language (DDL). This component of a database language is a notation for describing the data, the relationships among the data, and the constraints on the data and relationships. The DDL is used when the database is designed and is later used to modify the schema (Ullman and Widom 1997).

The data manipulation language (DML) is used to express operations on the database. The DML is sometimes referred to as a query language. The DBMS provides the DML so that users and application programmers can access data without having to know how or where these data are stored.

Fault Tolerance

The ability to remain available to provide reliable DBMS service despite faults is called *fault tolerance*. A failed database component produces a fault to other components that interact with it. Typical database faults include constraint violation and transaction timing faults. Recovery, as described previously, is closely related to fault tolerance, because recovery is a mechanism that ensures that faults causing transaction aborts are tolerated.

Data Catalog

The data catalog (sometimes called the data dictionary) is a system database containing descriptions of the data in the main database (sometimes referred to as metadata). It contains information about the data, relationships, constraints, and all the schemas that organize these features into a unified database. The catalog is considered a database, because it can be queried to get information about the structure of the main database.

Storage Management

The DBMS provides a mechanism for management of permanent storage of the data. The internal schema defines how the data should be stored by the storage management mechanism. The storage manager interfaces with the operating system in order to access physical storage.

Database Data Structuring Models

Database structuring models support the representation of the logical structuring of data items and the physical structuring of data items to isolate the various levels from each other. The models are dependent on the type of physical computer system the database resides on, and the degree of integration defines the number and composition of the layers of model specification. These structuring models are referred to as schema models, of which there are two widely accepted forms. The first form is the ANSI/SPARC three-layer schema model, and the second form adds additional layers to deal with distribution and heterogeneity.

The three-layer model (Figure 1.7) is the most common model used to introduce the concept of database metadata and the physical-to-logical mapping of the database logical model to the system physical model. In this model there are three levels of abstraction supported. The lowest ab-

Figure 1.7

Three-layer
ANSI/SPARC
schema model.

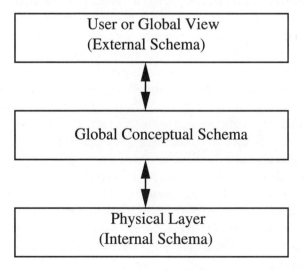

straction is the physical layer, referred to as the *internal schema*. The middle level defines the logical database structural elements and is referred to as the *global conceptual schema*. The third level defines the user's view of the database and is referred to as the *external schema*. The lowest layer of this model, the physical or internal schema, provides the map of the internal physical database storage structures (e.g., records, B-trees, linked lists, file organization, and so on). This layer fully defines how the physical data are allocated to physical storage structures and media. The function of this level is to isolate the physical data structures from the logical data structures of the database. This layer also provides a map of the logical schema relations, tuples, records, fields, and relationships to physical storage. By providing all bindings to physical storage in one layer, the database designers have isolated changes to this single layer. For example, if a new file organization is added to improve storage efficiency, only the internal schema needs to be changed to reflect the new storage structures. The middle layer, the global conceptual schema, represents the complete logical view of the database. For example, relations and their contents would be defined here if the relational model were being represented. All relations, tuples, and attributes would be logically defined here, as would relationships defined on or over attributes and relations in the database. The global conceptual schema represents a description of the logical structure of the data, not the physical realization of the data. The top layer, or view, of the schema may be only a partial description of the database. This layer may have separate names for relations, tuples, or attributes and may have them organized differently than in the global schema. This structuring allows for tailoring of the database to specific user applications and for isolating users from data they do not need or should not be allowed to view.

The second approach adds a distribution element, on top of the global conceptual schema, to define how the logical elements of the database are partitioned and/or distributed. In addition to this logical description, the distributed schema description could also add a mapping layer to define how one database looks to another database or translates from one to the other. For example, you can define a mapping between a relational database and a network database, or from an object-oriented database to a relational database. The idea is that simply by adding a layer of abstraction between systems, you can easily insert a new database or map an old database into a new one. This concept is embodied in the CORBA distributed systems specification. For details on these concepts, and others related to database design, refer to the bibliography.

Relational Database Support

The network database model's problems directly fed into the development of its successor, the relational database model. The complexity of a network database structure begged for simplification. The relational model provided this simplification. Relations organize as pieces of information into two-dimensional tables called *relations*. In Figure 1.8, each table consists of a set of rows, or tuples. Each row is exactly the same format. Each row has the same type of information in the same location. The items within a row are referred to as *attributes of the relation*. For example, a relation describing students could consist of a number of rows, where each row contains information representing a name, identification, Social Security number, major, and address. Each row within the student relation would contain the same format and the same placement of items in a row. In addition, the relations and their rows do not need links from one to the other to navigate through the information (as was the case in the network database model).

The columns of the relation represent the fields in the row. The relation, or table, has other desirable properties. There must be one attribute of a table where elements are unique for all rows of the relation. This unique item is used to select a row from all rows of a relation. For example, to select a single student from the student relation, the Social Security number or the student identifier number can be used as the unique identifier, or key, of a row in the relation. In either case, the desired effect is to use the unique identifier to differentiate one row from all the rows of the relation. Requiring tuples or rows to be unique removes any unwanted redundancy from the database and also removes problems that could occur due to the maintenance of redundant information.

Figure 1.8

Example of a relation.

Scientific Name	Common Name	Food Preference	Family	Max. Size	Geographic Range
Pomacanthus Imperator	Emperor Angelfish	Live	Angelfish	12	Red Sea
Chaetodon Xanthocephalus	Yellowhead Butterflyfish	Live	Butterfly-fish	10	Indo-Pacific
Parupeneus Indicus	Indian Goatfish	Scavanger	Goatfish	14	Hawaiian
Lutjanus Sanguineus	Red Snapper	Live	Snapper	15	Caribbean
Pterois Volitans	Lionfish	Live	Lionfish	20	Red Sea

Beyond the simplicity of the structure, the relational model also supports simple, yet powerful, data manipulation concepts based on relational algebra. Relational operators include SELECT, PROJECT, JOIN, UNION, DIFFERENCE, INTERSECT, and others. These operators provide easy-to-specify means for extracting wanted information without indicating how the extraction or operation is to be performed. To illustrate these concepts, the following simple database is described. There are two relations, Caribbean fish and Hawaiian fish, as shown in

Figure 1.9

Fish relations.

Caribbean Fish

Scientific Name	Common Name	Food Preference	Family	Max. Size	Geographic Range
Pomacanthus Imperator	Emperor Angelfish	Live	Angelfish	18	Caribbean
Chaetodon Xanthocephalus	Yellowhead Butterflyfish	Algae	Butterflyfish	12	Caribbean
Parupeneus Indicus	Indian Goatfish	Scavanger	Goatfish	15	Caribbean
Lutjanus Sanguineus	Red Snapper	Live	Snapper	20	Caribbean
Pterois Volitans	Lionfish	Live	Lionfish	15	Caribbean

Hawaiian Fish

Scientific Name	Common Name	Food Preference	Family	Max. Size	Geographic Range
Amphiprion Percula	Clown Anemone Fish	Algae	Anemone Fish	6	Hawaiian
Pterois Sphex	Hawaiian Lionfish	Live	Lionfish	15	Hawaiian
Parupeneus Indicus	Indian Goatfish	Scavenger	Goatfish	15	Hawaiian
Zebrasoma Flavescens	Yellow Tang	Algae	Tangs	10	Hawaiian
Zanclus Cornutus	Moorish Idol	Algae	Angelfish	8	Hawaiian
Lutjanus Deussatus	Checkered Snapper	Live	Snapper	22	Hawaiian
Lutjanus Sanguineus	Red Snapper	Live	Snapper	20	Caribbean

Figure 1.10

Result of the
SELECT statement.

Scientific Name	Common Name	Food Preference	Family	Max. Size	Geographic Range
Lutjanus Sanguineus	Red Snapper	Live	Snapper	20	Caribbean

Figure 1.9. To determine all types of snapper found in the Caribbean, you can use a simple SELECT statement:

```
SELECT * FROM Caribbean_fish WHERE species = 'snapper';
```

The simplicity of this operation illustrates the improvement from the network database model and storage. Within a network model, a program would need to be written in order to read the records of the Caribbean fish file one at a time, following the linked list chain of records until the answer was found.

The difference is that the relational model leaves it up to the database to determine how to access this piece of information; in the network model, the programmer would have to determine the best way to answer this query by writing a navigational program. The relational model is superior; relational query processors can be devised that optimize access to the data even when data structuring changes. The network model would have to rewrite the applications to take into account changes in physical database structuring. The SELECT statement example, as shown in Figure 1.10, results in a new relation, and contains the fish identifiers, the fish common names, and the species.

To select only one element of the relation—for example, the fish names—we simply need to include the item name in place of the asterisk (*) in the query above.

```
SELECT fish_name FROM Caribbean_fish WHERE species = 'snapper';
```

The result of this projection (Figure 1.11) is a new relation with only one column, which includes all the names of Caribbean snapper fish. You can see from this simple example how easy it is to write a directed query on the relational model. All you need to do is specify what you are looking for, not how to get it.

The relational model supports other desirable operations beyond the two unary operations just described. The relational model supports a

Figure 1.11

Result of SELECT
with PROJECT
statements.

Common Name
Red Snapper

variety of binary operations on multiple relations, which allow for the combination of information from relations supporting the relationship. For example, UNION, INTERSECT, EXCEPT, and JOIN operations allow for the integration or comparison of items within relations.

The UNION operator is a binary relational operation that acts on two relations and forms a third relation with all the elements from the other two (excluding any duplicates). The UNION operator can only be applied to relations that have the identical degree (number of attributes) and are from the same domain (characteristics of the attributes match). The resulting relation will have a cardinality that is equal to or less than the sum of the cardinalities (magnitude equal to the number of tuples in the relation) of the relations being unionized. For example, if you want to find all the species of snappers that are found in Hawaiian and Caribbean waters, you can write a query as:

```
SELECT * FROM Caribbean_fish WHERE species = 'snapper' UNION
SELECT * FROM Hawaiian_fish WHERE species = 'snapper';
```

Since the number of attributes of the two relations match, as do their types, the operation is legal and can proceed. The result of this query is a new relation, which contains all the attributes of the two relations in the same orientation, but only contains the tuples from Hawaiian fish and Caribbean fish that contained "snapper" as the species name. This is illustrated in Figure 1.12.

The second binary operation is INTERSECT. The INTERSECT operation is used to find the tuples that are common in the two relations being operated on. The operation is performed by taking one tuple at a time from the *first* relation and comparing it to each tuple in the *second* relation, looking for a match. If a match is found, the matched tuple is

Figure 1.12

Result of the UNION
operation.

Scientific Name	Common Name	Food Preference	Family	Max. Size	Geographic Range
Lutjanus Sanguineus	Red Snapper	Live	Snapper	20	Caribbean
Lutjanus Deussatus	Checkered Snapper	Live	Snapper	22	Hawaiian

Figure 1.13

Result of the
INTERSECT
operation.

Scientific Name	Common Name	Food Preference	Family	Max. Size	Geographic Range
Lutjanus Sanguineus	Red Snapper	Live	Snapper	20	Caribbean

copied into the resulting relation. If no match is found, the comparison continues with the second tuple of the first relation, and so on, until all tuples of the first relation have been compared to all tuples of the second relation. To determine which species of snapper are found in Hawaiian and Caribbean waters, you can use the query:

```
SELECT * FROM Caribbean_fish WHERE species = 'snapper' INTERSECT
    SELECT * FROM Hawaiian_fish WHERE species = 'snapper';
```

The result of this query is a new relation, as shown in Figure 1.13. The result clearly shows only those snapper species found in both places.

The EXCEPT binary operator, like the UNION operator, executes on two relations, forming another relation based on the relational EXCEPT operation. The EXCEPT operation requires that the two relations have the same degree (number of attributes), and the attributes of the two relations must match in terms of the domains of values for the attributes (in the same relative position in the relations) from the separate relations. The two relations are compared, tuple by tuple, to determine what is in one relation but not in the other. That is, you are looking for how the two relations differ, or what one possesses that the other does not. The cardinality (number of resulting tuples) is equal to or less than the cardinality of the first relation in the binary operations list.

Using our example, to find out which species of snapper are found in the Caribbean but not in Hawaii, the following query can be expressed:

```
SELECT * FROM Caribbean_fish WHERE species = 'snapper' EXCEPT
    SELECT * FROM Hawaiian_fish WHERE species = 'snapper';
```

The result of this query is shown in Figure 1.14. It shows the fish that are in the Caribbean but not found in Hawaii.

Figure 1.14

Result of the
EXCEPT operation.

Scientific Name	Common Name	Food Preference	Family	Max. Size	Geographic Range
Lutjanus Deussatus	Checkered Snapper	Live	Snapper	22	Hawaiian

Figure 1.15

Result of the JOIN
operation.

Scientific Name	Common Name	Food Preference	Family	Max. Size	Geographic Range
Lutjanus Deussatus	Checkered Snapper	Live	Snapper	22	Hawaiian
Lutjanus Sanguineus	Red Snapper	Live	Snapper	20	Caribbean

The binary relational JOIN operator merges two relations based on matching values from one attribute in each relation. The two relations are said to be *joined* over the two attributes. The JOIN condition, or test, can be viewed as selection criteria over the two relations. For example, you may want to join the Hawaiian fish relation and the geographical range relations, to find fish that exist in a variety of regions. The select criterion for this JOIN would be that the fish Fnum is equal to the geographical Fnum. The query would be:

```
SELECT * FROM Hawaiian_fish WHERE species = "snapper" JOIN
Geography
   ON Hawaiian_fish.Fnum = Geography.Fnum;
```

The resulting relation contains all the tuples from the Hawaiian fish relation, where the species is found to be a snapper, and all those from the geography relation (see Figure 1.15). The condition attribute used to match the two relations is not replicated; only one attribute is maintained to represent this value.

The JOIN operation is one of the most powerful relational operators and comes in a variety of options, such as the CROSS JOIN, the NATURAL JOIN, the CONDITION JOIN, the COLUMN NAME JOIN, and the INNER JOIN, LEFT OUTER JOIN, RIGHT OUTER JOIN, and FULL OUTER JOIN. Details on these variants will be discussed later in the book. You can also find more information in the bibliography.

Object Database Support

The object-oriented database model had its inception in computer-aided design systems, which needed ways to store, retrieve, and manipulate nontraditional data types. For example, a map, an illustration, a picture, or a solid object could be specified in the object model with appropriate methods or operators to manipulate these items. These same items would be difficult, if not impossible, to store, retrieve, and manipulate within the relational model.

Object-oriented database management systems are based on a more computationally complete model, possessing the natural features of a programming language, such as SmallTalk or C++, along with extensions to support database specification and maintenance. An object-oriented database consists of a schema, which is a nontrivial description of data structure and meaning. The database structuring policies and mechanisms should provide for forming data items into meaningful elements and for grouping them into more complex, useful data structures. Basic operations must be provided to create, delete, insert, and modify data structures. Means for accessing the stored information using powerful query mechanisms are a major part of a database management system.

An important component of database data structuring is the representation of relationships between data items or data structures within the database schema. Relationships are named structures, which can themselves have valued components. Relationships provide the means to link naturally unrelated data items, or structures, to model more advanced data semantics. In addition to relationships, a database provides for persistence and storage for these persistent data items. Persistence, a fundamental requirement of a database management system, implies that data have a lifetime beyond the process that created them. Data are created and persistently stored in the database so that they may be shared by more than the process that created them in a simultaneous manner (concurrency). Other features of data within a database and of database management systems include data integrity constraints used to define ranges of correct states for data items and their relationships in the database, database security, database query processing, semantic and restricted views of the database, and data administration concepts. Security provides for access authorization and authentication, as well as access control. Query processing is a facility of databases that provides for the specification of what action on the database is desired without specifying how it is to be performed. Without these and other fundamental features of database systems, the object-oriented paradigm cannot be brought into the database paradigm.

The fundamental concept in an object-oriented database system and the object-oriented database model is the object (see Figure 1.16). An object is an abstract representation of a real-world entity consisting of two parts: a state that defines the meaning of the object at a point in time and an interface representing the only means through which the state

Figure 1.16

A fish object.

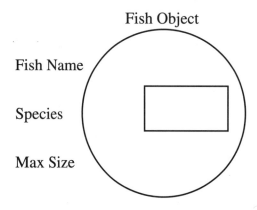

Fish Object

Fish Name

Species

Max Size

of the object can be referenced. The maintenance of the privacy of an object's state is crucial to the fundamental concept. Objects encapsulate their private parts (state) and reveal only their public parts (interface). The interface to an object consists of a set of operations that return values for the state of an object (e.g., the object's encapsulated attributes) or that simply perform some hidden operation on the encapsulated state. Operations on objects are invoked through the sending of a request or message (operation and parameters) to the named object, which contains the requested operation and stored state. As long as the types of the message parameters match the interface types, the operation requested can be performed. If they do not match, an error occurs. The operations act on the stored state, based on the defined operation and parameters—similar to a procedure call or a function call in contemporary programming languages. Object operations are implemented by *methods,* which are pieces of code that perform the desired operations on the encapsulated object state. Methods have privileges not available to users of the object. A method can access the private encapsulated state (memory) of the referenced object.

Object methods can have their name overloaded with many possible method implementations for the same named method. For example, you can specify a method, ADDER, which takes as parameters two data items, which must be of the same type:

```
ADDER ( TypeA: parameter one, Type A: parameter two)
```

The ADDER method adds the two provided parameters, returning the result in the same type as the parameters. This method can then be used to add two integers, two reals, two complex numbers, two binary numbers, or two characters. The underlying object would be required to have a separate implementation for each of the possible different parameter types. The object-oriented type system contains several rules, which are used to determine the correct implementation to use at run time.

The object-oriented database does not possess inherent operations as does the relational database system. Object-oriented databases must specify basic operations on objects, which can then be used to specify a query on the object. Unlike the relational database, the objects do not all share a common query language, unless this is specified as a supertype inherited by all objects. For example, every attribute of an object can have a generic overloaded operator to select an attribute and update an attribute of an object. Operators for more complex forms of selection, as allowed in the relational database, can be specified and have been for most object-oriented databases, such as the object query language. However, these have not gone far enough in providing a coherent, integrated language for application and database designers to use.

Object-Relational Database Support

The object-relational model was a natural progression based on the benefits of the combination of a relational database and an object-oriented database. This model extracts the best of each model and merges them into a single model. Relations form the foundation of the combined data model. Objects are constructed as in the object-oriented data model and can be made persistent by storing them within a relational table. For example, you can have a fish relation composed of the original fish relation in Figure 1.9, combined with added object fields, to represent the picture of the named fish, a map of the geographical areas where the fish is found, and so on (Figure 1.17). To query this relational object, we would need added syntax and semantics within the query language to name an object and to use its methods. For example, to extract the picture of the Moorish Idol fish from the Hawaiian relation, we would use the SELECT statement with the added operation to display (picture)— possibly like this:

```
SELECT Display(picture) FROM Hawaiian_fish WHERE species =
"tobies";
```

Figure 1.17
Relational/object
example.

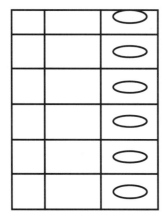

This query would result in the Moorish Idol fish, the only toby in the database, to be displayed on the screen. Likewise, for other operations defined on objects stored in the database, similar syntax would apply. The SQL-3 language takes this concept a step further and completely defines the rules and conventions for generating such queries on an object-relational database.

Database SQL Standards

You can see from this progression of languages that if standards are not put in place, database languages of every variety will evolve, leaving the application developers and users to wade through the many dialects to select one, or a few, that meets their needs. Standards have been fostered to alleviate this and many other problems with information interchange. Programming language standards evolved to allow computer designers to fix designs on a specific language and to allow application developers to port code from one machine to another. As the hardware changes or demands grow, users can keep their operational environment stable.

Standards typically evolve through the demands of users. As a new dialect arrives, it may enjoy early success as a de facto standard—as was the case with the early programming languages. Once a language arrives at the de facto state, it has arrived at the entry stage toward standardization. Language variants, developed by numerous vendors, are brought together through a process of consensus acceptance of the variant features. Bringing vendors together to discuss their variants and to decide on accepted features to include in all future releases constitutes the process of developing a language standard specification. This alone, however, will not result in useful open products. If vendors do not have a means to validate their products against the standard, then there is no true conformance and users are no better off than they were before the standard was developed.

This process occurred in the early days of the database community. The CODASYL database specification and the resulting NDL standard, in 1986, fall into this category. Even though a standard for the language was produced, there were no validation tests written, and products therefore implemented features as they interpreted them—not always as the language designers had intended. SQL has learned from this first failure of the database standards process and has, along with the National Institute of Standards and Technology (NIST), developed validation tests to determine if vendor products do indeed adhere to the standard's specifications and intentions.

SQL Database Language Development History

The history of the SQL language began with Ted Codd's first papers in the 1970s on the relational model and its mathematical foundations. Dr. Codd's work dealt with the specification of the basic unit of the model, the relation, and the relational algebraic means through which relations can be manipulated and transformed. Dr. Codd's work led to IBM's pioneering research work on developing the first relational database system, called System R, and its application programming interface, called SEQUEL (Structured English Query Language). SEQUEL was initially developed and implemented in 1974–1975 and was revised in 1977. Recognizing the significance of this development, a U.S. database project was initiated in 1977. In 1978, ANSI approved the SQL database language project, which led to the formulation of the initial SQL standard language. ISO followed suit with ANSI and initiated its own database standardization effort in 1979, based on ANSI's and IBM's early SQL efforts. In 1982–1983, these efforts continued with a decision to split the database standardization effort into NDL and SQL at both ANSI and ISO. The standardization developments continued, culminating in 1986 with the ANSI release of the NDL database language standard and the SQL standard. This was followed one year later by the ISO release of the SQL standard.

Closely associated with the development of the SQL standard, was the initiation of test development to validate conformance to the standard. The majority of this work followed the effort to refine and clean up the SQL language. The SQL-89 standard was released along with the FIPS 127-1 specification. NIST set out to develop test suites to allow the validation of this and the evolving SQL-92 language. The SQL-92 release was broken into three levels for conformance testing and development. These levels were entry, intermediate, and full. This release of the language corrected many of the shortcomings that were defined over the brief history of the language and were realized through its extensive use.

Following this change to the base language, the SQL committee, under the guidance of ANSI and ISO, began a wide-sweeping change of the SQL language in 1992. This revision, called SQL-3, is the focus of the remainder of this book. The SQL-3 language was released as a draft standard in 1999, resulting in elevation to standard level later in the same year.

Object-Relational Language Support

The SQL-3 data model enhances and extends the basic relational data model by including objects and abstract data types in the basic data types supported, which also form relational tables. New data types initially added include enumeration, Boolean, character large objects (text), national character large object, binary large object, row type, set type, multiset, list, and abstract data type. These new data types can be combined in a variety of ways within relations (e.g., as parameters, columns, domains, and variables in relations, abstract data types (ADTs), objects, and object operations).

Motivation

Why is such a new language needed? To answer this question you need to look at the variety of new applications where databases are being applied. With the advent of object-oriented programming languages and object-oriented databases, application information can now be seamlessly moved in and out of a persistent secure medium, the database. Application developers have seen the advantages of this approach and have begun to demand that their present databases be upgraded to allow the storage, retrieval, and manipulation of nonstandard database data types. Vendors have answered the call by including nonstandard enhancements to the baseline SQL standard and the storage and retrieval of nonstandard items. They have also added other features, closing in on those being specified within the SQL-3 standard.

Approaches

Many approaches to integrating the relational model with the object model have been proposed. The tack taken by the SQL-3 committee was to add enhanced attribute specifications for the basic table of the relational model. Instead of the simple table with simple data types used for attributes of the tables, the SQL-3 data model allows for enhancements to the basic structure. A table can consist of attributes of the classic model, along with enhanced attributes, such as a row within a row, or an ADT within an attribute, or even an object within an attribute field. This results in a model flexible enough to represent and store any data type supported by the relational and object-oriented models, as well as some in between, as will be illustrated later.

Relational Object Concepts within SQL-3

The SQL-3 data model still relies on the table as the fundamental structure by which data are organized and through which data are stored and manipulated. The difference lies in how table structures are allowed to be altered. Tables need not be strictly regular. A field can have rows within it, or an object or ADT embedded within it. Beyond the table alterations, the ADT represents the most significant change seen in SQL-3. The ADT specification in SQL-3 consists of two parts: an attribute specification and function specifications. Both are contained within an ADT type definition. ADT behavior is entirely encapsulated within the type definition. The only externally visible entities are the function interface and attribute definitions. No implementation details are visible outside the type.

ADT attributes and function interface can be further restricted through definitions of public, private, or protected modifiers to their specification. Public specification allows attributes or functions to be available to all users of an ADT. Private specification limits access to internal ADT code, and protected specification limits access to all subtypes of an ADT and local ADT code. These access scopes can be further restricted by privilege mechanisms.

ADTs within SQL-3 are either specified as value ADTs or object ADTs. A value ADT has no unique identifier, but simply has a value for the instance variable. The value ADT acts as primitive data types, which have a value associated with their location identified within a relation by tuple and attribute. Object ADTs differ in that each instance of an ADT has an object identifier (OID) bound to the ADT that uniquely identifies the ADT instance. ADTs can also be used as data types for columns in a table, attributes of other ADT definitions, parameters in procedures or functions, and variables in SQL statements.

Beyond the major addition of abstract data types, SQL-3 also proposes support for data types beyond those of SQL-92, including enumeration, Boolean, character large object, binary large object, distinct types, row types, set types, multiset types, and list types. Some may be deferred to the SQL-4 language upgrade due to their complexity and inability for consensus to be derived at this point. We will, however, discuss them all for completeness, and set the direction the language will ultimately reach.

The second major change to the foundation relational SQL model deals with computational completeness. SQL-3 has extended SQL-2 by incorporating functions, procedures, modules, and associated flow of control statements. Basic flow of control statements, such as the compound statement with block delimiters BEGIN and END; loop control, such as WHILE, IF THEN ELSE, REPEAT, FOR, and LOOP; and the selection statement CASE, are all basic elements of the SQL-3 language and do not need to be borrowed from host languages, as was the case in pre-SQL-3 languages. The addition of these statements has made the SQL-3 language more computationally complete.

For example, to send notices to the electrical and computer engineering (ECE) students and to the computer science (CS) students for an upcoming IEEE and ACM meeting, respectively, the following code segment can be generated:

```
IF      (SELECT major
         FROM students
         WHERE club = 'IEEE') = ECE
THEN INSERT INTO send_mail(IEEE . . .

ELSEIF (SELECT major
         FROM students
         WHERE club = 'ACM') = CIS
THEN INSERT INTO send_mail(ACM . . .

ENDIF
```

To make this complete would require the IF statement to be encased in another statement, which would continue to iterate over all the students in the student table. This can be performed by a FOR loop:

```
FOR stu AS SELECT * FROM students
          WHERE college = 'engineering'

          DO

          \* Do some computation *\

END FOR;
```

The other statements operate in similar fashion to their programming language counterparts. BEGIN – END forms a group of statements to be executed sequentially, within their defined scope. The Bacus Naur Form (BNF) format of the compound statement formed using BEGIN and END is:

```
<compound statement> ::=
    [ <beginning label> <colon> ]
    BEGIN [ [NOT] ATOMIC]
    [<local declaration list>]
    [<local handler declaration list>]
    [<SQL statement list>]
    END [ <ending label> ]
```

Declarations within a BEGIN – END compound statement have a lifetime and scope defined by the containing compound statement. For example, a declaration made within the BEGIN – END block exists only during the execution of the block. Compound statements can contain control structures, data manipulation language statements, transaction control statements, session management statements, diagnostic management statements, data definition statements, dynamic statements, and connection statements.

The CASE statement provides a means to select one of many options based on a key value. The format of the CASE statement is:

```
CASE ( selection variable or statement )

WHEN 'value1' THEN

     .
     .
     .


WHEN 'value n' THEN

ELSE  SQL-statements     \* no matches do else clause
END CASE
```

The CASE statement has two versions. The first version has one selection variable or statement being evaluated for the CASE statement. The second version of the CASE statement has no value expression associated with the keyword CASE. Instead, a separate condition for each WHEN clause is allowed:

```
CASE

WHEN 'cond' THEN
     .
     .
     .
WHEN 'cond n' THEN

ELSE      SQL-statements      \* no matches do else clause
END CASE
```

Other iteration statements are provided. LOOP allows for iteration over SQL statements encased in a loop indefinitely. Once a loop has begun, the code encased in the loop will be executed over and over until a LEAVE statement is encountered, which allows for exiting the loop. The structure of the LOOP statement is:

```
Loop_label: LOOP
            SQL-statement
            IF condition      THEN
                LEAVE Loop_label
            END IF;
            SQL-statement
END LOOP;
```

SQL-3 also includes the WHILE and REPEAT statements to allow iteration with testing for completion at the top or bottom of the structure.

```
Loop_label: WHILE condition_false
            DO
                SQL-statements
            END WHILE;
Loop_label: REPEAT
            SQL-statements
            UNTIL condition_true
            END REPEAT;
```

An addition to the SQL-3 language are condition handling statements and the semantics to support them. Condition handling provides a means to define where and how exceptions (errors as well as positive events) are to be handled. Exceptions must be explicitly defined, have names associated with them, and have an SQLSTATE code associated with them. Exception conditions can be raised explicitly using the SIGNAL or RESIGNAL keywords, or they can be raised implicitly. The SIGNAL statement explicitly raises a named exception and empties the previously defined diagnostic area.

Exception handlers can follow one of three execution styles: UNDO, CONTINUE, and EXIT. The scope of an exception handler is the scope of the compound statement that contains the defined exception handler. The UNDO handler is used to undo the changes made by a compound statement before the exception was raised. UNDO handlers are allowed for atomic compound statements only. Upon completion of the UNDO handler, flow of control continues at the end of the compound statement where the exception was raised. The CONTINUE handler is used to perform some designed condition fix and then return control to the statement following the statement that raised the exception. Finally, the EXIT handler style is used if the intent of the condition handling is to perform the handling function and then exit the compound statement from where the condition derived.

To explicitly cause an exception to be executed requires the SIGNAL statement. The format is SIGNAL `condition_handler_name`; the statement requires that the condition handler name was declared earlier in the compound statement structure. If a handler out of the immediate scope of this compound statement is appropriate for handling the condition, the RESIGNAL statement is used to pass the call outside of the compound statement. The RESIGNAL statement can only be used within an exception handler to change the handler for a given condition. When the RESIGNAL is called, the existing compound statement and the handler issuing the RESIGNAL are terminated, and control passes to the next outer exception handler.

Functions, procedures, and modules were added to SQL to support the requirements of ADTs and advanced database applications. Routines are necessary to support the concept of object and object operation. Object operations may be realized through code segments embedded within stored data, through stored data, or through another object's inherited instance. Inherited object data structures and ADT behavior (code) are stored together and are accessible through an object's OID and methods.

Functions associated with ADTs are used to compute single-valued data type results or return Boolean designations. Functions can have parameters passed in to use in their computations, or they can be parameterless. For example, a function to return the time may be parameterless; one to determine a relative time may need the geographical region being referred to for the computation of the correct value.

Functions can be constructed completely from SQL code, may be defined in an SQL schema definition (persistent stored module), or may be implemented in a separate host language as a host language function.

A function may be either a *destructor* or an *actor*. A destructor function destroys ADT instances, and an actor function is any function that reads, updates, or creates an ADT instance or accesses any component of an ADT.

ADT methods can also be implemented using procedures that do not return a value. Procedures can have parameter lists, which can be in parameters, out parameters, or in-out parameters. Procedures can include data structure definitions, database access statements, flow of control statements, functions, objects, and special database operation statements (e.g., BEGIN ATOMIC).

Functions and procedures may be encapsulated within an ADT's definition or defined externally. Encapsulated routines and externally defined routines have access to the private attributes of the ADT when associated with a specific ADT. All ADTs have one specific routine automatically defined, called a *constructor*, which is used to create new instances of the ADT type. The constructor takes on the same name as the ADT type and has zero arguments. When called, it returns a new instance of the type with a unique OID and uninitiated attributes.

Functions and procedures associated with an ADT implement ADT type-specific behaviors. For example, an ADT of type student may have functions or procedures to access or update the student's name, address, age, major, phone number, Social Security number, photo, mother, father, daughter, son, sibling of, and whatever else the ADT designer developed and coded into the ADT to give the user-defined type the specific behavior. Functions and procedures may also be constrained to act on rows of tables, allowing for object-like operations to be constructed for rows.

A structural component of SQL-3, which differs from SQL-2 and other relational database languages, is the module and persistent stored routines. Modules can contain functions and procedures, as well as shared declarations for cursors, variables, and tables. Modules can be schema objects and thus can be persistent. Persistent stored modules and procedures can be called in any other SQL statement, function, procedure, or module that is linked to the database schema and contains the stored element. The calling routine or statement uses the names of routines as though they had been defined within the context of the executing routine, statement, or SQL code segment.

Summary

The SQL-3 language represents a drastic change from the database systems of the 1980s and early 1990s. This model is complex, as represented by the difference in the size of the specifications. The SQL-89 specification was about 120 pages, the SQL-92 specification was approximately 579 pages, and the SQL-3 language specification now stands at 1,500+ pages. The complexities aside, the language will provide database support to a wider range of applications than is now possible with both relational and object-oriented database languages. This model extracts and uses the best of each language and embellishes them to further support the needs of advanced applications. The remainder of this book presents some of the major SQL-3 language features and their use.

SQL-92 Overview

T he SQL-86 and SQL-89 database languages were functional, but were found to be inadequate in numerous areas by the user community, as users gained more experience with the database languages. Some fundamental flaws included the ability to alter schema items after initial construction and user controls over data specifications. Users could not change the database tables configuration, or even add new tables within the context of the language, without closing down and rebuilding a database. Some products provided these features, but they were not implemented the same way from one product to another product, causing portability problems. SQL-92 was started to fix these and numerous other problems discovered in the earlier versions of the language. The following sections provide a high-level overview of the SQL-92 language. The interested reader can seek out further resources, such as Jim Melton and Alan Simon's *Understanding the New SQL: A Complete Guide* (see the bibliography).

The Foundation of the Language: Concepts and Features

The SQL-92 language was under research and development from 1989 to 1992 by the X3H2 National Database Committee under the auspices of ANSI and an international database language (DBL) committee under ISO. The resulting SQL standards, both ANSI and ISO, were identical. The standards of the various countries were published under their standards body; for example, AFNOR in France or DIN in Germany. Countries involved in the SQL standards development included Australia, Canada, Denmark, France, Germany, Italy, Japan, the Netherlands, the United Kingdom and the United States. The language was designed as a superset of the SQL-89 standard with a few exceptions expressed in an addendum to the standard. The major features of SQL-89 are maintained in SQL-92; many areas have been enhanced. The SQL-89 standard is 120 pages and the SQL-92 standard is 579 pages, representing the many changes to the language.

ANSI's SQL-92 major new features compared with SQL-89 were:

- Greater orthoganality within the language
- Extended data types (varchar, bit, character sets, date, time, interval)

- Enhanced JOIN operators (UNION JOIN, NATURAL JOIN)
- Enhanced SET operators (SET DIFFERENCE, SET INTERSECTION)
- Catalog management and specification (constraints, domains, assertions)
- Domain definitions (represents a range of acceptable values or structure limits)
- Derived tables in FROM clause
- Additional referential integrity support (user control of statement deferral, assertions, subqueries in check constraints)
- Temporary table support
- Schema manipulation language additions (ADD, DROP, ALTER applied to tables, constraints, columns)
- Dynamic SQL language support
- Scrolled cursor support
- Remote data access support using connections
- Information schema tables
- Additional programming language linkage and support (ADA, C, etc.)

How ANSI SQL Database Language Conformance Is Defined

The SQL-92 standard specifies what conforming to the standard language features means. Conformance in SQL-92 is measured on three levels: entry, intermediate, and full. Each conformance level builds on the lower level. For example, the intermediate level must conform to the entry level. The features of the language are assigned to conformance levels. To conform to a level, a product must adequately implement all features defined within the level. Conformance must be tested through a set of application test suites applied to a vendor product, and then the evaluation of the results are delivered. The tests must examine all features of the SQL language, and they must produce the same desired result for two products that conform to the standard at the specified level of conformance. If the product does not provide the desired response to the test suite, it is deemed nonconforming. Nonconformance can range from missing one or more features to not exhibiting any of the desired features. Testing agencies deliver test results to the vendors that indicate which features of the language were validated and which features were not validated. Products that pass the conformance tests are issued a validation certificate, which allows them to advertise their product as conforming to this tested level of conformance. At the time of writing this chapter, the National Institute of Standards and Technology (NIST) is the only agency in the United States performing conformance tests; but this is changing. NIST has indicated that they will no longer provide this service to the community. The indication is that the government would like some third-party organization, such as Underwriters Laboratory, to take over this function. Many leading vendors in the database industry have indicated their displeasure with this option. They feel that such a situation may result in some vendors not receiving the same or fair service. We will have to wait and see what the outcome of this action will be.

At present, there is no conformance test for the full ANSI standard. However, there is a set of tests for entry-level and intermediate-level SQL-92, written to the federal information processing standard (FIPS), which closely follows the SQL-92 standard. At the present time, there is much debate in the SQL committee as to how to test, or even define, conformance to the new standard. Proposals are coming to the standards committee and associated bodies to form a subcommittee of SQL to define and generate test suites and to test database conformance for the new products.

Another problem is that of "implementation-defined" behaviors and "implementation-dependent" features. These items are defined within the standard to differ, by definition, from one vendor to another. This issue will remain open and debated for some time to come regarding how this affects portability and conformance. All of these issues are of primary interest to the users, who will be required to determine if the applications they have on one platform—even those from a single vendor—will interoperate.

SQL-92 Entry-Level Features

For a product to be entry-level compliant with the NIST, FIPS 127 specification, the product must exhibit all of the SQL-89 features (excluding those removed or altered), plus only a few extensions. This conformance level is the easiest for the vendors to claim conformance to and to test to. The added features over SQL-89 include the SQLSTATE feature, which is used to provide enhanced diagnostic information back to the application about the execution of the SQL statements presented to the database for processing. A second difference over SQL-89 is the delimited identifier, which allows the user to use an SQL reserved word as a reference. You can create a table with the name of the reserve word SELECT; for example:

```
CREATE TABLE "SELECT" . . .
```

In prior implementations, a compiler error would have resulted.

Another added feature is the named expressions in the SELECT list; for example:

```
SELECT name, sal+comm AS pay
    FROM employee
    ORDER BY pay
```

In this example, the computation, sal+comm, is restated as the name pay. This causes the result to be associated with the name pay, giving more flexibility to users operating on data in the database.

The SQL-89 standard includes the ability to define a database, define database tables, insert data into database tables, update column values in a base table, query information within a base table, use the SELECT statement to find a tuple or data item within a table, and combine information within tables using UNION, INTERSECT, EXCEPT, and JOIN operators. To illustrate a few of these concepts, you can create a simple aquarium management database, which consists of 16 base database tables, covering the full spectrum of information that can be stored in an SQL database.

```
CREATE SCHEMA aquarium
    AUTHORIZATION DBN_associates
    DEFAULT CHARACTER SET "latin-1"
```

This statement allows you to create a database repository within the database with the name aquarium. The named schema has a user-defined group called DBN_associates. This group is authorized to operate upon this database schema, using the Latin-1 defined character set.

```
CREATE DOMAIN price AS DECIMAL (5,2)
    CONSTRAINT price_not_negative CHECK (VALUE >= 0) NOT DEFERRABLE
```

```
CREATE DOMAIN revenue AS DECIMAL (9,2)
    CONSTRAINT revenue_not_negative CHECK (VALUE >= 0) NOT
DEFERRABLE

CREATE DOMAIN name AS CHARACTER VARYING (50) COLLATE
american_english

CREATE DOMAIN food AS CHARACTER VARYING (50) COLLATE
american_english

CREATE DOMAIN region AS CHARACTER VARYING (50) COLLATE
american_english

CREATE DOMAIN temperment AS CHARACTER VARYING (50) COLLATE
american_english

CREATE DOMAIN day_shift AS CHARACTER VARYING (50) COLLATE
american_english

CREATE DOMAIN liters AS DECIMAL (5,2)
    CONSTRAINT liters_not_negative CHECK (VALUE >= 0) NOT
DEFERRABLE

CREATE DOMAIN milligram AS DECIMAL (6,2)
    CONSTRAINT milligram_not_negative CHECK (VALUE >= 0) NOT
DEFERRABLE
```

The CREATE DOMAIN statements allow you to specify a variety of named data types that have an associated base data type from the elemental data types. The data types available for the definitions must come from the elemental types, such as character, number, and so on. In the example above, you created a domain called name by using the syntax:

```
CREATE DOMAIN name AS CHARACTER VARYING (50) COLLATE
american_english,
```

This replaces the character varying data type as the type to be used in specifying names later in the database.

In addition to these definitions, the domain can also be a place where the possible values of a data type can be further restricted. In the previous examples, you added some additional constraints, which restrict the values possible for some of the domains to be positive. These named types may make more sense to database designers and applications developers, who will need to use and maintain this schema. Using these defined domain data types and base data types, the following base tables are defined:

```
CREATE TABLE marine_fish (
    scientific_name     name,
    common_name         name,
    fish_species        name,
    max_size            DECIMAL (5,2)
    food_preference     food,
    geographic_range    region,
    fish_disposition    temperment,
    fish_activity       day_shift
);

CREATE TABLE fresh_water_fish (
    scientific_name     name,
    common_name         name,
    fish_species        name,
    max_size            DECIMAL (5,2)
    food_preference     food,
    geographic_range    region,
    fish_disposition    temperment,
    fish_activity       day_shift
);

CREATE TABLE marine_plants (
    scientific_name     name,
    common_name         name,
    plant_species       name,
    max_size            DECIMAL (5,2)
    geographic_range    region,
    plant_light_needs   CHARACTER (3)
    water_quality_tol   CHARACTER (3)
);

CREATE TABLE fresh_water_plants (
    scientific_name     name,
    common_name         name,
    plant_species       name,
    max_size            DECIMAL (5,2)
    geographic_range    region,
    plant_light_needs   CHARACTER (3)
    water_quality_tol   CHARACTER (3)
);

CREATE TABLE marine_invertebrates (
    scientific_name     name
    common_name         name,
    invertebrate_group  name,
    max_size            DECIMAL (5,2),
    food_preference     food,
    geographic_range    region,
    invert_disposition  temperment,
    invert_activity     day_shift
);

CREATE TABLE fresh_water_invertebrates (
    scientific_name     name,
    common_name         name,
```

```
        invertebrate_group    name,
        max_size              DECIMAL (5,2),
        food_preference       food,
        geographic_range      region,
        invert_disposition    temperment,
        invert_activity       day_shift
    );

CREATE TABLE marine_fish_disease (
        scientific_name       name,
        common_name           name,
        root_cause            CHARACTER VARYING (15),
        affected_area         CHARACTER VARYING (15),
        mortality_rate        DECIMAL (5,2),
        treatment             CHARACTER VARYING (20),
        t_concentration       DECIMAL (8,4)
    );

CREATE TABLE fresh_water_fish_disease (
        scientific_name       name,
        common_name           name,
        root_cause            CHARACTER VARYING (15),
        affected_area         CHARACTER VARYING (15),
        mortality_rate        DECIMAL (5,2),
        treatment             CHARACTER VARYING (20),
        t_concentration       DECIMAL (8,4)
    );

CREATE TABLE marine_invertebrate_disease (
        scientific_name       name,
        common_name           name,
        root_cause            CHARACTER VARYING (15),
        affected_area         CHARACTER VARYING (15),
        mortality_rate        DECIMAL (5,2),
        treatment             CHARACTER VARYING (20),
        t_concentration       DECIMAL (8,4)
    );

CREATE TABLE fresh_water_invertebrate_disease (
        scientific_name       name,
        common_name           name,
        root_cause            CHARACTER VARYING (15),
        affected_area         CHARACTER VARYING (15),
        mortality_rate        DECIMAL (5,2),
        treatment             CHARACTER VARYING (20),
        t_concentration       DECIMAL (8,4)
    );

CREATE TABLE customers (
        cust_id               INTEGER
          CONSTRAINT customers_cust_id_pk PRIMARY KEY,
        cust_last_name        name
          CONSTRAINT customers_cust_last_name_not_null NOT NULL,
        cust_first_name       name
          CONSTRAINT customers_cust_first_name_not_null NOT NULL,
        cust_address          CHARACTER VARYING (30),
        cust_city             CHARACTER VARYING (20),
        cust_state            CHARACTER (2),
```

```
    cust_zip              CHARACTER VARYING (9),
    cust_phone            CHARACTER (10),
    cust_credit_id        CHARACTER VARYING (20),
    cust_current_bal      DECIMAL (7,2),
    cust_ytd              DECIMAL (9,2),
    num_complaints        INTEGER,
    num_returns           INTEGER,
    cust_rating           INTEGER,
    last_purchase         TIMESTAMP
);

CREATE TABLE employees (
    emp_id                INTEGER
        CONSTRAINT employees_emp_id_pk PRIMARY KEY,
    emp_title             name,
    emp_last_name         name
        CONSTRAINT customers_cust_last_name_not_null NOT NULL,
    emp_first_name        name
        CONSTRAINT customers_cust_first_name_not_null NOT NULL,
    emp_address           CHARACTER VARYING (30),
    emp_city              CHARACTER VARYING (20),
    emp_state             CHARACTER (2),
    emp_zip               CHARACTER VARYING (9),
    emp_phone             CHARACTER (10),
    emp_start_date        TIMESTAMP,
    emp_pay_rate          DECIMAL (7,2),
    emp_com_rate          DECIMAL (5,2)
);


CREATE TABLE sales (
    sale_id               INTEGER
        CONSTRAINT sales_sale_id_pk PRIMARY KEY,
    stock_id              INTEGER,
    sale_item_name        name,
    sale_price            price,
    cust_id               INTEGER );

CREATE TABLE aquarium_supplies (
    stock_id              INTEGER
        CONSTRAINT aquarium_supplies_stock_id_pk PRIMARY KEY,
    item_name             name
        CONSTRAINT supplies_item_name_not_null NOT NULL,
    number_in_stock       INTEGER,
    current_price         price );

CREATE TABLE aquatic_organism_stock (
    stock_id              INTEGER,
        CONSTRAINT aquatic_organism_stock_id_pk PRIMARY KEY,
    scientific_name       name
        CONSTRAINT aquatic_organism_name_not_null NOT NULL,
    number_in_stock       INTEGER,
    current_price         price
);

CREATE TABLE aquatic_stock_tanks (
    tank_id               INTEGER
        CONSTRAINT aquatic_stock_tanks_tank_id_pk PRIMARY KEY,
```

```
        water_vol               liters,
          CONSTRAINT aquatic_stock_tanks_water_not_negative CHECK
          (VALUE >= 0)          NOT DEFERRABLE,
        water_type              CHARACTER VARYING (10),
        ph          DECIMAL (4,2),
        salinity                DECIMAL (4,3),
        nitrates                miligram,
        nitrites                miligram,
        temperature             DECIMAL (5,2),
        trace_elements          miligram
);

CREATE TABLE aquarium_revenues (
        employee_id             INTEGER,
        daily_sales             revenue,
        monthly_sales           revenue,
        year_to_date            revenue,
        commissions             revenue
);
```

You created tables for saltwater fish, freshwater fish, saltwater plants, freshwater plants, and saltwater and freshwater invertebrates. You also created tables to maintain information on fish and invertebrate diseases and their treatment. The business aspects of the database tables include tables to maintain customer and employee information, and to track sales, hardware supplies, live stock supplies, display tanks, and overall revenues. This information represents a subset of information needed by a full application implementation.

Using this database definition and table definitions, you can create a variety of user views on this database, as well as grant privileges regarding who can view, alter, insert, or delete items from the database. You can also set up assertions or constraints on the value of various attributes in the database or on composite information from the database. The application designer can then use this information to construct an aquarium management database, which can be used by the proprietor of the business to manage his or her assets. This basic database will be used throughout the remainder of this book to illustrate the concepts being presented.

SQL-92 Intermediate-Level Features

The intermediate level of SQL-92 contains the bulk of the new features added to the SQL-89 standard. This level adds data types DATE, TIME, TIMESTAMP, INTERVAL, CHARACTER VARYING (n), and data type operators LENGTH, SUBSTR, TRIM and ‖ (concatenation) operators, as well as date and time arithmetic operations. Referential integrity constraints with cascade deletes were also added. SQL-92 intermediate adds new types of JOINs to the equi-JOIN of SQL-89, including the NATURAL JOIN, LEFT and RIGHT OUTER JOIN, and the FULL OUTER JOIN. Dynamic SQL (ad hoc) is enhanced to include prepare, execute, and describe. The ability to alter the schema of a created and populated database is added to the specification. This facility permits altering a table description to add or drop a column of a table, removing a table from the database, and revoking privileges that were given when the database was initially created. You can use online data definition language features to add a table to the schema. Within the DDL, you can define domains that can be viewed as a "macro" facility for data type, default values, nullability, and check constraints. The domain facility in SQL-92 does not possess strong type checking; however, the type checking is performed based on the underlying data type. This concept is not the same as domains defined by Codd's original concept of the domain of values for an item.

To provide an application requirement to alter the types of data items in the database at run time, SQL-92 provides a CAST function, which allows for the conversion between numeric types, numeric and character types, and character and date time types. Casting can be implicit, where a scalar-valued subquery can be used in place of any scalar. The schema catalogs have been augmented to provide a set of standard catalogs for tables, views, columns, privileges, constraints, usage, domains, and assertions. You can, in addition, possess multiple schemas, whereas in the past only one set of schema catalogs was allowed per user. The view mechanism is augmented to include the UNION operator, providing more flexibility in constraining view creation and materialization. The transaction is improved to permit transaction isolation levels. These include the read uncommitted, read committed, repeatable read, and serializable levels of operation.

The data manipulation capabilities of SQL-92 are improved through the use of scrollable cursors, with commands to fetch prior (tuple), relative access, absolute access, and last item access in a queriable table. Additional SET operations are supported between query blocks to allow UNION, INTERSECT, and EXCEPT on subqueries and even on subelements of a table, using the CORRESPONDING operator applied to like columns of tables. A CASE expression is added to the basic SELECT statement to allow conditional access to stored data, based on retrieved or provided values.

Tests on the uniqueness of a query's result can be easily found by applying the UNIQUE predicate to a subquery, which will return TRUE or FALSE based on the outcome of the query. The intermediate conformance level of SQL also improves the readability of generated code by increasing the size of character identifiers to 128 and allowing multiple character sets to be represented—for example, the Kanji or Russian character sets. Finally, the intermediate level extends the SQL flagger to recognize extensions and nonconforming uses of the language features. Details and specific examples of these features can be found in Jim Melton and Alan Simon's *Understanding the New SQL: A Complete Guide*, which is listed in the bibliography.

SQL-92 Full-Level Features

The full level of SQL-92 continues to extend the basic features of the language. Added data types BIT (n) and BIT VARYING (n) are now included. Tables and their semantics are enhanced in a variety of ways. For example, tables can be temporary (vanishing at the end of a transaction), derived, and explicit, and table rows can have constructors applied to them. More unary and binary operations are allowed (e.g., the CROSS JOIN and UNION JOIN). The predicates applied to the SELECT statement are further enhanced—for example, there is now a MATCH predicate. SQL-3 full-conformance level provides more character string operators based on position in a string (e.g., upper, lower position). Security is enhanced; for example, the insert privilege on individual columns is now allowed, as are update and delete with subqueries on the same table. Further enhancement of the DISTINCT operator allows for the application to subqueries and enhancements of the cursor. Again, for further details and a finer definition of what is in the full level of SQL conformance, see Jim Melton and Alan Simon's *Understanding the New SQL: A Complete Guide*.

SQL-92 Basic Operators and Features

To understand the fundamentals of the SQL language, and to give some background for the SQL-3 extensions to be discussed in later chapters, you need to get acquainted with some of the basic data manipulation statements and how they are used in performing operations on the database. The most fundamental data manipulation element in the database language is SQL's SELECT statement and its syntax for manipulating data within the database. The basic structure of the manipulation statement is found in the BNF syntax for the SELECT statement:

```
SELECT [DISTINCT] <column-name(s) | *>
   FROM <table-name>;
```

As an example, to find the common names for all marine fish in the database, issue the SQL statement:

```
SELECT common_name
FROM marine_fish;
```

This returns a list of common names for the fish in the marine fish table:

```
Emperor Angelfish
Yellowhead Butterflyfish
Indian Goatfish
Red Snapper
Lionfish
   .
   .
   .
```

The SQL SELECT statement can be refined to force an ordering on the retrieval and display of extracted information by adding the ORDER BY optional syntax to the SELECT statement:

```
SELECT [DISTINCT] <column-name(s) | *>
FROM <table-name>
ORDER BY <column-name(s) | column-number(s)>[ASC | DESC];
```

In the example above, to retrieve the given list in alphabetical order, alter the SELECT statement by adding ORDER BY common_name ASC (ascending):

```
SELECT common_name
FROM marine_fish
ORDER BY common_name ASC;
```

The result is now in alphabetical order:

```
Emperor Angelfish
Indian Goatfish
Lionfish
Red Snapper
Yellowhead Butterflyfish
```

The SELECT statement can be further refined to select only specific rows within the named table that meet some selection restriction criteria. The refinement is accomplished with the SELECT statement's restriction clause formed with the keyword WHERE and the restriction expression:

```
SELECT <column-name(s) >
FROM <table-name>
WHERE <column-name><comparison operator><value>;
```

As an example, to refine the search further to retrieve only the fish that are found in the Caribbean, use the restriction clause and semantics:

```
SELECT common_name
FROM marine_fish
WHERE geographic_range = 'caribbean';
```

If only the Red Snapper and Emperor Angelfish are from this region, then only their names would be found in the resulting list. Comparison operators can be included—equal to (=), less than (<), not equal to (!=), less than or equal to (<=), greater than (>), and greater than or equal to (>=). Any of these operators can be used to restrict what is retrieved from the database.

SELECT statements, which search for rows within a table, can have more than a single search or restriction condition by using the AND keyword to link multiple search conditions into a single, larger search condition. The BNF syntax for the additional restrictions is:

```
SELECT <column-name(s) >
FROM <table-name>
WHERE <column-name><comparison operator><value>
AND <column-name><comparison operator><value>;
```

As an example, to find out if marine plants from the Caribbean region grow to a maximum of ten inches and have low light needs, write a query as follows:

```
SELECT common_name
FROM marine_plant
WHERE geographic_range = 'caribbean'
AND max_size <= 10
AND plant_light_needs = 'low';
```

The database scans through the tuples of the marine plant table to determine which tuples meet the three conditions specified. If even one condition is not met, the tuple is not included in the resulting list.

If, on the other hand, you want to retrieve results even if all conditions are not met, you can further refine the query. The search can be further restricted by allowing for the selection of multiple rows, which meet either one of the search conditions, using the OR keyword, with the BNF as:

```
SELECT <column-name(s) >
FROM <table-name>
WHERE <column-name><comparison operator><value>
OR <column-name><comparison operator><value>;
```

In the example for the marine plants, if you include plants that meet conditions one and two or just condition three, you can easily refine the query to look like:

```
SELECT common_name
FROM marine_plant
WHERE geographic_range = 'caribbean'
AND max_size <= 10
OR plant_light_needs = 'low';
```

The result has tuples where some would have plants from the Caribbean, which do not grow greater than ten inches, and other tuples that only meet the criterion that the plant requires low light resources to grow.

Instead of looking for specific values or values above or below some elements, you may want to perform range searches, finding all elements between some values or outside of some set of values. This is accomplished by using the SQL-92's range search syntax and the BETWEEN keyword. The BNF for the BETWEEN syntax is:

```
SELECT <column-name(s) >
FROM <table-name>
WHERE <column-name>
[NOT] BETWEEN <value-1> AND <value-2>;
```

Alternatively, instead of looking at a single column, you can look at values found within multiple columns, as:

```
SELECT <column-name(s) >
FROM <table-name>
WHERE <value>
[NOT] BETWEEN <column-name-1> AND <column-name-2>;
```

In the database, as an example, you may wish to find all the invertebrates that are found in the Caribbean and that grow to a maximum size of between 3.5 and 5.5 inches. This query involves two of the restrictions you have looked at up to this point—the specific match and an alternative match—which also must be evaluated to true. The query may look like:

```
SELECT common_name
FROM marine_invertibrates
WHERE geographic_range = 'caribbean'
AND max_size BETWEEN 3.5 AND 5.5;
```

The query is not that different from what you had in the first place. The only added feature is the syntax, BETWEEN 3.5 AND 5.5, which indicates the added condition of wanting to see any tuple that falls beteen these two boundary values.

In many cases, not all the information being looked for is known. For example, if you do not know what the exact value of an attribute should be, or the exact content of a character string you are looking for, you can use SQL-92's matching character patterns syntax. The BNF for this syntax looks like:

```
SELECT <column-name(s) >
FROM <table-name>
WHERE <column-name>
[NOT] LIKE <'character-string'>;
```

As an example of this syntax, assume you are interested in determining the symptoms and treatment of the marine fish disease commonly known as white spot disease, but you can't remember if this is the correct name. In addition, you know that the major affected area is the skin. You can specify the following query to extract all diseases with the first name "white."

```
SELECT common_name, scientific_name, treatment
FROM marine_fish_disease
WHERE common_name LIKE 'white%'
AND affected_area = 'skin';
```

The resulting table may have information such as:

white spot	oodinium	copper sulfate
white fin rot		copper malichite

Not all information is complete; therefore, an important base element within the SQL-92 and successor languages is the base value NULL. NULL implies that no data are found in the location. It does not imply that it is zero or some other element; it implies that no value exists. It is important to be able to look for the presence of, or lack of, the NULL character string within a column or within a table. The form of SELECT used for this is shown in the BNF as:

```
SELECT <column-name(s) >
FROM <table-name>
WHERE <column-name> IS [NOT] NULL;
```

The example above retrieves a row from the disease table, which did not have a value for the scientific name for the disease white fin rot. If you want to retrieve only this item, or not have this item show up in the list, specify that you do not want any tuples where the scientific name is NULL:

```
SELECT common_name, scientific_name, treatment
FROM marine_fish_disease
WHERE common_name LIKE 'white%'
AND affected_area = 'skin'
AND scientific_name IS NOT NULL;
```

The result now is just the single tuple:

white spot	oodinium	copper sulfate

The second tuple was removed as part of the restriction derived from the statement AND scientific_name IS NOT NULL.

If, instead of looking for a single value, you want to consider some larger set of values, you need some additional syntax and symantics. For example, to search for some set of values within some column of a table, the SELECT statement offers syntax to list a set of values to search on, as shown in the following BNF syntax:

```
SELECT <column-name(s) >
FROM <table-name>
WHERE <column-name>
[NOT] IN (<value-1>, <value-2>, . . . );
```

As an example, you want to find all the freshwater fish that are found in any of the following lakes: Superior, Huron, Okeechobee, George, Titicaca, and Champlain. Use the following query:

```
SELECT common_name
FROM fresh_water_fish
WHERE geographic_range
IN ('lake superior', 'lake huron', 'lake okeechobee', 'lake
george', 'lake titicaca', 'lake champlain');
```

The result may look something like:

pike
trout
bass
eel
garr

The idea is to allow the user to further refine the search within the database, and let the database do the job of performing the multiple searches necessary to find the information.

SQL-92 and SQL-3 also offer many built-in functions, which can be used to operate upon data within a query. These operators include the aggregate functions average, summation, minimum, maximum, and count. They are applied to columns extracted with a SELECT statement using the BNF syntax, as shown below:

```
SELECT AVG ([DISTINCT] <column-name(s) >)
FROM <table-name>
[WHERE <condition>];
```

In the example database, if you want to find out what the average size is of all the fish itemized within the database, use the following query:

```
SELECT AVG(max_size)
FROM marine_fish;
```

This returns a number that is equivalent to the sum of the size of all fish found in the marine fish table, divided by the number of fish in the table. If you happen to have many fish of the same size, and want to have these redundant pieces of information removed from the calculation, you can refine this query to look only at the distinct items found:

```
SELECT AVG( DISTINCT max_size)
FROM marine_fish;
```

If, instead of an average, you want to know a total income for the day, use the built-in SUM function, whose syntax is:

```
SELECT SUM ([DISTINCT] <column-name(s) >)
FROM <table-name>
[WHERE <condition>];
```

By applying this syntax to the database, you can determine what the total value of all sales recorded in the database is by issuing the following query:

```
SELECT SUM (sale_price)
FROM sales;
```

If, instead, you want to know the sales for a customer only, whose identifier is 12344, you refine this query to look like:

```
SELECT SUM (sale_price)
FROM sales
WHERE cust_id = 12344;
```

This returns a number that represents all the sales generated by the customer identified by ID number 12344.

If, instead, you want to find the minimum amount spent by anyone, you can generate a list of all customers' minimum purchases. Use the BNF grammar below:

```
SELECT MIN ([DISTINCT] <column-name(s) >)
FROM <table-name>
[WHERE <condition>];
```

The minimum can be generated with the following syntax:

```
SELECT MIN (sale_price) , stock item
FROM sales;
```

Similarly, if you want to find the sale that had the greatest value, use the keyword MAX in place of the keyword MIN. The result is the sales item with the greatest value. The BNF for this syntax is:

```
SELECT MAX ([DISTINCT] <column-name(s) >)
FROM <table-name>
[WHERE <condition>];

SELECT MAX (sale_price) , stock item
FROM sales;
```

Another aggregate, which is very useful to know, is how many of something exists within a list of items. For example, how many fish in the fish description list have the word "angel" in their name? This can easily be found by mixing a few of the search restrictions you used before, with the new search restriction that counts how many meet a criterion. The BNF syntax for this form of the statement is:

```
SELECT COUNT ([DISTINCT] <column-name(s) >)
FROM <table-name>
[WHERE <condition>];
```

The actual query may look like this:

```
SELECT COUNT(*)
FROM marine_fish
WHERE common_name LIKE '%angel%';
```

The result of this query is a whole number representing how many fish in the table have at a minimum the word "angel" in their name.

SQL-92 allows computations to be included within the SELECT statement syntax. Computations with multiplication, division, addition, and subtraction are possible. The statement BNF syntax is:

```
SELECT <column-name(s) >, <arithmetic expression>
FROM <table-name>
[WHERE <condition>]
[ORDER BY <column-name(s) | column-number(s)>[ASC | DESC]];
```

An arithmetic statement can be used to determine an employee's total compensation in commissions for the year by selecting the employee's total sales and multiplying this by the employee's commission rate. The query might look something like this:

```
SELECT employee_id, year_to_date * .05
FROM aquarium_revenues;
```

The `year_to_date * .05` portion of the query takes the value of each employee's sales and multiplies that by a commission rate of 5 percent. This will then be listed next to each employee's identifier, indicating the value of the employee's yearly commissions.

Queries do not need to be standalone. Queries can be embedded within each other to cascade or nest the selection process. The BNF form of such a query appears as follows:

```
SELECT <column-name(s) >
FROM <table-name>
WHERE <comparison operator | IN>
        SELECT <column-name(s) >
        FROM <table-name>
        WHERE <condition>;
```

In a database, you may need to extract information from one table based on facts from another table. For example, an employee, Jane Doe, works for you, and you want to find out how her sales were for the last week, month, and year, but you cannot remember her employee identifier. You can find the appropriate information using a nested query with the syntax as follows:

```
SELECT employee_id, daily_sales, monthly_sales, year-to_date
FROM sales
WHERE employee_id = (SELECT emp_id
                     FROM employees
                     WHERE emp_last_name = 'Doe'
                     AND emp_first_name = 'Jane');
```

The result of this query is the identifier for Jane Doe, listed with her daily, monthly, and year-to-date sales figures.

Often you need to view information as grouped collections, related by one or more of the categories of the collection. Queries can be formulated and operated on to order and cluster the resulting table, based on the categorization needs of the query generator, using the GROUP BY operation. The BNF syntax looks like:

```
SELECT <column-name(s) >
FROM <table-name>
[WHERE<condition>]
GROUP BY <column-name(s)>
[HAVING <condition>]
[ORDER BY <column-name(s) | column-number(s)>[ASC | DESC]];
```

As an example, if you want to determine where all fish are from, and form these into groups, you can generate the following query:

```
SELECT geographic_range, common_name
FROM marine_fish
GROUP BY geographic_range, common_name
```

The resulting table is first grouped by geographic region clusters, and then, within each of these clusters, are the common names. This is a useful way to order and cluster results of queries. A more common use of the clustering mechanism is to look at aggregates within a clustered group of items. For example, you may want to examine the sales table to see how many of each item was sold and the aggregate return in sales from those sales. This query may look something like the following:

```
SELECT sale_item_name, COUNT(sale_price), SUM(sale_price)
FROM sales
GROUP BY sale_item_name;
```

You can refine this query further to look only at the items purchased by a single customer in quantities greater than 1, by augmenting the previous query, as follows:

```
SELECT sale_item_name, COUNT(sale_price), SUM(sale_price)
FROM sales
WHERE cust_id = 12344
GROUP BY sale_item_name
HAVING COUNT(sale_price) >1;
```

The result of this query is categories of goods purchased by customer 12344, with the number of times the item was purchased and the total revenue generated by these sales.

Tables can be combined in numerous ways using relational binary operations, such as the JOIN, UNION, INTERSECT, and DIFFERENCE operators. One of the most important of these binary operators is the JOIN operation. This operation is based on the basic SELECT statement, using multiple tables as the input for the selection, and a condition on the JOIN, which equates items in one table with those in another table. The BNF syntax generally looks like:

```
SELECT <column-name(s) >
FROM <table-name>,<table-name>,[<table-name>]
[WHERE<join-condition>]
[AND | OR <condition>]
[ORDER BY <column-name(s) | column-number(s)>;
```

As an example, you may want to retrieve the common names for marine fish sold. The query joins the three tables using stock_id and scientific_name as the JOIN conditions. The query may look something like this:

```
SELECT m.common_name, s.sale_price
FROM marine_fish m, sales s, aquatic_organism_stock a
WHERE m.scientific_name = a.scientific_name
AND a.stock_id = s.stock_id;
```

The result is a list of marine fish common names and the prices they sold for. This result was constructed by combining the tuples in aquatic_organism_stock with those that match in stock_id in the sales table. The resulting table then combined with the marine fish table to extract those tuples that have a scientific name found within the fish table.

Other binary operations, such as the UNION, EXCEPT, and INTERSECT operators, are used to compare the contents of one table with those of another. The tables must have the same structure in each column and in the same order. For example, you can combine the contents of the marine fish and freshwater fish tables simply by using the following operator:

```
(SELECT * FROM marine_fish)
UNION
(SELECT * FROM fresh_water_fish);
```

This can be refined to provide a list of all the common names for marine and freshwater fish. Select the common names from each and then union them together:

```
(SELECT common_name FROM marine_fish)
UNION
(SELECT common_name FROM fresh_water_fish);
```

The result of this operation is a combined list, with those fish found in each list displayed only once. The redundant columns are cut from the final list; only the unique tuples remain. If you want to see which items are found in both, you can use the INTERSECT operation as follows:

```
(SELECT * FROM marine_fish)
INTERSECT
(SELECT * FROM fresh_water_fish);
```

The result includes only the items that are in both tables—for example, bass may not have been discerned as sea bass or lake bass. If, on the other hand, you want to know all the items that are found in one table but not in the other, use the EXCEPT binary operator:

```
(SELECT * FROM marine_fish)
EXCEPT
(SELECT * FROM fresh_water_fish);
```

The result here is all the marine fish (except the bass, if this is the only fish found in each table with the same common name).

Beyond basic search conditions, SQL-92 allows the user to insert and delete items from tables, as well as to change values within the tables using the INSERT, DELETE, and UPDATE statements.

To insert new information into the database use the basic INSERT statement. The statement has a BNF format:

```
INSERT INTO <table-name>
[(<column-name-1>,<column-name-2>, . . .)]
VALUES (<value-1>,<value-2>, . . .);
```

For example, to insert a new fish into the fish table, the Rock Beauty, you use the following syntax:

```
INSERT INTO marine_fish
(scientific_name, common_name, fish_species, max_size,
food_preference,
geographic_range, fish_disposition, fish_activity)
VALUES ('Holocanthus tricolor', 'Rock beauty', 'Chaetodontidae',
10.0,
'live and frozen','Tropical Atlantic', 'aggressive', 'grazer');
```

Or, if you want to make the insert a bit easier, and know you are placing the values in appropriate order, then use the BNF form:

```
INSERT INTO <table-name>
VALUES (<value-1>,<value-2>, . . .)

INSERT INTO marine_fish
VALUES ('Holocanthus tricolor', 'Rock beauty', 'Chaetodontidae',
10.0,
'live and frozen','Tropical Atlantic', 'aggressive', 'grazer');
```

If you enter the value erroneously, or must remove an item from the database, use the DELETE statement. DELETE completely removes the named tuple or tuples from the database; therefore, it must be carefully applied. The syntax of DELETE is:

```
DELETE FROM <table-name>
[WHERE <condition>];
```

To delete the tuple just inserted from the marine fish table, you need to uniquely identify the tuple within the statement's syntax. In this case, the scientific name is the key; you can use this to uniquely define the tuple for removal:

```
DELETE FROM marine_fish
WHERE scientific_name = 'Holocanthus tricolor';
```

If you did not provide the restriction clause, this statement would have deleted all tuples from the marine fish table. You may not have wanted that result. Many actions within the SQL language can have dire effects on the database; you need to be careful when applying these operators to the database.

If, instead of inserting or deleting information from the database, you want to alter information persistently stored within the database, you need to use the UPDATE statement. The UPDATE statement has syntax similar to that of the SELECT statement, and it permits the unique identification of a tuple or tuples for alteration within the database. The BNF syntax of the statement is:

```
UPDATE <table-name> | <view-name>
SET <column-name-1> = <value> | <expression>,
    .         .         .
<column-name-n> = <value> | <expression>
[WHERE <condition>];
```

To illustrate this statement: If you want to alter the entry for the Rock Beauty to indicate that instead of being a grazer, the fish is a predator, you can use the following statement:

```
UPDATE marine_fish
SET fish_activity = 'preditor'
WHERE common_name ='rock beauty'
AND scientific_name = 'Holocanthus tricolor';
```

The condition clause is redundant, but was used to make a point. If one field is empty, another can be used as the selection criterion. The UPDATE statement does not dictate that it must be used in this way. You can also use it to update an entire table. For example, if you want to increase the current price of the organisms in the aquarium stock table, you can use the following statement:

```
UPDATE aquatic_organism_stock
SET current_price = current_price + current_price *.05;
```

The result is that the price of every organism represented in the database, in this table, has had its price changed from its present value to 5 percent higher.

The basic features of the data definition portion of SQL-92 permit the creation, deletion, and altering of tables. The basic operators are the CREATE, ALTER, and DROP statements. The general form of these statements is:

```
CREATE TABLE <table-name>
(<column-name-1><data-type> [NOT NULL],
(<column-name-2><data-type> [NOT NULL],

(<column-name-n><data-type> [NOT NULL]);

ALTER TABLE <table-name>
ADD <column-nmae><data-type>;

DROP TABLE <table-name>;
```

The statements were described in examples at the beginning of this chapter. These statements can be modified to create, drop, or alter a view on a table.

Finally, there are the data control language features within the SQL-92 language. Some of them have been investigated through the GRANT and REVOKE statements. For completeness within this quick overview of the language, the following represents the syntax for the data control statements GRANT and REVOKE:

```
GRANT <ALL | SELECT | UPDATE | INSERT | DELETE | INDEX | ALTER>
ON <table-name(s)> | <view-name(s)>
TO <user-name(s)>;
```

In the database, you may wish to allow customers to select information about fish and diseases from the database, but not allow them to alter, insert, or delete information. To give these rights, you first make an assumption that a "role" exists for customers, and that each customer has access to the database. This can easily be accomplished by providing an obelisk with a query terminal in the store. To give the appropriate access, use the following two statements:

```
GRANT SELECT ON marine_fish TO customer;

GRANT SELECT ON marine_fish_disease TO customer;
```

Similarly, if you grant rights to these tables, views, and procedures, you also have to be able to remove these rights when they are no longer required. SQL-92 provides a REVOKE statement to remove the rights. The format of this statement is:

```
REVOKE <ALL | SELECT | UPDATE | INSERT | DELETE | INDEX | ALTER>
ON <table-name(s)> | <view-name(s)>
TO <user-name(s)>;
```

Summary

This chapter highlighted some of the basic features of the SQL-92 language. Details of the syntax are provided through the BNF described in the chapter. However, this coverage provides only the general form of the language statements. For details and examples of the SQL-92 language, the reader is directed to the bibiliography.

SQL-3 Overview

The SQL-3 language standard has been designed so that parts of the language and the standard can be processed at different speeds as they are accepted and published by national and international standards bodies. Some portions of the SQL-3 standard were started and initially published under the SQL-2 standard (e.g., the SQL CLI [call-level interface] and the SQL PSM [persistent stored modules]). Beyond these components, which have been added to the SQL-2 language, most aspects of SQL-3 replace components within SQL-2. For example, SQL/foundations, SQL/binding, and SQL/objects replace parts of SQL-2 and go well beyond what would be found in SQL-2. The SQL-3 language standard consists of eight accepted parts, and a few additional study areas, which may become parts of the standard in future releases. The eight parts of the SQL-3 standard language are framework, foundation, call-level interface, persistent stored modules, bindings, transactions, temporal, and object. Two possible future extensions include real time and multimedia (MM).

SQL-3 Introduction

The SQL-3 language has been designed as an upwardly compatible extension to the SQL-92 standard (Melton and Simon 1992). This implies that an SQL-2 database and applications could be run, without change, under the SQL-3 data model. The SQL-2 model is a pure relational database model with the relational table as the fundamental data structure and with relational operations provided for data manipulation.

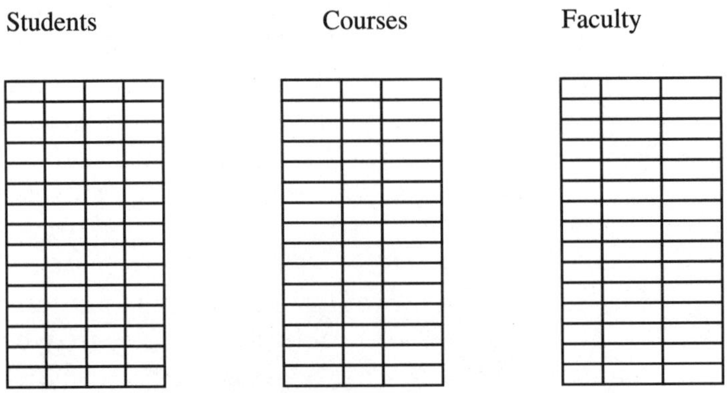

Figure 3.1
SQL-2 data model.

Students   Courses   Faculty

Figure 3.2

SQL-3 data model.

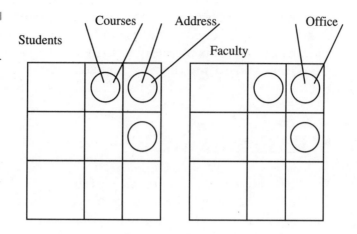

SQL-2 supports standard data types such as variable character, bit, numeric, decimal, integer, real, date, time, timestamp, interval, and others. Base data types can only be combined into base relational tables (Figure 3.1). Relational tables can have views defined on them, restrictions through domains, referential constraints, assertions, and schema modifications. Enhancements at the query level have resulted in new JOIN types for the NATURAL JOIN, and LEFT and RIGHT OUTER JOINs. Dynamic SQL provides additional features to describe, execute, and prepare SQL code segments. SQL-2 enhanced transactions give transaction writers semantic control over execution through expanded degrees of isolation (Gray and Reuter 1993).

The SQL-3 data model (Figure 3.2) enhances and extends the basic SQL-2 relational data model by including objects, row types, collections, and abstract data types into the basic, supported data types that form relational tables. New data types added to the language include enumeration, Boolean, character large objects (text), national character large object, binary large object, row type, set type, multiset, list, and abstract data type. These new data types can be combined in a variety of ways within relations (e.g., as parameters, columns, domains and variables in relations, ADTs, objects, and object operations).

The fundamental components of SQL-2 and SQL-3 have not changed. The relational table is still the only means through which data can become persistent and be included as part of the stored database and its schema. The difference is in how relations are composed. Relations need not be normalized (Date 1990);. that is, they may be composed of repeating groups and nonsingular data types. These include embedded rows, embedded objects, or abstract data types. Details of these structures will be revealed in this chapter and expanded as the book progresses. The remainder of the chapter briefly describes the eight present portions of the SQL-3 standard and the two proposed extensions.

SQL Framework

The SQL framework provides an overview of the complete standard, and documents how the various components that make up the SQL-3 language fit together. This component of the standard can be thought of as a map, or index, to the rest of the standard and a way by which vendors will build conforming products. The main contribution of this element is to provide a repository for common specifications, such as definitions, conventions used in the standard, and concepts applied to the standard. In addition, the SQL framework contains overall conformance clauses for the language.

SQL Foundation

The SQL foundation contains most of the major changes applied to the SQL-2 relational language. This portion of the language contains descriptions for triggers, roles, recursion, new built-in data types, type system extensions, stored routines, user-defined tables, subtables, and other language extensions.

Triggers enhance the ability of the database users to make the database respond actively to changes within the database or external interfaces. Triggers can be used to enhance the integrity of the database by making the database an active element within information management. Database actions can be specified to occur on a variety of system actions, such as an update, deletion, or insertion of informational elements. Triggers can be selectively activated using conditions or temporally based on timing boundaries using before or after controls. Triggers can be specified on individual items within a table, on rows or columns of a table, or the table itself. Triggers can act upon multiple elements and be simple or fairly complex. Applications developers and users can determine the ordering of triggers using SQL-3 syntax and can define the extent of the triggers based on the appropriate definition of scope.

Roles are used to enhance security within the database system. Privileges to roles can be granted or revoked. Roles can be granted and revoked to users or other roles. Roles are used to form groups of users or views into specific domains, which have rights granted to or removed as a unit.

Recursion, a powerful feature of modern programming languages, has been added to the foundation of SQL-3. The primary reason for adding recursive support was to increase the efficiency and power of SQL's query language. Linear recursion, allowing one routine to call itself successively, is provided. A variety of search strategies are supported by recursion, such as depth first and breadth first searching capabilities. Recursion, with added query optimization techniques, provides SQL-3 a powerful mechanism to find information hidden within the database and supports new applications, such as data mining.

A variety of new built-in data types and operations are included in the basic SQL extensions, which are found in SQL's foundation. These new built-in types include Boolean and a variety of large object data types. In addition to these basic built-in data types, there are a variety of other type extensions. The most significant is the abstract data type, which allows applications to define their own database types and is understandable and processible by the database system. There are many advantages as a result of this extension. For example, application data can now map one-to-one with database items (no data impedance mismatch). Complex objects can be represented and processed by the database. Enhanced reusability of data items is possible by making available the combined concepts of object-oriented and relational databases in one place.

The abstract data type (ADT) represents one of the most significant changes within SQL-3. An ADT specification in SQL-3 consists of two parts: an attribute specification and ADT function specifications. Both parts are contained within an ADT type definition. ADT behavior is entirely encapsulated within the type definition. The only externally visible entities are the function interface and attribute definitions. No implementation details are visible outside the type.

ADT attributes and function interface can be further restricted through definitions of public, private, or protected modifiers to their specification. Public specification allows attributes or functions to be available to all users of an ADT. Private specification limits access to internal ADT code, and protected specification limits access to all subtypes of an ADT and local ADT code. These access scopes can be further restricted by privilege mechanisms.

ADTs within SQL-3 are either specified as value ADTs or object ADTs. A value ADT has no unique identifier, but simply has a value for the instance variable. The value ADT acts as primitive data types, which have a value associated with their location identified within a relation by tuple and attribute. Object ADTs differ in that each instance of an ADT has an object identifier (OID) bound to the ADT that uniquely identifies the ADT's instance within the database.

ADTs can also be used as data types for columns in a table, attributes of other ADT definitions, parameters in procedures, parameters in procedures or functions, and variables in SQL statements.

Beyond the major addition of abstract data types, SQL-3 also supports added data types beyond those of SQL-92, including enumeration, Boolean, character large object, binary large object, distinct types, row, set, multiset, and list.

Boolean types allow definition of Boolean functions to use in user-defined operators and predicates where true or false values are wanted. For example, you can create a table for students as:

```
CREATE TABLE students
  (stuid           INTEGER,
   name            VARCHAR (30),
   major           VARCHAR (20),

   . . .

   finaid          BOOLEAN)
```

This table can then be used in a query to find students who are on financial aid:

```
SELECT stuid, name
  FROM students
  WHERE finaid = TRUE;
```

The large object types, character large object (CLOB) and binary large object (BLOB), are additions to the SQL language that provide the basic mechanisms to construct multimedia data storage and retrieval. Data specified as CLOB or BLOB are stored within the database, not as external, noncontrolled files. For example, the student table could be expanded to include an academic vita, the student's transcript, a picture of the student, and an electronic representation of the student's signature:

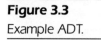

Figure 3.3

Example ADT.

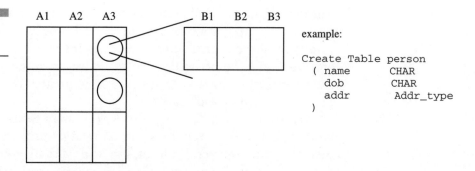

What CLOB and BLOB provide is another type of useful data and the means through which these data may be managed and protected by the database management systems services. These specialized data types do not support all the built-in operators, such as less than, greater than, and union. Operators such as retrieve, replace, like, and concatenation are supported, as are others that allow BLOB and CLOB manipulations on the database side, as well as the applications side, enhancing their usefulness and performance.

Distinct types are the most basic form of user-defined types. A distinct type is defined as a construction or redefinition of base types. Equivalence of distinct types is defined based on name equivalence. For example, two distinct types defined as integers, but with separate names, will not be equivalent. Continuing with the student type, a separate attribute for student identifiers, based on country of legal domicile, could be formed as follows:

```
CREATE DISTINCT TYPE canadianid as integer (9)

CREATE DISTINCT TYPE americanid as integer (9)

CREATE DISTINCT TYPE britishid as integer (9)

                          .
                          .
                          .


CREATE TABLE british_students
     (stuid             britishid,
      name              VARCHAR (30),
      major             VARCHAR (20),

       . . .

      finaid            BOOLEAN)
```

You are required to build tables for each nationality. What distinct type allows is the reuse of a base type or related type (even an ADT) as a separate type, without creating a new, complex ADT. Distinct typing permits ignoring the structural equivalence as a means to determine equivalence, thereby giving the specifier greater control over a data type's specification and use.

All of these added data types and ADTs may be used in SQL-3 as parameters, columns in relations, domains, and variables. Of these added data types, the row, set, multiset, list, and ADT diverge most from past SQL and relational concepts. These data types permit relations to take on forms not possible within the confines of the classical flat relational model of SQL-3's predecessors. In particular, these additions allow SQL-3 to take on some of the qualities of the network database, where repeating groups could be formed within a record's structure. The difference is that the SQL-3 language supports these without the need for navigation to find information, as will be seen in later chapters.

The row type is composed of a row name and sequence of data types, similar to the definition of a flat relation. For example, a row type for address can be specified for the student relation defined in Figure 3.3, as follows:

```
CREATE DOMAIN address_dom ROW
   (street_no       VARCHAR (20),
    street_name     VARCHAR (20),
    city            VARCHAR (20),
    state           VARCHAR (20),
    zip_code        VARCHAR (20),
    )
```

This definition can then be used to embed a row within an attribute holder in an ADT. For the student example, the specification includes just one additional entry, address, of type address_dom, which specifies that the type of the attribute address is the row type address_dom. This implies that each of the address entries for students will have an entry for street number, street name, city, state, and zip code.

```
CREATE TABLE students
   (stuid            INTEGER,
    name             VARCHAR (30),
    address          address_dom,
    major            VARCHAR (20),

      . . .

    finaid           BOOLEAN,
    vita             CLOB(50K),
```

```
transcript          CLOB(50K),
picture             BLOB(10M),
signature           BLOB(1M))
```

Figure 3.4 shows the table created with entries that expand into larger collections of base types. In this example, the address attribute expands to include all the attributes specified in the row type definition. With the row type, as with any type in SQL-3, you can query and operate on these expanded types. For example, to insert a new student instance into the student table:

```
INSERT INTO students VALUES (
     '999-99-9999', 'Jane Doe',
     ROW('118', 'Holly lane', 'SQLville', 'Ca', '99999'),
     'Computer Science', . . . );
```

This only requires the addition of the ROW keyword and parentheses to indicate that these items are part of an embedded row within this relation.

To examine elements of this table you could generate a query, such as:

```
SELECT          name, address..city
FROM            students
WHERE           students.major = 'Computer Science' ;
```

The difference in these specifications from past SQL notation is in how the row type contents for insert uses the keyword ROW, and for que-

Figure 3.4

Table with row type.

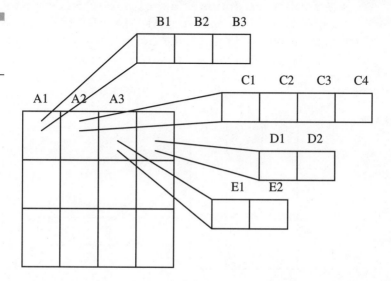

ries, a double dot notation to specify a subpart (row type element) of a column within a table.

Row types are also used to define subtables composed of a base table and, possibly, added column definitions. The subtype/supertype relationship is defined within SQL-3 using the keyword UNDER in a subtype clause. A type S is a supertype of T, if T is a subtype of S. Similar to ADT inheritance in the object model, a subtype specification takes on all the specifications of the supertype, incorporating these into the subtype specification along with any other definitions (see Figure 3.5). For example, using the type students previously defined, you can define a subtype, research_assitants, by specifying:

```
CREATE TYPE research_assistants UNDER students
(RA_ID           INTEGER,
 hire_date       DATE,
 salary          INTEGER,
 department      u_department,
 review_date     DATE
);
```

The subtype research_assistant also includes all the specifications for students. The idea is that the table research_assistants automatically creates a row type for students as part of the research_assistants table. The subtype inherits every column from the supertype table and may define its own columns. The supertable becomes a column in the subtable and is represented by a row type. Actions on a supertype or subtype will affect the related type (inheritance).

To allow definition of more complex data structures, SQL-3 provides a number of *collection* types: ARRAY, SET, LIST, and MULTISET. (These may be deferred until SQL-4 due to national and international commit-

Figure 3.5

Table structure with subtyping.

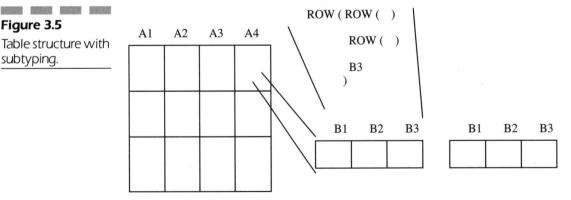

tee concerns.) The components of these collection types can be simple elementary data types, such as character, strings, integers, and so on; more complex types, such as row or ADT; or major types, such as tables.

The SET data type facilitates the grouping of a collection of related instances of the same data type into a single data structure, which will have no duplicates. For example, a SET could contain the names of a collection of students or a collection of phone numbers. SET provides a means to collect similar elements for added semantic richness. As an example, if a student has multiple addresses (say a home address and a school address), as well as a number of phone numbers where the student can be reached (e.g., a lab, dorm room, or work/study office), SETs could be used to group these under the student using the following syntax (assuming the types address and phone numbers are created):

```
CREATE TABLE students (
            s_name          name,
            s_id            INTEGER,


                              .
                              .
                              .


            s_address       SET(address),
            s_phone         SET(phone_no)
        );
```

To insert an item into the student table you can use the following syntax:

```
INSERT INTO students VALUES (
    ROW('Jane','Doe'),
    '000112222',
 .

    SET(ROW('285','Old Westport rd', 'N.Dartmouth', 'Ma.', '02747'),
ROW('1199', 'West 69th st', 'New York', 'NY', '10021'))
    SET( '5089991122', '2029991111')
     );
```

To construct a data structure with order, the LIST collection type of SQL-3 can be used. By using this type of structure, a list of students or a list of faculty could be constructed with the property that each of the collections would have an ordering based on the types of implied ordering. For example, if you want a list of students in a particular class, the list can be ordered based on the students' IDs or their names.

Another collection type is the MULTISET. MULTISET is a collection type that, unlike the other two types, allows duplicates. As a fundamental definition, the relation or table is a MULTISET of rows. MULTISET provides the means to collect a set of items together, irrespective of duplicate values. In general, collections are value typed and thus have no object identifier (OID) and must be declared as types of table columns for instances of the collection to be persistently stored in the database.

Another addition to the SQL-3 language is the condition handling statement and the semantics to support them. Condition handling provides users with a means to define where and how exceptions (errors as well as positive events) are to be handled. Exceptions must be explicitly defined, have names associated with them, and have an SQLSTATE code associated with them. Exception conditions can be raised explicitly using the SIGNAL or RESIGNAL keywords, or they can be raised implicitly. The SIGNAL statement explicitly raises a named exception and empties the previously defined diagnostic area.

Exception handlers can follow one of three execution styles: UNDO, CONTINUE, and EXIT. The scope of an exception handler is the scope of the compound statement that contains the defined exception handler. The UNDO handler is used to undo the changes made by a compound statement before the exception was raised. UNDO handlers are allowed for atomic compound statements only. Upon completion of the UNDO handler, flow of control continues at the end of the compound statement where the exception was raised. The CONTINUE handler is used to perform some designed condition fix and then return control to the statement following the statement that raised the exception. Finally, the EXIT handler style is used if the intent of the condition handling is to perform the handling function and then exit the compound statement from where the condition derived.

To explicitly cause an exception to be executed requires the use of the SIGNAL statement. The format is SIGNAL condition_handler_name. The statement requires that the condition handler name was declared earlier in the compound statement structure. If a handler out of the immediate scope of this compound statement is appropriate for handling the condition, the RESIGNAL statement is used to pass the call outside of the compound statement. The RESIGNAL statement can only be used within an exception handler to change the handler for a given condition. When RESIGNAL is called, the existing compound statement and the handler issuing RESIGNAL are terminated, and control passes to the next outer exception handler.

These are highlights of some of the extensions found within this dynamic and far-reaching change to the SQL-2 database definition, manipulation, and management language. Many other features, such as subtables, save points, and cursor extensions, will be discussed in following chapters.

SQL Call-Level Interface

A call-level interface (CLI) is a binding between an SQL database and a user-interface language. A CLI binding forms a cross between dynamic SQL and static SQL supported in a server. SQL CLI operates by passing SQL statements as parameters to a support subroutine (an ad hoc SQL interface server), which interprets the passed statement and returns responses to the calling CLI routine. SQL-3's call-level interface (SQL/CLI) supports an alternative means for invoking SQL code from application programs. SQL/CLI is based on the SQL access group and X/Open's call-level interface definitions, along with open database connection specifications. CLI does not support a non standard means to access distributed databases, as supported through ISO's remote database access (RDA) standard protocols.

What CLI does provide is a means for noncompiled programs to access an existing SQL database or SQL-supported product, without recompilation of the SQL database or compiled product. The view to a server is an application opening a session, issuing dynamic SQL statements, waiting for responses interacting with the server, and, finally, closing the session (see Figure 3.6). CLI provides a functional interface to a database. These functions are used to control the connection of the application to an SQL server to allocate and deallocate resources, execute SQL statements, obtain diagnostic information, control transaction termination, and acquire information about underlying database management system implementation.

CLI supported applications interact with underlying SQL databases using the CLI call handler as the middleman. CLI handlers take as input CLI "handles," which in turn are converted to SQL server commands through appropriate conversions and processing. A CLI-supported application initiates an SQL command by first issuing an SQL alloc environment call, which creates a CLI environment handle. Then the application must issue an SQL alloc connect handle to control the connection to the target database. If the SQL connect command is successful, implying the server has opened the connection, the CLI can

Figure 3.6
CLI interface.

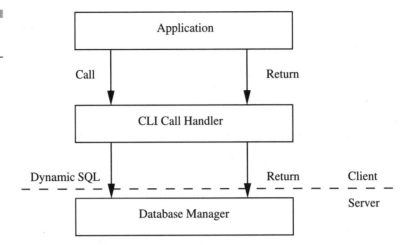

package the SQL statements for execution on the server using the SQL alloc statement function. This function provides the packaging and protocols for CLI to issue an "execute immediate" command with the packaged statement as its operation. If ready, the CLI can issue a commit using CLI SQL transac statements with the appropriate SQL server command through the middleman. Once completed, the CLI manager must release the statement handles, disconnect from the database, free the connect handle, and, finally, free the environment handle.

A number of statements can be included in the environment's body that run interactively with SQL servers under CLI management. CLI provides more than 50 functions to support interactive access to an SQL server environment. Details of these CLI function definitions and their use can be found in (Melton 1998a). CLI permits the execution of applications and SQL code without the need to possess the source code on this site. CLI permits access to external data through a simple interface, which avoids the need for a preprocessor. The CLI behaves similarly to dynamic SQL in that access is limited to simple requests and performance will be reduced.

SQL Persistent Stored Modules

SQL-3 added a significant feature to the language with SQL persistent stored modules (PSM). SQL-3's stored procedures and user-defined functions can be written in a 3GL or in SQL. PSM gives great power to the database management system and improves performance through pre-compilation, compile time type checking, and optimization. Modules in PSM support overloading of names, with resolution of which implementation to use based on evaluating all arguments passed to the module at run time and matching to the closest implementation. Users can define paths to implementations as part of the design-time specification.

Functions, procedures, and modules were added to SQL to support the requirements of ADTs and advanced database applications. Routines are necessary to support the concept of object and object operation. Object operations may be realized through code segments embedded within stored data, through stored data only, or through another object's inherited instance. Inherited object data structures and ADT behavior (code) are stored together and are accessible through an object's OID and methods.

Functions associated with ADTs are used to compute single-valued data type results or return Boolean designations. Functions can have parameters passed in to use in their computations, or they can be parameterless. For example, a function to return the time may be without parameters; a function to determine a relative time may need the geographical region being referred to for computation of the correct value:

```
CREATE FUNCTION l_time() RETURNS time

    BEGIN

  /* extract current time from the database */

    END;

CREATE FUNCTION r_time(t_zone CHAR) RETURN time
    BEGIN

  /* extract current relative time from the database */

    END;
```

Functions can be constructed completely from SQL code, may be defined in an SQL schema definition (persistent stored module), or may be implemented in a separate host language as a host language function.

Functions may be either a *destructor* or an *actor*. Destructor functions destroy ADT instances, whereas actor functions are any function that reads, updates, or creates an ADT instance or accesses any component of an ADT.

ADT methods can also be implemented using procedures that do not return a value. Procedures can have parameter lists, which can be simply in parameters, out parameters, or in-out parameters. Procedures can include data structure definitions, database access statements, flow of control statements, functions, objects, and special database operation statements (e.g., BEGIN ATOMIC).

Functions and procedures may be encapsulated within an ADT's definition or defined externally. Encapsulated routines and externally defined routines have access to the private attributes of the ADT when associated with a specific ADT. All ADTs have one specific routine automatically defined, called a *constructor,* which is used to create new instances of the ADT type. The constructor takes on the same name as the ADT type and has zero arguments. When called, it returns a new instance of the type with a unique OID and uninitiated attributes.

Functions and procedures associated with an ADT implement ADT type-specific behaviors. For example, an ADT of type student may have functions or procedures to access or update the students name, address, age, major, phone number, Social Security number, photo, mother, father, daughter, son, sibling of, and whatever else the ADT designer developed and coded into the ADT to give the user-defined type the specific behavior. Functions and procedures may also be constrained to act on rows of tables, allowing for object-like operations to be constructed for rows.

A structural component of SQL-3, which differs from SQL2 and other relational database languages, is the module and persistent stored routines. Modules can contain functions and procedures, as well as shared declarations for cursors, variables, and tables. Modules can be schema objects and thus can be persistent. Persistent stored modules and procedures can be called in any other SQL statement, function, procedure, or module that is linked to the database schema and contains the stored element. The calling routine or statement uses the names of routines as though they had been defined within the context of the executing routine, statement, or SQL code segment.

As an example, the module student_actions is defined to describe all the actions required on the student objects of a database:

```
CREATE MODULE student_actions
LANGUAGE SQL

PROCEDURE enroll(. . . )        PROCEDURE gpa ( . . . )
BEGIN                           BEGIN

END                             END
```

```
PROCEDURE add_class( . . . )      PROCEDURE get_transcript( . . . )
BEGIN                             BEGIN

END                              END

PROCEDURE drop_class( . . . )     PROCEDURE get_advisor( . . . )
BEGIN                             BEGIN

END                              END

PROCEDURE graduate( . . . )
BEGIN

END

END MODULE student_actions;
```

To use the module and procedures in an application requires the use of CALL statements:

```
EXEC SQL

  CALL student_actions.enroll ('Nicole', 'Pediatrics',
   '999 88 7777', '1',
   'America's Cup Ave','Newport', 'RI', '02840');

EXEC SQL

  CALL student_actions.add_class('Anatomy', 'BIO121', '01',
   'Nicole', '999 88 7777');
```

The names of the routines defined within the module are used later, as if they were defined in the direct context of the executing SQL code. The modules form a structure that can encase data specification and data manipulation actions separately from ADT declarations and operations. As such, the module can be used as an area to capture sets of specialized data and operations in a single schema object, which then decomposes into its constructed components.

Routines, however, do not need to be defined only within the context of an SQL schema element. Routines can be defined external to the SQL language in some other host language. External routines, to be accessible to SQL statements, must have an SQL signature. The signature includes definition of the external name by which the routine can be accessed, the implementation language, the parameter style used by the routine, the SQL state, and other specifications as needed.

The signature is shown in the following code segment:

```
CREATE FUNCTION grade_point_avg ( x CHAR ) RETURNS FLOAT;
EXTERNAL NAME gpa
LANGUAGE C++
PARAMETER STYLE SQL
NOT VARIANT;
```

The new, externally defined function and SQL statement use the SQL signature definition:

```
SELECT gpa ( 'Nicole') FROM . . .
```

PSM SQL 3 Flow of Control Structures

Another major change to the relational SQL model deals with computational completeness. SQL-3's PSM has extended SQL-2 by incorporating functions, procedures, modules, and associated flow of control statements. Basic flow of control statements, such as the compound statement with block delimiters BEGIN and END; loop control such as WHILE, IF THEN ELSE, REPEAT, FOR, and LOOP; and the selection statement CASE, are all basic elements of the SQL-3 language and do not need to be borrowed from host languages, as was the case in pre-SQL-3 languages. The addition of these statements has made the SQL-3 language more computationally complete.

For example, to send notices to the electrical and computer engineering (ECE) students and to the computer science (CS) students for an upcoming IEEE and ACM meeting, respectively, the following code segment can be generated:

```
IF    ( SELECT major
         FROM students
         WHERE club = 'IEEE') = ECE
THEN INSERT INTO send_mail(IEEE . . .

ELSEIF (SELECT major
    FROM students
    WHERE club = 'ACM') = CIS
THEN INSERT INTO send_mail(ACM . . .

ENDIF
```

To make this complete would require that the IF statement be encased in another statement, which would continue to iterate over all the students in the student table. This could be performed by a FOR loop:

```
FOR stu AS SELECT * FROM students
        WHERE college = 'engineering'

        DO

        \* Do some computation *\

END FOR;
```

Other statements operate in similar fashion based on their programming language counterparts. The BEGIN – END forms a group of statements to be executed sequentially, within their defined scope. The BNF format of the compound statement formed using BEGIN and END is:

```
<compound statement> ::=
[ <beginning label> <colon> ]
BEGIN [ [NOT] ATOMIC]
[<local declaration list>]
[<local handler declaration list>]
[<SQL statement list>]
END [ <ending label>]
```

Declarations within a BEGIN – END compound statement have a lifetime and scope defined by the containing compound statement. For example, a declaration made within the BEGIN – END block exists only during the execution of the block. Compound statements can contain control structures, data manipulation language statements, transaction control statements, session management statements, diagnostic management statements, data definition statements, dynamic statements, and connection statements.

The CASE statement provides a means to select one of many options based on a key value. The format of the CASE statement is:

```
CASE ( selection variable or statement )

WHEN 'value1' THEN
        .
        .
        .
WHEN 'value n' THEN

ELSE  SQL-statements        \* no matches do else clause
END CASE
```

The CASE statement has two versions. The first version includes one selection variable or statement being evaluated for the CASE statement. The second version of the CASE statement has no value expression associated with the keyword CASE. Instead, a separate condition for each WHEN clause is allowed:

```
CASE

WHEN 'cond' THEN
            .
            .
            .
WHEN 'cond n' THEN

ELSE       SQL-statements      \* no matches do else clause
END CASE
```

Other iteration statements are provided. LOOP allows for iteration over SQL statements encased in the loop indefinitely. Once a loop has begun, the code encased in the loop will be executed over and over until a LEAVE statement is encountered, which allows for exiting the loop. The structure of the LOOP statement is:

```
Loop_label:   LOOP
                 SQL-statement
              IF condition      THEN
                 LEAVE Loop_label
              END IF;
                 SQL-statement
              END LOOP;
```

SQL-3 also includes the WHILE and REPEAT statements to allow iteration with testing for completion at the top or bottom of the structure:

```
Loop_label:   WHILE condition_false
                 DO
                        SQL-statements
              END WHILE;

Loop_label:   REPEAT
                        SQL-statements
              UNTIL condition_true
              END REPEAT;
```

Further details and a more thorough example will be provided in later chapters.

SQL Bindings

The SQL bindings specify the relationship and operations between the SQL-3 language and other application-specific languages. SQL bindings exist to provide dynamic invocation of SQL code embedded in a host language. The most common form of binding is the EXEC SQL statement, which permits the initiation of an embedded SQL data manipulation statement. Bindings statements exist to create tables, manipulate data, extract SQL state, examine and evaluate constraints, execute an SQL exception, and issue SQL warnings. Further extensions are forthcoming to support client modules and definers' rights. Bindings have been defined between the C and C++, Basic, Ada, and COBOL languages.

SQL Transactions

Transactions represent a complete unit of work in a database system that exhibits the *ACID* properties (Atomic, Consistent, Isolated, and Durable) (Date 1990). Transactions may encase many tasks requiring communication, user interface, and data manipulation. The SQL transaction, or SQL/XA specification, depicts the policies and mechanisms through which application programs interact with isolated resource managers under the control of a transaction manager.

The typical instantiation of distributed processing is the client/server class of system and processing. The transaction manager has the job of coordinating the operations of the various resource managers (which could be separate database systems) to encase them in a larger sphere of control (Gray and Reuter 1993), so that coordination of actions can ensue (Figure 3.7). The resource managers use two-phase commit operations to ensure correctness. First, all resource managers are asked to prepare to commit. If all resource managers involved within a transaction manager's scope are ready to commit, the manager will then either issue commit or issue rollbacks to all.

Figure 3.7

Distributed
transaction
processing model
and components.

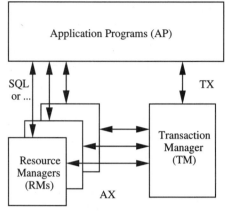

(1) AP uses
resources from
a set of RMs

(2) AP defines
transaction boundaries
through the
TX interface

(3) TM and RMs exchange transaction information

The interface to complete this coordination requires that added functional calls be provided to the applications in order to construct transactions. The commands include:

xa_reg	To register a resource manager as part of a transaction T
ax_unreg	To unregister a resource manager
xa_close	To terminate an application's use of a resource manager
xa_commit	To command the resource manager to commit under a transaction's control
xa_complete	To test if an asynchronous xa_ operation has completed
xa_end	To disassociate a thread from a transactional branch
xa_forget	To allow a resource manager to discard knowledge of a heuristically completed transactional branch
xa_open	To initialize a resource manager for use by an application
xa_prepare	To indicate to a joined resource manager to prepare to commit a transaction branch

xa_recover   To acquire a list of transaction identifiers for prepared or completed transactions on a resource manager

xa_rollback   To indicate to a resource manager to roll back a transactional branch

xa_start   To initiate or resume a transactional branch on a resource manager

The scope of this specification is distributed transactions, which are comprised of actions on a variety of database engines or platforms, which coordinate actions to complete a joined piece of work into a single transactional thread. The SQL Transaction specification (Melton 1998b) describes the details of these operations, and the scope of how and when they may be used by applications to construct distributed transactional units of work. This extension to the foundation SQL-3 language builds a specialization for the XA interface defined by X/Open, and has been accepted as an international standard. This component of the standard is specific for SQL and defines the binding of XA parameters to SQL data types.

SQL Temporal

The SQL temporal portion of the SQL-3 standard describes additions to the language to support temporal data storage and retrieval. Temporal data are used to describe information of historical interest, such as time of change intervals, historical events, versions, and so on. The SQL temporal standard describes additions to the SQL-2 and SQL-3 base data types for the DATETIME, INTERVAL, and PERIOD types. The DATE-TIME data type allows the representation and asking of questions as to the actual time an event occurred. The DATETIME data type is an extension of the TIMESTAMP data type, which includes year, month, day, and timestamp. The INTERVAL data type returns a value commensurate with the base types of the interval and indicates the relative *age* (begin time up to end time or present time) of a data object (e.g., the age of a person, the age of a process, etc.). The PERIOD data type is composed of two data types, which include the begin time and end time of a data item explicitly stored with the item. For example, the period a student spent in school could be September 3, 1990, to June 5, 1994. These

Figure 3.8

Example temporal
data table.

Name	Salary	Title	Date of Birth	Start	Stop
Cousteau	15000	Collector	1-1-20	1-1-80	1-1-85
Cousteau	25000	Curator	1-1-20	1-2-85	1-1-89
Cousteau	35000	Biologist	1-1-20	1-2-89	1-1-93
Cousteau	45000	Explorer	1-1-20	1-2-93	1-1-95
Cousteau	55000	Explorer	1-1-20	1-2-95	1-1-97
Cousteau	15000	Collector	1-1-20	1-2-97	1-1-99

two dates together form the period of the data type associated with the student.

These base data types are then expanded on functionally to include predicates on how these types are related. For example, one data item X *precedes* a data item Y, a data item X = Y, X *meets* Y, X *overlaps* Y, and X *contains* Y. These temporal data types support low-level arithmetic operations, such as addition, subtraction, and so on; support logical operations, such as <, >, and so on; as well as some of the SQL aggregate operations. Time can be tested for its validity in reference to base types and the present time.

The goal of these extensions is to provide SQL-3 with the expressiveness and manipulation power to support time-varying data. Time-varying data are found naturally in applications such as personnel operations, accounting, financial, budgets, geographical information, decision support, and numerous others (Figure 3.8). Further details about the SQL temporal language specification can be found in (Melton 1998c).

SQL Object

The SQL object component delivers a means whereby application-specific data types can be understood by the database management system. The addition of application-defined abstract data types into the database increases the database's ability to model more complex objects and increases the range of possible application requirements that can be met. The impedance mismatch between applications and the database can further be closed through the use of this component of the SQL-3 language. A further benefit of this capability is the possibility of sharing existing type libraries with applications and the database. SQL objects will enable the integration of object-oriented and relational concepts in a single language.

The major change is to extend the row type to include row objects. Row objects have an identity for rows in a table, such as an OID. Row objects can have references to other row objects, allowing for sharing, and can have path expression operations that allow for dereferencing operations. This component of the SQL-3 language is presently in committee draft form and is anticipated to progress forward toward a standard later in 1999 or sometime in 2000.

Proposed SQL-3 Extensions

There are two proposed extensions to the SQL-3 standard. They are multimedia (MM) and real time. These are discussed in the following text.

Multimedia (MM)

SQL-3 can allow definition of user-defined, application-specific data types, user-defined functions to operate on the data types, storage of large binary and character objects, powerful triggers, and constraints for semantic integrity maintenance on these new types. SQL-3 also allows persistent stored modules and procedures. This has enabled the development of user-defined types, functions, procedures, and controls integral with the database management system operational functions. These user-defined collections can be formed into *libraries,* which can be shared or transferred among users of conforming systems. SQL multimedia data types and operations form such *libraries.* These multimedia libraries themselves, if defined to be interoperable and portable (use only standard SQL-3 syntax and semantics), can be created by a variety of database vendors, software vendors, or users to support their multimedia data management needs.

Specifying these specialized abstract data types and operations upon these abstract data types, within the database's language boundaries and in a standard way, delivers consistent semantics and syntax for application development using these multimedia data types and their operations. Productivity improves development. As with other generalized data types supported in the database, multimedia data types can be optimized by specialists and can be readily used by applications developers. The standard multimedia data types integrate cleanly and completely with the database, whereas user-specified data types may not be as seamlessly integrated and reusable.

The SQL multimedia portion of the standard is being developed by a separate committee within ANSI and ISO. This committee has the charter to develop a set of multimedia library specifications, which define specialized SQL abstract data types and their operations for multimedia objects. The present effort has defined a baseline document, which includes initial multimedia objects for spatial and full-text objects, still image, and general-purpose abstract data types, such as complex numbers, vectors, Euclidean 2 and 3 space, and Boolean set. Additional generalized data types for coordinates, geometry (point, line, circle, ellipse, polygon, etc.), and their operations (area, intersection of spatial objects, volume, etc.) are under development. Present efforts are examining audio and video specifications as additions to the library of SQL multimedia abstract data types and operations. Details and status of the multimedia component of the SQL-3 database language can be found in the ANSI baseline document for the language (Melton 1998d).

Real Time

The real-time database language efforts under the SQL language are only in their initial concept development phase. Presentations to the SQL committee have been for informational and educational purposes, with the intent being to develop a baseline document describing the foundations of the SQL Real-Time (SQL/RT) component by the end of 2000. Real-time database systems have three distinguishing features compared with their conventional counterparts: the concept of temporally consistent data, the ability to place real-time constraints on data processing requests, and the requirement that certain executions exhibit predictable timing behavior (Fortier 1994; Prichard 1995).

Data in a real-time system must not only be logically consistent, but temporally consistent as well. Such requirements stem from a real-time application's need to acquire information that closely reflects the state of the application's interacting environment, which the database is trying to mimic. Data are collected at intervals and hence represents an approximation of reality. As time passes, this approximation is less accurate, until a point is reached when the information value is no longer reflective of the environment it is meant to model. At this point these data are said to be temporally inconsistent. Temporal consistency can be measured in two ways: *absolute* and *relative* consistency. Absolute consistency is assured if the value of a data item is within some given *age.* Relative consistency deals with the time validity of a data item *relative* to the value and absolute time of other data items.

Transactions, as with data, can have temporal constraints defined on their operations. Timing constraints on transactions and embedded actions define the period of time imposed on the completion of a transaction or action. This constraint can be absolute or periodic. Absolute timing constraints are used to express earliest start times, latest start times, and latest finish times and can be specified using the absolute clock or a relative time (interval). Periodic timing constraints are used to express periodic executions of actions that can be based upon absolute time intervals of action initiation and completion.

This proposal focuses on the definition of additional data types, extension to basic data types with transaction specification, transaction structure, transaction initiation and completion predicates, and on recovery of all, based on the concept of real-time actions on data and transactions (Prichard 1995).

Summary

The SQL-3 language specification and its implementation is a monumental task. The national and international standards organizations embarked on this ambitious undertaking in 1992, just as the SQL-2 standard was released. The work was spurred on by the needs of the information management community, applications developers, and end users. These diverse groups have wide-ranging informational needs, which far outstripped SQL-2's capabilities. Because of this, advanced concepts beyond the relational model were undertaken. SQL-3 embodies the best of two worlds—the highly successful relational database community and the dynamic and flexible object-oriented database community. The new model is a combination of these two models and is referred to as the relational-object or object-relational model, depending on which side of the database community your roots lie.

The SQL-3 language is a very complicated work of standards documentation encompassing about 1,500 pages of specifications and clarifications. The language is broken up into eight existing components, with two additional portions under development for possible future inclusion. It is anticipated that the language, once released as a standard, will be implemented in pieces. How these pieces are evaluated for conformance to the standard is still a matter of conjecture. It is hoped that either some government organization, or independent arm of the standards community, will come up with a description of the levels of conformance and tests against which products can be evaluated. Without such capabilities, this new SQL standard may go the route of the network database standard and have no means by which a product can be classified as conforming. This is a plight no vendor or user wishes to see happen.

SQL-3 represents a revolution in how databases are constructed and operated. If the full standard and proposed extensions are realized, database applications developers, database vendors, and, most importantly, database users will have a product that is poised to support the community for some time into the future. The standard will evolve and be introduced to the community in sections. Users and designers alike are urged to participate and respond to requests from the database standards community and vendors to indicate features needed by their respective application domains. SQL-4 is closer than we think. Many features originally envisioned for the SQL-3 standard have been pushed out to its successor, SQL-4, to improve the likelihood of progression of the SQL-3 standard to final international standards status. It is anticipated that by the time this book is published, the SQL-3 foundation will be moving into the final stages toward standardization and release.

CHAPTER **4**

SQL-3 Model and
Language Basics

Introduction to the Object-Relational SQL-3 Data Model

Databases have been developed to provide a set of basic data types, used to construct the representation of real data within an application's domain. Database management systems are then developed to provide a set of operations, allowing for the manipulation of this stored information in some meaningful way. Application complexity has continued to grow, as the ability and desire to model further real-world objects in useful ways within a computer's digital environment has progressed. This trend is not likely to change within the foreseeable future and is, indeed, expected to grow in complexity. Such application requirements spurred the database community and software developers to find ways to more completely represent information desirable to users and applications developers.

One way of providing for application-specific data types is to extend the possible data types supported by the language to include new built-in data types. The problem with this simplistic approach is that application-specific data types come in many forms. One application may need a map data type, another may need a fish data type, and a third may need a disease data type. How could a database include all these and many more application-specific data types as built-in data types to the database? The answer is that it cannot. The basic data types, along with some needed extensions, must possess the ability to be organized into more complex user-defined, *new* data types. These new application-specific data types will have their own structure and behavior separate from all other database types. The new data types, however, must exist at the database level and be processible by the data management system, if the qualities of a database management system are to be available to the new applications using the database.

The approach taken by the SQL-3 committee is to provide a means through which user-defined *objects* can be specified within the framework of the database and the database's schema, can be manipulated by the underlying database management system, and can be used directly by users. The result is a highly integrated data typing system with supporting database processing software. Objects and their behaviors can be specified by users; stored within the database; and, through user-provided add-on actions, managed and manipulated by the database system.

Basic Database Structures

The basic element within the SQL-3 database system is still the table or relation. However, the structure has taken on significantly more semantic meaning. The table is the sole means through which any data can become persistent, as in past SQL databases. The table and descriptive information about the table are the sole means for constructing the database schema. The table is not as rigid in its structure, syntax, or semantic meaning as in the original relational database model. Tables need not adhere to the strict normal forms of relational design. Instead, they are allowed to take on more flexible forms in support of application requirements.

The Relation

In the beginning, there were relations, a fundamental property of the relational database model. All information entities are represented as two-dimensional arrays of data items called *relations,* or *tables.* These data structures are not just randomly ordered or loosely organized. The definition and structure of a relation forces numerous properties to be applied to the stored data items. A relation is structured in the form of a uniquely named table consisting of a fixed number of columns and rows, all having the same number and types of columns, and all in the same location within the row. A table name represents the relation's name within the database. Once a relation is placed into a database it is a time-invariant specification. Thus, the name of this relation cannot be changed, duplicated, or altered within this database over its lifetime. The columns of the table represent the attributes or components that make up a relation's entries. For example, an employee relation from the aquarium management database informally described in Chapter 2 may be comprised of the attribute's employee identifier (`emp_ID`), employee name (`emp_last_name`, `emp_first_name`), employee job title (`emp_title`), employee address (`emp_street`, `emp_city`, `emp_state`, `emp_zip`), employee phone number (`emp_phone`), employee start date (`emp_start_date`), employee commission rate (`emp_com_rate`), and employee salary (`emp_pay_rate`). This can be represented in SQL data definition language as follows:

```
CREATE TABLE employees (
    emp_id          INTEGER
      CONSTRAINT employees_emp_id_pk PRIMARY KEY,
    emp_title       CHARACTER VARYING (50),
    last_name       CHARACTER VARYING (50),
      CONSTRAINT employees_last_name_not_null NOT NULL,
    first_name      CHARACTER VARYING (50),
      CONSTRAINT employees_first_name_not_null NOT NULL,
    emp_street      CHARACTER VARYING (30),
    emp_city        CHARACTER VARYING (20),
    emp_state       CHARACTER (2),
    emp_zip         CHARACTER VARYING (9),
    emp_phone       CHARACTER (10),
    emp_start_date  TIMESTAMP,
    emp_pay_rate    DECIMAL (7,2)
    emp_com_rate    DECIMAL (5,2)
)
```

These attributes form the definition for an entity's instance to be represented within this relation. The name of attributes defined for a relation are also time invariant. Thus, their name and specification cannot be altered, changed, or duplicated within this relation once they have been defined within the schema for this database. In addition, the specification of a relation includes the specification of the set of possible values that each attribute can possess. In the employee example above, the Employee relation consists of 12 attributes, where their domains of possible values are chosen from the sets of characters (CHAR) or integers (INT), TIMESTAMP, and DECIMAL types. The attributes are limited to some number of characters, integer size (based on the descriptor for the data type), timestamp, and decimal. In addition, some attributes (e.g., emp_ID) have the additional constraint that they must always have a value. The value is a primary key for this relation, implying that this field must also be unique for each row within this relation. It cannot be undefined or unambiguous. We will see why later.

The attribute names within a relation are required to be unique in order to differentiate between attributes within a relation, though the name used to describe an attribute in one relation can be reused within another relation within the same database. For example, in the Employee relation above you can have another relation in the database, Customer, that also includes the attribute's name and address.

```
CREATE TABLE customers (
    cust_id         INTEGER
      CONSTRAINT customers_cust_id_pk PRIMARY KEY,
    last_name       CHARACTER VARYING (50)
      CONSTRAINT customers_last_name_not_null NOT NULL,
    first_name      CHARACTER VARYING (50)
      CONSTRAINT customers_first_name_not_null NOT NULL,
```

```
        cust_address      CHARACTER VARYING (30),
        cust_city         CHARACTER VARYING (20),
        cust_state        CHARACTER (2),
        cust_zip          CHARACTER VARYING (9),
        cust_phone        CHARACTER (10),
        cust_credit_id    CHARACTER VARYING (20),
        cust_current_bal  DECIMAL (7,2),
        cust_ytd          DECIMAL (9,2),
        num_complaints    INTEGER,
        num_returns       INTEGER,
        cust_rating       INTEGER,
        last_purchase     TIMESTAMP
    )
```

Even though many of the attributes in the Customer relation have the same definition as the Employee relation, the elements themselves are still unique and can therefore be differentiated from each other, since they are from separate relations. Addressing them as separate attributes is as easy as referring to the two relations and their attributes with a dot notation. This form of addressing is:

```
ename := EMPLOYEE.last_name;
```

or

```
cname := CUSTOMER.last_name;
```

The name of a relation in the database, however, cannot be reused within the specification of the entire database. This means, within the aquarium management example, that you cannot have another relation within the database that has the name Employee or Customer.

The specification of the attributes within a relation must be separate from the specification for an attribute's domain of values the attribute can take on. In the example above, the attribute name is specified first, followed by the domain of the values for the employee name attribute. The domain of values is specified as a character string, which consists of up to 50 characters for both the first and last name. The employee's salary rate is specified first by an attribute name or identifier called emp_pay_rate, followed by a specification for the domain of possible values that salary can be (e.g., positive decimal values with a range of three integers and two decimal places). This allows representation of an employee salary rate from $0.00 to $999.99.

Similarly, to guarantee that the tuples within a relation can be differentiated from each other, you must specify a unique identifier. In the Employee relation, the employee identifier is specified as a non-null value with a range of possible integer locations. This gives you a range of zero to the integer limitation of the implementation for employee identifiers. In addition, we need to specify that this is the primary key for the relation to limit its representation further. As a key, the attribute is further constrained to require that each occurrence of a data item of this type be unique across all such data items within this relation only. What this means is that no two employee identifiers can have the same value, or an SQL error would be raised.

A relation can have numerous types of key attributes. The first and most important is the *primary key*. A primary key is the attribute within a relation that, by itself, uniquely defines any tuple within the relation. A primary key also cannot possess the null value. A key can also be constructed from multiple attributes. For example, if you had a supplies database table where the item identifiers were not unique, a primary key could be constructed by combining the item identifier with a vendor identifier:

```
SUPPLIES(item-id, vendor-id, item_name, unit-cost);
```

The combination of the two attributes, if they provide a unique value, would represent the primary key for the relation. A key constructed in this manner is called a compound key. Compound keys are common in relational databases for use as relationship implementers. For example, the simple Supplies relation above could be used as the relationship construct to link manufacturers (VENDORS) with items (SUPPLIES). In this way you can represent the relationship where a particular item is purchasable from multiple vendors or a relationship where a vendor supplies multiple items.

There can also be times when a relation has numerous attributes that could qualify as a primary key. For example, in the Employee relation from above, if we add an additional attribute called Social Security number (ss#), a second attribute now exists that, by definition, has a unique representation for each person in the company. Both of the attributes could therefore act as the key for this relation. They are then both called *candidate keys*. Candidate keys can be used in numerous ways: as the primary indices into a relation, as secondary indices into a relation, or as a means to provide a path for the combination of relations during relational operations.

The fourth form of key found in the relational model is the foreign key. A foreign key is an attribute in one relation that has a matching attribute in another relation, where the match is to a primary key in the foreign relation. From this definition, if an attribute, A, from relation R is a foreign key in relation S, then there must be elements in S such that for each value of A in R, there is a match to a primary key value in S. Three example relations are shown below.

```
VENDOR( Vendor-No, Vendor-id, Vendor-name, Vendor-city)

SUPPLY( Vendor-No, Item-No, Qty)

ITEM( Item-No, Item-name)
```

If Item-No is a foreign key in SUPPLY, by the definition above, there must be a matching value in ITEM for Item-No, the primary key in the Item relation.

Relational Operations

The most fundamental property of the classical relational database system is that data are presented to the user as tables. All actions performed on relations within the database result in new relations, with a cardinality and degree derived from the combination of the relations being operated on and the relational operator being applied. To access the new data produced, you must place the results of a relational operation into a user program data structure. The relational data manipulation model provides a variety of relational operators to examine and restructure stored relations for user purposes. Unary and binary are two basic types of classical relational operations. The unary operations are used to access singular attributes, tuples, multiple values of a single attribute, or tuples within a single relation. The binary operators are used to combine multiple relations in a variety of forms, with the results placed into a new relation. The unary operators are the SELECT operator and the PROJECT operator. The main binary operators include the JOIN, UNION, INTERSECT, and EXCEPT. These operators are each addressed briefly in the following sections.

Select Operator   The SELECT operator is one of the most basic of the relational unary operations. The SELECT operator is used to choose one row, or some subset of rows, from a named relation based on given selection criteria. Selected tuples are used to construct a new relation. The

TABLE 4.1   Aquarium Employee Relation Example

emp_ID	first_name	last_name	emp_address	emp_title	emp_hire_date	emp_pay_rate
100	Jacques	Cousteau	125 elm st	oceanographer	12/25/98	55000
200	James	Balfour	2 clark st	sales	11/21/98	25000
300	Jane	Curtain	1 wake st	stock	10/20/98	15000
400	Joan	Rivers	25 5th st	sales	10/22/98	25000
500	Jake	Smith	12 first st	stock	09/09/98	18000

selection criteria can be based on the specific value of one or more attributes of a tuple or can specify a range of values for attributes of a tuple.

To select the row with employee Cousteau (see Table 4.1), you can write a variety of queries that use unique values within this tuple. For example:

```
SELECT emp_ID, first_name, last_name, emp_title, emp_hire_date,
emp_pay_rate
    FROM Employee WHERE name = 'Cousteau'
```

or

```
SELECT emp_ID, first_name, last_name, emp_title, emp_hire_date,
emp_pay_rate
    FROM Employee WHERE emp_title = 'oceanographer'
```

or

```
SELECT emp_ID, first_name, last_name, emp_title, emp_hire_date,
emp_pay_rate
    FROM Employee WHERE salary <= '50,000'
```

The result in all three cases is to retreive the tuple from the employee with Cousteau's information into a temporary relation.

In all cases, the SELECT statement results in some subset of the total tuples in the database to be retrieved (Figure 4.1). The SELECT operator is used the most in the relational database manipulation language repertoire. The basic operation is a comparison on a row-by-row basis and a search for matches to the selection criteria. If a tuple does not match, the tuple is eliminated from incorporation within the resulting table. If the tuple matches, it is copied into the resulting tempory relation. For a

Figure 4.1

SELECT operation result.

emp_ID	first_name	last_name	emp_address	emp_title	emp_hire_date	emp_pay_rate
100	Jacques	Cousteau	125 elm st	oceanographer	12/25/98	55000
200	James	Balfour	2 clark st	sales	11/21/98	25000
300	Jane	Curtain	1 wake st	stock	10/20/98	15000
400	Joan	Rivers	25 5th st	sales	10/22/98	25000
500	Jake	Smith	12 first st	stock	09/09/98	18000

Result of Query

emp_ID	first_name	last_name	emp_address	emp_title	emp_hire_date	emp_pay_rate
100	Jacques	Cousteau	125 elm st	oceanographer	12/25/98	55000

full SELECT of all attributes, the degree of the resulting table will be the same, but the cardinality will be equal to, or less than, the cardinality of the relations being queried.

If you issued the following query:

```
SELECT emp_ID, first_name, last_name, emp_title, emp_hire_date,
emp_pay_rate
    FROM Employee WHERE salary > '24,000'
```

the resulting relation (Table 4.2) would have three tuples. In such a way, the SELECT operator can be used to restrict retrieval to specific tuples only, or it can be used as a tool to browse through the tuples of a relation within the database.

The selection criteria can have numerous attributes to search for and match on as well as to support a variety of comparison operations. For example, you can write a query that searches for matches on one attribute only, as above, or that searches on all of the attributes for a specific match, as shown in the following code segment:

```
SELECT emp_ID, first_name, last_name, emp_title, emp_hire_date,
emp_pay_rate
    FROM Employee WHERE emp_ID = '100' AND name = 'Cousteau'
        AND emp_hire_date = '12/25/98' AND job = 'Oceanographer'
        AND dept = 'Field Research' AND salary = '55,000'
```

In reality, most queries will fall somewhere between these two extremes. Also, typically you do not know specifically what you are looking for. You know only some criteria about the boundaries that you want to search around. The connecting operations of AND, OR, and

TABLE 4.2 *Resulting Relation from SELECT Example*

emp_ID	first_name	last_name	emp_address	emp_title	emp_hire_date	emp_pay_rate
100	Jacques	Cousteau	125 elm st	oceanographer	12/25/98	55000
200	James	Balfour	2 clark st	sales	11/21/98	25000
400	Joan	Rivers	25 5th st	sales	10/22/98	25000

NOT are supported to connect search conditions. The comparison operations do not need to be only equal (=). The search operations can be less than (<), greater than (>), not equal to (≠), less than or equal to (≤), and greater than or equal to (≥).

In addition, you can set the SELECT conditions to be specific values that an attribute could possess. For example, you can write a query on the employee database to look for employees who perform specific jobs, such as stock and disease treatment:

```
SELECT emp_ID, first_name, last_name, emp_title, emp_hire_date,
emp_pay_rate
    FROM Employee WHERE job IN ['stock', 'disease treatment']
```

This query results in a relation with two tuples, as shown in Table 4.3.

Selections that request a range of values also can be easily written. For example, to select the employees who make a salary between $10,000 and $30,000 requires a query that uses the AND operation range restriction:

```
SELECT emp_ID, first_name, last_name, emp_title, emp_hire_date,
emp_pay_rate
    FROM Employee WHERE salary ≥ '10,000' AND salary ≤ '30,000'
```

The result of this query (Table 4.4) is a new table with four tuples, where each of the tuples has a salary field between the search boundaries. If you had set the boundary as salary > 17,500 AND salary < 25,000, the resulting table would have only one entry, employee 500, whose salary is the only one within the range. Even though employee 400 makes

TABLE 4.3 *SELECT Operation Result on Employee Relation*

emp_ID	first_name	last_name	emp_title	emp_hire_date	emp_pay_rate
300	Jane	Curtain	stock	10/20/98	15000
500	Jake	Smith	stock	09/09/98	18000

TABLE 4.4 Employee Relation Example with NULL Values

emp_ID	first_name	last_name	emp_title	emp_hire_date	emp_pay_rate
200	James	Balfour	sales	11/21/98	25000
300	Jane	Curtain	stock	10/20/98	15000
400	Joan	Rivers	sales	10/22/98	25000
500	Jake	Smith	stock	09/09/98	18000

$25,000 and employee 200 makes $25,000, the operations do not include equality; therefore, these tuples are not matched.

PROJECT Operator The second unary operator is the PROJECT operator. The PROJECT operator is used to select specific columns and eliminate other columns from the resulting table (Figure 4.2). The table

Figure 4.2

PROJECT operation.

Emp-ID	Name	age	job	dept	salary	tele_num
100	Adams	60	Admin	Prsnl	50,000	6171234567
200	Jones	30	Mangr	Prod	40,000	4018413666
300	Smith	35	Weldr	Prod	25,000	5089999991
400	Doe	28	Cuter	Prod	22,500	4016836835
500	Kent	25	Asmby	Prod	15,750	5083219877
600	Wilson	32	Suply	Ship	17,500	NULL

PROJECT Name
Result Table

Name
Adams
Jones
Smith
Doe
Kent
Wilson

TABLE 4.5 Employee Relation Example with NULL Values

emp_ID	first_name	last_name	emp_address	emp_title	emp_hire_date	emp_pay_rate
100	Jacques	Cousteau	125 elm st	oceanographer	12/25/98	55000
200	James	Balfour	2 clark st	sales	11/21/98	25000
300	Jane	Curtain	1 wake st	stock	10/20/98	15000
400	Joan	Rivers	25 5th st	sales	10/22/98	25000
500	Jake	Smith	12 first st	stock	09/09/98	18000

may have some rows with duplicate fields. If this occurs, the duplicates are removed from the table to maintain the relational property that all tuples must be unique. For example, if you have the employee database shown in Table 4.5, and you write a projection query, which selects the employee title and hire date attributes, the resulting table will initially have duplicate entries, which must be pruned.

```
PROJECT emp_title, emp_hire_date FROM Employee
```

The PROJECT operator is not actually found in the relational standard SQL language, but is inferred by removal of some of the SELECT attributes in the list, after the keyword SELECT. For clarity of presentation, the keyword PROJECT is used to differentiate the two.

Table 4.6 shows that the result has no duplicate tuples and will not need any alterations. The resulting final relation has five tuples with no duplicates.

Just as with the SELECT operation, the PROJECT operation can have restriction clauses associated with it to allow further pruning of tuples from the resulting relation. However, this is not the intended use of the initial PROJECT operation. It is more common to group the SELECT and PROJECT operators into the same query when this form is applied. In this form, a query would have only the listed attributes to PROJECT from the relation in the SELECT list after the keyword SELECT, and the remainder of the SELECT operation would be as shown previously in the SELECT operator section. As an example, if you want to project only the names and ages of all employees who make between $15,000 and $30,000, you can write the following query:

```
SELECT last_name, emp_title FROM Employee
    WHERE salary >= '15,000' AND salary <= '30,000'
```

TABLE 4.6

Initial PROJECT
Result for
Employee
Relation Example

emp_title	emp_hire_date
oceanographer	12/25/98
sales	11/21/98
stock	10/20/98
sales	10/22/98
stock	09/09/98

TABLE 4.7

SELECT and
PROJECT Applied
to Employee
Relation

last_name	emp_title
Cousteau	oceanographer
Balfour	sales
Curtain	stock
Rivers	sales
Smith	stock

This query results in a table with five tuples and two attributes. You can see from this example that the combination of the SELECT and PROJECT operators gives you the ability to isolate even single data items from a large relation. SELECT allows access to only the desired tuples and PROJECT allows you to retrieve only the wanted attributes from the reduced table. (See Table 4.7.)

UNION Operator   The UNION operator is a binary relational operation that acts on two relations, forming a third relation with all the elements from the other two, excluding any duplicates (Figure 4.3). The UNION operator can only be applied to relations that have the identical degree (number of attributes) and that are from the same domain (characteristic of the attributes' match). The resulting relation will have a cardinality that is equal to or less than the sum of the cardinalities (magnitude equal to the number of tuples in the relation) of the relations being UNIONed. In the following example there are three relations.

The first relation (Table 4.8) represents a list of suppliers that an aquarium company may keep.

Figure 4.3

UNION operation.

Emp-ID	Name	age	job	dept	salary	tele_num
100	Adams	60	Admin	Prsnl	50,000	6171234567
200	Jones	30	Mangr	Prod	40,000	4018413666
300	Smith	35	Weldr	Prod	25,000	5089999991

Emp-ID	Name	age	job	dept	salary	tele_num
400	Ashton	50	Admin	Prsnl	45,000	617889222
500	Fields	36	Mangr	Prod	30,000	5083337736
600	Smith	32	Cutter	Prod	25,000	5082101233

Result Table after UNION

Emp-ID	Name	age	job	dept	salary	tele_num
100	Adams	60	Admin	Prsnl	50,000	6171234567
200	Jones	30	Mangr	Prod	40,000	4018413666
300	Smith	35	Weldr	Prod	25,000	5089999991
400	Ashton	50	Admin	Prsnl	45,000	617889222
500	Fields	36	Mangr	Prod	30,000	5083337736
600	Smith	32	Cutter	Prod	25,000	5082101233

The second relation (Table 4.9) represents a list of the companies and their addresses. This relation has the same degree and matching domains with the first relation, the Suppliers relation.

The third relation (Table 4.10) represents a list of suppliers that supply a particular item, and have some quantity of that item on hand.

TABLE 4.8

Supplier Relation

supplier_id	supplier_name	supplier_address
1001	Acme	Walla Walla, WA
1002	Floatsom	Kings Bay, GA
1003	Fish-R-US	Georgetown, CA
1004	Tank Supplies	Honolulu, HI

TABLE 4.9

Company
Relation

company_id	company_name	company_address
1001	Acme	Walla Walla, WA
1002	Fathom	Newport, VA
1003	Divers World	Sydney, FL
1004	Tanks Plus	Providence, RI

The UNION operation can be applied to these relations, resulting in new combinations of the data. For example, if you want to take the UNION of the vendor and the company relations, Supplier UNION Company, the operation checks whether the degree of the relations match and whether the domains of the attributes in the same columns of the two relations match. Since they do match in this case (supplier number, supplier name, supplier city), the UNION operation can proceed. The UNION operation executes by first taking all the elements in one relation and copying them into the resulting relation. Then, one by one, the UNION operation inserts tuples from the second relation, if they have no exact match in the resulting relation.

Using our relations above, the resulting relation (Table 4.11) will have seven tuples, four contributed from relation one and three from rela-

TABLE 4.10

Supply Relation

supplier_id	item_name	Quantity
1001	filter	100
1002	coral	26
1003	fish	1000
1004	air pumps	25

company_id	company_name	company_address
1001	Acme	Walla Walla, WA
1002	Flotsam	Kings Bay, GA
1003	Fish-R-US	Georgetown, Ca
1004	Tank Supplies	Honolulu, HI
1002	Fathom	Newport, VA
1003	Divers World	Sydney, FL
1004	Tanks Plus	Providence, RI

tion two. In addition, notice that one tuple from relation two (1001, Acme, Walla Walla, WA) has been eliminated from the final relation, since it represents a duplicate tuple in the UNIONed relation.

If you attempt to perform the UNION of the Supplier relation and the Supply relation, Supplier UNION Supply, you find that the operation cannot occur. An error condition would be sent back to the user or the program issuing the query. The error occurs because the relations are not "UNIONable." One of the requirements was not met for the UNION operation. The two relations do have the same degree, but the individual attribute domains are not consistent. The first attributes in each match, so this is not the error. The second and third attributes from the two separate relations, however, do not match. This mismatch error causes the UNION operation request to be denied. The result, therefore, is no new relation.

EXCEPT Operator The EXCEPT binary operator, as with the UNION operator, executes on two relations, forming another relation based on the relational difference operation. In this operation, the two relations must have the same degree (number of attributes), and the attributes of the two relations must match in terms of the domains of values for the attributes (in the same relative position in the relations) from the separate relations. The two relations are compared tuple by tuple to determine what is in one relation, but not in the other. That is, you are looking for how the two relations differ—what one possesses that the other does not. The cardinality (number of resulting tuples) is equal to or less than the cardinality of the first relation in the binary operations list.

For example, if you first try to determine the difference between the Supplier relation and the Company relation (Supplier EXCEPT Company), the following operation must be performed. First, the supplier table structure and component types are compared with the Company relation structure and types to see if the operation is even possible. In this example, the degree of the Supplier relation matches the degree of the Company relation. The second check looks at the individual attributes of the two relations to see if they match in terms of data type. In the example, the first attribute of the Supplier relation matches the first attribute of the Company relation. The check succeeds and goes on to the second attribute in supplier and company. These, too, are found to match in terms of data type. The final match checks the third attributes from the two relations and finds they also match in terms of data types. Not only do these relations and their attributes data types match, but they have the same names. This does not have to be the case for the relations to be UNIONable or EXCEPTional. They must only match in terms of degree and attribute base types, not by the field name. For example, if the company name is "company name" instead of "name," the two fields still match. There is no problem with mismatched attribute names, only with the types of the attribute data fields. (See Figure 4.4.)

The operation is then released for execution to the underlying EXCEPT operator. The EXCEPT operation performs its function by examining the first tuple in the Supplier relation, V100, Smith, Boston, and comparing this tuple with each tuple of the Company relation, one at a time. If (V100, Smith, Boston) is not found in the Company relation, it is placed in the result relation for the difference operation. Since it is in the Company relation, the operation goes on to the second tuple of the Supplier relation, having copied no tuples into the result relation.

The second tuple from the Supplier relation, V200, Jones, Chicago, is removed and compared to each of the tuples in the Company relation. Since the company has no tuple that matches this tuple, it is placed into the resulting relation. This selection of a tuple from the Vendor relation and its comparison to all tuples in the Company relation continues until all the tuples in the Vendor relation have been examined this way. (See Table 4.12.)

The resulting relation (Table 4.13) has only two tuples in it, V200, Jones, Chicago and V400, Franklin, Las Vegas. All other tuples of the Vendor relation have matches in the Company relation and therefore are not reflected in the resulting relation.

Figure 4.4

Vendor, company,
supply relations.

VENDOR

Vendor number	Vendor name	Vendor city
V100	Smith	Boston
V200	Jones	Chicago
V300	Brown	Houston
V400	Franklin	Las Vegas

COMPANY

Vendor number	Vendor name	Vendor city
V100	Smith	Boston
V500	O'Beirne	Lowell
V600	Jezak	Lenox
V300	Brown	Houston

SUPPLY RELATION

Vendor number	Part number	Quantity
V100	P25	12
V200	P31	5
V300	P35	10
V100	P1	32

If the operation is reversed, and you perform the operation, Company EXCEPT Supplier, a different relation may occur because of the method of operation. You are comparing the *first* relation with the *sec-*

TABLE 4.12

Vendor-Company
Relations

VENDOR-COMPANY

Vendor number	Vendor name	Vendor city
V200	Jones	Chicago
V400	Franklin	Las Vegas

TABLE 4.13

Resulting Supplier-
Company EXCEPT
Relation

VENDOR-COMPANY

Vendor number	Vendor name	Vendor city
V200	Jones	Chicago
V200	Franklin	Las Vegas

TABLE 4.14

Resulting Company-
Supplier EXCEPT
Relation

VENDOR-COMPANY

Vendor number	Vendor name	Vendor city
V500	O'Beirne	Lowell
V600	Jezak	Lenox

ond relation, looking to see what tuples are in the first relation but *not* in the second relation. In this binary relational operation, you can see that there are only two tuples in the Company relation that are not in the Supplier relation (Table 4.14). These tuples are V500, O'Beirne, Lowell and V600, Jezak, Lenox.

INTERSECT Operator The third binary operation is the INTER-SECT operator. This operator is used to find tuples that are common in the two relations operated on. The INTERSECT operation is performed by taking one tuple at a time from the first relation and comparing it to each tuple in the second relation, looking for a match. If a match is found, the matched tuple is copied into the resulting relation. If no match is found, the comparison continues with the second tuple of the first relation, and so on, until all tuples of the first relation have been compared to all tuples of the second relation.

The binary INTERSECT operator executes similarly to the UNION and EXCEPT operators shown in the example relations, Supplier and Company, introduced earlier. The first step in the execution is to check if the two relations' degree is the same. If not, the INTERSECT operation is aborted. If the degrees match, the second check is to determine if the attributes of the two relations match in terms of base types. If they match, the INTERSECT operation is allowed to continue.

The INTERSECT operation follows that of the UNION and EXCEPT operations. The test is to see what tuples in the first relation are also in the second relation. In this example, the binary operation being performed is Supplier INTERSECT Company. The operation executes by taking the first tuple from the Supplier relation, V100, Smith, Boston, and comparing it with each of the tuples in the Company relation, one at a time. If the comparison finds that the tuple V100, Smith, Boston is in the Company relation (which it is), then the tuple is copied into the resulting relation. The operation continues by taking the second tuple from the Supplier relation, V200, Jones, Chicago, and comparing it with each tuple in the Company relation. Since the tuple V200, Jones, Chicago has no match in the Company relation, it is not copied into the resulting relation. This selection of the next tuple in the Supplier relation, and comparison with each tuple in the Company relation, continues until there are no more tuples in the Supplier relation. The resulting relation (Table 4.15) has two tuples, V100, Smith, Boston and V300, Brown, Houston.

Reversing the order of the relations in the INTERSECT operation's execution does not have an effect on the outcome. The INTERSECT operation compares the two relations, looking for all tuples that are in both of them. Therefore, whether you place Company first or Supplier first, you are still looking for all matches, not differences (as in the DIFFERENCE operation), and all tuples, including the matches (as in the UNION operation).

TABLE 4.15

Supplier INTERSECT Company Resulting Relation

VENDOR-COMPANY

Vendor number	Vendor name	Vendor city
V100	Smith	Boston
V300	Brown	Houston

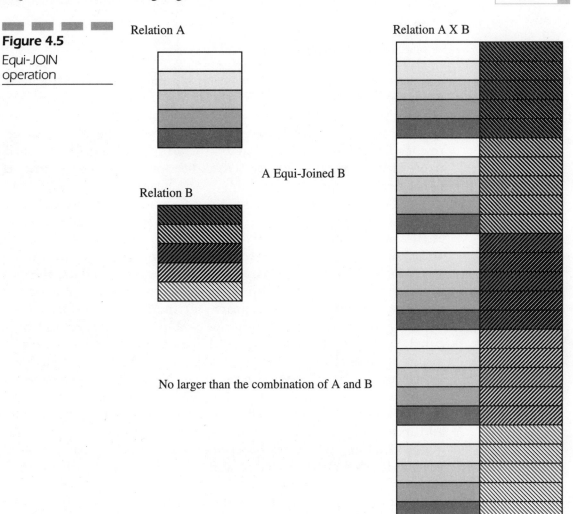

Figure 4.5

Equi-JOIN
operation

Relation A

Relation A X B

A Equi-Joined B

Relation B

No larger than the combination of A and B

JOIN Operator The binary relational JOIN operator merges two relations based on matching values from one attribute in each relation (Figure 4.5). The two relations are said to be joined over the two attributes. The JOIN condition, or test, can be viewed as selection criteria over the two relations. For example, you may want to join the Supplier relation and the Supply relations to find suppliers of parts and the quantities. The SELECT criterion for this JOIN is that the Vendor vnum is equal to the Supply vnum. This query is as follows:

```
DOMAIN of V IS Supplier;
DOMAIN of S IS Supply;
Supplier JOIN Supply WHERE V.Vnum = S.Vnum;
```

The result of the equi-JOIN operation is a new relation with a maximum degree of the magnitude of the sum of the Supplier and the Supply relations minus one. There is one less attribute, because the attribute used in the selection criteria does not need to be repeated. It would represent a redundant data item and can therefore be discarded. The cardinality of the result lies between zero and the cardinality of the product of the two relations.

The JOIN operation conceptually works much like the Cartesian product. Before the JOIN operation can begin, the two relations' *match* attributes are checked to see that they are of the equivalent base types and that their domain of values is within ranges that would allow a JOIN to proceed. The JOIN operation then begins by taking the first tuple of relation one and, using the match attribute, looking for a matching *value* in the selected match attribute of relation two. If no match is found, the second relation's next tuple is selected and compared, looking for the same match. This selection and checking continues until a match is found. When a match of the two values in the match attributes from both relations is found, the two tuples are merged into a single new tuple and placed in the resulting relation. The search then continues using the same tuple from the first relation until all tuples of the second relation are exhausted. When this occurs, the JOIN operation then selects the second tuple of the first relation and repeats the above selection, comparisons, matching, and creation of new tuples until all the tuples of the first relation have been compared with all the tuples in the second. This search and comparison requires that the second relation be searched as many times as there are tuples in the first relation. To put this another way, given that R1 is the cardinality of the first relation and R2 the cardinality of the second relation, we performed R1 * R2 selections and comparisons to join the two relations.

As an example, you can join the Supplier relation and the Supply relation by searching and matching the supplier number from the Supplier relation with the vendor number from the Supply relation. To perform the JOIN, you first must be sure that the JOIN is possible by checking that the JOIN match attributes have the same base type and come from a compatible domain of values. In the example, since the two attributes represent the same values—that of vendor numbers—and the numbers are constructed from an alphanumeric followed by three dig-

■ ■ ■ ■

Figure 4.6

Supply relation.

Vendor number	Part number	Quantity
V100	P25	12
V200	P31	5
V300	P35	10
V100	P1	32

it integers in both relations, the JOIN can proceed. The join BEGINS by selecting tuple one, V100, Smith, Boston, from the Supplier relation and placing the value of the match attribute (Vendor number) into a match register. This value is then used as the value to look for a match with the value in the Supply relation's first attribute (Vendor number). In the example (Figure 4.6), the first tuple in the Supply relation matches the vendor numbers. The tuple V100, Smith, Boston from Supplier is merged with tuple V100, P25, 12 from the Supply relation, forming a new tuple, V100, Smith, Boston, P25, 12, which is placed in the resulting relation (Table 4.16).

The search continues, comparing tuple V100, Smith, Boston to tuples two and three in the Supply relation, finding no match. On comparison with tuple four, V100, P1, 32, from the Supply relation, we find another match. The tuple V100, Smith, Boston is once again merged with the new matched tuple from the Supply relation, V100, P1, 32, forming a new tuple, V100, Smith, Boston, P1, 32, which is then stored in the resulting relation. After this match, we are at the end of the Supply relation. The JOIN operation then continues by selecting the second tuple from the Supplier relation, V200, Jones, Chicago, and performing the same selection and comparison of each tuple in the Supply relation against this new search tuple.

The scan of the second relation finds one match with tuple V200, P31, 5. This match results in a new merged tuple, which is created and placed in the resulting relation (Table 4.17). The search continues until all the tuples in the Supplier relation have been compared and possibly matched with all tuples from the Supply relation. The resulting final relation is shown in Table 4.18.

The JOIN operation is a powerful operator when used in conjunction with the other unary and binary relational operators. A database

TABLE 4.16

Partial Resulting
JOINed Supplier and
Supply Relation

Vendor-Parts

Vendor number	Vendor name	Vendor city	Part number	Quantity
V100	Smith	Boston	P25	12
V100	Smith	Boston	P1	32

TABLE 4.17

Partial Relation

Vendor-Supply

Vendor number	Vendor name	Vendor city	Part number	Quantity
V100	Smith	Boston	P25	12
V100	Smith	Boston	P1	32
V200	Jones	Chicago	P31	5

TABLE 4.18

Resulting JOINed
Supplier and Supply
Relation

Vendor-Supply

Vendor number	Vendor name	Vendor city	Part number	Quantity
V100	Smith	Boston	P25	12
V100	Smith	Boston	P1	32
V200	Jones	Chicago	P31	5
V300	Brown	Houston	P35	10

user can create and perform powerful searches on a relational database
using these operators.

Extended Relations

This book is not simply about the relational model, but is also about the
new, extended relational-object model. This model extends the relation
in many ways and extends the way in which relations are operated upon. The ways in which we can expand relations are left up to the imagination of the applications designers, with but a few new rules. First,
relations are not what they used to be. They are now tables, since they
do not have all the relational baggage to bring with them. Second, they

are flexible, leaving the operations to be used up to the database designers' imagination, augmented by the old, dependable relational operators.

Tables change by allowing attributes to be more than simply singular respositories of data. An attribute position in a relation can hold an array of base types, an array of abstract data types, row types, objects, or simply object identifiers. By using these elements, very flexible user-defined tables can be constructed that naturally match the data types and structures needed by an application, as will be seen in later chapters.

Operations have also changed. The SELECT, UNION, EXCEPT, INTERSECT, and JOIN operations are still available, as are numerous other operators, to support these new data structures. In the following chapters, these will be revealed by using the aquarium data management example described earlier.

Basic Data Types

The set of atomic data types supported in SQL-3 possess all of those within SQL-2 plus some additional base data types. All of these can be used to define tables, row types, ADT types, and objects. In the SQL-2 version of the standard, the atomic data types were limited to exact numerics, approximate numerics, character strings, bit strings, datetimes, and intervals. Following is a discussion of each of these categories.

Numbers

In this category, many types defined in the SQL-3 standard that have the ability to represent numbers in a variety of applications. (For example, exact numbers, such as two Moorish idols or three moray eels, or approximate numbers, such as 3.33 E 5 parts per million or 2.333 E 2 parts per million.) One category of these representations is the integers, or counting numbers. In SQL-3 this is referred to as an INTEGER, abbreviated as INT and SMALLINT. Other forms of exact numerics include those to represent fractional numbers with specific significance—for example, money.

- INTEGER: The integer data type represents a whole number used in counting (e.g., 1, 2, 3, and so on). Its precision (the largest and smallest number supported) is implementation-defined, allowing for the product to be supported on machines with differing ranges. To declare a column or item within a constructed data type as an integer, simply assign the attribute to the item using the keyword INTEGER—there are no parameters associated with this. For example, specifying the employee identifier in the employee table as an integer, requires the following syntax:

```
CREATE TABLE employees (
    emp_id   INTEGER,
    .
    .
    .
```

- SMALLINT: The small integer data type is also used to represent integer values. The realization of this data type is also implementation-defined, but allows the implementer to provide a repository where a smaller value using less storage can be supported. For example, the employee identifier attribute may only need to support up to 1,000 employees, not 1,000,000 as supported by the INTEGER representation. SMALLINT can be used to conserve memory. SMALLINT, as with INTEGER, requires no optional parameters in the specification:

```
CREATE TABLE employees (
    emp_id   SMALLINT,
    .
    .
    .
```

- NUMERIC: The numeric data type differs from the INTEGER and SMALLINT in that it does not support just the counting of whole numbers, but also counts numbers with a specific decimal component—for example, money or percentages. The specification has two parameters: a precision and a scale. The precision (p) represents the range requested in the specification and supported for the implementation. The scale (s) is decimal locations allocated or supported by the implementation. The result gives you the exact precision you specified. To specify an attribute as NUMERIC in SQL-3, you can use one of three possible means: the keyword NUMERIC, NUMERIC(p), or NUMERIC(p,s). If NUMERIC is used without parameters, the implementation-defined default representation is used.

```
CREATE TABLE employees (
    emp_id          INTEGER
    emp_title       name,
    emp_last_name   name,
    emp_pay_rate    NUMERIC (7,2)
)
```

- **DECIMAL:** The decimal data type is similar to the numeric data type, though the precision used by the implementation can be greater than the precision you specify within your declaration. The scale is exactly as specified within the declaration. As with the numeric data type, you can specify a decimal using the keyword DECIMAL alone or using the precision and scale fields as DECIMAL (p) or DECIMAL (p,s).

```
CREATE TABLE employees (
    emp_id           INTEGER,
    emp_last_name    name,
    emp_first_name   name
    emp_pay_rate     NUMERIC (7,2)
    emp_com_rate     DECIMAL (5,2)
)
```

Not all values are exact or can be represented within a computer to their exact values. In cases such as this, approximate numbers are required. In SQL-3 there are three means by which you can specify which data item is to be represented by an approximate value. These are the REAL, DOUBLE PRECISION, and FLOAT data types.

- **REAL:** The real number data type represents floating-point numbers using a single-word format. Single precision floating-point numbers are different from machine to machine and therefore can have problems with portability. To specify an attribute as real, simply use the keyword REAL. In the example below, the aquatic tanks nitrates and nitrites are specified to be of the type REAL.

```
CREATE TABLE aquatic_stock_tanks (
    tank_id         INTEGER,
    water_vol       DOUBLE PRECISION,
    ph              DECIMAL (4,2),
    salinity        DECIMAL (4,3),
    nitrates        REAL,
    nitrites        REAL,
    temperature     DECIMAL (5,2),
    trace_elements  FLOAT
)
```

- DOUBLE PRECISION: The double precision data type is implementation-defined for precision. However, the precision must be greater than that of a real data type. In most implementations, this translates to a double precision floating-point data item within the computer system where the implementation is located. As an example, in the aquatic stock tanks table, the water volume is specified to be of type double precision.

- FLOAT: The float data type gives you a bit more control by allowing you to specify the precision wanted as FLOAT (p). The optional parameter will give the implementation a specific precision to be adhered to. The specification can be made with or without the optional parameter. Without the parameter, the implementation can decide which prevailing precision of float to use. As an example of this specification, the value of trace elements in the aquatic stock tank table is specified to be of the type FLOAT.

Characters

SQL-3 has two main character data types, with some variations to allow for shortened specifications and for differing character sets. The two major character types are CHARACTER and CHARACTER VARYING. In addition, there are also NATIONAL CHARACTER and NATIONAL CHARACTER VARYING, along with abbreviations for their specification. The national variants of the character data types allow for the internationalization of the SQL language. Implementations can use non-English character sets, such as Japanese Kanji. More will be said about these later.

- CHARACTER: The character data type is used to specify character strings. The form of the character set is typically ASCII strings or Latin-1, depending on your implementation. The specification is either CHARACTER or CHARACTER (x). CHARACTER is the same as specifying CHARACTER (1). If you specify some character string size—for example, CHARACTER (5)—and try to store anything smaller, the remainder of the string will be filled with blanks. In the employee example, an employee's job title can be specified to consist of five characters.

```
CREATE TABLE employees (
    emp_id          INTEGER
    emp_title       CHARACTER(5),
```

```
    emp_last_name   CHARACTER VARYING (25),
    emp_pay_rate    NUMERIC (7,2)
)
```

- CHARACTER VARYING: The character varying data type is used when the number of characters for an attribute is not uniform. For example, a name or address will have a varying number of characters to represent different names and addresses. This implementation allows you to store only the number of characters used; blanks are not needed or added. To specify this data type, you use CHARACTER VARYING (x), where x is the limit on the number of characters that can be placed into this string. In the employee example above, the employee's last name can be specified as character varying with a limit of 25 characters.

- NATIONAL CHARACTER: The national character set data type specifies the default data type for the country of implementation. The character set can be specified explicitly by using the specification CHARACTER CHARACTER SET char_set_name. For example, if the implementation had the Kanji character set available, you could specify the name of the employee using the Kanji character set.

```
CREATE TABLE employees (
    emp_id          INTEGER
    emp_title       CHARACTER(5),
    emp_last_name   CHARACTER VARYING (25)   CHARACTER SET Kanji,
    emp_pay_rate    NUMERIC (7,2)
)
```

The variety of national and specific character sets is dependent on the implementation and what has been defined as a character set within the implementation.

Bit Strings

The bit and bit varying data types support the storage and management of binary data types of specific or varying lengths. These data types allow the applications developer to store and retrieve any bit-based data type.

- BIT: The bit data type supports fixed-length bit fields from 1 bit up to the maximum size supported by the implementation, which can be as high as a few megabits. Once specified, all stored values must have the same number of bits. The specification can use a parameter or not. If no parameter is specified, then the string is 1 bit. An example specification is as follows:

```
low_stock_flag  BIT
```

- BIT VARYING: The bit varying data type allows for specification of a variable bit field, from 1 bit up to the limit of the implementation. The number of bits stored can be different each time, varying from 1 to the limit specified and can be specified as BIT VARYING (x). An example is as follows:

```
low_stock_encoded_flag  BIT VARYING (16)
```

Datetimes

The need to store date and time information is essential to most application information. To facilitate this, the SQL language supports the DATE, TIME, and TIMESTAMP data types.

- DATE: The date data type specifies the structure and range of values the elements of the type can take on. The format specifies that the data type consist of a year, month, and day element. The year is specified as four digits, allowing for representation of dates from 0000 to 9999. The month is specified as two digits, with a range of 01 to 12, representing the 12 months of the year. The day field is specified as two digits and can range from 1 to 31 for the days of any month. The length of the DATE type is specified as ten positions, allowing for a variety of implementations as characters, digits, or some other representation. An example specification from the sales table of our aquarium management schema follows:

```
sale_date  DATE,
```

- TIME: The time data type is used to specify a time value type consisting of hour, minute, and second components. The hour component is two digits and ranges from 00 through 23, allowing for the representation of military or civilian time formats. The minute component is two digits and ranges from 00 through 59.

The second component is also two digits and ranges from 00 through 61. The second component can also have an optional fractional part, which allows the range to be from 00.000 through 61.999. The range value greater than 59 allows for the representation of leap seconds, which occasionally are added to earth's time-clock systems. The time data type ranges from six to eight positions with no fractions and up to nine positions plus additional positions for fractional components. Added positions are used to hold separator characters, such as the colon or period (e.g., 12:24:35.333). To specify a time type, use either TIME or TIME (p). An example specification follows:

```
store_open_time TIME,
```

■ TIMESTAMP: The timestamp data type can facilitate a combined date and time specification. The specification includes the year, month, day, hour, minute, and second elements. The restrictions on this type are the same as on the DATE and TIME types. A valid timestamp could be 1997-06-23,13:12:34.123. To specify the timestamp type, use TIMESTAMP or the expanded TIMESTAMP (p). An example follows:

```
tax_deadline  TIMESTAMP,
```

Some additional date and time types are included in SQL to allow for world time differentials within a database. For example, if you want to specify how this value differs from the UTC, the specification is similar to the TIME data type except for the addition of an offset from UTC. The range of the offset is from –12:59 to +13:00. The wider time zone difference accounts for country differences with summer and winter time differentials (e.g., in the United States, the spring forward and fall back practice of seasonal time shifts).

■ TIME WITH TIME ZONE: This data type extends the basic TIME type with time zone information. The number of digits to specify this data type is 14 or 15, plus the number of fractional units on time. An example specification follows:

```
store_open_time  TIME WITH TIME ZONE,
```

■ TIMESTAMP WITH TIME ZONE: This data type extends the TIMESTAMP data type with the time zone data extension. The number of digits to specify this data type is 25 or 26, plus the number of fractional seconds digits. An example specification follows:

```
tax_deadline   TIMESTAMP WITH TIME ZONE,
```

Intervals

The interval is a useful extension to the basic time and timestamp types. In numerous cases, it is important for an application to be able to specify an interval of time (e.g., the time between orders, the time of an employee's employment with the company, and so on). An interval is defined as the difference between two dates or times. For example, the difference between December 12, 1956, and December 12, 1997, is 42 years. SQL defines two basic types of intervals: year-month and day-time. Further extensions will be defined in the temporal SQL-3 standard, which is still being worked on.

■ Year-month intervals: This data type is used when the interval you want is years, months, or a combination of the two. This interval type includes a qualifier for the interval you want, YEAR, MONTH, YEAR TO MONTH. To be sure you have adequate accuracy, the precision parameter is provided as an option. An example specification follows:

```
Emp_longevity   INTERVAL YEAR (4) TO MONTH,
```

■ Day-time intervals: As with the year-month intervals, this class can only contain the specified types, day, time, or day and time, as the measures of the interval. The available intervals are day value only, hour value only, minute value, or second field. If multiple types are wanted, all logical values between must also be included. The length of an interval is computed as the length of the leading field plus the lengths of each smaller field (e.g., 3 days + 5 hours). An example specification is:

```
Emp_month_hours   INTERVAL DAY TO HOUR,
```

Logic and Null

SQL supports the concept of unknown values for some fields. This data type is useful in realistic situations where not all information is known about a subject, but sufficient information is known to make the remainder of the information useful. In SQL, to facilitate the condition where something is true, false, or not known, a three-valued logic system is used. This allows for partial information to be represented without causing added invalid combinations. SQL-2 does not, however, have a specific data type for the null value or for Boolean data types. SQL-3 extends this. This will be discussed later.

Type Equivalence

Type equivalence in SQL-3 differs from that applied to SQL-2 out of necessity. SQL-3 has extended what can be in a table and what its semantics are. Equivalence looks at what the meaning of a definition is and how it relates to other definitions. There are two definitions of equivalence in the SQL language: name equivalence and structural equivalence.

Name Equivalence   For two items to be name equivalent, they must have the same name. This applies to types whose type equivalence is defined by means of the type name. In addition to this condition, the underlying structural types must also be equivalent. For example, two types, last_name VARCHAR (30) and first_name VARCHAR(30), appear to have the same underlying structure—that is, they both are of type VARCHAR(30). However, since the type names are not the same, they cannot be equivalent. To be name equivalent they both must have the same type and name. As an example, we define a domain name as follows:

```
CREATE DOMAIN name AS CHARACTER VARYING (50),
```

Use this to define the following employee and customer tables:

```
CREATE TABLE customers (
    cust_id           INTEGER
        CONSTRAINT customers_cust_id_pk PRIMARY KEY,
```

```
    last_name          name
        CONSTRAINT customers_last_name_not_null NOT NULL,
    first_name         name
        CONSTRAINT customers_first_name_not_null NOT NULL,
    cust_address       CHARACTER VARYING (30),
    cust_city          CHARACTER VARYING (20),
    cust_state         CHARACTER (2),
    cust_zip           CHARACTER VARYING (9),
    cust_phone         CHARACTER (10),
    cust_credit_id     CHARACTER VARYING (20),
    cust_current_bal   DECIMAL (7,2),
    cust_ytd           DECIMAL (9,2),
    num_complaints     INTEGER,
    num_returns        INTEGER,
    cust_rating        INTEGER,
    last_purchase      TIMESTAMP
)

CREATE TABLE employees (
    emp_id             INTEGER
        CONSTRAINT employees_emp_id_pk PRIMARY KEY,
    emp_title          name,
    last_name          name
        CONSTRAINT employees_last_name_not_null NOT NULL,
    first_name         name
        CONSTRAINT employees_first_name_not_null NOT NULL,
    emp_address        CHARACTER VARYING (30),
    emp_city           CHARACTER VARYING (20),
    emp_state          CHARACTER (2),
    emp_zip            CHARACTER VARYING (9),
    emp_phone          CHARACTER (10),
    emp_start_date     TIMESTAMP,
    emp_pay_rate       DECIMAL (7,2),
    emp_com_rate       DECIMAL (5,2)
)
```

last_name and first_name in the employee table are name equivalent to last_name and first_name in the customer table. This is true because the names of the two attributes in the two tables match in specific name and type.

Structural Equivalence For two defined types to be structurally equivalent, they must have the same number of elements and the elements must be pairwise type equivalent. This implies that to be structurally equivalent, two items must have the same underlying structure, and each element of the structure must be in exactly the same location in one item as in the other. Using the example above, the employee and customer identifiers are structurally equivalent, as are their name, address, and phone number attribute fields. The two tables, however, are not either name or structurally equivalent because the fields differ in some locations.

As another example, if a type, *sale*, is defined as (sale_id INTEGER, sale_date DATE) and another type, *purchase*, is defined as (purchase_id INTEGER, purchase_date DATE), the two types are not name equivalent, because the names are different and the names used within the types are different. However, these two types are structurally equivalent, because the two types have the same number of elements, in the same locations, with matching data types.

How Equivalence Is Applied to SQL In SQL-2, type equivalence is defined by the operations on rows and tables and is based on structural equivalence. For example, for two tables to be unionable they must have the same number of attributes, and each of the attributes in the equivalent position within each table must be of the same type, as shown in the following code segment:

```
CREATE TABLE customers (
    cust_id          INTEGER
        CONSTRAINT customers_cust_id_pk PRIMARY KEY,
    last_name        name
        CONSTRAINT customers_last_name_not_null NOT NULL,
    first_name       name
        CONSTRAINT customers_first_name_not_null NOT NULL,
    cust_address     CHARACTER VARYING (30),
    cust_city        CHARACTER VARYING (20),
    cust_state       CHARACTER (2),
    cust_zip         CHARACTER VARYING (9),
    cust_phone       CHARACTER (10),
)

CREATE TABLE employees (
    emp_id           INTEGER
        CONSTRAINT employees_emp_id_pk PRIMARY KEY,
    last_name        name
        CONSTRAINT employees_last_name_not_null NOT NULL,
    first_name       name
        CONSTRAINT employees_first_name_not_null NOT NULL,
    emp_address      CHARACTER VARYING (30),
    emp_city         CHARACTER VARYING (20),
    emp_state        CHARACTER (2),
    emp_zip          CHARACTER VARYING (9),
    emp_phone        CHARACTER (10),
)
```

Since the types within Employees and within Customers are the same in all positions, these two tables are considered to be structurally equivalent and can be unioned.

Operations on columns of tables are restricted to name equivalence. This implies that the only columns within the two tables that are name equivalent are last_name and first_name, and these, therefore, can be used to perform column operations, such as a JOIN:

```
employee JOIN customer WHERE employee.last_name =
customer.last_name
```

Rows in an SQL-2 database are instances of structural types, and values in columns are instances of named types. This statement implies that rows in a relation each must have the same structural members in the same position in the table, and the elements of a table can be equivalent if the values in a single row are the same. For example, in the employee table defined above, the column emp_title can have elements within the table where the elements have the same "value," such as marine biologist, sales, or service.

SQL-3 changes some of these conditions to support extended data types. Operations on rows and on tables within SQL-3 are based on applying structural equivalence (which is the same for both SQL-2 and SQL-3). The difference is in how columns are viewed. Operations on columns are based on the name and structural equivalence. This is essential, since columns can now have nested rows or tables and ADTs. For example, the customer table can be reorganized to include a nested row for address, as follows:

```
CREATE TABLE customers (
    cust_id       INTEGER
       CONSTRAINT customers_cust_id_pk PRIMARY KEY,
    last_name     name
       CONSTRAINT customers_last_name_not_null NOT NULL,
    first_name    name
       CONSTRAINT customers_first_name_not_null NOT NULL,
    cust_address  ROW(
                  address       CHARACTER VARYING (30),
                  cust_city     CHARACTER VARYING (20),
                  cust_state    CHARACTER (2),
                  cust_zip      CHARACTER VARYING (9)),
    cust_phone    CHARACTER (10)
)
```

Rows are instances of structural types, and values in columns are instances of named or unnamed rows or table types.

Type System Extensions

SQL-3 has extended the basic type system of SQL-2 in a variety of areas. Specific changes are the Boolean data type, the large binary object, large character object, row type, and abstract data type. In addition to these, further extensions were proposed and made their way into early base documents to ultimately be deferred to SQL-4. These include the collection types and a few others, which will be briefly discussed because of their importance to applications writers.

Boolean

The explicit BOOLEAN data type included in SQL-3 differs from the logic operators in SQL-2. The Boolean is a true Boolean, with just true or false values. These data types can be used anywhere these values are needed. The Boolean data type allows definition of Boolean functions where predicates are expected and enables support for user-defined operations.

```
CREATE TABLE employees (
    emp_id          INTEGER
        CONSTRAINT employees_emp_id_pk PRIMARY KEY,
    last_name       name
        CONSTRAINT employees_last_name_not_null NOT NULL,
    first_name      name
        CONSTRAINT employees_first_name_not_null NOT NULL,
    emp_address     CHARACTER VARYING (30),
    emp_city        CHARACTER VARYING (20),
    emp_state       CHARACTER (2),
    emp_zip         CHARACTER VARYING (9),
    emp_phone       CHARACTER (10),
    emp_full_time   BOOLEAN
)
```

For example, in the employee table above, you can insert a new attribute called emp_full_time of type Boolean to indicate whether or not the employee is full time. This can then be used in queries as with any other attribute in the WHERE clause or as the result of a query. For example, if you want to get a list of all the full-time employees, write the following query:

```
SELECT emp_id, fist_name, last_name FROM employees
    WHERE emp_full_time = TRUE
```

Large Binary Objects

SQL-3 adds some other very useful new data types. One is the large binary object, or BLOB. The BLOB is a database holder for a binary piece of data (e.g., a digital representation of an individual's signature or a picture). In the employee table we could expand the definition to include additional attributes, which further describe the employee using the BLOB data type as follows:

```
CREATE TABLE employees (
    emp_id          INTEGER
      CONSTRAINT employees_emp_id_pk PRIMARY KEY,
    last_name       name
      CONSTRAINT employees_last_name_not_null NOT NULL,
    first_name      name
      CONSTRAINT employees_first_name_not_null NOT NULL,
    emp_address     CHARACTER VARYING (30),
    emp_city        CHARACTER VARYING (20),
    emp_state       CHARACTER (2),
    emp_zip         CHARACTER VARYING (9),
    emp_phone       CHARACTER (10),
    emp_full_time   BOOLEAN,
    emp_signature   BLOB (1M),
    emp_picture     BLOB (10M)
)
```

The employee table now has two new attributes, `emp_signature` and `emp_picture`, each of which are to be stored in the database (not in a separate file) as a binary large object. The BLOB is not simply a holder for more complex data. Some built-in database operations are provided for the management and manipulation of such database items. BLOBs can be stored and retrieved and their contents can be partially retrieved. A BLOB can be replaced by another BLOB. BLOBs with similar characteristics (e.g., signatures) can be retrieved using the LIKE predicate. BLOBs can be concatenated, and they can be checked for length. In some cases, UNION ALL can be applied. The EQUAL and NOT EQUAL operators can be applied to BLOBs. Conversely, some operators are not allowed, such as the GREATER THAN and LESS THAN operators. The concepts of primary key, unique key, and foreign key do not hold with the BLOB. Also, BLOBs cannot use the GROUP BY and ORDER BY operators, nor can they use the PARTIAL UNION operator.

BLOB data types use a different concept for key or locator in an SQL-3 database. The BLOB locators are used to uniquely define and locate BLOBs within the database. BLOBs are manipulated on the database side of a system, not in the application side. This avoids unnecessary data movement, as well as application-side data buffering, which could be excessive if numerous BLOBs were being accessed by a particular application. BLOB manipulation on the database side allows for as needed access and provides for deferring BLOB expression evaluation and for BLOB copies. The BLOB locators can, however, be held by an application for quicker access. Since they can be held, they also can be released at some later time. Some examples will be given later in the book.

Large Character Objects

Similar to the BLOB, the character large object, or CLOB, is a holder for nondatabase structured data (e.g., an employee's resume or a collection of papers written by employees on topics of interest to the database users). As an example, the employee table is modified to include the employee's rèsumè. In addition, a new table is defined, which includes CLOBs for research papers and aquarium enthusiast help papers.

```
CREATE TABLE employees (
    emp_id          INTEGER
        CONSTRAINT employees_emp_id_pk PRIMARY KEY,
    last_name       name
        CONSTRAINT employees_last_name_not_null NOT NULL,
    first_name      name
        CONSTRAINT employees_first_name_not_null NOT NULL,
    emp_address     CHARACTER VARYING (30),
    emp_city        CHARACTER VARYING (20),
    emp_state       CHARACTER (2),
    emp_zip         CHARACTER VARYING (9),
    emp_phone       CHARACTER (10),
    emp_full_time   BOOLEAN,
    emp_signature   BLOB (1M),
    emp_picture     BLOB (10M),
    emp_resume      CLOB (50K)
)

CREATE TABLE employee_publications (
    paper_id        INTEGER
        CONSTRAINT employee_publication_paper_id_pk PRIMARY KEY,
    emp_id          INTEGER,
    paper_title     CHARACTER VARYING (150),
    paper           CLOB (200K)
)
```

As with the BLOB, the CLOB is used to allow the database to store and manage large objects for applications, bringing the database power and support to the management of the object. The CLOB, like the BLOB, cannot use all the operators in SQL-3. The GREATER THAN and LESS THAN operators, as well as the primary key, unique key, and foreign key are not allowed in their definitions. The GROUP BY and OR-DER BY operators, as well as the UNION operator, are not available. As with the BLOB, the CLOB can be operated on to retrieve the full object or some partial object, can be replaced by another CLOB, can be operated upon using the LIKE predicate, and can be concatenated with other CLOBs. CLOBs can be operated on using the substring, position, and length functions, as well as the UNION ALL operator.

Similar to the BLOB, CLOBs use LOB locators to define their location within the database. The LOB locator is used on the database side to locate and manipulate the CLOB for the user application. As in the BLOB case, this is done to limit the excess data movement between the database and user application. The LOB locator allows the application to access the CLOB in chunks. The CLOB locators, as with the BLOB locators, can be held on the application side to facilitate manipulation and can be released when no longer needed.

Row Types

The row type is a divergence from what was allowed in the SQL-2 database model. The row type provides a means to explicitly define a structural type within the larger context of the table structure. A row type is defined as a sequence of attribute names and defined data type pairs, just like the definition of a flat table. In essence, the row is a table nested within a table (Figure 4.7). The BNF for the row type is as follows:

```
<row type> ::=
    ROW <row type body>

<row type body> ::=
    <left paren>
      <field definition> [ { <comma> <field definition> }... ]
    <right paren>

<field definition> ::=
    <field name> { <data type> | <domain name> }
    [ <collate clause> ]

<field name> ::= <identifier>

<domain name> ::= <schema qualified name>
```

Figure 4.7
Row data type
example.

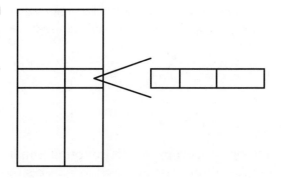

As an example, we can refine the definition of the employee table to include a subtable containing all the employee address information as an encased row type. The row contains the employee's street, city, state, and zip code information.

```
CREATE TABLE employees (
    emp_id          INTEGER
        CONSTRAINT employees_emp_id_pk PRIMARY KEY,
    last_name       name
        CONSTRAINT employees_last_name_not_null NOT NULL,
    first_name      name
        CONSTRAINT employees_first_name_not_null NOT NULL,
    emp_address     ROW (
                        street CHARACTER VARYING (30),
                        city   CHARACTER VARYING (20),
                        state  CHARACTER (2),
                        zip    CHARACTER VARYING (9)
            ),
    emp_phone       CHARACTER (10),
    emp_full_time   BOOLEAN,
    emp_signature   BLOB (1M),
    emp_picture     BLOB (10M),
    emp_resume      CLOB (50K)
)
```

The remainder of the employee table is exactly as it was before. The row type can be used anywhere a predefined data type can be used. The row can be an instance of types in a table, as described above, or a result of a query or view.

The row type uses structural equivalence for type checking, implying that the number of fields must be the same, and the data type of the corresponding fields must be the same. Row types can be unnamed, as in the example above, or can be defined separately, with a named type associated with the row. For example, you could have defined a base row type address and used this in the above employee table specification to simplify the description of the table. To create the named row type address, the following specification could be used:

```
CREATE ROW TYPE address_t (
        street   CHARACTER VARYING (30),
        city   CHARACTER VARYING (20),
        state   CHARACTER (2),
        zip   CHARACTER VARYING (9)
        );
```

This can then be used in the definition of employee in place of the original row definition. The declaration replaces the simple row name with the actual type in the schema. In this way, the row type replaces the definition of the subelements of the original specification. It also provides a means to specify data types in a general way, which can then be used by other tables within the database in a uniform manner. For example, this new data type address_t can be used in the customer table or in the supplier table to define their address locations. These definitions will now have the same uniform way of describing this information without any special nuances.

```
CREATE TABLE employees (
    emp_id          INTEGER
       CONSTRAINT  employees_emp_id_pk PRIMARY KEY,
    last_name       name
       CONSTRAINT  employees_last_name_not_null NOT NULL,
    first_name      name
       CONSTRAINT  employees_first_name_not_null NOT NULL,
    emp_address     address_t,
    emp_phone       CHARACTER (10),
    emp_full_time   BOOLEAN,
    emp_signature   BLOB (1M),
    emp_picture     BLOB (10M),
    emp_resume      CLOB (50K)
)
```

The row type is a powerful means to refine the information capture and modeling capability of the SQL data model. The row type permits the specification of varying levels of nesting, which may more nearly model real-world information and semantics than a simple flat table.

Array Types

The array data type is specified as a collection type, which provides a means to specify a varying cardinality list of elements for a field. The array type allows the specification of an array of built-in types (e.g., arrays of integers, abstract data types, named row types, and reference data types). Instead of being a distinct type, the array type is simply a refinement, allowing elements in tables or rows to have multiple instances. For example, an employee could have multiple phone numbers or multiple addresses. To specify an element of a table as an array simply requires the addition of the keyword ARRAY, followed by the number of elements to be allowed. In the employee table, if we allow multiple phone numbers, the specification could look like this:

```
CREATE TABLE employees (
    emp_id          INTEGER
        CONSTRAINT employees_emp_id_pk PRIMARY KEY,
    last_name       name
        CONSTRAINT employees_last_name_not_null NOT NULL,
    first_name      name
        CONSTRAINT employees_first_name_not_null NOT NULL,
    emp_address     address_t,
    emp_phone       CHARACTER (10) ARRAY (5),
    emp_full_time   BOOLEAN,
    emp_signature   BLOB (1M),
    emp_picture     BLOB (10M),
    emp_resume      CLOB (50K)
)
```

The specification now allows an employee to have up to five telephone numbers stored in the database as an array of phone numbers in the employee table. The array data type is a means whereby repeating groups can be readily incorporated into an SQL table much like that of the earlier network data models.

Abstract Data Types

Abstract data types are one of the most important changes to the type system defined within SQL-3. Abstract data types are named user-defined data types, which possess a behavior and encapsulated internal structure unique to the ADT. An ADT allows users to define and support the storage and manipulation of complex structures. For example, in the aquarium management system, you can define an abstract data type for the online description and viewing of the aquatic stock tanks by using an ADT.

```
CREATE TYPE aquatic_stock_tank_view (
        tank_size        INTEGER,
        text_description VARCHAR (2048),
        front_view_image BLOB,
```

```
left_side_image    BLOB,
right_side_image   BLOB,
top_view_image     BLOB,
specimens          BLOB ARRAY(25),
setting_objects    BLOB ARRAY(25),
setup_document     CLOB)
```

This ADT provides a means whereby the aquarium company can show off its stock to prospective customers using the database system. Each tank in the shop can be defined as an instance of this ADT, with the contents of the tank scanned into the database as BLOBs. The design of the tank can be specified in a PostScript document, which can be extracted and viewed using a PostScript viewer application integrated into the database system. For each of the attributes within the ADT, the designer must define the behavior of the attribute with the outside world. For example, front_view_image could have a function to show the image and zoom in on a section of the image (which could expand internally to open and view a specimen or setting object). More will be said about these in Chapters 5 and 6.

Abstract data types, by definition, are completely encapsulated. Access to instances of an ADT are restricted to operations supplied through the ADTs functions. ADTs are defined by their visible functional interface, with internals encapsulated and protected by the ADT's structure and semantics. There is no distinction between functions and stored or virtual attributes at the interface. Stored attributes and virtual derived attributes are indistinguishable. Every attribute of an ADT has an observer and a mutator function defined on it, allowing for viewing and altering the ADT instance. As with object-oriented systems, an ADT's internals can change without affecting any application using the ADT, as long as no changes to the interface are specified.

Attributes of an ADT have a name and a type. The names of the attributes in an ADT cannot be repeated—that is, an ADT definition may specify only one attribute of any given name. The types of an ADTs attributes can be predefined (built-in types or distinct types) or any other user-defined type, including other ADTs. Definition, access, and manipulation of ADTs will be described in further detail in later chapters.

Distinct Type

The distinct type is a specialization of basic data types by users and represents the most basic form of user-defined data types. Distinct type equivalence is based on applying name equivalence, implying that two types with the same structure, which have been defined as distinct types, will not be equivalent under any circumstances. The BNF definition of the distinct type is:

```
<distinct type definition> ::=
    CREATE DISTINCT TYPE <distinct type name>
      AS <data type>
      [ <cast to distinct> ] [ <cast to source> ]
```

For example, you can define different types of money using this data type specification. If the aquarium management system is to be used in different countries, you can define a different currency and sales table for each country, as defined below.

```
CREATE DISTINCT TYPE US_dollar AS DECIMAL (7,2)
```

and

```
CREATE DISTINCT TYPE CAN_dollar AS DECIMAL (7,2)
```

The sales tables can be defined as:

```
CREATE TABLE CAN_sales (
      order_id      INTEGER,
      cust_id       INTEGER,
      emp_id        INTEGER,
      sale_amt      CAN_dollar
)

CREATE TABLE US_sales (
      order_id      INTEGER,
      cust_id       INTEGER,
      emp_id        INTEGER,
      sale_amt      US_dollar
)
```

You now have two distinct types, which can be used in place of any base data type definition. The distinct type is a renamed basic data type, which typically will have a behavior different from the base type from which it is derived. The internal representation of the distinct type is the same as the base type; however, the base type and the distinct types are not directly comparable. The distinct type has some defined operators derivable from the base type from which they are constructed (comparison operators). The distinct type can be transformed into the base type through casting. Distinct types cannot be used with each other, unless there are defined functions to convert from one to the other. For example, Canadian dollars would need to be converted into U.S. dollars before operations using comparisons from both could be performed. The main feature of distinct types is their adherence to strong typing, which guarantees correctness and intended type behavior.

Some Possible SQL-4 Deferred Data Types

To allow definition of more complex data structures, SQL-3 (possibly deferred to SQL-4) provides a number of *collection* types: SET, LIST, and MULTISET. The components of these collection types can be simple elementary data types, such as character, strings, integers, and so on; or more complex types, such as row or ADT; or major types, such as tables or objects.

SET   The SET data type facilitates the grouping of a collection of related instances of the same data type into a single data structure, which will have no duplicates. For example, a SET could contain the names of a collection of students or a collection of phone numbers. The SET provides a means to collect similar elements for added semantic richness. As an example, a student could have multiple addresses (say a home address and a school address) and a number of phone numbers (e.g., a lab, dorm room, or work/study office). SETs can be used to group these data under the student by using the following syntax (assuming the types address and phone numbers are created).

```
CREATE TABLE students (
        s_name          name,
        s_id            INTEGER,

                        .
                        .
                        .

        s_address       SET(address),
        s_phone         SET(phone_no)
        );
```

To insert an item into the student table you can use the following:

```
INSERT INTO students VALUES (
   ROW('Jane','Doe'),
   '000112222',
             .
             .
```

```
SET(ROW('285','Old Westport rd', 'N.Dartmouth', 'Ma.', '02747'),
    ROW('1199', 'West 69th st', 'New York', 'NY', '10021'))
SET( '5089991122', '2029991111')
  );
```

LIST   Similarly, to construct a data structure with order, the SQL-3 LIST collection type can be used. By using this type of structure, a list of students or a list of faculty members can be constructed with the property that each of the collections has an order based on the type's implied ordering. For example, if you want a list of students in a particular class, the list can be ordered by student IDs or names.

MULTISET   Another collection type is the MULTISET. MULTISET is a collection type that, unlike the other two described types, allows duplicates. As a fundamental definition, the relation or table is a MULTISET of rows. MULTISET provides the means to collect a set of items together, irrespective of duplicate values. In general, collections are value typed and thus have no object identifier (OID) and must be declared as types of table columns for instances of the collection to be persistently stored in the database.

Subtables and Supertables

Subtables and supertables are used in SQL-3 to model collection hierarchies. The supertable is the top-level base table defined. The subtable inherits every column and respective definitions from the supertable. If any name conflicts are present, the columns must be renamed to rectify the conflict. The rows of the subtable correspond to one, and only one, row from the supertable, and every row in the supertable corresponds to, at most, one row in the subtable. This implies that a row in the subtable must have row elements from a supertable, but not the other way around. Some rows in a supertable may not be present in a subtable.

If an item is updated, a new item inserted, or an item deleted, the effects propagate among the derived tables. For example, if a row in a supertable is deleted, the corresponding row in the subtable must also be deleted if the database is to remain correct and consistent.

As an example of this concept, you can produce a set of tables for classifying marine fish by their geographical areas, using the marine fish supertable as the basis for the construction. First, we define the marine fish table as follows, assuming the domain types for `name`, `food`, `region`, `temperament`, and `day_shift` are already defined:

```
CREATE TABLE marine_fish (
    scientific_name    name,
    common_name        name,
    fish_species       name,
    max_size           DECIMAL (5,2)
    food_preference    food,
    geographic_range   region,
    fish_disposition   temperament,
    fish_activity      day_shift
)
```

Second, you form subtables comprised of elements from the supertable using the notation UNDER to specify that this new table is defined as consisting of the supertable, plus possibly some new information:

```
CREATE TABLE caribbean_marine_fish UNDER marine_fish;
CREATE TABLE red_sea_marine_fish UNDER marine_fish;
```

and so on, until all the regions are defined. You can then use further refinements or SELECT statements to populate these new tables from the existing table. In addition to inheriting all the attributes from the supertable, you can add attributes to the subtables, if there is a need for them. For example, you can add some subregional information within each of the subtables:

```
CREATE TABLE caribbean_marine_fish UNDER marine_fish (
    Subregion    VARCHAR(15) ARRAY (6)
)
```

You can now specify that a specific fish is found in the western and eastern Caribbean, but nowhere else in this major region. This is a powerful modeling and database design tool to minimize redundancy and to reuse specifications already performed.

Another example defines a supertype for person, which then can be refined into employees and customers in the aquarium database. These concepts will be explored in later chapters.

Summary

In this chapter, background information about basic information representation in the SQL-3 language was examined. In particular, the basic built-in data types, which can be used to construct the fundamental component of an SQL database table, were discussed. Beyond the basic data types, there are new added data types available, including the Boolean, distinct, array, abstract data type, binary large objects, and character large objects. This discussion presented these extended data types within the context of the working database example, the aquarium management system.

To be complete, some controversial extended data types were included, which have been deferred to SQL-4 due to their immaturity and/or controversial nature. It is assumed that these extended data types will show up in some early SQL-3 products, because application developers and users want to use them. Collection types are viewed as important where query processing is concerned. They give users or applications developers another tool through which they can direct the underlying system to cluster data in storage for improved performance.

Abstract Data Types

Introduction

The type system of SQL-3 extends that of SQL-2 in numerous ways, as shown in Chapter 4, and maintains upward compatibility with SQL-2's type system. SQL-3 provides the same set of built-in types supported in SQL, along with operations upon those types. The fundamental storage repository in SQL-3, the table, remains the same as that in SQL-2. However, the table takes on significantly more meaning in the SQL-3 system. Among the numerous changes to the type system in SQL-3 is the ability to specify new abstract data types, which capture application-specific behavior within the database. Types in SQL-3 hide implementation from clients (abstraction and encapsulation) and are viewed in the system the same as built-in types. Abstract data types have properties such as object identity, inheritance, polymorphism, and other properties formerly reserved only for objects without object-oriented database systems.

Abstract Data Type

What is an abstract data type? An abstract data type (ADT) can be anything a user can imagine and represent within the confines of the language. For example, an ADT can represent a map, a marine fish, an aquatic environment, an employee, and so on. The fundamental concept behind an ADT is that it has encapsulated information and specific behaviors relevant to the encapsulated information.

An abstract data type specification in SQL-3 defines the contents of the ADT (stored information) and the behavior to be exhibited by instances of the ADT. The specification of an ADT consists of *attribute* specifications and *function* specifications encased within the ADT type specification. The BNF for the SQL-3 abstract data type indicates that it is a user-defined data type, which is defined within the schema using a qualified schema name:

```
<type predicate item> ::=
    <expression type>
  | TYPE <data type>
```

```
<expression type> ::=
    TYPE <left paren> <value expression> <right paren>

<data type> ::=
      <predefined type>
    | <row type>
    | <user-defined data type>
    | <collection type>

<user-defined data type> ::=
      <abstract data type>
    | <distinct type name>

<abstract data type> ::=
    <abstract data type name>

<abstract data type name> ::= <local or schema qualified name>
```

An ADT in SQL-3 is defined within the schema using the following syntax:

```
CREATE TYPE address

   <ADT address body>
```

The body of the ADT contains specifications for stored information, routines that provide the desired behavior, operators, ordering, cast, table constraints, and, possibly, default values.

The behavior of an ADT is completely encapsulated in the type definition, leaving only public attributes and function interfaces visible to clients—though users can only access stored attributes using defined routine interfaces. The encapsulation level associated with the attribute or function can further control attribute and function visibility. SQL-3 defines three encapsulation levels: public, private, and protected. Public attributes and functions are visible to all authorized users of the defined ADT. Private attributes and functions are visible only within the lexical scope of the ADT. Protected attributes and functions are visible both within their own ADT and within the definition of all subtypes of the ADT. The ADT is defined as public, private, or protected using the tags PUBLIC, PRIVATE, or PROTECTED (this may be deferred to SQL-4). The tag can be associated with any attribute or function of the abstract data type. If no tag is present with an attribute or function, the previous tag used is defined. If no tags are used at all, the default is public.

Access to public attributes and functions can be further restricted by privilege mechanisms. Privilege mechanisms can be applied to control whether a given user is authorized to use a particular public attribute or function. Below is an example of some ADT attribute definitions:

```
CREATE TYPE address (
        street          VARCHAR (20),
        city            VARCHAR (20),
        state           VARCHAR (20),
        zip             CHAR (5),
        ext_            CHAR (10))

CREATE TYPE person (
        ss_num          CHAR (11),
        first_name      VARCHAR (20),
        middle_name     VARCHAR (20),
        last_name       VARCHAR (20),
        domicile        address,
        birth_date      date,
        sex             CONSTANT CHAR (1))
```

The definitions above look very much like the definitions for tables shown in previous chapters. The difference lies in the means through which access to the encapsulated attributes is allowed.

For every attribute defined for an ADT, an *observer* and a *mutator* function are automatically generated, allowing access and setting of the ADT's attributes. For example, in the address ADT defined above, observer and mutator functions are generated with the following interfaces:

```
FUNCTION street (address) RETURNS VARCHAR (20)
FUNCTION street (address, VARCHAR (20)) RETURNS address

FUNCTION city (address) RETURNS VARCHAR (20)
FUNCTION city (address, VARCHAR (20)) RETURNS address

FUNCTION state (address) RETURNS VARCHAR (20)
FUNCTION state (address, VARCHAR (20)) RETURNS address

FUNCTION zip (address) RETURNS CHAR (5)
FUNCTION zip (address, CHAR (5)) RETURNS address

FUNCTION ext_zip (address) RETURNS CHAR (4)
FUNCTION ext_zip (address, CHAR (4)) RETURNS address
```

These observer and mutator functions can then be used to access or change the named attribute's values. For example, if the street address is 285 Old Westport Road, the observer function:

```
s = street (address)
```

returns the value 285 Old Westport Road. The mutator function can be used to change the address:

```
a = street (address, '385 Old Westport Road')
```

and returns an entire instance of the address ADT with the new value set.

Abstract Data Type Attributes

The attributes of an ADT have a name and a type. For example, the attribute "street" of the address ADT, has a type VARCHAR(20). The names used to describe attributes within an ADT must be unique for the ADT, though an attribute name can be reused in a separate ADT specification. For example, if you use the attribute first_name in the person data type, this attribute name cannot be used again to define any other attribute in the person abstract data type. It can be used in another abstract data type, such as the employee described in Chapter 4.

Attribute Definition

Attributes in an ADT can be defined using any nonreserved word in the SQL language specification. For example, you cannot define an ADT with the name SELECT, but you can use the name USER_SELECT or some other literal not on the reserved word list. Once an ADT attribute name has been chosen, it must be defined to have a type associated with it. The type of the named attribute can be one of the predefined data types, such as: INTEGER, DECIMAL, REAL, FLOAT, CHARACTER, CHARACTER VARYING, VARCHAR, BIT, BIT VARYING, DATE, TIME, TIMESTAMP, INTERVAL, BOOLEAN, BLOB, CLOB, and so on. The attribute definition is not limited to these built-in data types. The attribute data type can be a user-defined enumerated type, DISTINCT data type, ROW type, SET, MULTISET, LIST, or even another ADT. For example, if you define an ADT address as shown previously, this ADT can then be used to define the type of an attribute in another ADT named person or employee, customer ADTs, or tables. In the person

ADT below, the domicile attribute is defined as type address, using the address ADT as the type of the domicile attribute:

```
CREATE TYPE person (
        ss_num        CHAR (11),
        first_name    VARCHAR (20),
        middle_name   VARCHAR (20),
        last_name     VARCHAR (20),
        domicile      address,
        birth_date    date,
        sex           CONSTANT CHAR (1))
```

The above type specification nests the ADT address within the ADT person. If further nesting is required, the model supports additional depth in the definition of data types.

Attributes defined in this way can be further refined to be viewable from certain perspectives of the defined ADT. PUBLIC attributes are visible from the ADT's interface to users of the ADT. PRIVATE attributes are not visible to the user interface, but only to the ADT's implementation. Finally, PROTECTED attributes are visible only to subtypes. For example, if an employee type is given attributes that are not to be automatically visible to the outside world, they can be declared as PRIVATE:

```
PRIVATE   emp_salary    DECIMAL (9,2),
PRIVATE   emp_com_rate  DECIMAL (3,3)
```

Alternatively, these can be defined as PROTECTED, allowing any subtype inheriting this data type to have direct access to their interface.

Stored and Virtual Attributes

The attributes of an ADT have one of two representations: stored or virtual. The difference is in how the "value" of the attribute of the ADT is represented and determined. As defined previously, an attribute is specified using a name and an associated data type. The data type can be a built-in or user-defined type. Stored attributes are represented by the stored data associated with an ADT instance. Each ADT attribute instance is associated with a value from the possible collection of values stored in all instances of the ADT. This is similar to the class concept within C++.

Contrary to stored attributes, virtual attributes do not necessarily correspond directly to stored data. Virtual attribute values are derived through the execution of a user-defined function. For example, in the person data type you can define a virtual attribute, age, using the present date minus the person's birth date. Unlike stored attributes, where observer and mutator functions are implicitly defined, you must specify observer and mutator functions explicitly when defining a value ADT attribute. For example, for the age virtual attribute, you must define functions to set and retrieve the virtual attribute age:

```
PUBLIC FUNCTION age ( p person) RETURNS REAL
  BEGIN
   DECLARE : p person;
   DECLARE :a REAL;
      SET a = CURRENT_DATE - birth_date(p);
      RETURN a;
  END;
```

You also need a set_age function to change the age of this person if necessary. The value associated with an ADT's attribute, stored or virtual, can be accessed using two forms of notation: Simple implicit interface—for example, name (person) returns name; and dot notation, where you declare an item of type person and then use p..name as the means to extract the name value stored in the ADT.

Abstract Data Type Creation and Initialization

ADTs are not simply defined with encapsulated attributes; an ADT can have numerous other components. ADTs are of no use if they are not created and instantiated in the database. The BNF notation used to define an ADT in SQL-3 (which could change before publication) is shown below and highlights some of the elements that can be found within an ADT definition:

```
<abstract data type definition> ::=
    CREATE <abstract data type body>

<abstract data type body> ::=
    ABSTRACT DATA TYPE
        <abstract data type name>
    [ <subtype clause> ]
    [ <constructor option> ]
    [ <member list> ]
    [ <type default> ]
```

The following clause allows for defining an ADT under another ADT definition. For example, the employee ADT can be defined UNDER the person ADT. The syntax using the BNF description would be as follows:

```
CREATE TYPE employee UNDER person (
    remainder if ADT definition );

<subtype clause> ::=
    UNDER <supertype clause>
        [ { <comma> <supertype clause> }... ]

<supertype clause> ::=
    <abstract data type name>
```

ADTs can optionally define their own constructor routines separate from the automatically defined constructor, using the following syntax:

```
<constructor option> ::=
    CONSTRUCTOR [ <routine name> ]

<member list> ::=
    <left paren> <member> [ { <comma> <member> }... ] <right paren>

<member> ::=
      <attribute definition>
    | <ordering clause>

<attribute definition> ::=
    <attribute name>
    { <data type> | <domain name> }
    | [ <attribute default> ]
    [ <collate clause> ]

<attribute name> ::=
    <identifier>

<attribute default> ::=
    <default clause>
```

The instances of ADTs defined using the ADT definition can be further constrained to exhibit ordering properties using this syntax:

```
<ordering clause> ::=
    EQUALS ONLY BY <ordering method>
    | ORDER FULL BY
        <ordering method>
```

The ordering can be performed using methods described as relative, hash, or state. The relative method is a function that returns a 0 for equal, – for less than, and + for greater than. The hash method uses a hash function, which takes a single argument of the ADT type and returns a predefined data type. Comparing two ADTs is accomplished by comparing the two hash values associated with them. The state method compares the attributes of the operands to determine an order. These methods are used throughout the language where clauses to select items by order are needed:

```
<ordering method> ::=
      RELATIVE <relative function specification>
    | HASH <hash function specification>
    | STATE

<relative function specification> ::=
    <specific routine designator>

<specific routine designator> ::=
      SPECIFIC <routine type> <specific name>
    | <routine type> <member name>
```

The implementation of observer and mutators can be a routine, function, or procedure. Routines are externally defined in a host language. Functions are routines that return a single value or structure (an ADT instance). A procedure is also a routine and can have input, output, or input-output parameters associated with it. The syntax for specifying which one is being defined is as follows:

```
<routine type> ::=
      ROUTINE
    | FUNCTION
    | PROCEDURE

<specific name> ::= <schema qualified name>

<member name> ::= <routine name> [ <data type list> ]

<data type list> ::=
    <left paren> [ <data type> [ { <comma> <data type> }... ] ]
    <right paren>

<hash function specification> ::=
    <specific routine designator>

<type default> ::=
    TYPE <default clause>
```

Defining an ADT creates the interface to the outside world; however, an ADT is not realized in the database until it has been created and instantiated in the database. An ADT is not created by simply defining its external interface, as defined through encapsulated attributes. For example, the address ADT is not realized simply through the definition of the ADT type address. Its attributes and their types are as follows:

```
CREATE TYPE address (
        street   VARCHAR (20),
        city     VARCHAR (20),
        state    VARCHAR (20),
        zip      CHAR (5),
        ext_zip  CHAR (10))
```

In addition, the definition requires the implicit observer and mutator function and a constructor and destructor function. The constructor and destructor functions are used to create an instance (realization) of the ADT in the database.

Constructor Functions

To create an instance of an ADT you must specify a constructor function for the ADT type. The constructor function for an ADT instance has the form:

```
CONSTRUCTOR FUNCTION <adt name> ( optional parameter list ) RETURNS
<adt type>
   <function declarations>
   <body of constructor>
```

The constructor can have specific default values (defined during the ADT specification), which will result in each new instance being created with the same default values, or it can be parameterized, permitting user-defined initializations. Once an ADT instance is instantiated, the built-in functions can be used to set stored and virtual values. For example, for the address data type defined earlier, a constructor and destructor function with NULL defaults may appear as follows:

```
CONSTRUCTOR FUNCTION address() RETURNS address
   DECLARE :a address
   BEGIN
      NEW :a;
      SET :a.street = NULL;
      SET :a.city = NULL;
      SET :a.state = NULL;
      SET :a.zip = NULL;
      SET a.exp_zip = NULL;
      RETURN a;
   END;
END FUNCTION
```

Or, using explicit values to write into the instance, you can use a parameterized version, such as:

```
CONSTRUCTOR FUNCTION address
    (s VARCHAR(20), c VARCHAR(20), t VARCHAR(20),
     z VARCHAR(5), e VARCHAR(4)) RETURNS address
    DECLARE :a address
    BEGIN
       NEW :a;
       SET :a.street =s;
       SET :a.city = c;
       SET :a.state = t;
       SET :a.zip = z;
       SET a.exp_zip = e;
       RETURN a;
    END;
END FUNCTION
```

Or, simply leave the initialization of defaults and the selection of default values to the system-supplied constructor function. In this case, the defaults become the defaults for the data types—for example, NULL for CHAR and VARCHAR, and so on.

Destructor Functions

If an instance can be created, it must also have the capability to be removed from the database. To remove an instance of an ADT, you must specify a destructor function for the ADT type. The format of a destructor function is:

```
DESTRUCTOR FUNCTION <adt name> ( :P parameter ) RETURNS <adt name>
    BEGIN
       clean up work
       DESTROY :P;
       RETURN :P;
    END;
END FUNCTION
```

For the example ADT address, the destructor may appear as:

```
DESTRUCTOR FUNCTION remove_address ( :a address ) RETURNS address
    BEGIN
       DESTROY :a;
       RETURN :a;
    END;
END FUNCTION
```

The constructor and destructor functions, as well as the observer and mutator functions, do not need to be functions; they can also be implemented using procedures or external routines.

Accessing Attributes of an ADT

To access an instance of an ADT requires using automatically generated or user-defined observer functions and mutator functions, along with the semantics of their use. In addition, user-defined functions are required for accessing virtual attributes. To use these functions requires that you declare a variable of the ADT type first. Once the ADT has been declared and an instance located (typically through the use of a higher-order SQL data manipulation statement), access can be performed using one of two methods.

Observer Functions

The first method to access the attributes of an ADT is by using the function name and parameters with the automatically generated observer function. For example, in the address ADT, to access the street name requires that first an ADT reference type is declared in the user's code:

```
DECLARE a address;
```

You can access the attributes using this variable of type address as the base access pointer in the parameter list for a specific ADT (which can be located using the SELECT statement). To extract the street address from an instance of the ADT address, simply request:

```
DECLARE st VARCHAR(20);
st = street (a);
```

The variable st is declared to be of the same type as the stored attribute, allowing for the value to be copied from the database to the declared variable. The second statement causes the observer function street to be invoked on the instance of the ADT address pointed to by the ADT locator (previously defined) and allocated to an instance of the address data type.

Mutator Functions

Conversely, to set the value of the address ADT's street attribute to "1997 East Main Road" from its present value would require use of the automatically generated mutator function for the street attribute of the address ADT. The mutator function requires that two parameters be passed into it: the base ADT reference to an instance of the ADT and the named attribute value to be stored. To set the street address to the value above requires the same declarations for an instance of the address ADT, followed by its use in the function call:

```
street ( a, '1997 East Main Road' );
```

Again, this statement is most likely to be embedded in an UPDATE statement or some other SQL-3 data manipulation statement.

Dot Notation for Access

A second method to access an ADT's attributes is to use the dot notation. Dot notation is simply another syntactic means by which ADT attribute observer and mutator functions can be invoked. The notation uses the ADT instance variable followed by the double dot, which is then followed by the name of the function to invoke. Using the same example above, to extract the street address from an instance of the address ADT would require the following:

```
DECLARE a address;
    DECLARE st VARCHAR (20);
    SET st = a..street;
```

The syntax supports multiple levels of ADT navigational access. The multiple levels require a path expression describing how the multiple levels of nested ADT instances are to be perused. However, dot notation does not reveal the underlying physical representation, which can be very different. As an example of the multiple level access capabilities, define an ADT person as shown below:

```
CREATE TYPE person (
        ss_num        CHAR (11),
        first_name    VARCHAR (20),
        middle_name   VARCHAR (20),
        last_name     VARCHAR (20),
```

```
domicile        address,
birth_date      date,
sex             CONSTANT CHAR (1))
```

The nested, previously defined, ADT address defines the domicile attribute. The following nested dot notation form can then be used to access the street attribute:

```
SET st = P..domicile..street;
```

This assumes you have declared a variable P of type person and a variable st to store the recovered attribute value. Dot notation provides an easy and powerful method to extract information from encapsulated ADT stored and virtual attributes.

Abstract Data Type Interface

The visible interface to an ADT is defined using the definition of the ADT's attributes and the designation of what degree of visibility the attributes are to have. As discribed in the introduction, attributes and routines of an ADT can be specified as being public, private, or protected. These qualifiers indicate the degree to which the defined attribute or routine is to be visible outside the ADT's scope. Similar to degrees of isolation when dealing with transactions in SQL-2, these declarations allow users to use data in different ways or to restrict how the data are to be used. The concept behind providing these levels of visibility is to give the database ADT designer control over how the encapsulated attributes and routines become usable by external users.

Public Interface

The first level of visible interface is the public declaration. Public attributes and routines are visible from the ADT's interface. The attributes themselves are not directly accessible at the interface; however, the attributes' automatically generated observer and mutator functions are. To be declared as public, an attribute or routine declaration must be preceded with the reserved word PUBLIC. In the definition of the employee type, to make all the attribute definitions public requires only the specification of the first attribute as public. All other attributes fol-

lowing a declaration have the same declaration, unless another is specified. In the employees type below, specifying the `emp_id` as PUBLIC
"tags" all following untagged attributes with the same designation, unless altered by a subsequent tag specification:

```
CREATE TYPE employees (
PUBLIC    emp_id           INTEGER .
          emp_title        name,
          emp_last_name    name,
          emp_first_name   name,
          emp_address      address,
          emp_phone        CHARACTER (10),
          emp_start_date   TIMESTAMP,
          emp_pay_rate     DECIMAL (7,2)
          emp_com_rate     DECIMAL (5,2)
    )
```

The employees data type is declared to be all public, since no other tag
is specified after the first tag on the `emp_id` attribute. In SQL-3, if no tag
is supplied for any attribute or routine of an ADT, then all items are by
default declared to be public.

Private Interface

The second format for attribute and routine declarations is the private
declaration. An attribute or routine is considered private only if the attribute or routine is available from within the ADT where the attribute
or routine was specified. This implies that an attribute or routine defined as private will be accessible from an internal routine and will not
be visible from outside the ADT's specification. For example, in the employees type defined below you may not want to allow access to an employee's salary or commission rate except by this ADT. You may want to
provide functions that allow virtual access to these values, based on
some further constraints specified in the routine definitions.

In the following employees example, the employee identification,
pay rate, and commission rate are specified as private. This implies that
these attributes are not available from outside this ADT's definition. To
access values stored in these attributes requires that additional routines
be provided to allow indirect access to these data items. These indirect
routes must, however, be defined by the ADT type specifier:

```
CREATE TYPE employees (
PRIVATE   emp_id           INTEGER
PUBLIC    emp_title        name,
```

```
          emp_last_name    name,
          emp_first_name   name,
          emp_address      address,
          emp_phone        CHARACTER (10),
          emp_start_date   TIMESTAMP,
PRIVATE   emp_pay_rate     DECIMAL (7,2)
PRIVATE   emp_com_rate     DECIMAL (5,2)

)
```

The attributes and routines defined in this way are only available to the internal implementation code of the ADT. To access any of these attributes, or hidden routines, requires that you leave some derivable means to extract this information.

Protected Interface

The final form of attribute and routine tagging for ADTs is the protected tag. A protected tagged attribute or routine is protected from external users viewing or accessing its stored values. A protected attribute or routine, however, is accessible from any table, routine, or ADT that uses this attribute as a subtype. For example, in the person type, you can declare the phone attribute to be protected. As a result, the phone attribute is available only to the internal components of the employees type and in any type derived using this type as a subtype in its type specification:

```
CREATE DOMAIN name AS CHARACTER VARYING (25) COLLATE
american_english

      CREATE TYPE employees (
PRIVATE     emp_id           INTEGER
PUBLIC      emp_title        name,
            emp_last_name    name,
            emp_first_name   name,
            emp_address      address,
PROTECTED   emp_phone        CHARACTER (10),
            emp_start_date   TIMESTAMP,
PRIVATE     emp_pay_rate     DECIMAL (7,2)
PRIVATE     emp_com_rate     DECIMAL (5,2)

)
```

To access a protected type, an internal routine must be defined that uses the attribute as an input to its computations. Private and protected designations are meant to provide a means through which access to items can be restricted to only routines or subfunctions that the database designers deem acceptable.

Summary

This chapter introduced some of the fundamental aspects of abstract data type specification in the SQL-3 language. ADTs in SQL-3 provide a means to define application-specific data structures within the context of the database and make these data types available for processing and storage using the facilities of the database system. SQL-3 has extended the capabilities of the previous SQL database language to allow user-defined data types. Later, the ADT will be shown to be one of the most important extensions introduced into the SQL-2 language.

CHAPTER **6**

Using Abstract
Data Types

One of the largest alterations to the typing system of SQL-3, as compared with that of its predecessors, is the abstract data type. The abstract data type allows users to specify data types that naturally map to data types used in an application. This change allows SQL-3 to avoid the data type mismatch found in most prior standardized relational database languages. This concept came from the prototype object-oriented databases and extended relational products on the market today. As users have begun to accept the capabilities of the object model and object-relational model into a wider range of applications, it was inevitable that these new data types would find their way into the domain of standardized production-level database systems. In this chapter, the abstract data type is further examined in terms of where it can be used in an SQL database and how example abstract data types can be used in SQL's unary and binary operations.

Abstract Data Type Use in Expanded Type Definitions

In Chapter 5, the application-specific, abstract data type and its specification was presented. Abstract data type specification allows users of SQL-3 to define tables and their contents, which are mapped to the needs of applications, not the needs of data management functions. Abstract data types can be specified and used where any other predefined data types can be used. Abstract data types can be used to define the type of attributes within another abstract data type (called subtyping), as the type of the domain of columns in a table, as the type of an SQL variable, or as the type of parameters for functions or procedures. In short, an abstract data type is treated the same as the SQL-2 base types were in previous standardized SQL database systems products.

The BNF specification for an ADT is defined in the standard as follows:

```
<user-defined type definition> ::= CREATE TYPE <user-defined type
body>

<user-defined type body> ::=
   <user-defined type name>
   [ <subtype clause> ]
```

```
      [ AS <representation> ]
      [ <instantiable clause> ]
      <finality>
      [ <cast option> ]

<subtype clause> ::=
   UNDER <supertype name> [ { <comma> <supertype name>} . . .]

<supertype name> ::= <user-defined type>

<representation> ::=
   <predefined type>
   |<member list>

<member list> ::=
   <left paren> <member> [ { <comma> <member> } . . .] <right
paren>

<member> ::=
   <attribute definition>

<instantiable clause> ::=
   INSTANTIABLE
   |NOT INSTANTIABLE

<finality> ::=
   FINAL
   |NOT FINAL

<cast option> ::=
   [ <cast to distinct> ]
   [ <cast to source> ]

<cast to distinct> ::=
   CAST <left paren> SOURCE AS DISTINCT <right paren>
   WITH <cast to distinct identifier>

<cast to source> ::=
   CAST < left paren> DISTINCT TO SOURCE <right paren>
   WITH <cast to source identifier>

<cast to source identifier> ::= <identifier>
```

ADTs in Attributes of Other ADTs

The first extended use of abstract data types is to use a previous ADT specification as the type of an attribute in another abstract data type. To declare an ADT using another ADT as a subpart, you first must declare a base ADT type, which will then be used in the declaration to follow. If you want to change the aquarium employees' pay rate from a simple decimal value to an ADT with added security and functionality, you can redefine the base type from DECIMAL (7,2) to an abstract data type, as follows:

```
CREATE TYPE salary (
      value    DECIMAL (7,2),

      <body of ADT salary>

);
```

With this new data type, you can redefine the employee abstract data type, as follows:

```
CREATE TYPE employees (
PUBLIC   emp_id          INTEGER
      emp_title          name,
      emp_last_name      name,
      emp_first_name     name,
      emp_address        address,
      emp_phone          CHARACTER (10),
      emp_start_date     TIMESTAMP,
      emp_pay_rate       salary,
      emp_com_rate       DECIMAL (5,2)
)
```

In this manner, any attribute of an abstract data type can itself be composed of another abstract data type. The level of nesting supported is implementation-defined, but is expected to be fairly robust in most vendor implementations.

Another use of this technique is to define a new ADT using another ADT as the base type. For example, assume you have an abstract data type person, as follows:

```
CREATE TYPE person (
      ss_num       CHARACTER(9),
      last_name    name,
      first_name   name,
      address      address,
      phone        CHARACTER (10)
)
```

You can use this base abstract data type in the definition of another abstract data type (subtyping) by combining all the specifications of the person ADT in some other ADT. To redefine the aquarium employee using the person ADT, you can use the person ADT, as follows:

```
CREATE TYPE employee UNDER person (
      emp_id          INTEGER
      emp_title       name,
      emp_start_date  TIMESTAMP,
      emp_pay_rate    salary,
      emp_com_rate    DECIMAL (5,2)
)
```

This specification uses the SQL-3 BNF subtype clause:

```
<subtype clause> ::=
   UNDER <supertype name> [ { <comma> <supertype name>} . . .]

<supertype name> ::= <user-defined type>
```

This specification results in the employee abstract data type aquiring all the attributes and functionality of the person abstract data type, as well as the additional attributes and functionality defined specifically for the employee abstract data type.

Parameter Types in Procedures or Functions

An abstract data type can also be used as an input, output, or input/output parameter for a procedure or as input parameters for functions. For example, if you have a function to compute the total salary of employees as the sum of their salaries and commissions, the following declaration can be used:

```
CREATE FUNCTION total_compensation (e employee) RETURNS
         DECIMAL (9,2)
   RETURN ((emp_pay_rate (e) * total_hours) + (emp_com_rate (e) *
         total_emp_sales));
```

In this function, the abstract data type employee is used to define the type of the parameter to be passed into the function for use in computing the result defined for this function. The passed-in employee parameter would have pay and commission rate read; then the employee's total compensation for the year to date would be computed. This function is not complete, however, since the employee's total hours worked to date and his or her total sales also would need to be extracted from some other table or abstract data type. In the database being constructed, these values could come from the payroll table and the revenue table. To make this function complete, you would need to embed SQL code within the function to access these data values. To look at these, the table specifications are shown here:

```
CREATE TABLE aquarium_revenues (
    employee_id    INTEGER,
    daily_sales    revenue,
    monthly_sales  revenue,
    year_to_date   revenue,
    commissions    revenue
)

CREATE TABLE aquarium_debits (
    debit_id       INTEGER,
    debit_amount   payment,
    debit_name     CHARACTER VARYING
)

CREATE  TABLE aquarium_payroll (
    emp_id         INTEGER,
    ytd_reg_hours  FLOAT,
    ytd_ovt_hours  FLOAT
)

CREATE FUNCTION total_compensation (e employee) RETURNS DECIMAL
(9,2)

    r_hours          FLOAT;
    o_hours          FLOAT;
    total_hours      FLOAT;
    total_emp_sales  revenue;

BEGIN

    SELECT ytd_reg_hours
    INTO r_hours
    FROM aquarium_payroll
    WHERE aquarium_payroll.emp_id = e.emp_id;

    SELECT ytd_ovt_hours
    INTO o_hours
    FROM aquarium_payroll
    WHERE aquarium_payroll.emp_id = e.emp_id;

    total_hours = r_hours + o_hours;

    SELECT year_to_date
    INTO total_emp_sales
    FROM aquarium_revenues
    WHERE aquarium_revenues.emp_id = e.emp_id;

END;
    RETURN ((emp_pay_rate (e) * total_hours) + (emp_com_rate (e) *
total_emp_sales));
```

You can see from this example that the embedded abstract data type passed into a function as a parameter, or as an input or output parameter in a procedure, results in very powerful access capabilities. The BNF for the procedure declaration is as follows:

```
<schema procedure> ::=
    CREATE <SQL-invoked procedure>

<SQL-invoked procedure> ::=
    PROCEDURE <routine name>
<SQL parameter declaration list>
[ <language clause> ]
[ SPECIFIC <specific name> ]
[ DYNAMIC RESULT SETS <maximum dynamic result sets> ]
<routine body>

<SQL parameter declaration list> ::=
    <left paren>
[ <SQL parameter declaration> [ {  <comma> <SQL parameter
declaration> }... ] ]
    <right paren>

<SQL parameter declaration> ::=
[ <parameter mode> ] [ <SQL parameter name> ]
<parameter type>
[ RESULT ]
[ <default clause> ]

<parameter mode> ::=
IN
    | OUT
    | INOUT
```

This indicates that procedure parameters can be IN, OUT, or of the INOUT modes. For use in a procedure, ADTs can be specified as the types of the parameters being passed in or being extracted from a procedure, as defined above. For example, a procedure could be specified that updates our employee file when a new employee is hired or that enters the results of a sale into the elements of our database. To hire an employee, you can use the following procedure specification:

```
PROCEDURE hire ( IN p person, OUT e employee );
    BEGIN
<code to take an instance of a person and create an instance of an
employee>
    END;
```

A procedure is normally defined in a module (a package specification) and can then be used in an application as if it were defined in the application's boundaries.

SQL Variable Type

To make any language useful requires the ability to create and use variables within your code. SQL-3 allows use of built-in types when declaring variables. For example, you can declare a variable v_name to be of type VARCHAR(20) or declare another, v_id, as INTEGER simply by using the keyword DECLARE, followed by the variable name and the type of the named variable:

```
DECLARE v_name VARCHAR(20);
DECLARE v_id as INTEGER;
```

Similar to defining components of another abstract data type, or parameters in a procedure or routine, an abstract data type can also be used as a method to declare a variable having the same type as the abstract data type. For example, you can define a variable for use in manipulating employee information outside the table or SQL functions as follows:

```
DECLARE v_emp employee;
```

You can then use this variable in any location where a data type employee is expected. You can pass the variable into a procedure as a parameter or use it as the holder of the result of a procedure in an OUT parameter. The declared variable can be used as the result holder for selection of a particular employee's instance information:

```
SELECT *
INTO v_emp
FROM employee
WHERE employee.emp_id = '00100';
```

The benefit of this language construct is that dummy declarations mimicking the structure of a stored item in a table are not necessary. The actual type can be used to declare the variable of the same matched type, not some constructed or composite type.

Domain or Column Type in Tables

An abstract data type can be used as the source type for an attribute of a column in a table or as the domain of a column in a table—for example:

```
CREATE DOMAIN revenue AS money;
```

You can then use the newly created domain revenue to define a column in a table or any other place where the ADT money can be applied. In the example shown previously for the revenue generated by employees' sales, the domain revenue is used to define the majority of the attributes of the table:

```
CREATE TABLE aquarium_revenues (
    employee_id      INTEGER,
    daily_sales      revenue,
    monthly_sales    revenue,
    year_to_date     revenue,
    commissions      revenue
)
```

Conversely, instead of defining the new domain type revenue, you can use the abstract data type money directly to define each of the columns in the table aquarium_revenues, as follows:

```
CREATE TABLE aquarium_revenues (
    employee_id      INTEGER,
    daily_sales      money,
    monthly_sales    money,
    year_to_date     oney,
    commissions      money
)
```

Either method of defining the type of the columns would have resulted in the same abstract data type, money, being applied as the type of the columns in the table. The main difference is in the added semantics possible with the domain. Recall from Chapter 3 that the domain is a means to define a "macro," which defines the type as well as possibly some additional information about a specific attribute—for example, that the attribute cannot be null or that it can only have a specific set of values associated with it. As an example, by using a check constraint, you can refine the domain revenue to make sure that the value of money in revenue is greater than or equal to 0 by specifying a default value of 0 as the lower bounds of the abstract data type:

```
CREATE DOMAIN revenue AS money
    CHECK (value(m) >= 0)
    DEFAULT 0;
```

Source Type in Distinct Types

An abstract data type can also be used as the type of a distinct data type. For example, once you have declared a type revenue, you can refine this to represent different types of revenue. In the aquarium database, you may want to distinguish between revenue generated from the sale of saltwater fish and freshwater fish or between aquarium equipment and fish food. This can be accomplished by declaring the different categories of revenue as distinct types:

```
CREATE DISTINCT TYPE salt_water_fish_revenue AS money;
CREATE DISTINCT TYPE fresh_water_fish_revenue AS money;
CREATE DISTINCT TYPE aquarium_equipment_revenue AS money;
CREATE DISTINCT TYPE fish_food_revenue AS money;
```

These specifications result in four distinct data types, which can be used as the type of money being taken into the aquarium store. You also need to implement different methods to store and retrieve the revenues to make sense of this distinct type. You may want, for example, to compose the revenue portion of an array so that you can insert the values for a particular sale type or make the class of the sale item one of the four types. There will be more discussion on this later.

Abstract Data Type Manipulations

You have declared the new abstract data types and made them part of the durable database by incorporating them into the specification of the tables that comprise the database. Now, how can you use these applications' unique data types in a meaningful way in the database? To make this work, you need to examine how the specifications of these abstract data types now fit into the unary and binary operators built into the SQL data manipulation model. First, you need to determine how to extract individual items from an embedded abstract data type and how to extract values using the more complex binary operators. As mentioned in Chapter 2, the most simple forms of access are the SELECT and PROJECT operations, which, in SQL, are both implemented with the SELECT statement with added semantics wrapped around the applied SELECT criteria.

SELECT Operator

The SELECT operator is the most fundamental method of extracting information from an SQL persistent database. The SELECT statement has the BNF form:

```
<query specification> ::=
    SELECT [ <set quantifier> ] <select list>
    <table expression>

<select list> ::=
    <asterisk>
    | <select sublist> [ { <comma> <select sublist> }... ]

<select sublist> ::=
    <derived column>
    | <item qualifier> <period> <asterisk>

<derived column> ::=
    <value expression> [ <as clause> ]

<as clause> ::= [ AS ] <column name>

<table expression> ::=
    <from clause>
    [ <where clause> ]
    [ <group by clause> ]
    [ <having clause> ]

<from clause> ::=
    FROM <table reference list>

<where clause> ::= WHERE <search condition>
```

This generally looks for information about what is being looked for, where the information is found, and what restrictions are applied to the search. The general structure of the SELECT statement is:

```
SELECT   something    (columns, attributes, ADTs, etc.)
FROM     somewhere    (table)
WHERE    qualities    (predicates or restrictions)
```

In SQL-3, this is still the basic form, even when abstract data types are being applied. For example, to find an employee's address, who has a salary greater than $100,000, use the table structure defined below:

```
CREATE TYPE employees (
PUBLIC   emp_id          INTEGER
         emp_title       name,
         emp_last_name   name,
         emp_first_name  name,
```

```
        emp_address     address,
        emp_phone       CHARACTER (10),
        emp_start_date  TIMESTAMP,
        emp_pay_rate    salary,
        emp_com_rate    DECIMAL (5,2)
)
```

Then use the following SQL syntax:

```
SELECT    *
FROM      employees
WHERE     employees..emp_pay_rate > 100000;
```

This query results in a new table, which contains all the information for employees who make more than $100,000 per year. Using the wildcard entry (*) in the query asks for all the information about the tuples that meet this criterion. Here is a subset of our employee table:

00100	Manager	Jones	Reginald	125 Town Newport, RI 02810	4011112222	01-01-56	100001	0.00
00200	Sales	Simon	Sally	1 Fifth St. Fall River, MA 02746	5089999999	01-06-56	20000	0.05
00300	Biologist	Jewels	George	2 S. Main Marion, MA 02738	6171234567	10-15-62	80000	0.00
00400	Stock	Barr	Terisa	4 School Dighton, MA 02771	6172221111	12-20-65	25000	0.00
00500	Sales	Stevens	Gregory	12 Fourth Fall River, MA 02746	5089099911	12-20-65	20000	0.05

The resulting table has only one entry for the manager, Reginald Jones, since he makes $100,001 per year:

| 00100 | Manager | Jones | Reginald | 125 Town Newport, RI 02810 | 4011112222 | 01-01-56 | 100001 | 0.00 |

If you want to refine this query from a classic SELECT into a PROJECT, where you want only a subset of the entire tuple of the table, you can add access restrictions to what you are extracting from the table. For example, if you want only the addresses of employees who make more than $100,000 per year, you can generate the following query:

```
SELECT employees..street, employees..city, employees..state,
employees..zip
FROM      employees
WHERE     employees..emp_pay_rate > 100000;
```

This query results in a new table, whose elements contain the addresses of employees who make morethan $100,000 per year:

125 Town	Newport	RI	02810

SELECT statements can be further restricted to remove duplicates, which may occur during a query using the restriction DISTINCT. For example, in the query above, more than one employee can live at the same address. In this case, to make sure you only get distinct addresses, you can use the modified query:

```
SELECT DISTINCT employees..street, employees..city,
employees..state, employees..zip
FROM     employees
WHERE    employees..emp_pay_rate > 100000;
```

Another possible version of this query is to order the results in some meaningful way. For example, you may want to have the result ordered by street address, city, or state. To order the query above by street, you can alter the query by including the ORDER BY clause:

```
SELECT employees..street, employees..city, employees..state,
employees..zip
FROM       employees
WHERE      employees..emp_pay_rate > 100000
ORDER BY   employees..street ASC;
```

The added keyword `ASC` indicates that the ordering is to be done in ascending order. If you want the results to be ordered in descending order, use the keyword `DESC`.

This simple query included a restriction clause, or predicate, applied to the search, which resulted in the selection of some subset of the tuples (rows) of the table. The search condition does not need to be singular; it can include a number of predicates linked using the logical operators AND, OR, and other search conditions. For example, you can look for employees who make more than $100,000 and less than $150,000 by adding the predicate `employees..emp_pay_rate > 150000` and linking them together using the `AND` logical operator:

```
SELECT employees..street, employees..city, employees..state,
employees..zip
FROM       employees
WHERE      employees..emp_pay_rate > 100000
   AND     employees..emp_pay_rate < 150000;
```

The abstract data types were used in the above SELECT statements in a manner similar to how the SELECT statement used the built-in data types. The difference is that the abstract data types need to be accessed using dot notation or the functional interface provided by their built-in or defined operations.

INSERT Operator

To add new instances of a tuple or row into a table, use the SQL INSERT operator. The version available in SQL-3 acts much like that of its predecessors. The difference is in the extensions used to support added data types, such as the abstract data type, collection data types, row data type, and the object. Of interest here is the use of INSERT with abstract data types. In the example above, to add a new employee to the database, you need to supply the information required of the base attributes and the embedded abstract data type function parameters, so that the new instantiation becomes available:

```
CREATE TABLE employee AS employees;
```

The INSERT operation needs to use the abstract data type's constructor function to create a new instance of the type. For the `employees` type defined above, you need a constructor function for the `employees` and for the embedded address abstract data types. The constructors follow the classic INSERT syntax, with some added meaning, behind the embedded function calls to the constructors. To insert an employee you can use the statement:

```
INSERT INTO employee
VALUES ( emp_id(00600), emp_title('marine biologist'),
        emp_last_name('cousteau'), emp_first_name('Jacques'),
        emp_address (street('rue triumph'), city('paris'), state
('france'), zip(00110)),
        '5559991111',
      '01-JAN-1955',
      emp_pay_rate(value('50,000.00')),
      '10.00'

);
```

00100	Manager	Jones	Reginald	125 Town Newport, RI 02810	4011112222	01-01-56	100001	0.00
00200	Sales	Simon	Sally	1 Fifth St. Fall River, MA 02746	5089999999	01-06-56	20000	0.05
00300	Biologist	Jewels	George	2 S. Main Marion, MA 02738	6171234567	10-15-62	80000	0.00
00400	Stock	Barr	Terisa	4 School Dighton, MA 02771	6172221111	12-20-65	25000	0.00
00500	Sales	Stevens	Gregory	12 Fourth Fall River, MA 02746	5089099911	12-20-65	20000	0.05
00600	Marine Biologist	Cousteau	Jacques	rue Triumph Paris, France 00110	5559991111	01-10-55	50000	10.00

UPDATE Operator

Stored information does not stay static throughout the lifetime of a data item. Information changes; to make these changes visible within the database requires that an operator control and perform changes as needed. SQL uses the UPDATE operator to alter the contents of tuples or rows in a stored table. The UPDATE operator functions somewhat like the SELECT operator in that you must "find" the row to be updated. For example, if an employee has moved, you need to adjust the fields of that employee's tuple to reflect the change. If the inserted tuple above for employee 00600, Jacques Cousteau, must be changed, since he does not live at rue Triumph anymore, you need to use the UPDATE statement. If he has moved to rue St. Jacques, still in Paris, France, you need to update the attribute for street using the following syntax:

```
UPDATE employee
SET emp_address..street = street ('rue St. Jacques')
WHERE emp_id = '00600';
```

00100	Manager	Jones	Reginald	125 Town Newport, RI 02810	4011112222	01-01-56	100001	0.00
00200	Sales	Simon	Sally	1 Fifth St. Fall River, MA 02746	5089999999	01-06-56	20000	0.05
00300	Biologist	Jewels	George	2 S. Main Marion, MA 02738	6171234567	10-15-62	80000	0.00
00400	Stock	Barr	Terisa	4 School Dighton, MA 02771	6172221111	12-20-65	25000	0.00
00500	Sales	Stevens	Gregory	12 Fourth Fall River, MA 02746	5089099911	12-20-65	20000	0.05
00600	Marine Biologist	Cousteau	Jacques	rue St. Jacques Paris, France 00110	5559991111	01-10-55	50000	10.00

The statement works by defining which table, columns, ADT attributes, or other components are to be updated; it defines what the value of the item is to become and which specific row or tuple is to be affected by this update. Just as with the SELECT statement, a variety of predicates can be specified on the search condition. UPDATE can also be used to compute new values for an item. For example, if you want to give all employees with salaries less than $50,000 a raise of 10 percent, you can use the UPDATE statement, as shown here:

```
UPDATE employee
SET emp_pay_rate..value = (emp_pay_rate..value +
(emp_pay_rate..value * .10))
WHERE emp_pay_rate..value < 50000;
```

00100	Manager	Jones	Reginald	125 Town Newport, RI 02810	4011112222	01-01-56	100001	0.00
00200	Sales	Simon	Sally	1 Fifth St. Fall River, MA 02746	5089999999	01-06-56	22000	0.05
00300	Biologist	Jewels	George	2 S. Main Marion, MA 02738	6171234567	10-15-62	80000	0.00
00400	Stock	Barr	Terisa	4 School Dighton, MA 02771	6172221111	12-20-65	27500	0.00
00500	Sales	Stevens	Gregory	12 Fourth Fall River, MA 02746	5089099911	12-20-65	22000	0.05
00600	Marine Biologist	Cousteau	Jacques	rue Triumph Paris, France 00110	5559991111	01-10-55	50000	10.00

UNION Operator

The UNION binary operator provides mechanisms to take two tables of the same structure and combine them into a single table. In SQL-3, the UNION operator works just as it did in prior SQL releases, with some additional features. The UNION can now also provide for the union of tables containing abstract data types, as well as the built-in data types supported by SQL-3. To begin, you have the definitions of two tables for marine fish and freshwater fish, with the scientific name defined as an abstract data type, lat_name, consisting of two fields—one for the general class and the other for the specific name of the fish, as follows:

```
CREATE TABLE marine_fish (
    scientific_name    lat_name,
    common_name        name,
    fish_species       name,
    max_size           DECIMAL (5,2)
    food_preference    food,
    geographic_range   region,
    fish_disposition   temperment,
    fish_activity      day_shift
)

CREATE TABLE fresh_water_fish (
    scientific_name    lat_name,
    common_name        name,
    fish_species       name,
    max_size           DECIMAL (5,2)
    food_preference    food,
    geographic_range   region,
    fish_disposition   temperment,
    fish_activity      day_shift
)
```

These tables can be UNIONed to provide a list of all the freshwater and saltwater fish known to the database. To UNION these two tables, they must have the same structure and the same "equivalent" types for all attributes within the tables. Equivalence implies that the types must be name equivalent as well as structurally equivalent. They must have the same types defined for all attributes of the table. Abstract data types, built-in data types, and distinct types must match in placement and specification. If there is not a complete match, they cannot be UNIONed. For the example tables above, all attributes of the marine_fish and fresh_water_fish tables match in location and types. Since this is true, the tables are UNIONable. To UNION these two tables requires the use of the UNION operator, as follows:

```
SELECT * FROM marine_fish
UNION
SELECT * FROM fresh_water_fish;
```

The SELECT statements extract all the rows from the `marine_fish` and `fresh_water_fish` tables and put them together into a new, temporary table. If you only want to extract the Latin names of the fish, you can use the SELECT statements to reduce the number of attributes used to perform the UNION, as follows:

```
SELECT scientific_name..class, scientific_name..specific_name
FROM marine_fish

UNION

SELECT scientific_name..class, scientific_name..specific_name
FROM fresh_water_fish;
```

This operation results in a temporary table, which contains only the scientific names of the marine and freshwater fish. This form of UNION operation can be used when two tables do not match in all fields, but do match in the fields you are interested in. You first select the attributes from the tables that are to be UNIONed, and then perform the UNION. Since the selected attributes match, the UNION is allowed, even if the base tables used do not match in all columns.

INTERSECT Operator

As with its predecessors, SQL-3 supports the INTERSECT operator. The importance of this operator becomes evident when the application user must determine when an item exists in one portion of the database and also in another portion of the database (e.g., if a fish exists in both the marine fish and freshwater fish tables). This condition occurs when there are some fish that exist in the brackish regions between the open ocean and the rivers, streams, and estuaries. These fish will show up in both places and can actually live and thrive in both environments. Some aquarists may wish to build an environment where these fish in the middle layer are mixed and matched. Given the same tables as defined previously, this query for the marine and freshwater fish can be readily constructed using the INTERSECT operator.

The INTERSECT operation works by comparing two "matched" tables and looking for tuples (rows) that are found in both tables. The general form of this operation is:

```
SELECT * FROM table1
INTERSECT
SELECT * FROM table2;
```

This is only valid when `table1` and `table2` are equivalent—that is, they both match in all types of all attributes in the same locations in the tables. If an attribute is an abstract data type in one table, then it must also be the same abstract data type in the other table.

This does not imply that only 100 percent matched tables can be compared for INTERSECT. Tables that are "constructed" to be matched can also be combined using the INTERSECT operation. For example, if the two tables describing fish have a column that does not match, that column can be pruned out of the INTERSECT operation using the SELECT statements that access tuples from each of the tables for the INTERSECT operations. If the scientific names are not of the same type, they can be pruned out by using the SELECT statements to choose all the attributes of the two fish tables except the scientific name attribute. The resulting query appears as follows:

```
SELECT common_name, fish_species, max_size, food_preference,
       geographic_range, fish_disposition   , fish_activity
FROM marine_fish
INTERSECT
SELECT common_name, fish_species, max_size, food_preference,
       geographic_range, fish_disposition   , fish_activity
FROM fresh_water_fish;
```

This query selects all the attributes of the freshwater and marine fish tables, except their scientific names, to perform the binary INTERSECT operation. This concept can be taken to the extent necessary to determine the desired answer. Tables can be reduced, and then recombined, in a variety of ways through the combination of SELECT operations and binary operations such as the INTERSECT operation.

EXCEPT Operator

Not all queries want to combine and extract all the elements of two tables. Some may want to extract some subset, possibly a disjoint subset. The EXCEPT operator is used to return all the rows in the first table of the statement but not in the second table of the statement. The idea is to allow the application to test two tables and to determine what shows up in one but not in the other. For example, in the fish table, you may want to find out which fish are strictly freshwater. You can compare the freshwater fish table with the marine fish table to find out which fish are in the freshwater fish table but are not found in the marine fish table. The result is exactly opposite of what was found using the INTERSECT operation. (You expect that no item found using INTERSECT would appear in the resulting table using the EXCEPT operator.) Generally, the EXCEPT operator has the following syntax:

```
SELECT * FROM table1
EXCEPT
SELECT * FROM table2;
```

The items of `table1` are compared with the items selected from `table2`. Those in `table1`, but not in `table2`, are included in the result. As with the INTERSECT operation, the comparison requires that the tables be matched; that is, the types of each column in the two tables being compared must be equivalent and in the same locations in both tables. For the aquarium database, you can test for the difference between the freshwater fish table and the marine fish table by performing the EXCEPT operation:

```
SELECT * FROM marine_fish
EXCEPT
SELECT * FROM fresh_water_fish;
```

This query results in a new, temporary table, which contains the marine fish that do not show up in the freshwater fish table. This query can be reversed to find which freshwater fish do not show up in the marine fish table:

```
SELECT * FROM fresh_water_fish
EXCEPT
SELECT * FROM marine_fish;
```

As with INTERSECT, you can perform the EXCEPT operation on any constructed table where the types of attributes match in the same locations. Looking at the same example given for the INTERSECT operation, you can perform a selection on the fish tables to form a projection of the tables that are equivalent and therefore can be compared for their difference:

```
SELECT common_name, fish_species, max_size, food_preference,
       geographic_range, fish_disposition   , fish_activity
FROM marine_fish
INTERSECT
SELECT common_name, fish_species, max_size, food_preference,
       geographic_range, fish_disposition   , fish_activity
FROM fresh_water_fish;
```

The EXCEPT operation is a powerful built-in operation, which gives the applications designer an easy means to test two tables against each other to find where they differ.

Query Expressions and JOINs

The SELECT statement is much more complex than it first appears. It not only can be used to extract total or partial information from one table, but it can also be used to extract partial or complete information from multiple tables. To understand this further, let's look at the structure of a SELECT statement. The SELECT statement consists of the keyword SELECT, followed by a SELECT list. The SELECT list can include any number of attributes, abstract data type element accesses, or even a wild card (*), which extracts all items of the from clause:

```
<query specification> ::=
    SELECT [ <set quantifier> ] <select list>
    <table expression>

<select list> ::=
      <asterisk>
    | <select sublist> [ { <comma> <select sublist> }... ]

<select sublist> ::=
      <derived column>
    | <item qualifier> <period> <asterisk>

<derived column> ::=
    <value expression> [ <as clause> ]

<as clause> ::= [ AS ] <column name>
```

The second part of the SELECT is the table expression, indicating where the selected items are to be found. FROM points to one or more table

specifications, which contain all or part of the information being
looked for:

```
<table expression> ::=
    <from clause>
    [ <where clause> ]
    [ <group by clause> ]
    [ <having clause> ]

<from clause> ::=
    FROM <table reference list>
```

As an example, you can write a simple SELECT on the marine fish table
to retrieve the scientific and common names for all the fish, as follows:

```
SELECT scientific_name, common_name FROM marine_fish;
```

Finally, the SELECT statement has an optional qualifier list found in
the table expression clause. The major form of this qualifier is the
WHERE clause, which allows the query specification to have restrictions applied to the search specified in the first portion of the SELECT
statement. The qualifier allows a wide variety of search conditions to be
applied to the selection. One form of search condition results in the
combination of multiple tables into a larger table and is referred to as a
JOIN:

```
<where clause> ::= WHERE <search condition>
```

This form of the SELECT clause can be used to further restrict the rows
of the tables chosen for insertion into the resulting temporary table. For
example, if you want to see the scientific and common names for fish
only found in the Caribbean, you can alter the above query through
the addition of a where clause to restrict the selection:

```
SELECT scientific_name, common_name FROM marine_fish
WHERE geographic_region = 'Caribbean';
```

The other two possibilities for the table expression are the GROUP
BY and the HAVING clauses. These clauses allow for the ordering of a
selected list into sublists, based on the grouping selector chosen, or a further refinement of the selection criteria to look for columns with
specific values using the having clause:

```
<group by clause> ::=
    GROUP BY <grouping specifications>
```

The group by clause can be used to list fish based on the geographical region in which they are found. For example, you may want to see a list of Caribbean fish, Red Sea fish, Great Barrier Reef fish, or Hawaiian Islands fish. This can be accomplished using the GROUP BY clause:

```
SELECT scientific_name, common_name FROM marine_fish
GROUP BY geographic_region;
```

This results in a list of fish for each region grouped by the region forming our table.

The having clause can be used to search for specific instances of an attribute or attributes within the query. This clause is used much like the where clause. For example, you can use this clause to find which fish are also Caribbean fish:

```
<having clause> ::= HAVING <search condition>

SELECT scientific_name, common_name FROM marine_fish
HAVING geographic_region = 'Caribbean';
```

Query expressions do not have to have only one operation embedded in them. Queries can be constructed that include all the previously defined operators. For example, a query could examine the contents of multiple tables looking to perform a UNION, INTERSECT, and EXCEPT on them. As with an arithmetic expression in a mathematical formula, the operators are performed in a specific order, based on how they are syntactically organized. The organization can be specifically indicated by parentheses or can be implied by the operators provided. The INTERSECT has a higher precedence than UNION and EXCEPT.

For example, you can specify the UNION of two tables and the INTERSECT of the result of these tables with a third table, followed by the exception of this result with a fourth table, using the following specification:

```
SELECT * FROM (SELECT * FROM (Table1 UNION Table2)
INTERSECT Table3)
EXCEPT Table4;
```

In all cases, the item selected from the tables being operated on can be abstract data types. Abstract data types selected using any of these techniques would have their encapsulated attributes extracted using the built-in functions or user-defined functions. User functions requiring parameters would cause the query to pass in the needed parameters. But the query does not get any more complex than that. Abstract data types simply allow users the ability to define, store, and manipulate application-defined data using the database's built-in operators and the user-supplied extensions through the abstract data type functions and parameters.

One of the most powerful query capabilities in the SQL data model since its inception, is the JOIN. The JOIN comes in a variety of flavors, each giving a unique means to manipulate multiple tables in useful ways. The JOIN is used to combine tables that do not need to match in all columns into larger composite temporary tables. As the BNF shown below indicates, the JOIN comes in many forms: traditional, NATURAL, CROSS, INNER, OUTER, LEFT and RIGHT, and others. They are formed by the use of keywords and SELECT statement syntax and semantics.

The old-style JOIN uses the SELECT statement over multiple tables, with restrictions placed on each table where one or more items from one table must equate to the same number of items in the other table. In the fish example, if the scientific name is the only unique name in each table, you can use this element as the JOIN condition to form a new table, which indicates the common name given for a saltwater and freshwater version of the same fish, as follows:

```
SELECT marine_fish.scientific_name, marine_fish.common_name,
       fresh_water_fish.common_name
FROM marine_fish, fresh_water_fish
WHERE marine_fish.scientific_name =
fresh_water_fish.scientific_name;
```

This query results in a new table with three columns, the common scientific name of the two fish and the common names for both the saltwater and freshwater habitats.

The CROSS JOIN combines the tables referenced in the JOIN into a new table, which consists of the columns from both tables combined in all ways possible. That is, the number of columns is equal to the sum of the columns from the tables being JOINed, and the number of rows is equal to the number of rows in table1 times the number of rows in table2.

```
<cross join> ::=
    <table reference> CROSS JOIN <table reference>
```

You can see from this combination that many rows will contain useless or misleading information, although there may be some reason why such a combination is performed. For example, you can combine the `marine_fish` and `fresh_water_fish` tables using CROSS JOIN to create a new table, where, for each fish defined in a row in the `marine_fish` table, the row is combined once with every row of the `fresh_water_fish` table:

```
<qualified join> ::=
    <table reference> [ NATURAL ] [ <join type> ] JOIN
    <table reference> [ <join specification> ]
```

A more useful form of the JOIN is the NATURAL JOIN. This JOIN takes each row in one table and compares it to each row in the other, where the same name is used to define the column. For example, if you combine the `marine_fish` and `fresh_water_fish` tables using the NATURAL JOIN, each row of the `marine_fish` and `fresh_water_fish` tables is examined, comparing all the columns with each other. In both cases you use the same name for each. A more interesting case is when one table has only one column in common with another table. For example, if the fish tables only matched on the `scientific_name` column, the NATURAL JOIN would look for those rows in the `marine_fish` table where the scientific name is equivalent to the scientific name of a fish in the `fresh_water_fish` table. When an item is found, it would copy all the columns of the `marine_fish` and `fresh_water_fish` tables for these two rows into the temporary table. A new row would be formed from the two rows concatenated together.

This could be a useful way to select marine fish and marine plants from the same geographical region—for example, the Red Sea—to form a harmonious collection for a customer's aquarium. The problem with this JOIN is that it looks at all items with the same name in the columns and combines only those items where all the columns with the same names match. So this, too, will not work, since scientific names are used for the names of fish and plants:

```
marine_fish NATURAL JOIN marine_plants
```

This is equivalent to:

```
marine_fish JOIN marine_plants
ON marine_fish.scientific_name = marine_plant.scientific_name
AND marine_fish.common_name = marine_plant.common_name
AND marine_fish.geographic_region = marine_plant.geographic_region;
```

So, if you use the NATURAL JOIN or the CROSS JOIN, you must first be sure that the tables being combined will reveal what you are looking for. If not, a more restrictive, specific form of the JOIN, as shown above, may be more prudent.

There are also other forms of the JOIN operator. INNER JOIN is the form described so far. This operation results in tables where rows that do not match the search condition are kept as part of the resulting relation. This holds for all tables involved in the JOIN operation. The use of the keyword INNER has, therefore, no additional effect on the operations of the JOIN. It just specifies the code in an unambiguous manner, leaving nothing to chance.

On the other hand, OUTER JOIN has an effect on the resulting constructed table. OUTER JOINS, which can have FULL, LEFT, or RIGHT forms, preserve unmatched rows from one or both tables, using the keywords supplied. Different from the INNER JOIN, which discards any rows where the JOIN condition is not met, the OUTER JOINs keep some rows. The partial BNF showing the format for the OUTER JOIN is shown here:

```
<join type> ::=
      INNER
    | <outer join type> [ OUTER ]
    | UNION

<outer join type> ::=
      LEFT
    | RIGHT
    | FULL

<join specification> ::=
      <join condition>
    | <named columns join>

<join condition> ::= ON <search condition>

<named columns join> ::=
    USING <left paren> <join column list> <right paren>

<join column list> ::= <column name list>
```

LEFT OUTER JOIN preserves the unmatched rows from the "left" table involved in the JOIN. In the syntax of the LEFT JOIN, this is the table specification that precedes the keyword JOIN. For an example, let's explore the fish tables once again. If you want to list the scientific and common names for those fish found in the marine_fish and fresh_water_fish tables, you can use the OUTER JOIN:

```
SELECT marine_fish.scientific_name, marine_fish.common_name,
       fresh_water_fish.common_name
FROM marine_fish LEFT OUTER JOIN freah_water_fish
ON marine_fish.scientific_name = fresh_water_fish.scientific_name;
```

This query results in a new table consisting of three columns. The first two columns from the `marine_fish` table are populated with the scientific and common names for every marine fish in the table. The third column contains common names for those freshwater fish that have the same scientific name as their saltwater counterpart. For the most part, this column is filled with nulls, since most of the rows will have no match within the `marine_fish` table.

RIGHT OUTER JOIN operates in a similar manner, but maintains all the rows of the table on the right side of the RIGHT OUTER JOIN operator in the query. Using the same query for the `marine_fish` and `fresh_water_fish` tables, the RIGHT OUTER JOIN results indicate that all the scientific and common names for freshwater fish are being maintained, and only the common names for marine fish with matches to the scientific names in the `fresh_water_fish` table are being maintained:

```
SELECT marine_fish.scientific_name, marine_fish.common_name,
       fresh_water_fish.common_name
FROM marine_fish RIGHT OUTER JOIN freah_water_fish
ON marine_fish.scientific_name = fresh_water_fish.scientific_name;
```

The last form of the OUTER JOIN is FULL OUTER JOIN. The FULL OUTER JOIN behaves in a manner similar to the combination of the LEFT and RIGHT OUTER JOINs. For the `marine_fish` and `fresh_water_fish` tables, the FULL OUTER JOIN produces the union of the LEFT and RIGHT OUTER JOINs as its result. The query is as follows:

```
SELECT marine_fish.scientific_name, marine_fish.common_name,
       fresh_water_fish.common_name
FROM marine_fish FULL OUTER JOIN freah_water_fish
ON marine_fish.scientific_name = fresh_water_fish.scientific_name;
```

The abstract data type has added to the power of the SQL language, and, as the new SQL matures, it will find an increased importance in the language and in application use.

Abstract Data Type Privileges

A final note on abstract data types concerns the area of privileges. To be able to perform a variety of operations on, or even use, an abstract data type requires that the abstract data type be protected from unwanted access, manipulation, or alteration. The GRANT statement of SQL's data control language supplies the boundary on which further security is provided. The general form of the GRANT statement is depicted in the following BNF:

```
<grant statement> ::=
    GRANT <privileges>
    TO <grantee> [ { <comma> <grantee> }... ]
  [ WITH GRANT OPTION ]

<privileges> ::=
    <object privileges> ON <object name>

<object privileges> ::=
      ALL PRIVILEGES
    | <action> [ { <comma> <action> }... ]

<action> ::=
      SELECT [ <left paren> <privilege column list> <right paren> ]
    | DELETE
    | INSERT [ <left paren> <privilege column list> <right paren> ]
    | UPDATE [ <left paren> <privilege column list> <right paren> ]
    | REFERENCES [ <left paren> <privilege column list> <right
paren> ]
    | USAGE
    | TRIGGER
    | UNDER
    | EXECUTE

<privilege column list> ::= <column name list>

<object name> ::=
      [ TABLE ] <table name>
    | DOMAIN <domain name>
    | COLLATION <collation name>
    | CHARACTER SET <character set name>
    | TRANSLATION <translation name>
    | DATA TYPE <abstract data type name>
    | DATA TYPE <distinct type name>
    | <specific routine designator>

<grantee> ::=
      PUBLIC
    | <authorization identifier>
    | <role name>
```

The BNF defines the form of the SQL GRANT statement, what the GRANT statement is allowed to do, who is privileged to use the defined level of access, where the privilege is allocated, and on what object the definition is defined. Several rules apply to the usage privileges. Usage can be restricted to insert, update, select, delete, references, and triggers. The usage operator controls who is authorized to use an object defined in the GRANT statement. The GRANT statement is used to give privileges to various users:

```
GRANT SELECT
ON marine_fish
TO SALES_ASSOCIATE;
```

This statement gives viewing privileges for the `marine_fish` table to the selected user group identified as `SALES_ASSOCIATES`.

A second GRANT statement can be defined, which allows a specific user identified as the `STORE_MANAGER` to delete employee entries from the database:

```
GRANT DELETE
ON employees
TO STORE_MANAGER;
```

To allow only specific users the capability of updating the contents of a table, or only a specific attribute within a table, the GRANT UPDATE statement can be used. The following example allows the sales manager to update the price of the aquatic organism stock, which can include fish and plants presently in stock at the store:

```
GRANT UPDATE (current_price )
ON aquatic_organism_stock
TO SALES_MANAGER;
```

To make the database usable, the sales manager also needs to have privileges to insert new aquatic organisms into the `aquatic_organism_stock` table. This can be accomplished using the GRANT statement :

```
GRANT INSERT
ON aquatic_organism_stock
TO SALES_MANAGER;
```

Other privileges can be granted to users in the database. For example, the GRANT REFERENCES statement limits the ability for constructing views using foreign key access to tables.

The USAGE privilege can be used to control who is authorized to use an abstract data type to define columns of tables, to define variables of the abstract data type, and to create routines that use the abstract data type as parameters or return types. The USAGE privileges can be used to define the attributes of other abstract data types, to define domains on abstract data types, or to define distinct types:

```
GRANT USAGE
ON DATA TYPE person
TO EMPLOYEE_MANAGER;
```

This allows the user, identified as the employee manager, to use the abstract data type `person` as a basic type in creating distinct types, domains on abstract data types, attributes in another abstract data type, within routines, variable declarations or columns in tables.

Another privilege that can be granted to users is the UNDER privilege. The UNDER privilege controls who is authorized to define subtypes of an abstract data type. For example, you may want to give the employee manager the ability to use the `person` abstract data type to construct other abstract data types or tables. The abstract data type, `person`, can be used to define a new table, `employee_sales` or `customer_promotions`. To grant the authorization identifier, `MANAGER`, the ability to construct such tables, you can use the following statement:

```
GRANT UNDER
ON DATA TYPE person
TO EMPLOYEE_MANAGER;
```

This statement allows the database user, `EMPLOYEE_MANAGER`, to use the `person` abstract data type in the definition of other abstract data types or tables using the UNDER clause. For example, this user can now generate the specification:

```
CREATE TABLE employee_sales UNDER person (

    <body of table>
  )
```

Privileges can be granted to one or more users or groups of users. All privileges can be given to a named user using the GRANT ALL PRIVILEGES statement. The form is the same as the previous GRANT statements:

```
GRANT ALL PRIVILEGES
ON marine_fish
TO MARINE_BIOLOGIST;
```

This statement is used as shorthand to generate a list of privileges, including all those specified for a given object. This operation only works
on objects that the named user executing the GRANT statement can
grant privileges to.

Given that someone can grant privileges to an object he or she owns
or has been given the rights to, there must be an opposite operation to
take away or alter these privileges. For example, you may want to allow
a user temporary access to a specified table or abstract data type. SQL
uses the REVOKE statement to take away granted privileges:

```
<revoke statement> ::=

    REVOKE [ GRANT OPTION FOR ]
      <privileges>
    FROM <grantee> [ { <comma> <grantee> }... ] <drop behavior>

<drop behavior> ::= CASCADE | RESTRICT
```

The REVOKE statement performs the opposite function of the GRANT
statement. It removes some privileges from a particular user on a
named object in the database. For example, if you want to take away the
sales manager's ability to insert new aquatic organisms from the
aquatic_organism_stock table, the following statement can be used:

```
REVOKE INSERT
ON aquatic_organism_stock
FROM SALES_MANAGER RESTRICT;
```

The major difference from the GRANT statement is the additional
<drop behavior> functionality. The RESTRICT keyword indicates that
the system is to check if this removed privilege was granted to some other users by this user. If such a condition is found to be true, the system
will generate an error and will not perform the REVOKE. On the other
hand, if you were to use the CASCADE keyword in the statement, the
privilege will be revoked, and any dependent privileges will also be
revoked.

Summary

In this chapter, we examined how abstract data types can be used to enhance an SQL-3 database. Abstract data types can be used in most places where SQL's built-in data types can be used. An abstract data type can be used to define attributes in another abstract data type, as parameters in procedures or functions, to define variables to use in programs, as the domain or column type in tables, or as the source for a distinct data type specification.

The abstract data type is manipulated by using the observer and mutator functions or through user-defined functions. Abstract data type manipulation uses dot notation or a function call notation. These operations can be embedded in the various operational statements supported in SQL. Abstract data types can be operated on within the SELECT, INSERT, UPDATE, UNION, INTERSECT, EXCEPT, and JOIN operations.

Abstract data types can be controlled beyond their built-in encapsulation and internal function privileges with extensions on the SQL GRANT statement. The GRANT statement allows the owner of an object, typically the database administrator, to restrict how an object of the database can be used. Database objects can be restricted to SELECT, INSERT, UPDATE, DELETE, REFERENCES, UNDER, and USAGE. The objects that can be restricted with GRANT include database tables, domains of columns, character set, collations, abstract data types, BLOBs, CLOBs, and translations. The user is either a named user with an authorization identification or the general public. If privileges can be given, they must also be removable. The SQL REVOKE statement is used for this purpose. In SQL-3, these statements apply to abstract data types, as well as to the built-in types and tables.

For further details regarding the specifics of the GRANT and REVOKE operations, see the SQL-3 foundation document and vendor publications. In addition, the use of these statements has been described in past SQL-92 documentation and publications.

SQL-3 Specialized ADT Concepts

I n the previous two chapters, concepts for abstract data types in the context of the SQL-3 database language were investigated. In particular, the chapters looked at how these new data types can be used to construct tables (the fundamental database repository), whose data structure can map one to one with data structures required in advanced information processing applications. In addition to introducing the manner in which abstract data types can be used in the definition of the database, how abstract data types can be used in the relational operators found in the SQL database language was also investigated. These two aspects of abstract data types, however, do not fully define their place or use in applications and database management. To discover these further properties of abstract data types, this chapter examines them in greater detail. In particular, you will look at abstract data type properties for subtyping and inheritance, which have been briefly addressed in Chapter 5. Also included is an in-depth examination of abstract data type functions and their properties.

Subtyping and Inheritance

The SQL-3 database language differs from many of the modern programming languages in terms of how it treats subtyping and inheritance. In SQL-3, all attributes of a supertype (base or fundamental type) are inherited, as are their operational behaviors. These are defined through their functions. Any name conflicts that may occur in abstract data type function interpretation are resolved by the abstract data type function resolution scheme in SQL-3. The precedence of functions for a collection of abstract data types with the same function name, and their resolution, is defined by the order of supertypes used in the under clause. Functions of an embedded supertype can be overloaded by subtypes, with the restriction that signatures of the functions must be unique so that resolution can occur. Function resolution is performed by examining the types of all arguments passed into a function call looking for the best match. This occurs for both static and dynamic resolution. All arguments are considered at run time to determine the best match. In the following paragraphs, these properties will be looked at in further detail.

Subtyping

The abstract data type is a very versatile data type in SQL-3's arsenal of data types. The abstract data type allows the database designer the ability to construct and support user applications–specific data types in the database. This not only supports their definition and storage, but also their manipulation from in the database's built-in operations. The BNF for the abstract data type definition as follows:

```
<user-defined type definition> ::= CREATE TYPE <user-defined type
body>

<user-defined type body> ::=
    <user-defined type name>
    [ <subtype clause> ]
    [ AS <representation> ]
    [ <instantiable clause> ]
    <finality>
    [ <cast option> ]

<subtype clause> ::=
    UNDER <supertype name> [ { <comma> <supertype name>} . . .]

<supertype name> ::= <user-defined type>

<representation> ::=
    <predefined type>
    |<member list>

<member list> ::=
    <left paren> <member> [ { <comma> <member> } . . .] <right
paren>

<member> ::=
    <attribute definition>

<instantiable clause> ::=
    INSTANTIABLE
    |NOT INSTANTIABLE

<finality> ::=
    FINAL
    |NOT FINAL

<cast option> ::=
    [ <cast to distinct> ]
    [ <cast to source> ]

<cast to distinct> ::=
    CAST <left paren> SOURCE AS DISTINCT <right paren>
    WITH <cast to distinct identifier>
```

```
<cast to source> ::=
   CAST < left paren> DISTINCT TO SOURCE <right paren>
   WITH <cast to source identifier>

<cast to source identifier> ::= <identifier>
```

The definition of the abstract data type includes one clause of particular interest to this section of the text, the subtype clause. The subtype clause allows an abstract data type to be constructed using other abstract data types as supertypes (Figure 7.1). By examining the subtype clause, you will notice that it specifies that this abstract data type is being defined *under* another abstract data type or multiple abstract data types. The abstract data type being used as a supertype is also an abstract data type; therefore, it, too, could have been defined using another abstract data type and so on. This undefined level of definitions gives much power to the database systems designers. The problem comes with the additional complexity, which can occur when using these nested specifications. Abstract data types defined in this way inherit the structure (attributes, other abstract data types, and so on) and the behavior (functions) from the supertypes being used to define them. For example, to define the marine and freshwater fish tables, you can use this supertype, subtype concept, by first defining a type `fish` and then using this as a supertype from which to define the marine and freshwater fish.

Figure 7.1

Inheritance and subtyping.

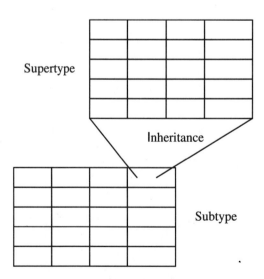

Supertype

Inheritance

Subtype

The abstract data type `fish` can be defined as:

```
CREATE TYPE fish (
       scientific_name   VARCHAR(40),
       common_name       VARCHAR(30),
       fish_species      VARCHAR(20),
       max_size          DECIMAL (5,2),
       body_type         VARCHAR(30)
)
```

Then, using this abstract data type specification, you can define two other abstract data types, `marine_fish` and `fresh_water_fish`, as follows:

```
CREATE TYPE marine_fish UNDER fish
       (food_preference   VARCHAR(20) ARRAY(5),
        geographic_range  VARCHAR(20) ARRAY(5),
        fish_disposition  temperament,
        fish_activity     day_shift
)
```

The `fresh_water_fish` abstract data type can be defined as:

```
CREATE TYPE fresh_water_fish UNDER fish
       (food_preference   VARCHAR(20) ARRAY(5),
        water_body_type   VARCHAR(20) ARRAY(5),
        geographic_range  VARCHAR(20) ARRAY(5),
        fish_disposition   temperament,
        fish_activity     day_shift
)
```

Upon close examination, the only difference in these two abstract data type specifications is in the `water_body_type`, which allows us to define if this freshwater fish is found in lakes, streams, estuaries, rivers, swamps, or other varieties of freshwater locations. If you think about it, other than their names and the types of water in which they are found, marine fish and freshwater fish have much in common. This similarity is true even if you were to break down the fish further into body shape types, which show how the fish operate in their watery realm.

Inheritance

In SQL-3, inheritance plays an important role in the definition of the database and the operations that are supported by the database. SQL-3 supports multiple levels of inheritance. For example, you can define the aquarium database fish in numerous ways, depending on what the needs of the applications are. The marine and freshwater fish abstract data types were already shown to be subtypes of the `fish` abstract data type. You can take this further and decide that the type of region or type of body of water can be a meaningful way to refine the definition of the fish as specialized subtypes. This can then be used to define marine fish of type `coral_marine_fish`, `open_marine_fish`, `coastal_marine_fish`, `estuary_fish`, and so on. Likewise, you can define the freshwater fish to be `lake_fish`, `river_fish`, `stream_fish`, or `swamp_fish` as follows:

```
CREATE TYPE coral_marine_fish UNDER marine_fish
```

or

```
CREATE TYPE open_marine_fish UNDER marine_fish
```

or

```
CREATE TYPE coastal_marine_fish UNDER marine_fish
```

or

```
CREATE TYPE estuary_marine_fish UNDER marine_fish
```

or

```
CREATE TYPE lake_fish UNDER fresh_water_fish
```

or

```
CREATE TYPE river_fish UNDER fresh_water _fish
```

or

```
CREATE TYPE stream_fish UNDER fresh_water _fish
```

or

```
CREATE TYPE swamp_fish UNDER fresh_water _fish
```

In each of these cases, you could have defined further attributes and functions for these new abstract data types. Each abstract data type would possess the same base attributes and functionality, but would be refined by the environment in which it is found.

You can also use multiple abstract data types as inherited supertypes of a new abstract data type. For example, to indicate some subtypes of `fish` as both `fresh_water_fish` and `marine_fish` you can use inheritance. In a salt marsh, brackish marshes, or in river estuaries some fish can survive in both saltwater and freshwater and also move freely between them. In these areas, fish can be classified as both marine and freshwater fish, since they move freely between these diverse environments. To hold an area where you can define the fish as existing in this shared free zone, you can define a new abstract data type, `marine_fresh_fish`, as follows:

```
CREATE TYPE marine_fresh_fish UNDER
         marine_fish, fresh_water_fish (
             . . .
         <body of ADT> )
```

The resulting data type has the qualities of both freshwater and marine water fish as its inherited attributes and, more importantly, its behavior properties. Of interest to the database designer is the ability to further enhance the abstract data types through more attribute definitions and functional interface definitions.

The new abstract data type "derived" from the supertype inherits "all" the attributes of the defining supertype, but, in addition, can define its own additional attributes and functions as required to refine the definition. Functions defined at the subtype level can overload function definitions at the supertype level. For example, in defining the marine fish as a subtype of the `fish` abstract data type, you can define an attribute, `body_type`, in the marine fish abstract data type, which means something different from using `fish`.

```
CREATE TYPE marine_fish UNDER fish
       (food_preference    VARCHAR(20) ARRAY(5),
        geographic_range   VARCHAR(20) ARRAY(5),
        fish_disposition   temperament,
        fish_activity      day_shift,
        body_type          VARCHAR(20)
     )
```

This definition for `marine_fish` has all the attributes of the fish data type: `scientific_name`, `common_name`, `fish_species`, `max_size`, and `body_type`, as well as those from the `marine_fish` definition: `food_preference`, `geographic_range`, `fish_disposition`, `fish_activity`, and `body_type`. The two definitions of `body_type` have the same name, and these conflicting definitions require function resolution to determine which is being operated on when a call is made to one of them. In one case, the function to extract `body_type` from the `fish` abstract data type expects to be given a parameter of type `fish` as input, while `marine_fish body_type` expects to see the parameter of type `marine_fish`. These differences allow function resolution to determine which operation is to be performed.

Any functions defined on a supertype can be invoked on an instance of a subtype. For example, an application using the `marine_fish` abstract data type can invoke the observer or mutator functions defined for the `fish` abstract data type. An application can invoke `scientific_name (fish)`, `common_name (fish)`, `fish_species (fish)`, `max_size (fish)`, and `body_type (fish)` observer functions or mutator functions `scientific_name (fish, VARCHAR (40))`, `common_name (fish, VARCHAR (30))`, `fish_species (fish, VARCHAR (20))`, `max_size (fish, DECIMAL(5,2))`, and `body_type (fish, VARCHAR (30)`. In addition to these, `marine_fish` also has its defined observer and mutator functions. Any additional functions defined in the abstract data types are also available to instances of `marine_fish` that have inherited them from the `fish` abstract data type.

Substitutability

SQL-3's enhanced type system provides some additional features to the database's ability to create, store, and retrieve information and is more closely matched to the needs of the applications designers. But SQL does not simply permit the creation of abstract data types and their behaviors; it also permits these new types to be used in quite interesting ways. One of these uses is in constructing database tables, where it may be desirable to store "different" subtypes derived from a single or multiple supertype. This concept of swapping subtypes is called *substitutability*. Of paramount importance is the uniqueness of an abstract data type's "instance." Each abstract data type instance has one specific type assigned at the time of its creation. For example, when an instance of the `marine_fish` abstract data type is created, it has the base type `marine_fish` as its most specific type, not the supertype `fish` under which the `marine_fish` is defined.

An important feature of abstract data types and inheritance is that for each instance of an abstract data type, an instance of a "subtype" can be used in every context where an instance of a supertype can be used. For example, you can define a table where one attribute is defined as the type `fish`. An instance of the type `marine_fish`, `fresh_water_fish`, or `mixed_fish` can be used in the same place. This, however, is not the only place where this substitution can be used. Since a subtype can be inserted in any place a supertype can be used, then any place an abstract data type can be used, is a place where substitutability can be used. Of course, this is only true when the defined types are subtypes and supertypes of each other.

A subtype can be used as the arguments of a function where the formal parameters are defined on the supertype. For example, if you have a function to determine the disease of a fish, which takes as its formal parameters the supertype `fish` and a supertype array of symptoms, you can pass in a `marine_fish`, `fresh_water_fish`, or `mixed_fish` type "substituted" for the supertype `fish`, which has been used to define the three subtypes:

```
CREATE FUNCTION disease ( f fish, s symptoms ARRAY(5) ) RETURNS
diagnosis
    <code to determine the diagnosis>;
```

You can then issue calls such as:

```
disease ( marine_fish, ARRAY['lesions', 'cloudy eyes', 'spots'])
```

The result can be assigned to a variable of type diagnosis or to a new temporary table if you have embedded this in a SELECT statement. This is the case if you assume that more than one possible diagnosis is possible from the given symptoms.

If the subtypes can be passed in as arguments to functions, then they also can be used as arguments passed in as input parameters of procedures defined on the supertype. Conversely, they can be used as returned results of a procedure, using output parameters, if these are defined as the supertype from which the subtype was derived. For example, you can have a procedure for ordering new fish when the quantity on hand reaches some level, and parameters are returned for the new fish instance for each of the new fish ordered:

```
PROCEDURE order_fish (IN f fish, OUT n fish);
BEGIN

    <code to check quantity on hand using input>

    <code to order new fish fish>
END
```

As was shown in the previous discussions, abstract data types can be used to define variables in a procedure, function, or user code segments. As such, subtypes can be used to assign instances of abstract data types defined as subtypes of a variable specified as the supertype of subtype instances. For example, if you have the abstract data type fish defined, and there is a declaration for a variable f of type fish:

```
DECLARE f fish;
```

This variable can be used to hold instances of fish or the subtypes defined on fish. For example, you can use this to set the values of fish or simply pass the result of some output parameter:

```
f := <instance of marine_fish>;
```

If you assign variables with the values of the instance of a subtype, then the results of a function, which can be defined to be of a defined abstract data type, can also substitute a subtype for a function that has been defined on a supertype. For example, the type of the function disease's return value is a subtype of fish; you can then return an instance of marine_fish or fresh_water_fish, along with the added attributes for the diagnosis abstract data type:

```
CREATE FUNCTION disease ( f fish, s symptoms ARRAY(5) ) RETURNS
diagnosis
    <code to determine the diagnosis>;
```

This is true if the diagnosis is defined under the fish type, with added attributes and functions as needed.

Finally, since abstract data types can be used to define columns in other abstract data types, then instances of subtypes of a supertype can be used as substitutions for the supertype when populating (creating) instances of the abstract data type. In the previous example, the subtype diagnosis could have as its attributes a `fish` supertype and further attributes as defined below:

```
CREATE TYPE diagnosis (
    afflicted_fish           fish,
    disease_scientific_name  name,
    disease_common_name      name,
    root_cause               CHARACTER VARYING (15),
    affected_area            CHARACTER VARYING (15),
    mortality_rate           DECIMAL (5,2),
    treatment                CHARACTER VARYING (20),
    t_concentration          DECIMAL (8,4)
)
```

When using this abstract data type to populate it with possible instances of a diagnosis, you can use subtypes `fresh_water_fish` or `marine_fish` to define the fish that can be afflicted with this type of disease. This definition could have been derived or extracted from the passed-in arguments to the disease function defined earlier.

Using these definitions, let's take a deeper look at the uses in a more detailed example. Assume you have an `inventory_purchase` table defined, which is to be used as a table to hold all purchases of the store inventory. You have defined a supertype, `inventory`, which only has as its attributes the item identifier and the quantity on hand:

```
CREATE TYPE inventory(
    item_id     INTEGER,
    quantity    INTEGER);
```

You can then use this to define further refinements on the inventory, such as `fish_inventory`, `marine_fish_inventory`, `tanks_inventory`, `fresh_water_fish_inventory`, `pumps_inventory`, and so on. These refinements use the supertype inventory as their base type. For example, to define the `fish_inventory`, use:

```
CREATE TYPE fish_inventory UNDER inventory (
    fish_item     fish);
```

Similarly, you can define the hardware in the store, the other organisms—such as plants and invertebrates, decorations, fish food, and so on—using the same inventory abstract data type as the supertype of all the inventory items. This, in turn, can be used to define a table to be stored in the database and used to keep track of inventory purchases from vendors throughout the world. To define such a table, you need a few more abstract data types; one will keep track of the different forms of money you must deal in and, through embedded functions, provide the appropriate conversions:

```
CREATE TYPE money
    (PRIVATE value DECIMAL(6,2),

        FUNCTION us_dollar

        FUNCTION cnd_dollar

        FUNCTION Mex_peso

        FUNCTION Caribbean_currency
            .
            .
            .
    );
```

Using the previously defined address abstract data type, with some alterations, make it include variations in address due to country of origin:

```
CREATE TYPE address

    (PRIVATE     <declarations for attributes>);

        FUNCTION us_address

        FUNCTION cnd_address

        FUNCTION Mex_address

        FUNCTION Caribbean_address
            .
            .
            .
    );
```

By using these abstract data types you can define the table, inventory_purchase, as follows:

```
CREATE TABLE inventory_purchase (
    item         inventory,
    supplier     VARCHAR(25),
    sup_address  address,
    price        money)
```

You can then use this table to insert a variety of items purchased for the store, as follows:

```
INSERT INTO inventory_purchase VALUES( marine_fish(item_no(00101),
    quantity_oh(10), 'pterois volitans', 'lionfish', . . .),
                    'RedSea Fisheries',
```

```
                caribbean_address('124 Front st', 'Georgetown', Grand Caymen',
                'Ht115', 'BWI'), Cayman_dollars (18.95));

        INSERT INTO inventory_sales VALUES ( fresh_water_fish
        (item_no(00011),
            quantity_oh(12), 'thayeria obliqua', 'penguinfish', . . ),
                            'Fish_R_US',
            us_address('1245 US 1', 'Miami', Fl., 00011, 'USA'),
        Us_dollars(9.95));

        INSERT INTO inventory_sales VALUES ( tank (item_no(10000),
        quantity_oh(3),
            '25 gallon' . . .), 'ACME Tanks', cnd_address('100 Rue Rouge',
            'Montreal', 'Quebec', 'Hc1', 'Canada'), cnd_dollars(19.95);
```

The resulting table is as follows:

inventory_purchase			
item	**supplier**	**sup_address**	**price**
<marine_fish> item_no: 00101 quantity_oh: 10 pterois volitans . . .	RedSea Fisheries	*< caribbean_address>* street: 124 Front St. city: Georgetown state: Grand Cayman . . . country: BWI	*<Cayman_dollars>* amount: 18.95
< fresh_water_fish> item_no: 00011 quantity_oh: 12 thayeria obliqua . . .	Fish_R_US	*<us_address>* street: 1245 US 1 city: Miami state: FL. zip: 00011 country: USA	*<us_dollars>* amount: 9.95
<tank> item_no: 10000 quantity_oh: 3 tank_size: 25 gallon . . .	ACME Tanks	cnd_address street: 100 Rue Rouge city: Montreal state: Quebec zip: Hc1 country: Canada	*<cnd_dollars>* amount: 19.95

Some additional information has been added to the table as hidden information to be used by the type-matching system during run time to match the types of attributes during accesses or alterations. What you will notice about the table above is that each of the rows in the table has a different instance of a different subtype of the supertype defined on the column. For instance, the item category for the table has subtypes `marine_fish`, `fresh_water_fish`, and `tank` as the type tag for the instances of inventory item. Similarly, each of the tuples (rows) has different type tags for the address of the supplier and the type of money used in the transaction.

One thing to consider when using such subtype substitutions is the issue of finding an instance of a subtype at run time. To find an instance, the system is required to use late binding and dynamic dispatching in locating the appropriate instance. For example, if you want to find the marine fish, lionfish, from a vendor that supplied them previously for less than $20 (U.S. currency), you can generate the following query:

```
SELECT inventory_purchase.supplier FROM inventory_purchase
    WHERE dollar_amount(price) < us_dollar(20.00) AND
        item..common_name = 'lionfish';
```

When generated, the query invokes one of the stored functions at run time, depending on the type of money and type of item stored in the columns price and item. For example, in this case the item uses `tank`, `marine_fish`, or `fresh_water_fish` at run time, and the price invokes `us_dollar`, `cnd_dollar`, or `Cayman_dollar` at run time. On each row accessed to determine if this is true, each attribute needs to be examined for the subtype used and the appropriate function to use.

Using Predicates for Type Checking at Run Time

The hidden type tags of subtype instances stored in tables can be used in application-generated table access to test for an appropriate run-time type of an abstract data type's instance. For example, the table specification for `inventory_purchase` in the following code segment:

```
CREATE TABLE inventory_purchase (
    item          inventory,
    supplier      VARCHAR(25),
    sup_address   address,
    price         money)
```

With the types of the abstract data type's attributes being defined as supertypes and the instances stored in instances (rows) of this table (consisting of the subtypes of previously defined supertypes), you can generate the following query to find fish purchased from Grand Cayman:

```
SELECT item, supplier, sup_address, price
    FROM inventory_purchase
    WHERE TYPE (price) IN (cayman_dollars);
```

This query uses the type tags of the attribute price to determine which rows to retrieve from the named table. In this example, you only have one row that can be retrieved, and it is shown below in the resulting table:

item	supplier	sup_address	price
<marine_fish> item_no: 00101 quantity_oh: 10 pterois volitans . . .	RedSea Fisheries	*< caribbean_address>* street: 124 Front St. city: Georgetown state: Grand Cayman . . . country: BWI	*<Cayman_dollars>* amount: 18.95

Similarly, you can generate queries using the `item` or `sup_address` types as the source for the type predicate. For example, to get the same single row, you can use one type predicate on the item attribute:

```
SELECT item, supplier, sup_address, price
    FROM inventory_purchase
    WHERE TYPE (item) IN (marine_fish);
```

Or, you can use a second type predicate on the `sup_address` type tag:

```
SELECT item, supplier, sup_address, price
    FROM inventory_purchase
    WHERE TYPE (sup_address) IN (cayman_address);
```

In both cases, these predicates retrieve the same row and no others. If other rows meet this type predicate, then they, too, are extracted and inserted into the resulting table. Using type predicates that use the abstract data type's type tags allows applications writers to select specific subtypes in a table, which may consist of numerous subtypes, based on the supertype used in the definition of the table's attributes.

Subtypes can be specified so that the type of an expression can be changed to that of one of its subtypes. For example, in the inventory_purchase table, you can generate a query that uses another subtype and coerces or changes it at run time into the subtype instance wanted. The following query uses the price attribute and changes it from whatever type it is into the us_dollar type, allowing the query retriever to see the price in U.S. dollars:

```
SELECT item, supplier, sup_address, TREAT (price AS us_dollar)
    FROM inventory_purchase
    WHERE TYPE (price) IN (cayman_dollars);
```

This concept of subtype specification can also allow you to pass a value, whose compile time type is a supertype, S, to a function whose parameter type is a subtype of the previously defined supertype, S, at run time For example, using a function that returns the dollar value of a given input of type money:

```
CREATE FUNCTION dollar_amount (Cayman_dollar) RETURNS us_dollar
    <code to do conversion>
```

This can then be used to allow the translation of the given value:

```
SELECT item, supplier, sup_address, TREAT (price AS Cayman_dollar)
    FROM inventory_purchase
    WHERE TYPE (price) IN (cayman_dollars);
```

The selection above provides the items in us_dollar form instead of the stored Grand Cayman dollar form. The coercion and changing can be done in statements in SQL also. The test is to determine if the value of the variable passed in is compatible for the translation to occur. If it has a common supertype, then this is possible. An exception is raised if the run-time type of the value (instance) does not correspond to the given subtype.

Abstract Data Type Functions

Abstract data types defined up to this point have not been too advanced. They include the built-in observer and mutator functions but do not fully address user-defined functions, which can also be (and often will be) part of an abstract data type's specification and use. For example, with the fish data type, you may want to include an attribute picture of data type BLOB, which has functions defined on it to display side, front, bottom, and top images of the fish. This allows a buyer to examine the fish online before he or she purchases one, or to order a fish if the aquarium shop does not have a particular fish in stock. The properties of abstract data types and their functions will be discussed in the following section.

Functions and ADT Operations

Up to this point, it has been suggested that abstract data types in SQL-3 allow access to encapsulated attributes through the implicitly created observer and mutator functions. These automatically generated functions take as their name the name of the attribute, and the type of the parameters, which is derived from the type of the attribute. For example, the fish abstract data type has the following specification:

```
CREATE TYPE fish (
    scientific_name   VARCHAR(40),
    common_name    VARCHAR(30),
    fish_species       VARCHAR(20),
    max_size       DECIMAL (5,2),
    body_type        VARCHAR(30)
)
```

Each of the attributes has an automatically generated observer and mutator function defined when an instance of the fish is created. For example, there is an observer for the attribute scientific_name, which has the signature:

```
FUNCTION scientific_name (arg1 fish) RETURNS VARCHAR(40);
```

and the scientific_name attribute also has a mutator function with the signature:

```
FUNCTION scientific_name (arg1 fish, arg2 VARCHAR(40)) RETURNS
fish;
```

These built-in operations, however, are not all that can be provided with abstract data types. If they were, true application-friendly abstract data types would not be possible. They would only be glorified subtables or subrows in tables. Thankfully, SQL-3 provides greater capabilities. You are allowed to define further encapsulated functions, which add additional capabilities and functionality to the abstract data types.

ADT Operations through Functions   Enhanced functions provided in the body of an abstract data type allow the designer to provide much more functionality and be tuned into the needs of the abstract data type user, rather than the needs of the database management system. For example, in the fish abstract data type, you may want, for classification reasons, to provide additional uses of the fish picture attribute in the fish abstract data type. You may want to provide functions that use the BLOB information to extract the caudal peduncle (fin), to compare this species with others, or to classify this species as having a specific type of fin. Or, you may want to get information on the makeup of the dorsal fin—for example, the spine type that supports the fin's webbing. To do this, you must be able to define further functions, which operate on encapsulated attributes, in more detailed ways. This is the job of abstract data type routines, which can be either procedures or functions:

```
CREATE TYPE fish (
         scientific_name   VARCHAR(40),
         common_name       VARCHAR(30),
         fish_species      VARCHAR(20),
         max_size          DECIMAL (5,2),
         body_type         VARCHAR(30),
         picture           BLOB(1M),
PUBLIC   FUNCTION display(P fish) RETURNS bitplane;
         <code to display fish picture>;
PUBLIC   FUNCTION fin(P fish) RETURNS fin_class;
         <code to determine the fin class>
PUBLIC   FUNCTION dorsal(P fish) RETURNS dorsal_class;
         <code to determine the dosal fin class>
PUBLIC   FUNCTION pectoral(P fish) RETURNS
         pectoral_class;
         <code to determine the pectoral fin class>
PUBLIC   FUNCTION latline(P fish) RETURNS latline_class;
         <code to determine the lateral fish line>
)
```

These new functions can then be used by code developers who have access to the signature of this abstract data type. These functions act just as the built-in observer and mutator functions in that the desired result is retrieved simply by providing the function call and the correct parameters for the function to operate on.

Function Overloading   Functions in SQL-3, as with functions in many modern programming languages, can have the function name overloaded. That is, there can exist multiple different instances of the same named function. For example, the function display used to return the picture of a fish in a bitmapped form to use in a system's display subsystem can act on different types of elements in the database. You can use the same name for functions to display `fish`, `marine_fish`, `fresh_water_fish`, `inventory_items`, `fresh_water_invertebrates`, `marine_invertebrates`, `marine_plants`, `fresh_water_plants`, `employees`, and so on. When the function is called, the type system must examine the parameter types to determine which implementation of display to use in performing the operation.

In some cases, multiple functions with the same name are essential to achieve a type-specific behavior. For example, you used a function called `dollar_amount` previously, alluding to the fact that this function would translate the given input data type into the desired output data type. If you use the same name for a set of different input data types, you need to provide a set of different implementations for the desired effect. To convert `Cayman_dollar` into `us_dollar` requires a function that takes the exchange rate of the Cayman dollar and for, each Cayman dollar, computes the U.S. equivalent.

```
Public FUNCTION dollar_amount (P Cayman_dollar) RETURNS us_dollar;
    BEGIN
        RETURN (P * 1.25);
    END;
```

Similarly, for the Canadian transformation, you can take the present exchange rate of .73 Canadian dollar for every U.S. dollar to compute the cost in U.S. dollars:

```
Public FUNCTION dollar_amount (P cnd_dollar) RETURNS us_dollar;
    BEGIN
        RETURN (P/.73);
    END;
```

When multiple functions with the same name are implemented in an abstract data type, or even outside of an abstract data type, dispatching of functions is based on the actual types of all the arguments passed into the function for invocation. Functions are not message based; they take in the parameters and perform the function. Functions must be examined by the underlying type rectification system. Arguments to the functions are passed in by reference, although the reference is hidden (protected). Modifications to abstract data types are accomplished by side effects of function operation.

Execution Privileges   Since function signatures embedded in an abstract data type are constructed at the time the function is defined, and functions may be reused or have a long life, you need a way to alter the embedded privileges. This statement is limited to the data control language component of SQL and requires that the application issuing this statement must have the appropriate rights to perform the statement. Within the context of the abstract data type, this statement can be used to restrict or to allow some users from accessing and/or modifying components (attributes) in an abstract data type. The general form of the two-function privilege statement follows that of the general GRANT and REVOKE statements of SQL:

```
<grant statement> ::=
 GRANT <privileges>
    TO <grantee> [ { <comma> <grantee> }... ]
      [ WITH GRANT OPTION ]

<privileges> ::=
 <object privileges> ON <object name>

<object privileges> ::=
    ALL PRIVILEGES
  | <action> [ { <comma> <action> }... ]

<action> ::=
    SELECT [ <left paren> <privilege column list> <right paren> ]
  | DELETE
  | INSERT [ <left paren> <privilege column list> <right paren> ]
  | UPDATE [ <left paren> <privilege column list> <right paren> ]
  | REFERENCES [ <left paren> <privilege column list> <right paren>
]
  | USAGE
  | TRIGGER
  | UNDER
  | EXECUTE

<revoke statement> ::=
 REVOKE [ GRANT OPTION FOR ]
     <privileges>
    FROM <grantee> [ { <comma> <grantee> }... ] <drop behavior>
```

The GRANT statement is used to give a particular user or group of users the rights to perform specific functions of the abstract data type. For example, you may want to give a user the ability to perform the display function on the abstract data type `fish`, while, at the same time, you do not want this same user to be able to alter the stored BLOB.

```
GRANT EXECUTE ON display(fish) TO PUBLIC;
```

This statement permits the general public having access to this database to perform the display function on the fish abstract data type.

Alternatively, by not giving the same group the ability to alter the stored bitmap for the fish, you can generate the following statement:

```
GRANT EXECUTE ON display(fish, bitmap) FROM PUBLIC;
```

With this statement, the system administrator tells the system to use not the named revoked functions to determine the routine for this user when a named function is invoked. This prunes the possible set of applicable functions when determining what to run. If a user attempts to invoke a function or procedure that has been removed from the list of executable functions, a system error is generated, indicating that no matching function exists or that the user does not have authorization to execute the function or procedure.

Function Definition and Scope

What are functions in relation to their use in the SQL-3 language? The answer is multifaceted. Functions can provide the behavior seen from the interface to an abstract data type, or they can be freestanding, existing in user code, or as part of a procedure or module in SQL-3. Functions can use abstract data types or embed SQL-3 code to perform some defined operation on the database or on some specific abstract data type or data structure. Similar to the function, the procedure can also have many faces. A procedure can be embedded in an abstract data type or can also be freestanding. The biggest difference and advantage of a function or procedure defined in the encapsulated domain of an abstract data type is the visibility gained by being part of the abstract data type. Functions or procedures defined in an abstract data type will have access to functions and procedures that may not be visible at the abstract data type's interface (e.g., functions or procedures that have been declared private or protected).

Definition within ADT   A function or procedure can be defined in the scope of an abstract data type definition. For example, in the `employees` abstract data type:

```
CREATE TYPE employees (
        emp_id              INTEGER,
        emp_title           name,

PUBLIC  emp_last_name       name,
        emp_first_name      name,
        emp_street          CHARACTER VARYING (30),
        emp_city            CHARACTER VARYING (20),
        emp_state           CHARACTER (2),
        emp_zip             CHARACTER VARYING (9),

PUBLIC  emp_phone           CHARACTER (10),
        emp_start_date      TIMESTAMP,
        emp_pay_rate        DECIMAL (7,2),
        emp_com_rate        DECIMAL (5,2),

PUBLIC  FUNCTION salary     (P employees) RETURNS DECIMAL

        <code to retreive number of hours worked and sales to
date>

RETURN Salary = (P..emp_pay_rate * (SELECT ytd_reg_hours
                                    FROM aquarium_payroll
                                    WHERE P..emp_id =
                                    aquarium_payroll.emp_id)
                + (P..emp_com_rate * (SELECT year_to_date
                                    FROM aquarium _revenues
                                    WHERE P..emp_id =
                                    aquarium_revenues.emp_id);

)
```

This function uses information internal to the abstract data type, employee, to compute an employee's total salary as a combination of the base hourly wage times the number of hours worked, plus the commission earned from total yearly sales to date multiplied by the commission rate set for this employee.

Definition outside an ADT   Just as easily, the same values from outside this abstract data type can be computed; the values you need are public in the new definition of the employee's abstract data type, as shown below, and are available to outside abstract data types. SQL code or applications code using the appropriate access methods can easily extract and use this information to compute the same result:

```
CREATE TYPE employees (
PUBLIC  emp_id              INTEGER,
        emp_title           name,
PUBLIC  emp_last_name       name,
        emp_first_name      name,
        emp_street          CHARACTER VARYING (30),
        emp_city            CHARACTER VARYING (20),
```

```
                     emp_state       CHARACTER (2),
                     emp_zip         CHARACTER VARYING (9),
         PUBLIC      emp_phone       CHARACTER (10),
                     emp_start_date  TIMESTAMP,
         PUBLIC      emp_pay_rate    DECIMAL (7,2),
         PUBLIC      emp_com_rate    DECIMAL (5,2)
         );
```

The abstract data type, employees, is then used, as are the tables aquarium_payroll and aquarium_revenues, to extract the necessary information from the repositories to compute the employees' salaries.

```
CREATE FUNCTION salary   (P employees) RETURNS DECIMAL

   <code to retrieve number of hours worked and sales to date>

   RETURN salary = (P..emp_pay_rate * (SELECT ytd_reg_hours
                                        FROM aquarium_payroll
                                        WHERE P..emp_id =
                                        aquarium_payroll.emp_id)
                  + (P..emp_com_rate * (SELECT year_to_date
                                        FROM aquarium _revenues
                                        WHERE P..emp_id =
                                        aquarium_revenues.emp_id);
```

You can see from this simple example that there is not much difference between the embedded and the external version of this function. The biggest difference lies in how the embedded information is used. If attributes are protected or private, the external routine cannot be generated, since it does not have access to the embedded attributes emp_id, emp_pay_rate, and emp_com_rate. Without access to these data items, this function cannot be generated.

Function Binding

Functions in SQL-3 can use the same name for function instances serving different input parameter data types. To determine which of the multiple instances of a function to use, the database management system must interrogate the input to the named function, looking for the closest match to the data types of the parameters, to determine which implementation to invoke. This can be performed in numerous ways. The matching can be done at the time of the function's definition, the time of the application's compilation, the time of call, or the time of execution. In each case, some syntax and semantics are required to make the appropriate choice.

Dynamic Dispatch of Functions   The most common form of function matching uses parameter checking at run time to define which implementation to use. Dynamic dispatch of functions operates by choosing an instance of a function to execute, depending on the evaluation of all the types of the actual arguments passed to the function during invocation at run time. The function chosen for execution is that which best matches the defined argument types in the function instances' definitions. The function that best matches the arguments is chosen as the one to invoke. For example, looking once again at the money conversion problem with purchasing fish from other countries, you need to deal with multiple currencies. The type of currency may not be known before run time of the inventory purchase function.

If the application has defined a variety of foreign currencies, and an application is performing some function on these currencies, you can use the following code to describe how dynamic dispatch occurs:

```
1      BEGIN

2          DECLARE m money;

3          DECLARE a DECIMAL (10,2);

4          SET m = Cayman_dollar (100.00);

5          SET a = dollar_amount(m);

6          SET m = cnd_dollar(100.00);

7          SET a = dollar_amount(m);

8      END;
```

In this simple code segment, lines 1 and 8 delineate the boundaries of this code block. Lines 2 and 3 are used to declare two variables: one as type money, a supertype, and one as a DECIMAL type. Line 4 sets the variable, m, of type money to the Cayman_dollar amount $100. This results in a data item that has a value and a type tag associated with it. Line 5 uses the amount of Cayman dollars and invokes the function dollar_amount using the implementation that operates on Cayman_dollars as the input parameter. The function will convert the Cayman dollars into U.S. dollars. Line 6 resets the variable, m, to $100 Canadian. This value is then used in line 7 to convert this amount from Canadian dollars into U.S. dollars. In both cases, the function call looks the same; the difference is in what occurs at run time for each of these calls. The first call to function dollar_amount uses as its input the subtype

`Cayman_dollar` as the input parameter. The functions' implementations are examined, and the closest match is found when the implementation with `Cayman_dollars` in the function parameter list is found. Similarly, on the second call to `dollar_amount`, the input parameter type is `can_dollar`, again, a subtype of the supertype `money`. The function call is taken as valid, and the search through the implementation lattice yields a match when the function implementation with the `can_dollar` type is found.

Type checking does not, however, only need to be performed at run time. Type checking of function invocations is also performed at compile time to eliminate run-time errors. Some forms of compile time type checking look to resolve functions for all forms of possible subtypes. The function types are checked to make sure that the return types of the functions share a common supertype.

Static Binding of Functions   If possible, a function is bound to a single implementation. This can be achieved when no arguments to the function are abstract data types or if no abstract data type arguments have subtypes. That is, there is only one type that is a supertype and has no subtypes defined on it. Finally, you can also statically bind a function to a single implementation when there is only one possible function instance for all possible function invocations. Using the same block of code, this can be illustrated by removing one of the different invocations:

```
1       BEGIN

2           DECLARE m money;

3           DECLARE a DECIMAL (10,2);

4           SET m = Cayman_dollar (100.00);

5           SET a = dollar_amount(m);

6       END;
```

In this example, there is only a single function call to `dollar_amount` and the input parameter is clearly defined. The compile time type checking can test for this match, and a priori assign the appropriate instance of the function to this code segment. This will alleviate having to perform more costly run-time type checking on this block of code.

Type Precedence   When a definitive match is not possible at compile time, a system service must be in place that allows the determination of an appropriate function instance to use at run time. The procedure used for this in the SQL-3 language proposal is type precedence. Type precedence defines how the subtypes are related to each other and to the supertype used in their definitions. The type precedence for a set of related abstract data types is constructed based on the order of the type names used in the subtype clause of the CREATE TYPE statement. For example, you defined the abstract data types `marine_fish` and `fresh_water_fish` as subtypes of the `fish` supertype. You can also use these to define other fish types, such as mixed saltwater and freshwater and fish that live in tropical, cool, or arctic waters, as separate subtypes of the marine fish and the freshwater fish.

The precedence defined in Figure 7.2 indicates that `tropical_fish`, `cool_fish`, and `arctic_fish` are subtypes of `marine_fish`, which is a subtype of the supertype `fish`. When checking for a match, you can traverse the precedence graph from the root toward the leaves looking for a match that closely resembles the input argument of the function.

Generalized Expressions   Function invocation, as defined in the previous sections, is dependent on the searching and matching of function arguments with stored function implementations. The implementation that has the closest match to all a function's passed-in arguments is the

Figure 7.2

Type hierarchy and precedence.

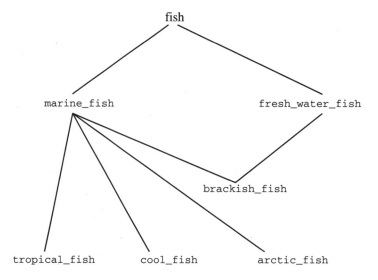

implementation used to perform the function. This dynamic binding, however, does not have to be used if the applications writer has specific knowledge of which implementation should be used. If information is available regarding which implementation to use, the applications writer can specify this using the generalized expression found as part of the routine invocation. The BNF for this sequence is as follows:

```
<routine invocation> ::=
 <routine name> <argument list>

<argument list> ::=
   <left paren> [ <positional arguments>]  <right paren>
 | <left paren> <positional arguments> <comma> <keyword arguments>
<right paren>
 | <left paren> <keyword arguments> <right paren>

<positional arguments> ::=
 <argument> [ { <comma> <argument> }... ]

<argument> ::=
   <value expression>
 | <generalized expression>

<generalized expression> ::=
 <value expression> AS <abstract data type name>
```

The generalized expression is embedded in the routine invocation's argument list. The generalized expression has the form:

```
(argument AS abstract data type)
```

This allows the calling statement to specify exactly which instance of the routine to use in performing the intended function. The concept being used is that an instance of a type can be treated as an instance of one of its supertypes for the purpose of function dispatch. As an example, look again at the fish abstract data types. First, extend the data types with a new attribute description, which is used to include a textual description of the fish and its habits:

```
CREATE TYPE marine_fish UNDER fish
       (food_preference   VARCHAR(20) ARRAY(5),
        geographic_range  VARCHAR(20) ARRAY(5),
        fish_disposition  temperament,
        fish_activity     day_shift,
        body_type         VARCHAR(20),
        .picture          BLOB(1M),
        description       CLOB(5K)
  )
```

```
CREATE TYPE fresh_water_fish UNDER fish
     (food_preference    VARCHAR(20) ARRAY(5),
      geographic_range   VARCHAR(20) ARRAY(5),
      fish_disposition   temperament,
      fish_activity      day_shift,
      body_type       VARCHAR(20),
      picture        BLOB(1M),
      description       CLOB(5K)
)
```

You can then generate queries to retrieve the fish description:

```
CREATE TABLE aquatic_organism_stock (
    stock_id           INTEGER,
        CONSTRAINT aquatic_organism_stock_id_pk PRIMARY KEY,
    scientific_name    name
        CONSTRAINT aquatic_organism_name_not_null NOT NULL,
    organism           fish,
    number_in_stock    INTEGER,
    current_price      price

)

        SELECT description(marine_fish) FROM
aquatic_organism_stock;

        SELECT description(fresh_water_fish) FROM
aquatic_organism_stock;
```

The queries return a text description of the fish selected in the marine and freshwater abstract data types. The return type must be a CLOB in order for the text description to be retrieved. In addition, for the queries to be truly accurate, you need to create two tables, with the tables' contents defined using the marine_fish and fresh_water_fish abstract data types.

These abstract data types, along with the text descriptor, can then be used to create a list of fish from a particular geographical region for both freshwater and saltwater varieties:

```
CREATE FUNCTION list_fish(lf fish)
    RETURNS CLOB(10K)
        .
        .
        .
    BEGIN
        RETURN description(lf)
            CONCAT    description(lf AS marine_fish)
            CONCAT    description(lf AS fresh_water_fish);
    END
```

To process the table you need to write a query with the following form:

```
SELECT description(lf) FROM aquatic_organism_stock
   WHERE aquatic_organism_stock..geographic(lf) = carribean;
```

This query uses the function description to search through the table of fish, both marine and freshwater, searching for matches where the geographical region is the Caribbean. Internally, the function has the statements:

```
CONCAT    description(lf AS marine_fish)
```

and

```
CONCAT    description(lf AS fresh_water_fish);
```

The statements treat the input to the function as both a marine fish and a freshwater fish to extract the information you want.

Paths   As a way of organizing data in the database, SQL uses a hierarchy of containers. The top level of the hierarchy is the database. The remaining components are the catalog, schema, tables, view, and the rows and columns. A user, application code, and even database code are defined in a schema. Each definer of database tables will have a defined schema. These schema names will be stored in the catalog system of the database. To access a procedure, function, table, or any structure stored in the database, users need to know the schema name where the appropriate database entity is stored. The path is the way SQL provides access conduits to the database users.

A path is a list of schema names that is to be searched when looking for the database element with which to access or operate. The paths can be defined for a variety of SQL components. The BNF format for defining and setting paths is as follows:

```
<module path specification> ::=
 <path specification>

<path specification> ::=
 PATH <schema name list>
```

Paths can be defined for modules in the SQL persistent stored module's elements. For example, if you defined multiple separate schemas for the aquatic store management system, then paths can be used to ensure that all the schemas are searched when an invocation is performed. If you have sales, service, marketing, accounting, personnel, biology, and training schemas, they can all be accessed by a module if the module contains a PATH statement:

```
CREATE MODULE testing

    ...

    PATH 'sales, service, marketing, accounting, personnel, biology,
          training'

    ...

END MODULE;
```

If a single schema is to have the ability to search through other schemas looking for appropriate tables, functions, and so on, a path must be defined in the schema definition:

```
CREATE SCHEMA fishes

    ...

    PATH 'sales, service, marketing, accounting, personnel, biology,
          training'
```

Beyond placing paths in modules and schemas, SQL also allows path expressions to be used in applications code, in dynamic SQL code segments, or in a transactional unit. The format for dynamic SQL uses the SET PATH statement, whose BNF is:

```
<set path statement> ::=
  SET <SQL-path attribute>

<SQL-path attribute> ::=
  PATH <value specification>
```

Setting the path in embedded SQL, in an application, requires that the code segment contain the following PATH statement:

```
PATH 'sales, service, marketing, accounting, personnel, biology,
      training'
```

To set the path in a dynamic SQL session or in an SQL-invoked routine requires this statement:

```
SET PATH 'sales, service, marketing, accounting, personnel,
biology, training'
```

Type Precedence

SQL allows multiple functions to have the same name and, therefore must have a means to determine which function instance is to be performed at run time. As was alluded to earlier, function instance selection is based on the types of all arguments of the functions. SQL will always succeed in finding a unique function if a suitable one exists. To perform this operation, SQL uses the precedence relationship that exists between function arguments and the types of these arguments. The precedence relationship for arguments is left to right. That is, the arguments on the left have a higher precedence than those on the right of the functions list or arguments:

```
CREATE FUNCTION list(arg1, arg2, . . .argn)
```

In the example above, `arg1` has higher precedence than `arg2` and all the other arguments through `argn`. Argument `arg2` has higher precedence than `argn`, but lower precedence than `arg1`.

The second form of precedence used for function definition is based on the precedence relationship between types. For the built-in types, the order is defined for each data type. For example, an argument of type SMALLINT has the precedence, SMALLINT, INTEGER, DECIMAL, NUMERIC, REAL, FLOAT, and DOUBLE. For the abstract data types, the precedence goes from left to right in lists of abstract types used to define an item and from subtype to supertype for inherited elements. For example, you defined a mixed fish type earlier as:

```
CREATE TYPE mixed_fish UNDER marine_fish, fresh_water_fish
```

In this example, the order of precedence is `mixed_fish`, `marine_fish`, `fresh_water_fish`, `fish`.

These rules aid in the system's ability to determine which instance of a function to invoke and helps users to have a better idea of which function will be performed when a given signature is used. In determining which function to perform, the system will only use the functions from schemas listed in the calling code's path definition. Functions where users have no execute privileges are not considered when determining which function to perform.

The system uses this information in determining which function to perform. The system first prunes all functions that a calling user has no execute rights for. Second, all functions that fall out of the defined path for the calling user's code are removed. Finally, the system examines the arguments of the call from left to right, comparing the argument in the call with parameters in the function definitions. The functions are eliminated from contention if this match test indicates that the parameter and the argument are not the same type or are not in the type precedence list for the argument being examined. The comparison is looking for the best match between the function parameters and the calling call arguments. If, when the search is complete, more than one function remains in the list of possible functions, the system will use the precedence of the path definition to pick the function from the first schema name. After this is performed, the system needs only to invoke the appropriately defined function at run time.

The main idea in subject function determination is that the mapping of function call to function invocation is performed on the closest match of arguments to function parameters, using the precedence in place, derived from fixed or created precedence.

Attribute Inheritance

You have learned about functions with the same name and how these can be rectified at run time or at compile time using subject function determination. This is not all that can occur when you are constructing tables, abstract data types, and attributes from other abstract data types. You can have the problem where multiple attributes with the same name can be defined in a single abstract data type instance. How is this possible? The answer is that two separate abstract data types can be used to define a new abstract data type or separate attributes in an SQL table. For example, if you use `fresh_water_fish` and `marine_fish` to form a new type, mixed_fish, then the new type, mixed_fish, would have many attributes with the same name but with different meanings:

```
CREATE TYPE mixed_fish UNDER marine_fish, fresh_water_fish( ....
```

In this case, a new subtype is formed through the combination of two supertypes, which happen to have many attributes with the same name.

A second possibility is that you use a supertype to form a new subtype, and then create new attributes of the subtype that have the same name as the supertype's attributes. For example, if you create the fish supertype, and then create the marine_fish subtype under fish and use the same name, common_name, as an attribute in each, you find a name conflict:

```
CREATE TYPE fish (
        scientific_name    VARCHAR(40),
        common_name        VARCHAR(30),
        fish_species       VARCHAR(20),
        max_size           DECIMAL (5,2),
        body_type          VARCHAR(30)
)
```

Then, using this abstract data type specification, you can define another abstract data type, marine_fish, as follows:

```
CREATE TYPE marine_fish UNDER fish
        (common_name       VARCHAR(30),
         food_preference   VARCHAR(20) ARRAY(5),
         geographic_range  VARCHAR(20) ARRAY(5),
         fish_disposition  temperament,
         fish_activity     day_shift
)
```

How does SQL propose to solve these types of name conflict problems? In the present proposal, it is envisioned that name conflict problems will be resolved by function resolution. Therefore, a reference will always resolve to the function that is the best match. For example, in the marine_fish abstract data type above, you can have some code in an application, such as:

```
BEGIN
    DECLARE mf      marine_fish;
    DECLARE f       VARCHAR(30);
    SET f = mf..common_name;
```

This always results in invoking the correct `common_name` observer function. In this case, the `marine_fish` function, `common_name`, is used to write into the variable `f`. The use of the nested observer and mutator functions eliminates the need for complex rules or precedence relationships to resolve this type of name problem.

A much more severe problem exists with naming in the example in defining a new `mixed_fish` abstract data type as a subtype of both `marine_fish` and `fresh_water_fish`. This new abstract data type has the problem of inheriting multiple attributes of the same name:

```
CREATE TYPE mixed_fish UNDER marine_fish, fresh_water_fish(
   common_name      VARCHAR(30),
   ....
   )
```

Multiple conflicts occur in this example. You have the use of the attribute `common_name` found in the `mixed_fish`, `marine_fish`, and `fresh_water_fish` abstract data types. If a specific instance is to be used, you can force this by using generalized expressions (discussed earlier in this chapter). For example, if you want to use `marine_fish` `common_name` as the name to assign to a variable, you can use the following generalized expression:

```
BEGIN
   DECLARE mf      mixed_fish;
   DECLARE f       VARCHAR(30);
   SET f = common_name( mf AS marine_fish )
END;
```

Beyond this, functions can be defined with the generalized expression to refer to inherited attributes. For example, to create a function, `common_name`, on the abstract data type `mixed_fish` to return `marine_fish` directly, you can write the following function:

```
CREATE FUNCTION common_name (mf mixed_fish) RETURNS VARCHAR (30)
   RETURN (common_name ( fmf AS marine_fish));
```

This will cause `mixed_fish` to be interpreted as its supertype `marine_fish`, and will cause the function `common_name` on `marine_fish` to be performed.

CAST Function on ADTs

An important feature in the SQL-92 and the SQL-3 languages is the CAST expression and function. At times you may want one data type to become or at least look like another data type. This becomes important when an application knows, for example, that it stored information in one type but needs it in another—for example, digits stored in a character string. The CAST expression in SQL-92 permitted changing one type into another in the CAST expression. For example, if you want to compare the capture date of a fish with the delivery date of a fish, you can alter `capture_date` to become simply a date data type, allowing comparison with any item of type `date`:

```
WHERE aquarium_order..deliver_date >
   (CAST( fish..capture_date AS DATE) + 5 DAYS)
```

In essence, it loses the added information about capture. Only the date becomes relevant in the search.

What is different in abstract data types is that the CAST function must be explicitly designated as a CAST function in the create abstract data type structure. For example, in the functions designed to translate money from one currency to another, you use the CAST function to alter the types, as follows:

```
CREATE TYPE us_dollar UNDER money

   CAST (us_dollar as Cayman_dollar) WITH us_dollar(Cayman_dollar)

           <other CAST expressions>

   FUNCTION us_dollar(c Cayman_dollar) RETURNS us_dollar
     BEGIN
     DECLARE u us_dollar;
     SET u = us_dollar;          /* create us_dollar value */
     SET u..amount - c..amount / .8;   /* exchange rate */
     RETURN u;
     END

<further function for other currencies>
```

This defined function can also be used by another CAST expression to alter an amount:

```
BEGIN
    DECLARE u us_dollar;
    DECLARE c Cayman_dollar;

    ...

    SET u = CAST (c AS Cayman_dollar); /* invokes us_dollar
(Cayman_dollar)*/

    ...
```

Either method will work to cause the values to be treated as another, not necessarily equivalent, data type.

Abstract Data Type Comparison

An important aspect of SQL-3's predecessors was the ability to take items from one table and compare them to items in another table. This allowed information from multiple sources to be integrated, based on the needs of the application users. For example, if you have the employees and customers tables, and you want to find out which employees had also been customers in the past, you can generate a query that selects employees whose Social Security number is the same as a customer's Social Security number:

```
SELECT employee.* FROM e AS employees, c AS customers
WHERE e.ss_numer = c.ss_number;
```

It is desirable, and even necessary, for abstract data types to act in the same way as simple base type attributes do when it comes to comparing attributes in one table with another. SQL-3 provides this feature through user-specified type-specific functions for comparing abstract data type instances. These functions overload the built-in comparison operators equal (=), less than (<), less than or equal (<=), greater than (>), greater than or equal to (>=), and not equal to (<>). In addition to these operators, SQL-3 also has relative and hash comparison capabilities.

Relative comparison of abstract data types permits the specification of ordering between two abstract data type instances. In this case, the user must specify a function, which will return an integer value for a pair of abstract data type instances, to indicate this relative positioning. If the result is negative, the first operand is less than the second operand. The following example shows order given to two instances of the `fish` data types:

```
RELATIVE (fish(), fish())
```

The BNF for this statement is shown as:

```
<ordering method> ::=
    RELATIVE <relative function specification>
  | HASH <hash function specification>
  | STATE
```

This operation can then be used to determine if one instance of the abstract data type comes before or after the abstract data type it is being compared with.

If the result is zero, then the two abstract data types being compared are the same abstract data type; that is, they are equivalent. Finally, if the result of the user-supplied function returns a positive value, then the first abstract data type instance is greater than the second abstract data type instance.

Another way to compare abstract data type instances uses the hash method. In this case, the ordering can be specified with a built-in data type. When this method is used, the result must be a value on a built-in data type (e.g., the size of the fish or the cost of the fish as an ordering method).

Summary

This chapter reviewed how the new abstract data type found in the SQL-3 language is constructed and how, based on this construction, the abstract data type functions. One of the most important topics covered in this chapter was the concept of supertype and subtypes derived from the supertype. The supertype is used to form the foundation of a subtype, and the subtype takes on all the attributes and characteristics of the supertype through abstract data type inheritance.

With these new abstract data types comes the ability to define behavior beyond the built-in observer and mutator functions. These user-defined functions give the abstract data types the ability to map one-to-one with the needs of advanced applications. However, with this new capability comes another problem for the database system to handle. How are functions seen from applications, from other abstract data types, and from SQL code? Functions can overload the function names and even the attributes in an abstract data type. This chapter defined some of the rules and procedures through which the SQL-3 language will rectify these conflicts in a run-time system. The methods for function scope definition and function binding were discussed. Function binding can be performed statically or dynamically, but in both cases it uses schema paths and defined precedence to determine the differences between conflicting implementations. Finally, the chapter looked at some of the ways to override the system's built-in functions for determining function invocation using the CAST expression.

CHAPTER 8

Database Persistence

Concept of Persistence

What does it mean for some information item to be "persistent"? The dictionary defines the term *persistent* as "existing for a long or longer than usual time or continuously." In a database system, the term is used in a different context. In a database, persistence is used to indicate that an information item will exist beyond the scope or existence of the entity (e.g., program) that created it. This implies that a program or SQL session, which creates a table, ultimately will exit, complete execution, and be removed from the system. However, the table that was created does not go away. It remains in the database storage subsystem, waiting to be extracted by some other transient program or session. A persistent informational item stays persistent as long as the database exists and is persistent or until the item is removed from the database.

In programming languages, information is created, used, and discarded for every instantiation of a program. Data can be stored in a file or in variables of a program. However, if the program ceases to execute, the data stored in the variables are lost. To rectify this, some programs use data files to extract and store information. There is a difference, though. There is no control over who, what, and when this file can be accessed, altered, or deleted. If a user or program has the authorization rights to the file, damage can be done. In addition, there are no controls over the concurrent access to the stored file. This is where a database, and its concept of persistence, and database properties come into play.

In a database, information and access protocols are said to exhibit the *ACID* properties. The first property implies that access to information is atomic *(A)*. All actions of a database service are performed on the underlying storage, or none of the actions is performed on the stored information. The second property is consistent *(C)*. The database's consistency constraints, which define the correct states of the database, are always true. This implies that the data stored in the database are correct and up-to-date. The third property of actions on the database is that they exhibit independence *(I)* of execution. Access to the database is performed in isolation (with no interference). The last property, durability *(D)*, indicates that changes to the database remain in the database. This is where and how the concept of persistence occurs.

In SQL-92 and its predecessors, the concept of persistence is attached to the fundamental database structures. First, to have persistence, you need a named database (a repository where information is to be maintained). Second, this database must have a catalog, which names instances of users' information embedded within this persistent storage realm. These catalogs, in addition, maintain links to schemas. That is, the catalog represents a collection of named schemas known to this database instance. A schema describes the relationships and structures that exist between elements of a particular user's data repository. A schema has information about the structure of tables in the user's database (true relations in earlier versions of SQL). The tables describe the structure of their columns and possible restrictions on what can actually be placed in these columns.

All these structures were developed to allow the database environment to support multiple users, with multiple database repositories, in a singular, distributed, or client/server environment. The concepts of database and schema have evolved since the early days of database systems to aid in the definition and, therefore, to aid in the location of unique database tables and entries in a larger database system.

Persistence for Tables in SQL-3

Tables or relations have always been the staple diet for SQL databases of the past, so they deserve to be the starting point in a discussion about persistence in the new SQL-3 database model. SQL has always provided several types of tables. The names have changed and the types of tables have grown, but there has always been variety. SQL-89 provided three types of tables: persistent base tables, view tables, and derived tables.

In most cases, these three table types are adequate, but in advanced applications, where abstract data types are the best match to the needs of advanced applications, these alone are not enough. These basic types, along with extended table types, are essential if the SQL-3 database model is to meet the specific information management needs of advanced applications. Persistent base tables are created and stored persistently in the database. View tables and derived tables are derived with base tables and the description formed on the stored base tables.

Table Persistence

A table in the SQL language is defined as a multiset of rows. A row is a nonempty sequence of values, implying that a row must have at least one row with a stored value. In addition, due to the structure of a table in the SQL database model, all rows must have the same data types for columns and be in the same location in each column. Every row in the table has the same number of columns and each row has the data type in each location: column 1 to column n are the same in each row of the table.

Base Tables A table can be a base table yet have a different definition of persistence. A base table can be a persistent base table, a global temporary table, a created local temporary table, or a declared local temporary table. A *persistent base table* is a named table defined using the CREATE TABLE statement. A *global temporary table* is a named table defined using the CREATE TABLE statement and the extension GLOBAL TEMPORARY, which is inserted before the CREATE TABLE keywords. A *created local temporary* table is a named table, also defined using the CREATE TABLE statement, preceded by the keywords LOCAL TEMPORARY. The *declared local temporary table* is a named table declared as a component of a module.

The persistent base table is defined using the CREATE TABLE statement. Once created, this table is placed into a schema, where it will stay until an explicit DROP TABLE statement is performed. Data inserted into a base table get stored in the database in a nonvolatile area, typically a disk. The database may, in addition, store a redundant table for reliability and recovery purposes.

Global temporary tables and created local temporary tables have some aspects in common with persistent base tables. The definitions of the global and local temporary tables, as with the base table, are stored in the database's schema, remaining there until they are explicitly removed. The difference lies in the creation and access of an instance of the defined table. Though the definition is stored in the database, the instance is created only when the global or local temporary table is referenced in an SQL session. Each reference to one of these tables from a separate SQL session or module creates a distinct instance of the table. Herein lies the main difference between these tables and the persistent base table. The contents of these temporary tables cannot be shared between SQL sessions or modules as the persistent base table can. Even more restrictive is the rule for the created local temporary table. The contents of this table cannot be shared between modules or embedded SQL programs defined and operated upon in an SQL session.

So what does this all mean? Why have these different types of tables if you cannot share their contents? The answer lies in how these elements of the database can be used. The global temporary table is

Figure 8.1

Tables and sessions.

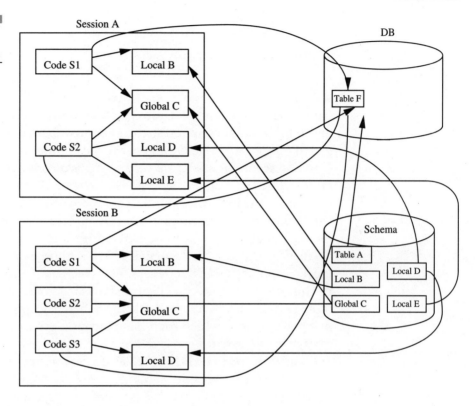

defined in a single SQL session, which may or may not have multiple modules, transactional sections of code, or other SQL code segments that share data being created during this session. For example, in Figure 8.1, there are two running sessions, defined as session A and session B.

Each of these sessions has embedded code segments, or modules, that access the lone persistent base table; the definitions for the local temporary tables B, D, and E; and the global temporary table C. To create these tables you can use definitions similar to these:

```
CREATE TABLE F( . . .)
   <persistent base table definition>

DECLARE LOCAL TEMPORARY TABLE A ( . . . )
   <local temporary table definition>

DECLARE LOCAL TEMPORARY TABLE B ( . . . )
   <local temporary table definition>

DECLARE LOCAL TEMPORARY TABLE D ( . . . )
   <local temporary table definition>
```

```
DECLARE LOCAL TEMPORARY TABLE E ( . . . )
   <local temporary table definition>

CREATE GLOBAL TEMPORARY TABLE C ( . . . )
   <local temporary table definition>
```

You can see in Figure 8.1 that there is only one copy of the persistent base table F stored in the database, which both sessions and their embedded components access and share. There is only one specification for the global temporary table C and for the local temporary tables B, D, and E. You also see in Figure 8.1 that there are two copies of global temporary table C, one for each of the sessions, and they are shared among the SQL code segments in the sessions, but not between the sessions. In session A, there are two local temporary tables B, one for each of the SQL code segments, which are separate, nonshared instances of the same table type defined in the database schema. There is another instance of the same local temporary table B in session B, linked to the top SQL code segment in this session. Finally, the figure shows instances of a local temporary table D in both sessions. As with the other example, these are different unique instances, which each have the same structure but do not share storage or information.

So why do you need these tables if they do not maintain persistence beyond the module, code segment, or session, in which they are instantiated? An application may need to create a repository for the results of some intermediate computations or data processing functions. A temporary table allows applications to create these holders and use them without having to explicitly remove the table at the end. Since the temporary table contents are eventually lost, you don't need to create a persistent base table and then drop the table before exiting a code segment. Another advantage of using these tables is security and privacy. Since the tables are only viewable and sharable in the single session or module, you don't need additional processing for concurrency control and recovery for the base table.

View and Derived Tables   A view is a constructed table, derived from one or more other tables through the evaluation of a query expression. For example, you have a table consisting of marine_fish:

```
CREATE TABLE marine_fish (
   scientific_name    name,
   common_name        name,
   fish_species       name,
   max_size           DECIMAL (5,2)
   food_preference    food,
```

```
    geographic_range   region,
    fish_disposition   temperament,
    fish_activity      day_shift
)
```

You want to create a partial representation of the data stored in the marine_fish table. You can use the view mechanism to form a derived, named table with an expression. Views are important when the database designer or administrator wants to restrict portions of a table from users or applications. For example, you want to form a view for an aquarist who wants to construct a tank containing only fish endemic to the Red Sea area. You can form a view to show just these fish, as follows:

```
CREATE VIEW Red_Sea_fish AS
    SELECT * FROM marine_fish
        WHERE geographic_region = 'redsea';
```

This results in a virtual table with all the marine fish from the Red Sea area viewable in this table. A view table does not exist on its own as a standalone table. In this example, a view table is formed by the query expression against the base table marine_fish. Once a named view has been specified, it can be used to write additional queries against, as if it were a physical table. Each time a user writes a query on the view, the view's SELECT statement is inserted for the view's named table, forming the query into an embedded subselection statement. For example, if you create the view above and then write a query to find all Red Sea fish that are nocturnal animals, you can write the following query:

```
SELECT * FROM Red_Sea_fish
    WHERE fish_activity = 'nocturnal';
```

This is is equivalent to:

```
SELECT * FROM (SELECT * FROM marine_fish
        WHERE geographic_region = 'redsea')

    WHERE fish_activity = 'nocturnal';
```

This is nothing more than a nested query. The view table is a mechanism to either aid in information hiding by restricting access to all the information, or it is a form of shorthand for commonly used groupings of data. Views do not need to name all the columns of a base table. A view can be constructed with any number of columns and in any order. A view can also be constructed using multiple tables. You use one table as the basis.

A derived view table can be further restricted to be updateable or read-only. The SQL operations INSERT, UPDATE, and DELETE are permitted on a derived view table that has been designated as updatable. These operations, however, are further restricted based on the privileges specified on the base table(s). When a view table is designated as read-only, DELETE, INSERT, and UPDATE are not allowed. On the other hand, a derived table is similar to a view table in that it is formed through the execution of a query statement on one or more base tables, but it is an unnamed temporary table. The values in the derived table are stored in the base tables that form the derived table. The derived table is the natural result of a query. SQL automatically generates a derived table instance, which exists in the buffer space of the database, upon execution of the query. Derived queries cannot be referred to again in any statements following the statement that generated the derived table. The derived table does not have a name or representation that can be referred to by any other statement. If a specific derived table is needed in another statement, it needs to be regenerated in the statement that wants it.

To generate the same derived table view that you saw earlier, a simple unnamed derived table can generate the query without the named view table designation:

```
SELECT * FROM marine_fish
   WHERE geographic_region = 'redsea';
```

This query results in a derived unnamed table, which contains the same information as the view table, Red_Sea_fish.

```
CREATE VIEW Red_Sea_fish AS
   SELECT * FROM marine_fish
      WHERE geographic_region = 'redsea';
```

What does all this mean in relation to the topic of this chapter, persistence in SQL? Each of these concepts deals with some element of persistence as used in the SQL-3 language. As with its predecessors, the concept of persistence in SQL-3 only maps to items that are in the schema and that represent base tables or the new SQL entity, a persistent stored module. In either case, the persistent base table or the persistent stored module uses the SQL keyword CREATE in the definition of the items that are to become persistent in the database. For example, the marine_fish table is a persistent base table, and the module sell_item is a persistent database item.

```
CREATE TABLE marine_fish (
   scientific_name   name,
   common_name       name,
   fish_species      name,
   max_size          DECIMAL (5,2)
   food_preference   food,
   geographic_range  region,
   fish_disposition  temperament,
   fish_activity     day_shift
)
CREATE MODULE sell_item
   LANGUAGE SQL
   SCHEMA catalog1.schema2.
   <declarations>
   <encapsulated procedures>
   <encapsulated functions>
   <other components of the module>
END MODULE;
```

Both these items are schema items, having a definition that can be recovered from our catalog and schema. In addition to these schema objects, SQL-3 also allows SQL routines (procedures and functions) and packages to also be declared as schema objects and, therefore, also be persistently stored in the database. The SQL-3 BNF for the schema procedure routines is as follows:

```
<schema routine> ::=
        <schema procedure>
    |   <schema function>
    |   <schema iterative routine>
  <schema procedure> ::=
     CREATE <SQL-invoked procedure>
  <SQL-invoked procedure> ::=
     PROCEDURE <routine name>
       <SQL parameter declaration list>
       [ <language clause> ]
       [ SPECIFIC <specific name> ]
       [ DYNAMIC RESULT SETS <maximum dynamic result sets> ]
       <routine body>
```

The SQL-3 BNF for the schema function routine is:

```
<schema function> ::=
      CREATE <SQL-invoked function>
  <SQL-invoked function> ::=
     FUNCTION <routine name>
       <SQL parameter declaration list>
       <returns clause>
       [ <language clause> ]
       [ SPECIFIC <specific name> ]
       <routine body>
```

These objects are persistent, because they have a specification, which is visible inside the database schema. This, however, is only part of the specification and the definition of persistence. To be persistent, the routines or modules must also be stored in the database nonvolatile storage subsystem, retrievable through client code having paths to the appropriate database, catalog, and schema to locate the persistent stored object.

So, the definition of persistence in SQL-3 has changed from that of SQL-92. Not only can base tables be persistent, but so can modules, procedures, and routines. These extensions allow SQL-3 to implement application-specific data types, routines, and programs (modules), making them durable and accessible through the database system's access mechanisms.

ADT Persistence

In an SQL-3 table, a persistent item must first exist in the database's catalog and schema metadata structures. That item must have a stored specification describing its structure and place within the database. The database can access and use this information to retrieve information from the database and interpret this information in the appropriate formats. The stored schema data are used to find an instance of an abstract data type's functions or procedures to receive a call or to retrieve and run a persistent stored schema module, procedure, or function (see Figure 8.2.).

An SQL database consists of the following components:

- An SQL environment (the database)
- A set of catalogs for users
- A set of schemas for these catalogs, describing the structure of the stored database
- A description of database tables
- A description of all defined domains
- A description of SQL-invoked function descriptions
- A set of SQL-invoked procedure definitions
- A set of SQL server module definitions
- Descriptions of SQL client modules and client procedures (possibly)

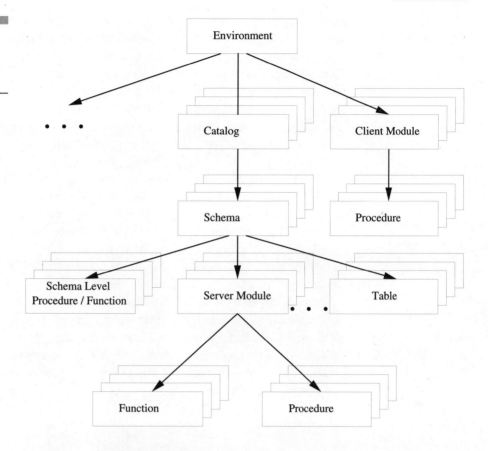

Figure 8.2

SQL database environment components.

Missing from this description are the abstract data types. Abstract data types, as described earlier, are created using the CREATE AB-STRACT DATA TYPE statement:

```
<abstract data type definition> ::=
     CREATE <abstract data type body>

  <abstract data type body> ::=
     TYPE
          <abstract data type name>
     [ <subtype clause> ]
     [ <constructor option> ]
     [ <member list> ]
     [ <type default> ]
```

This statement creates a schema description for an abstract data type. The abstract data type can then be recovered and used in the definition of attributes of an SQL table, in defining the type of a SQL variable or a user program variable. Missing from this form of the CREATE statement is a definition of how such an item becomes or can become persistent. An SQL variable or temporary structure cannot become persistent. An abstract data type is similar to a variable or temporary data structure. When it is instantiated, a unique instance of the abstract data type's description is created and populated with values based on the description in its constructor function. This instance, however, is not persistent. When the program or code segment that created this instance completes execution and exits the computer system, the abstract data type's instance is also removed from the system and its values are lost.

For an abstract data type to become persistent, it must be associated with an SQL-persistent base table. The abstract data type's instance must be stored as values of columns in the persistent base table. This is accomplished by defining a column of the base table as the same type as the abstract data type. Then you use the SQL INSERT or SQL UPDATE statements to place values for this abstract data type instance in the persistent table's storage. When an abstract data type is first created with its constructor function, the abstract data type is transient (temporary). The abstract data type only becomes persistent when the instance is placed into the persistent base table using the appropriate SQL storage statements. Until this occurs, the abstract data type instances are similar to the SQL temporary tables:

```
CREATE TYPE fish (
        scientific_name    VARCHAR(40),
        common_name        VARCHAR(30),
        fish_species       VARCHAR(20),
        max_size           DECIMAL (5,2),
        body_type          VARCHAR(30)
    )
```

For example, you can create an abstract data type fish as defined above and then create a persistent base table, marine_fish, as follows:

```
CREATE TABLE marine_fish
        (m_fish            fish,
         food_preference   VARCHAR(20) ARRAY(5),
         geographic_range  VARCHAR(20) ARRAY(5),
         fish_disposition  temperament,
         fish_activity     day_shift
    )
```

You can then create an instance of fish, where the marine_fish table has as a component the abstract data type fish—for example, a lionfish:

```
DECLARE :F fish;
   BEGIN
      NEW    :F;
      SET    :F.scientific_name = 'Pterois volitans';
      SET    :F.common_name = 'Lion fish';
      SET    :F.fish_species = 'Pterois';
      SET    :F.max_size = 14;
      SET    :F.body_type = 'Fusiform';
      RETURN :F;
   END;
```

The code segment above results in an instance of the fish abstract data type, which is transient (temporary). This fish instance becomes persistent only when you issue an SQL INSERT statement to place it into the table marine_fish.

```
INSERT INTO marine_fish VALUES
   (F, 'live', ARRAY['Red Sea', 'Indo-Pacific'], 'placid',
       'nocturnal');
```

The INSERT statement places the values for the marine_fish lionfish into the table marine_fish. The value is now persistent and will survive beyond the scope of the code segment that just created it. If you issued a SELECT statement looking for the scientific name of the lionfish, this value can be retrieved:

```
SELECT marine_fish..scientific_name FROM marine_fish
   WHERE marine_fish..common_name = 'Lion fish';
```

Once the abstract data type has been placed into persistent storage, it can only be altered or removed through the action of another SQL data manipulation statement. For example, if you find out that the lionfish is actually not placid but aggressive and you need to change this value, then you need to issue an SQL UPDATE statement:

```
UPDATE marine_fish SET fish_disposition = 'aggressive'
   WHERE m_fish..common_name = 'Lion fish';
```

Or, if you find out that there are no more lionfish alive on the planet and you need to remove them from the database, you need to use the SQL DELETE statement:

```
DELETE FROM marine_fish SET fish_disposition = 'aggressive'
   WHERE m_fish..common_name = 'Lion fish';
```

You can't simply remove the instance of the fish abstract data type from the table `marine_fish`. To remove an instance of the abstract data type, you need to use the UPDATE statement to place a new instance in place of the old instance or use the DELETE statement to remove the entire tuple (row) from the `marine_fish` table.

Summary

Without persistence of information, a database would be useless. Persistence, as defined for an SQL database system, has a specific meaning. To be persistent, data must be defined within the context of a persistent base table, defined in the schema of the database, and stored in the table's structure on nonvolatile storage. Abstract data types not defined or instantiated in the confines of a persistent base table are temporary program-scoped data types. For an abstract data type's instance to become persistent, the abstract data type must be used to define an attribute of a persistent base table, and the instance must be placed into the persistent base table using an SQL INSERT or SQL UPDATE statement.

SQL-3 adds to the classic SQL concept of table persistence by adding persistent stored modules, procedures, and functions. As with the persistent stored table, a persistent stored module, procedure, or function exists beyond the scope of the program, or SQL session, that defined it. To retrieve a persistent stored module, procedure, or function requires a call to the stored element, and must be accompanied by the calling session or program with a path to the schema location for the module, procedure, or function. More details of persistent stored modules, procedures, and functions will be covered in Chapter 12.

CHAPTER 9

Collection Types

Introduction

A database is used to store information for future reference and use. The data in the database are organized into collections of similar information. In an SQL-3 database, these collections are formed into tables, where each row of a table has the same organization, structure, and meaning as every other row in the same table. Organization permits the examination and interpretation of information in more meaningful ways. Collections can take on a variety of forms (e.g., a collection of cars, a list of cars, a sorted list of cars, and so on). In everyday life, we use collections and repositories designed to hold these collections (e.g., a bag of groceries, a case of soda, a bushel of clams). All these collections have two things in common. First, they are encased or collected into some structure (the bag, the case, the bushel). Second, there are the items being collected (the groceries, the soda, the clams). Each of the collections is grouping items of a similar type. The same is true in SQL. An SQL table is a collection of rows. The rows are of the same type. They may not hold the same values, but they are of the same type. As you will see, collections form the basis for the SQL table structure and form the foundation where SQL data manipulations are performed.

Collections of ADTs

Since so much time has been spent up to this point talking about the importance of the abstract data type, it is important to begin the discussion of collections in SQL-3 by focusing on collections of abstract data types. A collection of abstract data types can be constructed using the table. For example, to get a collection of the abstract data type fish, you can form a table consisting simply of instances of the fish abstract data type:

```
CREATE TYPE fish (
      scientific_name    VARCHAR(40),
      common_name        VARCHAR(30),
      fish_species       VARCHAR(20),
      max_size           DECIMAL (5,2),
      body_type          VARCHAR(30)
)

CREATE TABLE fishes ( f_fishfish);
```

This declaration forms a table consisting of a collection of fish defined using the abstract data type `fish`. This method of construction gives a simple means to model collections of abstract data types using the table as the repository for the items of the collection. The table can also be used to model different types of collections. For example, an ordered collection can be formed using the ORDER BY statement to extract items from one table and insert them in order in another table.

In this structure, there are many opportunities to construct a variety of collections. Subtypes in a table can be used to better model subcollections. For example, the aquarium database requires a means to monitor the accounts of customers and suppliers, so the application can manage the financial aspects of the enterprise. Since the enterprise has worldwide customers and suppliers, you need to be able to differentiate between a variety of currencies and different types of addresses from different countries. First, you define abstract data types with different implementations to support the different currency and address styles:

```
CREATE TYPE money
    (PRIVATE value DECIMAL(6,2),
        FUNCTION us_dollar
        FUNCTION cnd_dollar
        FUNCTION Mex_peso
        FUNCTION Caribbean_currency
            .
            .
            .
);

CREATE TYPE address
    (PRIVATE      <declarations for attributes>);
        FUNCTION us_address
        FUNCTION cnd_address
        FUNCTION Mex_address
        FUNCTION Caribbean_address
            .
            .
            .
);
```

You can then use these abstract data types to construct a table, accounts, as follows:

```
CREATE TABLE accounts
    (account_num        INTEGER,
     account_name       name,
     account_address    address,
     account_type       VARCHAR(6),
     account_balance    money
    );
```

By using this table and the embedded abstract data types, you can model different types of accounts as either sales or orders for different countries. The table allows you to have an instance of a different abstract data type (subtype) in each row of the table. The subtypes are used to capture the extended meanings of the abstract data types. One issue with this approach to supporting type extents is that subcollections must be specified in queries to extract the appropriate subtype. For example, if you want to select all the orders for supplies that have been placed in the Cayman islands, you need to specify the type of one of the two attributes supporting subtypes to specify either Cayman dollars or Cayman address:

```
SELECT account_num, account_name, balance
FROM accounts
WHERE account_type = 'order'
AND TYPE(account_balance) IN (Cayman_dollar)
AND TYPE(account_address) IN (Cayman_address);
```

In SQL-3, a second option to simulate extents is to use multiple subtables formed into explicit collections of the same subtype. The basic idea is that if there must be multiple subtypes to be managed, and you want to make the queries simpler at the cost of additional tables, you can form a new table under a base table, which will have specializations for each of the subtypes. Each of the tables formed as subtables under the base table will have a property indicating that each row of the table has an instance of the same abstract data type. Instances of subtypes are in separate tables, meaning that subcollections are directly expressed as subtables.

In the example for the aquarium orders and sales accounts, instead of having one table, accounts, you form multiple subtables under the basic accounts table, with the restriction that all the abstract data types found in each table will be uniform. For example, you will not find Cayman dollars mixed with U.S. dollars in the same table:

```
CREATE TABLE accounts
    (account_num        INTEGER,
     account_name       name,
     account_address    address
    CHECK (NOT TYPE (account_address) IN (US_address,
         Cayman_address, . . .),
     account_type       VARCHAR(6),
     account_balance    money
    CHECK (NOT TYPE (account_balance) IN (US_dollar,
         Cayman_dollar, . . .);
```

This creates a table, accounts, which has the same structure as before, except it now checks to make sure that types are not included and placed into specialized tables with the subtypes. Then, you create the subtables under this base table as follows:

```
CREATE TABLE us_accounts UNDER accounts
    ((CHECK (TYPE (account_address) IN (US_address)),
     (CHECK (TYPE (account_balance) IN (US_dollar))));
            .
            .
            .
    <other create table on other money and address types>
            .
            .
CREATE TABLE Cayman_accounts UNDER accounts
    ((CHECK (TYPE (account_address) IN (Cayman_address)),
     (CHECK (TYPE (account_balance) IN (Cayman_dollar))));
```

These distinct tables can now be accessed as any other SQL table through the SELECT statement and its variants. For example, to select only the orders generated from suppliers in the Cayman Islands, you can generate the following query:

```
SELECT account_num, account_name, balance
FROM Cayman_accounts
WHERE account_type = 'order';
```

You can see that we removed the need to determine the type of the abstract data type attributes during the query. This is not necessary, since all the abstract data types in this table are, by definition, the two types you want: Cayman_addresses and Cayman_dollars. The difference is that if you want to look for both Cayman and U.S. dollar accounts, you can do this in one query in the former case. In this case, however, you need to generate two queries—one to extract the Cayman accounts and the other to extract the U.S. accounts:

```
SELECT account_num, account_name, balance
FROM US_accounts
WHERE account_type = 'order';
```

If you want these results in one table, you need to coerce the types of the abstract data types and UNION the new temporary table results together. You will see later on in this chapter how the specialized collection types aid in modeling extents and collections.

Row Type

The row data type was first introduced in Chapter 4. The row data type provides a structure for refining attribute definitions (Figure 9.1). For example, you can define a row type for name, which includes a first, middle, and last component for a person's name. The row data type's specification is as follows:

```
<row type> ::=
    ROW <row type body>
<row type body> ::=
    <left paren>
      <field definition> [ { <comma> <field definition> }... ]
    <right paren>
<field definition> ::=
    <field name> { <data type> | <domain name> }
    [ <collate clause> ]
<field name> ::= <identifier>
<domain name> ::= <schema qualified name>
```

From the BNF specification for the row type, you can see that to define an attribute of a table as a row type requires the keyword ROW, followed by an open parenthesis and the definition of the row, using field name and data type pairs, closed with a right parenthesis. In the example above, to define the name attribute as a row you can use the following specification:

```
Name   ROW( first    VARCHAR(20),
             middle   CHAR(1),
             last     VARCHAR(20))
```

This definition can then be used to define an attribute in the construction of a table, such as the accounts table:

```
CREATE TABLE accounts
     (account_num       INTEGER,
      account_name      ROW( first        VARCHAR(20),
                        middle       CHAR(1),
                        last      VARCHAR(20)),
      account_address   address,
      account_type      VARCHAR(6),
      account_balance   money
      );
```

In this example, the account name is assumed to be a person's name, with a first name, middle initial, and last name. To insert an item into the row requires a nested structure of parentheses, which includes inner

Table A

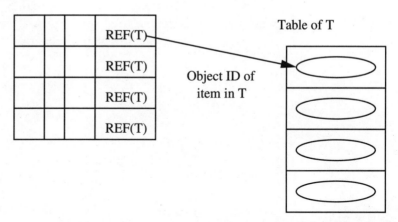

parentheses, where rows are found in the table. For example, to insert an item into the accounts table defined above, you use the following form of the INSERT statement:

```
INSERT INTO accounts VALUES( 1005, ('Thom', 'J.', 'Thumb'),
                  . . . );
```

The row values are inserted in the statement using parentheses as the boundaries for the data written in the row.

Rows can be nested (rows within rows). The row data type can be used anywhere that a predefined data type can be used: as instances of rows in base tables, as rows in a view table, or as rows in a query result. Type checking for the row data type is performed using structural equivalence. To be equivalent, the number of fields and the data type of the corresponding fields in the two rows being compared must be the same.

Named

Row types do not need to be unnamed. The row defined above in the accounts table was an unnamed row type. That is, it did not have a name associated with it. The named row type is a user-defined data type with a nonencapsulated internal structure. The fields of the structure are readily available to any SQL statements that have access to the table encasing the named row. This characteristic of named rows is different from the abstract data type's encapsulation, which permits hiding internal attributes from direct access by external operations. The named row allows a table to take on a non-normal form. The equivalence of two named rows is determined through structural equivalence. For example, you can create a row type name using the CREATE ROW TYPE statement:

```
CREATE ROW TYPE name_t ( first     VARCHAR(20),
                         middle    CHAR(1),
                         last      VARCHAR(20)
                       );
```

You can then use this named row type to create the table accounts as previously:

```
CREATE TABLE accounts
      (account_num       INTEGER,
       account_name      name_t,
       account_address   address,
       account_type      VARCHAR(6),
       account_balance   money
      );
```

The difference between this definition and the unnamed row type is that you do not need to include all the fields of the named row type. The named row can be used to define the entire row in a table or an attribute in a table.

Reference Types

Another important feature of SQL-3 is the reference type. A reference type is a means through which an instance of another type can be referenced (addressed) in a table or expression (Figure 9.2). References can be thought of as a way that a data item, row type, or abstract data type can be located. For example, in the definition for the accounts, you can replace the name with a reference to the customer or supplier records in another relation or as a standalone instance:

```
CREATE ROW TYPE account_t (
      account_num       INTEGER,
      account_name      REF(name_t),
      account_address   address,
      account_type      VARCHAR(6),
      account_balance   money
      );
```

Figure 9.2

Reference type
structure.

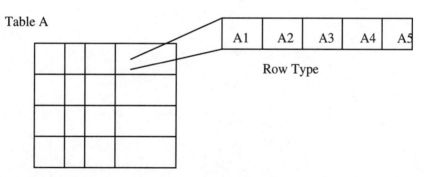

Table A

In this example, the `account_name` is not the row type; instead, it is a reference to an instance of the `name_t` type.

Reference types do not have the same semantic meaning as referential constraints. Referential constraints specify inclusion dependencies. For example, a constraint may indicate that an item cannot be null or that it must be within some range of values. Reference types have no concept of strong typing.

A reference type can be scoped. For example, using the row type `account_t`, you can form a table:

```
CREATE TABLE account OF account_t (
    PRIMARY KEY account_num,
    SCOPE FOR account_name IS name_t
);
```

This table indicates that the scope of the `account_name` is the `name_t` type reference in the `account_t` row type.

Access to the referenced table is limited to the top row in tables. Reference values never change as long as the corresponding tuple exists. The values of references are not reused, since they represent a unique instance of the referenced item. The reference values are unique in the database's catalog.

The reference values are obtained by using the REF operator. For example, `account_name` is of type `REF(name_t)`, indicating that the value for `account_name` is to be a reference value to an instance of `name_t`. Reference values can be materialized in an explicit column. For example, if you are defining a row type, `employee_t`, to refer to an instance of `employee_t`, a definition of this employee, and to other instances of `employee_t` for the employee's manager, you can use reference types to define these.

```
CREATE ROW TYPE employee_t(
        employee_id        REF(employee_t),
        employee_name      name,
        employee_address   address,
        employee_salary    money,
           .
           .
           .
        employee_image     BLOB(1M),
        employee_manager   REF(employee_t)
)
```

This can then be used to create a table of employees, as follows:

```
CREATE TABLE employees of TYPE employee_t(
    SCOPE FOR employee_manager IS employees,
    VALUES FOR employee_id ARE SYSYTEM GENERATED)
```

This creates a table of type `employee_t`, for reference by the employee's manager, from the table of employees and the values for references to the employee, generated by the system upon instantiation of an employee. This table can then be used to generate queries and to display results:

```
SELECT REF ROW e
FROM employees e
WHERE employee_name = 'Thomas T. Thumb';
```

This query returns the reference to the employee whose name is Thomas T. Thumb.

Reference types can be used in other SQL statements also. For example, you may want to use a reference value to help in locating a tuple to update:

```
UPDATE employees e
SET salary = salary + (salary * .10)
WHERE &ROW e = ( SELECT manager
                 FROM employees
                 WHERE name = 'jacques Cousteau');
```

Set Type

SQL-3 has proposed a number of extended collection types. These types allow the database designer to group database items into collections, which, in the future, may better support queries over the stored data

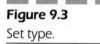

Figure 9.3

Set type.

Table A

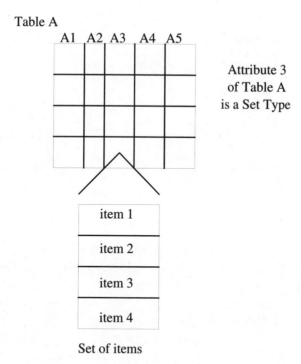

Attribute 3
of Table A
is a Set Type

Set of items

items. The proposed set data type facilitates grouping a collection of related instances of the same data type into a single data structure, which
has no duplicates (Figure 9.3). For example, you can have a collection of
fish disease symptoms, a collection of geographical regions where this
fish can be found, or a collection of phone numbers for a specific customer or supplier in the aquarium database. The set data type provides
a means to collect similar elements for added semantic richness.

As an example, look at the fish data types, a new data type, and table
for diseases. It is common for a marine fish to be found in more than
one geographical region. A grouper, for example, may be found in the
Caribbean, the waters off Bermuda, and the Baja Sea. Without the collection type, you may need to construct a separate table, which maintains this information through relationships formed using foreign keys.
With the set data type you can easily group similar items in a way that
enhances the usefulness and processing of queries on the database:

```
CREATE TABLE marine_fish_disease (
    scientific_name    name,
    common_name        name,
    root_cause         VARCHAR (15),
```

```
       symptoms           SET(VARCHAR(20)),
       affected_area      VARCHAR (15),
       mortality_rate     DECIMAL (5,2),
       treatment          SET(VARCHAR (20)),
       t_concentration    SET(DECIMAL (8,4))
)
```

You can then use this to have an entry for the vibrio anguillarum infection, as follows:

```
NULL, vibrio infection, vibrio anguillarum bacteria,
SET('skin hemorrage', 'inflamed fin edges', inflamed anal area',
'bloody fin edges', bloody anal area'), 'skin', 20.00,
SET('Copper Sulfate', 'Zinc sulfate', 'aureomycin',
'streptomycin'),
SET(0.25, 4.00, .015, .020)
```

This example shows how to use three set data types: the first contains the set of possible symptoms associated with this disease, the second contains the collection of treatments in order of importance, and the third, t_concentration, indicates the concentration of the treatments in grams per liter of water.

List Type

The proposed list collection data type is similar to the set collection data type in that it allows for organizing and holding items with the same data type. The main difference between the two collection types is that the list implies that an order exists and is enforced over the collection. Remember that set only had the concept that the collection can have no duplicates. An example of a good use for the list data type is with the employee table of our database. You can add an attribute in the employee table to hold a list of the children of an employee. This specification assumes that the abstract data type, person, has been previously defined. The children are represented by a list of person instances ordered by the primary key of the listed items. You can use the name, age, or placement in the list as the ordering mechanism:

```
CREATE TABLE employees (
    emp_id            INTEGER
       CONSTRAINT employees_emp_id_pk PRIMARY KEY,
    emp_title         name,
    emp_last_name     name
       CONSTRAINT customers_cust_last_name_not_null NOT NULL,
```

```
      emp_first_name  name
         CONSTRAINT customers_cust_first_name_not_null NOT NULL,
      emp_address     CHARACTER VARYING (30),
      emp_city        CHARACTER VARYING (20),
      emp_state       CHARACTER (2),
      emp_zip         CHARACTER VARYING (9),
      emp_phone       SET(CHARACTER (10)),
      emp_children    LIST(person),
      emp_start_date  TIMESTAMP,
      emp_pay_rate    DECIMAL (7,2)
      emp_com_rate    DECIMAL (5,2)
   )
```

You can then use this specification to store the instances of an employee's children as a list within the employee's record. This alleviates the need for a second table consisting of the children linked to their parents' table instance through a foreign key.

Multiset Type

The proposed multiset data type defines the basic concept of what a table is. That is, the multiset is defined as a collection of rows, where each of the rows has the same structure as all other rows in the set. The difference from the table definition is that the multiset allows for duplicate rows within the set. The multiset is defined using the keyword, MULTISET, followed by braces, which encase the set of items forming the multiset:

```
   Suppliers   MULTISET{suppliers_t},
```

The difference between the list and set types is that multiset allows this collection to contain duplicate items.

Collection Type Constructors

The collection types set, list, and multiset, consist of collections of elements. The elements that form a single item in the collection can be of any other type (e.g., any of the built-in basic types, the row types, abstract data types, or other collection types). The collection data type, as with the abstract data type and row types, can be used anywhere a predefined data type can be used. For a collection type to become persistent, it must, by definition, be placed in a persistent table. Collections cannot stand on their own, but are used as part of the rich data typing scheme in the new SQL database language.

Collections do not necessarily have to be statically derived. A collection type can be constructed using a query, just as many other temporary tables or views can be constructed using a query. SQL-3 allows queries to be written over these nested structures, as well as constructing the instances of these structures.

In the previous sections, you saw the basic form of the collection types:

```
collection type (<element list>)
```

Two examples are as follows:

```
SET ('red', 'blue', 'green', 'yellow')

LIST ('Amanda', 'Barbra', 'Catherine', . . .)
```

This, however, does not need to be the only way to perform and realize these collections. You can use an alternative form:

```
collection type (<expression>)
```

The expression can be any valid SQL expression, which results in the collection materialization in the database:

```
CREATE TABLE . . .
    .
    .
    caribbean_bat_fish    SET (SELECT m.common_name
                               FROM marine_fish m
                               WHERE m.common_name LIKE 'bat');
    )
```

This statement results in an attribute of this table, caribbean_bat_fish, which is constructed from the marine_fish table using an SQL SELECT statement to determine what the contents of this attribute will be. In this example, this attribute consists of a set of common names for Caribbean fish, with common names that have as part of their structure the term bat—for example, silver batfish, round_faced batfish, narrow_banded batfish, long-finned batfish, and so on.

The collection types themselves, once they exist within a table, can be treated as a subtable during access. For example, you can write a statement that looks for the diagnosis of diseases that have a skin condition in common:

```
SELECT m.scientific_name, m.common_name
    FROM marine_fish_disease m
    WHERE 'skin hemorage' IN (SELECT * FROM TABLE (m.symptoms) c);
```

This SELECT statement uses the set structure as if it were a table embedded in the main table. The result of this query is a list of diseases, with both the scientific name and the common name. The one thing in common for all these diseases is that they list, as one of their symptoms, skin hemorrhages.

Collection Type Manipulation

Collections, as with other extended data types in the SQL-3 language, require additional semantics to define what a user can do when manipulating these new data types and what the result will be. For example, how do you extract a piece of information from a multiset of rows, from a list, or from a set? How do these accesses differ in structure and operation from each other, or do they even differ? To answer these and other questions about how you can use collection types, look at the following two tables formed for the examples that follow:

```
CREATE TABLE marine_fish (
    Id                 INTEGER PRIMARY KEY,
    scientific_name    ROW( family      VARCHAR(15)
                            species     VARCHAR(15)
                       ),
    common_name        VARCHAR(20),
    max_size           DECIMAL (5,2)
    food_preference    LIST( food_t ),
    geographic_range   SET( habitats ),
    fish_disposition   temperment,
    fish_activity      activity_t
)

CREATE TABLE tank_displays (
    design_id          INTEGER PRIMARY KEY,
    design_type        VARCHAR(25),
    designer           INTEGER REFERENCES employee,
```

```
setup              TABLE (
                       variation_id   INTEGER,
                       design_name    VARCHAR(20),
                       view           BLOB(1M),
                       fish_t         SET(common_name),
                       invert_t       SET(common_name),
                       plant_t        SET(common_name))
                   )
```

These two SQL-3 tables can hold instances of marine fish representations and marine fish display tank designs. These tables can then be used by the aquarium applications and ad hoc query writers to extract information about marine fish and marine display tank setups. The marine fish table is composed of a row type, two SQL-3 collection types, a set type, and a list type. The marine fish tank display table consists of an embedded table (multiset of rows) and three set collection types, which are further embedded in the nested table. The embedded set types represent the marine fish in a tank, the marine plants, and the marine invertebrates found in a particular marine aquarium display tank. Using collection types allows for a more intuitive way of organizing information in a database; it models the real-world situation better.

Collection Transformations

Collection types can be transformed into constructed temporary tables through embedded SELECT statements and the application of the keyword TABLE over the queried collection. Collection types can be viewed as subtables for the purpose of querying their contents (Figure 9.4). The idea behind a collection query is to form a collection-derived table using the format shown in the BNF below. Such a query is similar to the view defined in the SQL-2 database language:

```
<collection derived table> ::=
    TABLE <left paren> <query expression> <right paren>
```

Additional qualifications can be added to the query expression if refinement is necessary. For example, using the optional "with" clauses to specify ordinalitypresents a more semantic meaning to the requester.

An example of such a collection transformation is described next in generating a query with the marine fish table. Within the marine fish table described above, you can generate a query to find all the marine fish located in more than three regions of the world. This query uses a

Figure 9.4

Nested collection types as tables embedded in a base table.

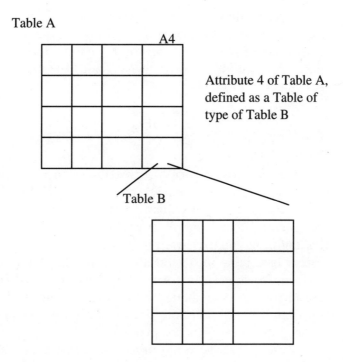

Table A

A4

Attribute 4 of Table A,
defined as a Table of
type of Table B

Table B

collection-derived table to extract the number of regions from the collection attribute, `geographic_range`, embedded within the `marine_fish` table:

```
SELECT common_name
    FROM marine_fish m
    WHERE 3 < (SELECT count (*) FROM TABLE ( m.geographic_range ) )
```

In this example, the embedded set collection type contains all the regions where a given fish is found and is treated as an embedded table. You want to ascertain from this embedded table the many separate geographical regions where a particular fish is found. To do this you simply need to know how many tuples are in the embedded collection subtable. The portion of the SELECT statement that performs this translation is the substatement, `TABLE (m.geographic_range)`, which replaces the normal `<table_name>` in a standard SQL SELECT statement. So, instead of saying `SELECT * FROM table_name`, you use the keyword `TABLE` to indicate an embedded table. This notation treats the set collection as a table, allowing querying in the same way that any base table would be accessed. Another feature of the SQL language in this statement is the aggregate function count, which returns a count of the number of elements (rows) found in this table that meet the condition being asked for. In this case, you have not added any additional conditions; you are just looking to find out how many items are in the set that meet your needs.

Collection Type as Query Return

You may want to return information from a query or subquery in the form of a collection type. The collections can also be viewed as separate structures by retrieving them from the repository where they have been persistently stored and placing these items in some temporary structure. For example, you may want to move a set of phone numbers from a persistent base table into a variable created as a set. Using the method described above, sets of information can be retrieved from the database to use in user code segments or in more complex SQL structures, such as procedures, functions, or triggers, simply by copying the result of the query into the temporary structure.

To use this feature requires some additional SQL query statement, syntax, and semantics. In particular, you use the additional keyword ITEM to form a multiset of returned items. Remember that a multiset is a collection of syntactically equivalent rows, which can have duplicates. Therefore, an SQL statement, which selects some item from one table into a temporary table, is actually forming a multiset collection of the selected items; that is, it is constructing a new table. As an example, if you want to determine the sizes of fish from the family "chaetodontidae" (butterfly fish) and construct a specific marine fish display tank for fish that will not be too big for the tank, you can write the following query statement:

```
SELECT ITEM m.common_name
   FROM marine_fish m
   WHERE m..family='chaetodontidae'
   AND m.max_size < 10;
```

This query results in the formation of a multiset of rows consisting of the common names for the butterfly fish from the family "chaetodontidae," that do not grow larger than ten inches. The resulting multiset can be defined structurally as follows:

```
MULTISET (VARCHAR(20))
```

This query permits duplicates, if some should exist in the collection, since a multiset does not exclude duplicates as part of its fundamental definition. In this example, however, it is highly unlikely that two fish will have the same common name. Therefore, you can expect this query to return the equivalent of a set, which has no duplicates.

If duplicates are specifically not wanted, you can refine this query to form a set collection as the returned structure, instead of a multiset, which does not allow for duplicates to be part of the structure:

```
SELECT DISTINCT ITEM m.common_name
   FROM marine_fish m
   WHERE m..family='chaetodontidae'
   AND m.max_size < 10;
```

The keyword DISTINCT, added to the original query, results in the removal of any duplicates that might occur. The two queries are exactly the same except for this single keyword. The distinction is important, however, when you want to deal with sets instead of multisets. One allows for duplicates; the other does not.

If you need to do some additional processing with the selected items, you can form these results into explicit sets or other programming language- or database-specific structures. Set data types, for example, can be part of a derived table resulting from a view specification. These derived collections are constructed using an embedded query specification. For example, you can create a view, which includes all the fish that do not grow greater than five inches, using this query:

```
CREATE VIEW small_fish (
small_fishes      SET (SELECT * FROM
                        marine_fish m
                        WHERE m.max_size <= 5);
```

You can also use this dynamic construction concept to build a collection type to represent a set structure, which includes all the fish that are not aggressive, as follows:

```
SET (TABLE marine_fishes
    EXCEPT
    (SELECT *
       FROM marine_fish m
       WHERE m.temperment='aggressive') )
```

This example executes by performing a SELECT of all elements in the marine fish table and then excluding all those in the table that have a temperament attribute containing the value "aggressive."

The concept of selecting collection types into other structures will be discussed in more detail in the following section.

Queries over Collections

Very often you want to extract information from stored relations without transforming data into some intermediate form. In the case of collection types that are embedded within tables, it is often useful and necessary to extract information from the embedded multiset, or set, directly into a defined SQL-3 variable—for example, if you want to build a collection of fish from the Cayman Islands' region of the Caribbean. First, you need to declare an SQL variable of type set of `marine_fish` common names to build the new collection. This specification is followed by a selection from the base marine fish table for those fish that have the Cayman Islands as their geographical range. You may want to add marine invertebrates and plants from the same region. These items also require the specification of set collection type SQL variables in the tank display construction process:

```
BEGIN
DECLARE marine_fish_var SET( VARCHAR(20) );
DECLARE marine_invrt_var SET(VARCHAR(20));
DECLARE marine_plant_var SET(VARCHAR(20));

SELECT common_name
   INTO marine_fish_var
   FROM marine_fish m
   WHERE 'Cayman Islands' IN (SELECT * FROM TABLE
(m.geographic_range) g);

SELECT common_name
   INTO marine_invrt_var
   FROM marine_invertabrates i
   WHERE 'Cayman Islands' IN (SELECT * FROM TABLE
(i.geographic_range) g);

SELECT common_name
   INTO marine_plant_var
   FROM marine_plant p
   WHERE 'Cayman Islands' IN (SELECT * FROM TABLE
(p.geographic_range) g);

END;
```

Once data have been extracted and placed in an SQL set variable, you typically want to do something with this information. For example, to extract an item from the new sets, you can use a query such as:

```
SELECT ITEM ROW m
    FROM m IN marine_fish_var
    WHERE m LIKE %angel fish%;
```

This query results in the name of the first fish from the marine fish variable that has as part of its name "angelfish." In addition, with simple forms such as these, you can add quantifiers to select the "*n*th" item meeting the requirement or to extract an item before or after some specific item in the set variable. For example, you know that your set has the following contents:

```
{Emperor angelfish, Koran angelfish, Queen angelfish}
```

The query is:

```
SELECT ITEM ROW m
    FROM m IN marine_fish_var
    WHERE m <= 'Koran angelfish';
```

This query statement results in the selection of the items that come before the given restriction item "Koran angelfish." The query can be additionally restricted with other SQL quantifiers. For example, you can replace the <= restriction operator with another SQL operator, such as a subselect on the marine fish table, qualified with an EXIST clause or any other valid operator.

Extracting Collections

Collections have proven to be a desirable modeling tool in realizing more natural combinations of related information. More natural combinations of information possess multiple distinct instances, which are related to a single item in a table (e.g., the children of an employee, the fry of a particular fish, multiple phone numbers for an employee, and so on). In the original example of marine fish, the information was described using a nested row, list, and set collection:

```
CREATE TABLE marine_fish (
    Id                  INTEGER PRIMARY KEY,
    scientific_name     ROW( family      VARCHAR(15)
                             species      VARCHAR(15)
                        ),
    common_name         VARCHAR(20),
    max_size            DECIMAL (5,2)
    food_preference     LIST( food_t ),
    geographic_range    SET( habitats ),
    fish_disposition    temperment,
    fish_activity       activity_t
)
```

To extract information from this nested structure requires some additional operations, or additional syntax and semantics, in the language. The added operation is referred to as un-nesting and flattening.

Un-nesting

Often, when you are working with nested data types, you need to retrieve the embedded information. In the marine fish table above, you can extract all the scientific names of the marine fish from the snapper family, scientific name Lutjanus, using the following query:

```
SELECT scientific_name
    FROM marine_fish m, TABLE (m.scientific_name) s (snappers)
    WHERE m.scientific_name..family = 'Lutjanus';
```

This query results in a new table, snappers, consisting of two attributes, family and species. The new table only contains the marine fish in the family Lutjanus (commonly known as snappers). The resulting table is the same one (a subset) that existed as a nested table in the original marine_fish table.

As a more interesting example, look at a table representing the employees who work for the aquarium shop. The table consists of two embedded row types, representing employee names and addressess, and two additional nested collection types, representing employee phone numbers and dependents:

```
CREATE TABLE employees (
    id          INTEGER   PRIMARY KEY,
    title       VARCHAR(15),
    name        ROW(last_name     VARCHAR(15),
                    first_name     VARCHAR(15),
                    middle_initl   CHAR(1)
                ),
```

```
        address      ROW(street        VARCHAR (30),
                         city           VARCHAR (20),
                         state          VARCHAR (2),
                         zip            VARCHAR (9)
                     ),
        phone        SET(CHAR (10)),
        start_date   DATE,
        pay_rate     DECIMAL (7,2),
        com_rate     DECIMAL (5,2),
        dependents   LIST(person)
   )
```

To determine the spouse of an employee, you can generate the following query:

```
SELECT spouse
   FROM employees e, TABLE (e.dependents) s (spouse)
   WHERE e.dependents..type ='spouse';
```

In countries other than the United States, such a query could deliver more than one entry in the new table. The resulting table, spouse, consists of all spouses of all employees. The entries in this table are the same type as the dependents, namely of type person.

To determine how many children the employees have (to order the correct number of fish posters for the holidays), you can generate the following query:

```
SELECT COUNT(child)
   FROM employees e, TABLE (e.children) c (child)
   WHERE e.dependents..type='daughter'
   OR e.dependents..type='son';
```

The result is a table called child, which contains an entry for all the employees' children, and a count of the total number of children found in the new table.

You can examine different information about the children by requesting more specific information. For example, if you want to retrieve the children in the order of their birthdays, the following query works:

```
SELECT c.name, c.birthday, e.name..last
   FROM employees e,
   TABLE (e.dependents) WITH ORDINALITY c (name, birthday)
   WHERE e.dependents..type='daughter'
   OR e.dependents..type='son'
   ORDER BY c.birthday;
```

Flattening

Not all queries over collections return multiple rows and multiple attributes in the rows. Many are aimed at returning a single row and a single attribute in a row. It is not as desirable to return a collection type in the case where only a single item is actually returned. It is more desirable to flatten out the collection into a simple item. Queries that operate on nested collections and return a single row and a single column can be flattened using the flattening subquery operator. The BNF is as follows:

```
<flattened subquery>::=
    THE (<query expression>)
```

As an example, you may want an employee's phone number. This works if you know that the employee has a single number, or at least a primary number, which is listed first:

```
THE (SELECT e.phone
    FROM employees e
    WHERE e.name..last = 'Cousteau');
```

The result reduces the operation from returning a row (set data type) to simply a data type. In the example, instead of returning a row containing a set of phone numbers, one phone number is returned. There may be some additional side effects of this operator; however, at this time these are not well defined. For specific effects, please refer to vendor documentation.

More Queries over Collections

Given the `marine_fish` and `tank_display` tables below, you can generate a variety of queries to extract information from these tables that further describes their stored collections.

```
CREATE TABLE marine_fish (
    Id                  INTEGER PRIMARY KEY,
    scientific_name     ROW( family      VARCHAR(15)
                             species     VARCHAR(15)
                        ),
    common_name         VARCHAR(20),
    max_size            DECIMAL (5,2)
    food_preference     LIST( food_t ),
```

```
            geographic_range   SET( habitats ),
            fish_disposition   temperament,
            fish_activity      activity_t
    )

    CREATE TABLE tank_displays (
        design_id          INTEGER PRIMARY KEY,
        design_type        VARCHAR(25),
        designer           INTEGER REFERENCES employee,
        setup              TABLE (
                               variation_id  INTEGER,
                               design_name   VARCHAR(20),
                               view          BLOB(1M),
                               fish_t        SET(common_name),
                               invert_t      SET(common_name),
                               plant_t       SET(common_name))

    )
```

As the first query, you want to find the employee who designed a specific display tank, so that the same employee can do something similar for a wealthy client. The following query can be used:

```
SELECT e.name..last
    FROM employees AS e, tank_designs AS t
    WHERE design_type='Cayman Reef'
    AND t.designer=e.id;
```

You can ask to find the employee and tank display designs and, in addition, get a list of all the designs the employee has constructed for the company:

```
SELECT e.name..last ,
    multiset (SELECT * FROM tank_displays as t
             WHERE e.id = t.designer)
    FROM employees as e;
```

This query examines the tank designs for each employee in the list. If an employee has not generated a design, that employee's name will not show up in the table of employees and designs.

If you have an additional function—for example, a PSM function called "most," which returns the ID of the designer with the most designs—you can alter this query to only display the top designer's name and designs, as follows:

```
SELECT e.name..last ,
    multiset (SELECT * FROM tank_displays as t
             WHERE e.id = most(t.designer)
    FROM employees as e;
```

The effect is to examine only the designers who have constructed the most designs. The result is a single employee name with the multiset describing the designs.

To get information about the employee who designed a Hawaiian Molikini display tank, you can generate the following query:

```
SELECT *
    FROM employees e
        WHERE e.id IN (SELECT * from tank_designs t
            WHERE t.setup..design_name='Hawaiian Molikini');
```

Summary

In this chapter, the extended collection data types were touched on briefly. These data types are important when there is a need to have one attribute contain more than one item. The collection types specified in SQL language are set, list, multiset, and row. The SQL-3 foundation has decided to defer these elements due to unresolved issues. It is anticipated that these data types will ultimately find their way into the standard. Beyond their ability to model a wider range of information structures, these data types will have a useful role in the construction of optimizers for the processing of queries. If collections of abstract data types can be formed into a table, then these can be used to aid information retrieval.

At this time, SQL-3 has included two collection types as part of the base language. One is the varying array type, which allows for a fixed-size collection to be specified. This type can have as its base type any valid SQL type, which implies that it can contain nested tables, rows, abstract data types, or any of the built-in types. What these lack, however, is the flexibility of set, list, and bag, which can grow as needed. VARRAY requires fixing the size of the embedded element, which may hinder growth. It is hoped that this restriction will be revisited.

CHAPTER **10**

Triggers

Introduction

Triggers, as with tables, objects, abstract data types, packages, procedures, and functions are schema objects in an SQL-3 database. These schema objects, however, provide the means for the database to "react" to changes in the database in a variety of ways. For example, you may want to insert a row into a log table in the national marine fisheries database when a marine mammal is sighted or captured by a fisherman. The trigger is a means to perform such an operation in the database without user-supplied procedures or code to "test" the condition of another table or event in the database. This schema object actively performs these checking functions.

Triggers are different from the simple constraints examined earlier. Simple constraints check a condition, either immediately or at the end of a transaction or session. In addition, these conditions are based on checking elements, such as the domain of values for an attribute or collection of attributes within a row or the existence of a referential constraint in another table. These conditions also only occur when a table's specific item is acquired. The trigger is different in that it allows the programmer to add other conditions regarding when to test for some condition and, more importantly, how to react to this condition when it occurs.

Triggers are similar to constraints in SQL-2 in that they react to changes to data, but they are extended to allow for the activation of a trigger based on some external event. The events tested for by a trigger are, at present, restricted in SQL-3. This feature will probably be extended by some vendors to provide even more flexibility to the database programmer.

Triggers have many benefits. The most important benefit is that triggers support improved application development. Since the trigger is stored in the database, the actions performed by the trigger do not need to be coded into all applications. They are tied to the table instead of to each application using the table. Due to the schema location of triggers, they support the global enforcement of business rules. The trigger only needs to be specified and activated once; then it can be used by any application acting on the bound table. In addition to global enforcement of business rules, triggers also support ease of maintenance. Since the triggering action is not found in all the applications acting on the triggered table, a change in business policy only needs to be changed in one place. One final benefit is the uniformity and correctness of consistency and enforcement through a system-controlled facility.

Trigger Definition

A trigger is a named database object, which is implicitly activated on its specified event. Triggers permit development of "active databases," which can react to changes made by applications or ad hoc users. Triggers differ from constraints and standards found in SQL-2-based products, as shown in the following list:

1. Triggers are only activated when a certain "event" or condition, specified within the triggers' condition clause, occurs. The types of conditions or events supported by SQL-3 are insert, delete, and update of columns or tables. Extensions being considered for future versions of SQL include transactional events and other database events, such as transaction initiation, commit, abort, and even mutation of tables. These are not specified in the current version of SQL-3.

2. Triggers do not "prevent" the action or event that activated the trigger; they "test" the condition for which they were designed. If the condition is not valid, the trigger performs no other action. If the condition is valid, the trigger's body (actions) is performed based on the interpretation of the condition.

3. The trigger, upon determining that the condition being tested for is satisfied, performs its intended function. This function could result in the removal of the triggering condition or the performance of some other action. The present trigger specification in SQL-3 does not allow mutation of the triggering table, which would result in the trigger's recursive invocation. Once valid rules for such an outcome can be devised to the satisfaction of the ANSI and ISO database language committees, it is anticipated that this feature will be allowed. You will need to wait at least until SQL-4, or until some vendors provide added features to their implementations.

Triggers fall into one of three major classes; they are related to inserting, deleting, or updating table items (Figure 10.1). The triggered event

Figure 10.1

Trigger types.

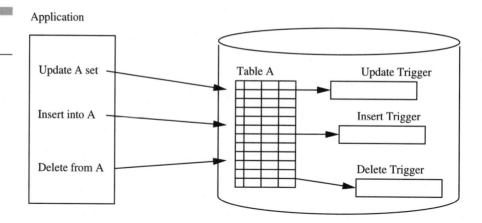

can be scoped to occur only once per statement or for all rows in the table which meet the condition. Triggers can be scoped to occur before the event it is constructed upon or after the event has occurred. In addition, triggers can be set to occur instead of the event that caused their invocation.

Triggers do not need to be isolated in the system. A trigger may cause another trigger to be invoked (Figure 10.2). A string of triggers is said to be "cascading." Cascading triggers must be carefully designed, but should be avoided if possible because of the complexity of maintaining them.

One trigger in particular, which at first appears to be quite useful, is an application that triggers itself. For example, you construct a trigger,

Figure 10.2

Cascading triggers.

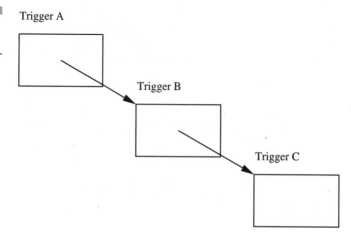

Figure 10.3
Mutating trigger.

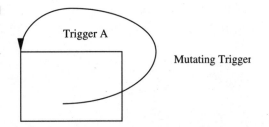

which detects an update to a field, and, because of the update, you want to alter some other field in the same table. The trigger, in essence, calls itself and may do this in an endless loop, depending on the clarity and completeness of the design. These triggers are called *mutating triggers* (Figure 10.3). They cause a mutation of the table that originally invoked the triggered action. Presently, in SQL-3, such mutating triggers are not allowed. These may, however, become useful and may be seen in future versions of the language.

Trigger Creation

Triggers have the general form shown in Figure 10.4 and consist of a trigger name, a triggering event, a trigger granularity specification, a triggering condition, and a triggered action.

Figure 10.4
Trigger structure.

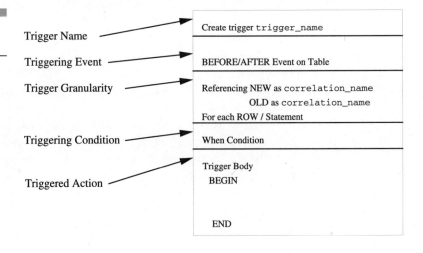

Triggers are written to respond to changes detected in the state of a table. For example, here is a specification for the `marine_fish` table:

```
CREATE TABLE marine_fish (
    scientific_name    name,
    common_name        name,
    fish_species       name,
    max_size           DECIMAL (5,2)
    food_preference    food,
    geographic_range   region,
    fish_disposition   temperament,
    fish_activity      day_shift
)
```

A trigger can be written that responds to adding a new fish species to the table. You increase the count of total species supported in the database and add a log entry into a log table, which is checked later for accuracy:

```
CREATE TRIGGER insert_marine_fish
    AFTER INSERT ON marine_fish
    REFERENCING NEW AS mf

    FOR EACH STATEMENT
        BEGIN
        UPDATE Total_species
            SET count = count + 1
            where fish_species = mf.fish_species;
        INSERT INTO mf_log Values (mf.scientific_name,
                                   mf.common_name,
                                   mf.fish_species, mf.max_size,
                                   mf.food_preference,
                                   mf.geographic_range,
                                   mf.fish_disposition,
                                   mf.fish_activity);
        END;
```

The named trigger, `insert_marine_fish`, responds to the addition of a new fish tuple into the `marine_fish` table by updating the number of fish of the same species in the `total_species` table. The trigger inserts a log tuple into the `mf_log` table for auditing purposes in the future. The trigger's timing is set to respond after the insertion is complete. In addition to the timing of the trigger, this trigger also has another restriction. The trigger only fires once for this condition. If the trigger had inserted multiple tuples, this trigger would react only to the first tuple and ignore all the others. If you want the trigger to respond to multiple insertions, then you need to specify FOR EACH ROW instead of FOR EACH STATEMENT.

The trigger above did not possess all the components possible in a trigger. To illustrate the possible components in a trigger, the specification of a trigger in the SQL-3 standard will be discussed first. The top-level BNF for CREATE TRIGGER is as follows:

```
<trigger definition> ::=
    CREATE TRIGGER <trigger name>
       <trigger action time> <trigger event>
       ON <table name>
          [ REFERENCING <old or new values alias list> ]
       <triggered action>

<trigger name> ::= <schema qualified name>
```

One property of the trigger is the ability to examine the old and new values for a row and column in the named triggering table. To access the old or new values, SQL uses transition variables. These variables permit the specification of how the old and new values are to be referenced in the body of the trigger. The BNF below shows the structure of the syntax for transition variables and correlation names in the trigger's body:

```
<old or new values alias list> ::=
    <old or new values alias>...

<old or new values alias> ::=
        OLD [ ROW ] [ AS ]
            <old values correlation name>
    | NEW [ ROW ] [ AS ]
            <new values correlation name>
    | OLD TABLE [ AS ]
            <old values table alias>
    | NEW TABLE [ AS ]
            <new values table alias>

<old values correlation name> ::= <correlation name>
<new values correlation name> ::= <correlation name>
<old values table alias> ::= <identifier>
<new values table alias> ::= <identifier>
```

An example of the use of transition variables is:

```
CREATE TRIGGER audit
    AFTER UPDATE OF balance ON accounts
    REFERENCING    OLD AS old_value
                   NEW AS new_value
    FOR EACH ROW
    WHEN (new_value.balance < 0)
        IF account_type = 'distributor' THEN INSERT INTO notices . .

        ELSE INSERT INTO invoices . . . . ;
```

In this example, the OLD and NEW values of the accounts are available through the transition variables and the correlation names applied to them. Each component of the BNF above is discussed further in the following sections.

Trigger Events

The first major element of the trigger structure is trigger events. These events fall into only a small subset of possible SQL statements. The allowable events in the present version of the SQL standard are shown in this BNF statement:

```
<trigger event> ::=
      INSERT
    | DELETE
    | UPDATE [ OF <trigger column list> ]

<trigger column list> ::= <column name list>
```

The triggering events are named over the total table or on some subset of the table's columns or rows. Allowable events are insertion, deletion, or update of tuples in a named table.

The triggered event can be named on specific components of the named table. For example, you may want to invoke a trigger only when the quantity on hand is updated. To accomplish this, you use the restriction that the triggering event is an update of the sales table, but only for the attribute quantity_on_hand. This can be shown as follows:

```
CREATE TRIGGER reorder
   AFTER UPDATE OF quantity_on_hand ON sales
   REFERENCING NEW AS nqoh
   FOR EACH ROW
   WHEN (nqoh < min_reorder)
   BEGIN ATOMIC
      INSERT INTO reorder
```

If any other column of the sales table is updated, the trigger is not fired and the triggered action is not performed. This additional property of the trigger gives the programmer the freedom to trigger only the corrective action instead of requiring the trigger to further filter the elements of the triggering table. In this way, the trigger is able to be constructed so that it responds only to desired conditions and not just a similar condition.

In the fish database, you can use such a mechanism to construct a trigger that responds to a 10 percent increase in the supplier's price of fish by adding 10 percent to the retail price charged to customers. In this way, the database can respond to changes from exterior forces. This active database is much more responsive to the needs and demands of on-line transaction processing systems.

Trigger Condition

The trigger condition can be any valid SQL condition. The condition to be met is specified in the WHEN clause of the trigger. The condition is satisfied, and the triggering action follows. The condition does not need to use the named table in its clause. It can reference any other table, object, valid package, function, or procedure in the database to determine validity. The programmer has a wide latitude in devising and generating triggering conditions.

For example, in the fish database, the inventory of clown fish is low, and you want to order additional clown fish, but only if the sales over the last month have been above some reference value. The trigger can be written using the following table description:

```
CREATE TABLE aquatic_organism_stock (
    stock_id           INTEGER,
       CONSTRAINT aquatic_organism_stock_id_pk PRIMARY KEY,
    scientific_name   name
       CONSTRAINT aquatic_organism_name_not_null NOT NULL,
    number_in_stock   INTEGER,
    current_price     price
)

CREATE TABLE sales (
    sale_id            INTEGER
       CONSTRAINT sales_sale_id_pk PRIMARY KEY,
    sale_date         DATE,
    stock_id          INTEGER,
    sale_item_name    name,
    sale_price        price,
    cust_id           INTEGER )
CREATE TABLE orders (
    order_id          INTEGER,
    stock_id          INTEGER,
    item_name         INTEGER,
    num_item          INTEGER
    )
```

The following trigger can be used to perform this function:

```
CREATE TRIGGER order_fish
   AFTER UPDATE ON aquatic_organism_stock
   REFERENCING NEW AS cn
   FOR EACH ROW
   WHEN( cn.number_in_stock < 5
      AND COUNT(SELECT * FROM sales WHERE
               cn.stock_id = sales.stock_id) > 3 )
      INSERT INTO orders VALUES (' ', cn.stock_id,
                                 cn.scientific_name,
                                 (cn.number_in_stock +5);
```

This trigger responds when the number of fish drops below the reference value. Then the trigger checks whether the number of this fish sold over the period of interest is greater than three. If this condition holds, then the fish are reordered. If the condition does not hold, then no reorder is issued. The outcome might be that fish that have not sold well are not reordered, and, in time, there will be no additional stock remaining for this fish.

Trigger Action

When a trigger is fired, the programmer's intention is to perform some predefined action designed to handle the condition being tested. This action can be any valid SQL statement, including SQL procedural statements. The action cannot be an SQL statement that alters the contents of the table that the trigger was written to act upon.

The triggered action is described using the following BNF notation:

```
<triggered action> ::=
    [ FOR EACH { ROW | STATEMENT } ]
      [ WHEN <left paren> <search condition> <right paren> ]
      <triggered SQL statement>

<triggered SQL statement> ::=
      <SQL procedure statement>
    | BEGIN ATOMIC
        { <SQL procedure statement> <semicolon> }...
      END
```

The BNF notation indicates that the triggered action can have multiple granularities. That is, it can act on each row affected by the triggered event, or it can execute only once, no matter how many rows are affected.

```
CREATE TRIGGER new_stock_item
    AFTER INSERT ON aquatic_stock_item
    FOR EACH ROW
        UPDATE audit_stats SET num_items = num_items + 1;

CREATE TRIGGER new_stock_item
    AFTER INSERT ON aquatic_stock_item
    FOR EACH STATEMENT
        UPDATE audit_stats SET num_items = num_items +
                (SELECT COUNT (*) FROM new_stock);
```

One important concept to consider when writing the trigger is the effect it will have on the database set (the set of rows in the subject table) it operates upon. For example, the statement below has an effect on all fish priced below $5.99. These fish will be updated and included in the affected set of tuples for the subject table:

```
UPDATE acquatic_stock_items
    SET price = price + (.1 * price)
    WHERE price < 5.99;
```

The trigger action itself is preceded by an optional conditional clause, which allows the programmer to restrict when the action is to be applied beyond the triggering event.

Trigger Activation

Triggers are activated when the triggering event occurs. As an added feature, you can also apply a time concept to the event. At present, there are two alternatives that can be applied to event timing: before the event occurs or after the event occurs. These alternatives are shown in the following BNF:

```
<trigger action time> ::=
        BEFORE
      | AFTER
```

The BEFORE alternative allows the trigger to block the execution of the event by causing some other action to occur. In essence, you can trap the event before it is applied to the base object. Similarly, the AFTER timing modifier allows the event to occur before the triggered action is performed. These modifiers permit the following six alternative triggering event sequences. In addition to the six combinations, these event combinations can also be modified to occur once for the statement or row affected:

1. BEFORE INSERT—The triggered action is performed before the insert operation is performed on the named table.

2. AFTER INSERT—The triggered action is performed after the insert is applied to the named table.

3. BEFORE DELETE—The triggered action is performed before the deletion of the rows from the named table.

4. AFTER DELETE—The triggered action is performed after the deletion of the rows from the named table.

5. BEFORE UPDATE—The triggered action is performed before the update operation is executed on the named table rows.

6. AFTER UPDATE—The triggered action is performed after the execution of the update operation on the named table rows.

Every event, and consequently every trigger, can be associated with exactly one subject table and exactly one triggering operation. In addition to this restriction, triggers also have additional restrictions based on the event type. For example, no other operation can be applied with the insert event. An UPDATE statement must also enforce referential constraint rules, or a DELETE statement must support the constraint rules on a delete cascade.

Trigger Operation

The trigger is not just a simple SQL statement. The trigger is more like a procedure or function for a persistent stored module. It performs more complex operations under the control of database kernel operations. Underneath the trigger is a set of operations, which trap triggering events and invoke the triggered procedure in very deliberate ways.

Execution Model

The trigger execution model (Figure 10.5) depicts the steps undertaken during the execution of any trigger. The underlying SQL execution engine must trap and test any operations on trigger-bound tables. The operation collects a set of affected rows, which is then used in the trigger execution. Once the set of affected rows is known, the triggering subsystem will process before triggering. Processing includes checking trigger conditions and performing actions defined in the body of the trigger. Once the trigger has been processed, the set of affected rows is applied to the target table. While applying the affected rows to the target table, additional constraints must be checked (e.g., restrict rules, cascade and set null rules, no action, check constraints, and check options). Once all these have been applied, the AFTER triggers can be processed. Again, this includes checking conditions and executing the trigger's body.

Figure 10.5

Trigger execution model.

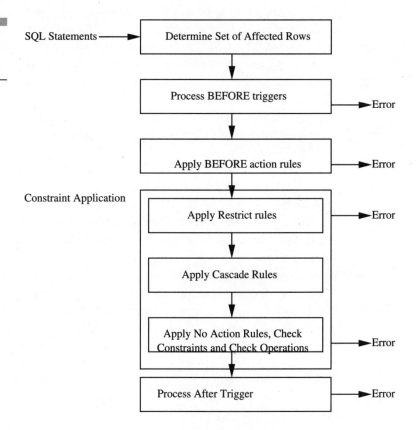

Trigger Activation Time

Trigger activation time specifies when the trigger should be activated. Triggers are activated based on the application of two qualifiers in the triggering statement. The first qualifier is the event being trapped by the trigger. The second qualifier is when, in relation to the trapped event, the body of the trigger is to be processed. These two possibilities are specified before or after the triggering event is applied to the named table. The BEFORE trigger activation time permits the triggering action to be performed before the events are installed on the affected rows of the triggering table. In essence, the BEFORE trigger is an extension to the SQL constraint subsystem. The trigger permits the validation of input data before installation into the constrained table. The BEFORE trigger permits the automatic insertion of audit rows for newly inserted or altered rows. The BEFORE trigger also can be used as a way to cross-reference values in other tables before new information is added or altered in a triggering table.

The BEFORE trigger has some drawbacks, however, when compared with constraints. The triggers are activated before the triggering SQL operation is applied to the database and, therefore, before any integrity constraints are checked. Due to these semantics of the BEFORE trigger, there is no guarantee that database integrity constraints will not be violated by the triggering SQL operation. Because of these properties of the BEFORE trigger, you should not use it for further modifying the database; unwanted side effects and errors may creep into the stored information.

The AFTER trigger, as with the BEFORE trigger, acts upon an affected set of tuples or a table, as defined by the triggering SQL operation. The triggered actions are only activated after the triggering SQL operation is performed on the affected set and after checking all constraints that could be affected. These constraints include actions of referential constraints. Unlike the BEFORE trigger, the AFTER trigger is a piece of application logic that runs in the database every time the specified triggering operation occurs. The AFTER trigger will always see the database in a consistent state, since it is applied only after all constraints have been validated. The trigger action can only occur after all constraints that affect the set are checked. An AFTER trigger, therefore, differs from the BEFORE trigger in that it cannot be used to check alternative conditions before the SQL operation is performed. It can, however, be used to perform follow-on operations, such as an audit trail on an affected set. The AFTER trigger can be used for the performance of operations outside the domain of a transaction operating on the affected set. For example, if a triggering operation, an update of some tuples in a named table, is later undone due to an abort, the triggered action that occurs on some other external table or data structure will not be rolled back later.

Trigger Granularity

Triggers are defined to respond to a specific SQL operation on some pre-defined portion of an affected set. The affected set may be an item within a single tuple, a single tuple, a set of tuples, or an entire table. The affected set, however, is only a part of the determination of the granularity of the trigger. The trigger can be refined to act on only a portion of the affected set derived from the defined SQL event. For example, the trigger can be defined to respond to each row of an affected set, for only one instance of an affected set, or the entire affected table as an aggregate. The keywords to select what should be applied are:

```
FOR EACH ROW or FOR EACH STATEMENT
```

Using FOR EACH ROW will cause the triggered action to be applied to all rows of the affected set, no matter how large or small this set may be. For example, in the following trigger, the affected set is all tuples, where the cost of the item is less than $5:

```
UPDATE sales SET cost = cost + Cost*.1 WHERE cost <5.00;
```

This statement results in an affected set consisting of all items from the sales table that have a cost of less than $5 to be updated. This set of updates causes the following trigger to be fired:

```
CREATE TRIGGER adjust_price
   AFTER UPDATE ON sales
   FOR EACH ROW
   UPDATE stats SET num_itemLT5 = num_itemLT5 + 1;
```

The result is a count of all the items that have been updated in the stats table. The trigger will be fired for all rows of the sales base table that have been updated by the UPDATE statement.

The alternative trigger, using the FOR EACH STATEMENT granularity syntax, results in the stats table being updated only once, no matter how many rows are affected by the triggering SQL update statement:

```
CREATE TRIGGER adjust_price
    AFTER UPDATE ON sales
    FOR EACH STATEMENT
    UPDATE stats SET num_itemLT5 = num_itemLT5 + 1;
```

Because of these differences, you need to be extremely careful of which syntax you use. For example, if you want to know that the UPDATE statement has occurred, and you are not interested in the magnitude of the affected set, then the FOR EACH STATEMENT is the appropriate syntax to use. However, if you are interested in how many items are in the affected set, then the syntax FOR EACH ROW is appropriate. The programmer must also be sure that the triggered action is appropriate for the granularity of the operation. For example, if you simply update some single item in a statistics table when a trigger is activated, the result may be that just the last update to the statistics table is seen. The design of the action to take, based on the set to operate on, is as important as deciding the affected set and what you want to do in response to it. The designer must keep in mind how often the action will be performed. If FOR EACH ROW is chosen, the action of the trigger will be executed once for each row of the affected set. If FOR EACH STATEMENT is used, the action will occur just once for the triggering statement, regardless of the magnitude of the affected set.

Transition Variables

If the set affected by the triggering operation is to be accessed at a finer granularity than simply the entire row, then it is necessary to use transition variables. Transition variables access values for the affected set and determine the trigger's action.

Transition variables are defined for both original and new relation tuple values for the affected set (Figure 10.6). The definition of transition variables uses the following syntax:

```
OLD correlation-name
```

or

```
NEW correlation-name
```

OLD specifies a correlation name, which captures the original state of the row in the affected set from the original relation (the old tuple's values before the triggering SQL operation is applied to the database relation). To use the old tuple values the following trigger structure is used:

```
CREATE TRIGGER REORDER
    AFTER UPDATE OF aquatic_stock_item
    REFERENCING OLD AS old_item
    FOR EACH ROW
    WHEN (old_item.on_hand < 5 )
        BEGIN ATOMIC
            triggering action
        END
```

The statement sequence REFERENCING OLD AS old_item is used to specify how the old values of the affected set are to be referred to in the conditional clause specified in the WHEN statement.

Figure 10.6

New and old
affected sets.

Item	Quantity	Cost
1	3	1.00
2	6	1.50
3	7	2.10
4	4	2.00

Relation A

Triggering Statement

UPDATE A SET Cost = Cost + (Cost *.1) WHERE Quantity < 5;

OLD Affected SET

1	3	1.00
4	4	2.00

NEW Affected SET

1	3	1.10
4	4	2.20

NEW is used to specify a correlation name, which captures the altered state of the rows in the affected set. That is, the new tuples' values, after the triggering SQL operation, have been applied to the database relation. To use the new tuples' values, the REFERENCING NEW AS correlation-name statement is required:

```
CREATE TRIGGER reorder
    AFTER UPDATE OF aquatic_stock
    REFERENCING NEW AS new_item
             OLD AS old_item
    FOR EACH ROW
    WHEN(new_item.qty < max_stocked
       AND old_item.order_pending = 'N')
    BEGIN ATOMIC
          perform trigger action
    END
```

There are some restrictions on using transition variables in a trigger. Transition variables are only supported with the FOR EACH ROW trigger granularity. Transition variables cannot be applied when the FOR EACH STATEMENT syntax is used. In addition, there is also a restriction on what type of transition variable can be applied to the triggering SQL operation. The UPDATE SQL operation can refer to both OLD and NEW transition variables. The INSERT SQL operation can refer only to NEW transition variables. Before the insertion, the affected row did not exist, so the OLD transition variable is undefined. Similarly, the DELETE SQL operation has the restriction that it can only refer to the OLD transition variable, since the affected set only has old values. The NEW transition variable is undefined for the DELETE operation.

Transition Tables

Another form of transition variable is the transition table. Transition tables are used when there is a need to view the totality of the table and affected set. In many cases, aggregates are needed to trigger an operation, not simply a single value. Transition variables over tables are written over the affected sets only, not the entire table. The aggregates, such as MAX, MIN, or AVG, are applied over some column values of the affected set. As with the transition variables, transition tables can specify the new or old affected set's aggregate. The form of the transition table specifying the original state of the set of affected rows is as follows:

```
OLD_TABLE AS correlation-name
```

The transition table variable captures the aggregate state of the table before the triggering SQL operation is applied to the named database table.

As with the old transition table reference, you can also specify and use a new table transition variable. The form of the transition table specifying the altered or new state of the set of affected rows is as follows:

```
NEW_TABLE AS correlation-name
```

The transition table variable captures the aggregate state value of the table after the triggering SQL operation is applied to the named database table. For example, if you want to check the aquatic_stock table for the remaining fish on hand after updating, the following trigger can be written:

```
CREATE TRIGGER reorder
    AFTER UPDATE OF quantity, max_qty_stocked ON aquatic_stock
    REFERENCING NEW_TABLE AS new-table
              NEW AS new-row
    FOR EACH ROW
    WHEN ((SELECT AVG(quantity) FROM new-table) < 5)
    BEGIN ATOMIC
       triggered action
    END
```

This simple example uses the new transition table to examine the remaining quantity of fish on hand in the aquatic_stock table. When the value of the stock is, on average, less than five, the triggering action is undertaken. In this way, you can further restrict how actions are taken, based on aggregated values. The transition table can be applied to triggers with granularity on each row or for each statement.

As with the transition variables, transition tables have restrictions placed upon them. Transition tables can be used in UPDATE statements. Both the NEW and OLD transition tables are supported in this structure. However, the INSERT and UPDATE SQL operations do have restrictions on using transition tables. The UPDATE SQL operation triggers can only use the NEW transition table; the DELETE SQL operation triggers can only use the OLD transition tables. In addition to these restrictions, transition tables can only be used in the read-only mode. A side property of transition tables is that their names (correlation names) take precedence over the names of any other tables with the same unqualified table names that may exist in the database's schema.

Trigger Action

Trigger actions are controlled by an optional trigger action condition or WHEN clause. The triggered action is composed of a set of triggered SQL statements. The form of the sequence is the WHEN clause followed by the triggered action block or statement. The triggered action can be any valid SQL statement except those that can alter any base tables the trigger was written to act on. Such an action is referred to as a *mutating action*. At present, this action is not allowed in the SQL-3 language. As more research is done, and when complete syntax and semantics are possible, such mutations may be allowed, possibly in SQL-4.

As an example of a triggered action, look back at the reorder trigger written to react to changes to the aquatic_stock table:

```
CREATE TRIGGER reorder
   AFTER UPDATE of quantity, max_stocked ON aquatic_stock
   REFERENCING NEW AS new-row
   FOR EACH ROW
   WHEN (new-row.quantity < .25*max_stocked)
   BEGIN ATOMIC
      CALL order(new-row.max_stocked-new-row.quantity,
            new-row.stock_id);
   END
```

This trigger acts by checking whether the quantity of the aquatic stock item, a fish species, has dropped to less than one-quarter of the maximum volume of the number typically kept in stock. When this condition is found, a new order is placed by calling the procedure order, which places a new order.

Trigger Action Condition

The trigger action condition encased in the WHEN clause is used as the last test that must be met for the triggered action to execute. If the WHEN clause is left out, the triggered action always occurs when the trigger is invoked. The WHEN clause is an optional syntax item and therefore can be left out. The specified result uses the trigger granularity clause as the means to determine how to apply the triggered action.

The trigger action condition evaluation frequency is dependent on the chosen trigger's granularity clause. If FOR EACH ROW is chosen, then the trigger action condition is checked once for each row in the trigger's affected set. If the trigger uses the FOR EACH STATEMENT clause, the trigger's action condition is evaluated once, no matter how many tuples are in the affected set of the triggering table.

The major benefit of the added trigger action condition is that it provides for further control in fine-tuning the actions activated on behalf of a trigger. The trigger action condition can be as simple or as complex as is needed to test for both pre- and posttriggering conditions. This added property's trigger can be designed to react to almost any imaginable information event in a database system.

Triggered SQL Statement

Once a trigger has been activated, it acts by executing an SQL statement or some other valid SQL program structure. As described up to this point, a trigger is a schema-level object, which has two major components. The first component is the triggering portion, which defines the table and the event on which the trigger is to activate. This triggering component also includes information about the granularity of the trigger and the scope of the action on the affected set. The second component of the trigger is the triggered action. Based on the action clause, the triggered action performs the desired action on the database or external elements. The action clause can be a simple SQL statement or some other more complex SQL or external structure.

Types of Statements

The triggered action, which follows the triggering event statement and conditions, can be one of many valid SQL-3 statements or structures. In general, any valid SQL-3 statement can be used in the trigger action portion of the SQL-3 trigger. The limitation is that the triggered action cannot be a mutation of the table the trigger is activated upon. The fundamental SQL data manipulation statements, along with any variants, are allowed in trigger action elements. For example, the INSERT, UPDATE, DELETE, or SELECT statements, with any restrictions or qualifiers, are allowed. If transition variables or tables have been defined as part of the trigger, these too can be used in the data manipulation statements as portions of the DML predicates. For example, you have the following trigger:

```
CREATE TRIGGER reorder
    AFTER UPDATE of quantity, max_stocked ON aquatic_stock
    REFERENCING NEW AS new-row
    FOR EACH ROW
    WHEN (new-row.quantity < .25*max_stocked)
    BEGIN ATOMIC
        INSERT INTO order VALUES(new-row.stock_id , new-
                row.item_name, new-row.max_stocked-
                new-row.quantity, new-row.cost_each
            );
    END
```

In this example, the INSERT data manipulation statement encased in an atomic execution block was used. The BEGIN ATOMIC – END structure is a persistent stored module construct, which permits the atomic execution of a block of SQL or extended SQL code.

In addition to supporting any SQL data manipulation statement, trigger actions can also be composed of any SQL control statement (e.g., any collection of valid SQL or PSM statements encased in a BEGIN ... END block). Iteration control statements, such as WHILE and REPEAT, are also supported within a trigger action sequence. Decision sequences using IF ... THEN ... ELSE syntax and exception conditionals are supported.

There are some limitations, however. The trigger action cannot include an SQL transaction statement such as a commit or rollback. Trigger actions cannot be used to connect to another database. They cannot be used to issue a new SQL session, which is equivalent to a new transaction being initiated.

Embedded Functions and Procedures

Functions and procedures, to be discussed at length in the next chapter, can also be embedded in a trigger action sequence. Functions and procedures are SQL programmer-defined services that are schema-level objects accessible from any valid SQL block. For example, a procedure order can be written to take as input the values of the quantity, the max_stock, item_name, and price and use this to insert a new order into the order table in the database. This procedure in turn can then be called from in the trigger to be executed externally within the persistent stored module engine:

```
CREATE TRIGGER reorder
   AFTER UPDATE of quantity, max_stocked ON aquatic_stock
   REFERENCING NEW AS new-row
   FOR EACH ROW
   WHEN (new-row.quantity < .25*max_stocked)
   BEGIN ATOMIC
      CALL order (new-row.stock_id , new-
            row.item_name, new-row.max_stocked-
            new-row.quantity, new-row.cost_each
            );
   END
```

The procedure order is external to the trigger, existing in the database as a separate unique schema object, which is located and executed in the database at the time of call, not at the time of trigger creation. This allows the programmer, at some later time, to alter or replace the procedure with another, possibly providing some different semantics. The only requirement is that the procedure's interface does not change.

Since the name of the procedure or function is a global schema object, it is resolved to a specific implementation based on the SQL path available at the time of creation of the trigger. If none exists, the procedure or function can be resolved dynamically at run time by traversing the lattice of schema objects of the same name, looking for a match between parameter types.

Execution of functions or procedures in the trigger action body can return an SQLSTATE variable value, indicating an error. Such a return results in the failure of the triggering SQL statement.

Cascading Triggers

Triggers may not be standalone entities. One trigger can use an SQL statement on a particular table, which already has another trigger on it. In this case, the root trigger initially fires, causing an action in the trigger's body, which, in turn, invokes the execution of another trigger (Figure 10.7). Such an effect can occur often if many tables have had a variety of triggers generated for them that the programmer does not know about. Because of this interaction, it is imperative that triggers are only used where they are necessary. In addition, the programmer must ensure that the triggers are well documented, so that their existence is known before an unwary programmer stumbles over one. Cascading triggers can become highly complex and may lead to mutations that were not intentional. Such mutations in the SQL-3 language will cause

Figure 10.7

Cascading triggers.

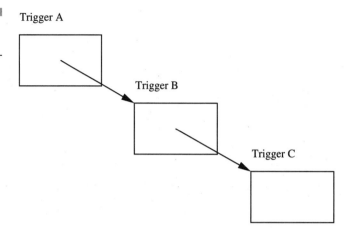

Trigger A

Trigger B

Trigger C

the failure of the cascading triggers, leaving it up to the programmer to find and trace the root and sequence.

Interactions with Referential Constraints

Referential constraints are important to the development of correct and consistent database systems. Referential constraints permit checking values in one table against those in another. For example, you cannot have a fish in the `acquatic_stock` table unless it has an entry in the `marine_fish` or `fresh_water_fish` tables. Using these constraints permits the enforcement of existential integrity and much more. The problem with referential integrity, from the perspective of triggers, is the possible side effect, or desirable effect, if designed correctly, of trigger firing due to referential constraint enforcement.

The triggering SQL operation can be the result of changes to tables caused by referential constraint enforcement, as shown in the following example:

```
CREATE TABLE sales
    (item_no   INTEGER (6) NOT NULL,
       .
       .
       .
    fish_name   CHARACTER VARYING(20)
       REFERENCES marine_fish,
       .
       .
    );
```

If a trigger is written on this table, and the `fish_name` is updated or deleted, there is a possibility of an additional action being required by the referential constraint on the item. The referential constraint indicates that an item with the same name must exist in the referenced table in order for this item to be correct and durable in the database. If the referential constraint is violated, and causes the table's tuple to be aborted, this change could fire a trigger defined on the item either before the violation or after the violation.

Of more interest to triggers is using added semantics on the referential constraints. For example, the referential constraint above can be modified to add a command directive on what to do if the referential constraint is violated or a change is made to the referencing table. The possibilities are examined in relation to the following alteration to the table specification above:

```
CREATE TABLE sales
   (item_no   INTEGER (6) NOT NULL,
      .
      .
      .
   fish_name   CHARACTER VARYING(20)
      REFERENCES marine_fish
        ON SQL_operation SQL_action,
      .
      .
      .
   );
```

The *SQL_operation* can be a DELETE or UPDATE and the *SQL_action* can be CASCADE, SET NULL, or SET DEFAULT. These operations and actions have the potential to affect triggers defined on the parent or referenced tables. The semantics of these constraints imply that on the given operation occurring on the referenced attribute the defined action is to be performed—for example, if the table above were defined as follows:

```
CREATE TABLE sales
   (item_no   INTEGER (6) NOT NULL,
      .
      .
      .
   fish_name   CHARACTER VARYING(20)
      REFERENCES marine_fish
        ON DELETE CASCADE,
      .
      .
      .
   );
```

This implies that if the referenced `fish_name` in the `marine_fish` table is deleted, then any item in this table with the same name is also to be deleted. The implication of the action is that if a DELETE trigger is defined on the sales table when a deletion of a particular fish is performed in the `marine_fish` table, this will cause the deletion of all tuples in the sales table with the same `fish_name`. This action in return fires the DELETE trigger you defined over the sales table.

If the referential constraint uses the syntax ON DELETE SET NULL, the delete trigger defined above is not fired. However, if an UPDATE trigger were defined on the sales table, and the `marine_fish` table has a `fish_name` deleted, the update trigger is fired on the sales table. The deletion of a `fish_name` from the `marine_fish` table causes all tuples with the named fish to have the `fish_name` updated to NULL. A similar effect occurs if the modification to the referential constraint uses the syntax ON DELETE SET DEFAULT. In this case, deletion of a `fish_name` in the `marine_fish` table causes the fish to be set to whatever the default name was. For example, if a fish is removed from the database (you no longer will carry it, but still have a few left), you may want to set the default to "discontinued stock item" or some other appropriate business name. However, the result, in terms of a trigger, is the same. Setting the default name is equivalent to an UPDATE operation and causes the UPDATE trigger to fire.

Instead of DELETE as a modifier to the referential constraints, you can use the UPDATE modifier, as shown here:

```
CREATE TABLE sales
    (item_no    INTEGER (6) NOT NULL,
         .
         .
         .
    fish_name    CHARACTER VARYING(20)
        REFERENCES marine_fish
          ON UPDATE CASCADE,
         .
         .
         .
    );
```

In this case, the desired result of the referential constraint and its modifier is to keep the names of fish the same in both the `marine_fish` table and the sales table. So, if you decide to change the name of the blue devil to the blue marauder in the `marine_fish` table, all entries in the sales table using the name blue devil would have the name changed to blue marauder. The enforcement of this constraint would cause the firing of any update trigger defined on the sales table.

Other alternatives for this modifier are similar to the delete modifiers above. The UPDATE can be modified to SET NULL or SET DEFAULT. In both cases, this is still equivalent to an update. Setting the value of fish_name to NULL, or some default, has the same effect as far as a trigger is concerned. The named table has changed and the trigger must respond to it.

The implication of these referential constraints is that you may need to go back to the referencing table to check the values to see what occurred and why. This is necessary to make sure that the trigger is doing what it is supposed to do. For example, if the trigger is supposed to keep track of the total sales, changing a fish name may cause the collection of a tuple's value several times, instead of once as was intended. When referential integrity is involved, use triggers carefully.

Trigger Ordering

Triggers are defined to cause automatic actions for predefined database operations. Triggers, however, do not always operate in a vacuum. There are many times when triggers are designed to work in conjunction with each other. In these situations, it may be important to have the triggers fire in a very precise, predefined sequence. You can design the trigger based on the implicit ordering of triggers by the database. At this time, the default ordering of triggers is specified using the creation time of the trigger. The creation time of the trigger is determined with a system-generated timestamp. The timestamp is registered with the trigger in the database schema for later use. Triggers are activated in ascending order of the triggers' timestamp values.

The implications of this are that old triggers are activated before new triggers. In this way, new triggers operate on known database states as defined by existing triggers. In addition, the new triggers are viewed as incremental additions to the changes already defined by an exiting trigger on a table. Activating triggers in ascending order of creation ensures that all triggers will be fired in a known consistent way, alleviating any side effects that may occur if triggers are allowed to fire in random order.

At the time of this writing, the committee was still in the process of reviewing the ordering of trigger firing. It seems desirable that in many circumstances the designer of the triggers may have a better understanding of the firing order than the system does, using such a simple mechanism of time of creation. By using time of creation, programmers can get the order they want, but this requires the deletion and redefinition of all triggers on a table. The redefinition needs to be done in the order of the trigger firings. By allowing programmers to choose the firing order, possibly with some additional syntax, the alteration of this arbitrary ordering would aid database maintenance and growth.

Summary

Standards evolve over time and by consensus. Therefore, it is not surprising that not all the features postulated for triggers were available to the programmer in SQL-3 at the time this book went to press. It is also very likely that as database system developers and programmers use more triggers and related mechanisms, we will see further enhancements to this very useful feature of the SQL language. Many vendors already support a variety of extensions to the triggers defined in this chapter in their SQL-3 products just beginning to be released. The programmer, however, should avoid these added features if portability of code from one vendor system to another is desirable. Vendors, such as IBM and Oracle, have implemented a variety of extensions to triggers in related database products that operate in and on top of their base systems. Oracle, for example, has added numerous extensions to triggers in its application development tools. It is very likely that many such features will find their way into the SQL standard language as it evolves over the coming years. SQL-3 has been released, and the ANSI NCITS and ISO DBL standards committees are already looking at SQL-4 and beyond.

SQL Persistent Stored Modules

One of the major additions to the SQL language at this time, beyond user-defined abstract data types, is the persistent stored module and related properties. This feature alone represents a major diversion from traditional SQL implementations, which relied heavily on host languages for their computational requirements and interface to applications. SQL/Persistent Stored Modules (SQL/PSM) are a major change from the past, providing computational completeness in the domain of the database. In addition to this major benefit, PSM also provides a variety of far-reaching enhancements that add to its importance in furthering SQL's dominance in the database community. With the addition of user-defined data types and persistent stored modules and related properties, SQL is positioned for the twenty-first century. Pure object-oriented languages, though new and unique, do not and will not demand the respect that SQL-3 will, nor will they provide the vendor and user base enjoyed by SQL.

SQL persistent stored modules provide syntactic and semantic constructs for the specification of stored modules, procedures, and functions. These stored routines may then be called from any SQL transaction or statement from the internal or external system. The design of these elements aids in the performance of SQL client/server environments. In addition to internal SQL routines, SQL/PSM provides properties for accessing and using 3GL (external) routines in SQL routines and/or statements. These procedures and functions are user-defined, but are standalone elements. That is, they do not need to be tied to a transaction or session to complete their execution.

SQL/PSM modules are computationally complete. This implies that these routines can perform all operations required by their applications designers without needing an external host language to provide computational semantics. The structure of the modules, procedures, and functions was designed with the best features of several existing languages. As in many of these languages, PSM modules, procedures, and functions can use overloading with resolution based on the mapping of input arguments to stored routine arguments to determine the best match. Beyond this, users can define the path to be searched in resolution.

The PSM modules use added procedural extensions beyond those of SQL. The PSM modules include new control statements, such as BEGIN – END, block structuring, assignment statements, CALL, CASE, IF-THEN-ELSE, looping structure, FOR loops, SIGNAL and RESIGNAL primitives, internal and external variables, and a powerful condition handling mechanism. The advent of the block gives SQL programmers the ability to encase multiple SQL statements in a single EXEC SQL statement in an ad hoc or host language environment.

The SQL/PSM portion of the language was released early as an extension for the SQL-2 relational system. It has been augmented and re-released with the SQL-3 object-relational language to take advantage of the new features available with SQL-3 and to complete and fix features that were deprecated at the time of the initial release. SQL/PSM will continue to be enhanced by the ANSI and ISO database language committees. The committees, vendors, and users will demand further features to improve the usefulness of the language to a larger mass of people. The language has already seen many vendors release early versions of this part of the language; these versions have been going through constant reevaluation and improvements since their initial release.

SQL Architecture

SQL/PSM modules, procedures, and functions are resident in, and managed by, the SQL environment: the database. These elements are stored persistently in the database and are managed much like an SQL relational table is managed. That is, they can be accessed, altered, or deleted from the persistent storage using the correct syntax, applied in a correct manner, adhering to any embedded constraints.

An SQL database system consists of a number of related components. First, there is the SQL environment, which defines a database space, where an instance of a database will exist. Within the scope of an SQL environment are SQL catalogs and client modules. An SQL catalog consists of a collection of SQL schemas (Figure 11.1). An SQL database can have more than one catalog. For example, the fish database can have a separate catalog for aquarium items and for aquaculture items that are available from the company. Separating the database into separate catalogs is at the discretion of the database administrator and designers.

A single database site can have one or more databases. Each of these logical databases can then have one or more schemas. A database site is equivalent to an SQL environment (Figure 11.1). An SQL catalog is equivalent to a logical database repository or a named database. For example, you can have a database named AFMIS, NOAA, or some other logical name. This named database can then be composed of a set of user sche-

Figure 11.1

SQL architecture.

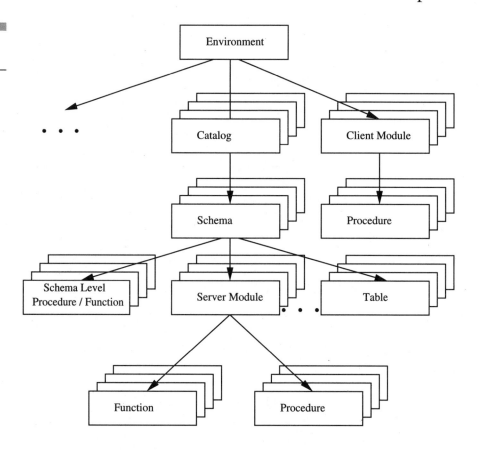

mas. The schema is composed of the basic elements of a database: tables. As discussed in previous chapters, this schema can also have numerous other elements, such as user abstract data types or user triggers. Both of these are also called schema objects. The SQL schema can also contain other items—domains, named constraints, privileges, and assertions.

The SQL module is one important item that is storable in the SQL hierarchy. A module is a schema object, which has an interface and a collection of functions and/or procedures that implement the interface. All of these items are also part of the persistent database connected to some named schema. The schema they are connected to is dependent on which user created the module and its embedded procedures and functions. Procedures and functions do not need to be embedded in an SQL module to exist in the database. A procedure or a function can be

defined and exist as a standalone object in an SQL schema. The difference is in how the procedures and functions are managed and how they
are accessed and utilized in the database.

An SQL environment can also include items that are outside of a specific database catalog. These are defined and referred to as client modules. In addition, client modules can have embedded procedures. These
database objects are persistently stored, but are out of the domain of a
particular named database instance and, as such, have a different set of
access and operational qualities.

SQL Client Modules

SQL client modules exist outside the catalog of a named database. That
is, they are defined and exist on a client of the database, not as an item
of the server. Client modules support the hosting of an SQL agent module on some other processor or even in some other space on the same
processor (Figure 11.2). SQL client modules consist of a variety of SQL
structures. The primary structure is embedded SQL procedures. The
BNF for the module specification is as follows:

```
<SQL-client module definition> ::=
    <module specification>

<module specification> ::=
    <module header>
    <module contents>...

<module header> ::=
    <module name clause>
    <language clause>
    <module authorization clause>
    [ <module path specification> ]

<module name clause> ::=
    MODULE [ <module name> ]
    [ <module character set specification> ]
```

The main denotational element in the specification is the keyword
MODULE. There is also an optional declaration of the character set to be
used in the module. An example of a module's main declaration is:

```
MODULE account_audit
```

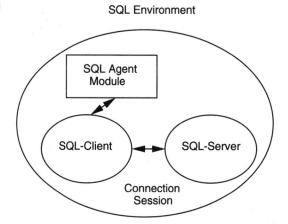

SQL Environment

This portion of the module declares a module of the name `account_audit`. The name used must be a valid SQL client module name and must be a valid identifier in the language:

```
<module name> ::=
    <SQL-client module name>

<SQL-client module name> ::= <identifier>

<module character set specification> ::=
    NAMES ARE <character set specification>
```

This statement fragment is followed by the remainder of the module definition, which includes a specification regarding which language is being used in the module's design and implementation. The valid languages presently supported by SQL are Ada, C, COBOL, FORTRAN, Mumps, Pascal, PL/I, and SQL:

```
<language clause> ::=
    LANGUAGE <language name>
<language name> ::=
    ADA | C | COBOL | FORTRAN | MUMPS | PASCAL | PLI | SQL
```

For the example, the initial module specification can be followed by the language specification for the programming language C as follows:

```
MODULE account_audit
    LANGUAGE C
```

The language specification is then followed by a module authorization clause, indicating who has the privileges to use this module. This identifier indicates either under which schema this module has the authority to run or which user or role has the authorization to run this module on the database:

```
<module authorization clause> ::=
      SCHEMA <schema name>
    | AUTHORIZATION <module authorization identifier>
    | SCHEMA <schema name> AUTHORIZATION <module authorization
identifier>

<module authorization identifier> ::=
    <authorization identifier>

<authorization identifier> ::= <identifier>
```

In the example, you can extend this module specification to indicate that the manager of the aquarium store will be allowed to run the named module by declaring:

```
MODULE account_audit
    LANGUAGE C
    AUTHORIZATION manager
```

In addition to this specification, the external module can also include the specification for a path where the external module can be found in a particular system:

```
<module path specification> ::=
    <path specification>

<path specification> ::=
    PATH <schema name list>

<schema name list> ::=
    <schema name> [ { <comma> <schema name> }... ]
```

In the example, you can also indicate that this particular function can be found in a particular list of schemas:

```
MODULE account_audit
    LANGUAGE C
    AUTHORIZATION manager
    PATH ORCL.manager, ORCL.accounts
```

This indicates where the named tables in the module's procedures can be found.

The module then has a collection of internal elements, which make up its possible implementation. This typically is a collection of procedures, which can be called from a host language. The procedure is the major element found in external client modules. The module contents can also include cursors, which are usable in the embedded module's procedures:

```
<module contents> ::=
      <declare cursor>
    | <externally-invoked procedure> <semicolon>
    | <SQL-invoked routine> <semicolon>
    | <global declaration>

<SQL-invoked routine> ::=
      <schema routine>

<global declaration> ::=
      <temporary table declaration>
```

An external client module procedure has the BNF shown below. The main declaration is the same as an internal SQL procedure. The keyword PROCEDURE indicates the beginning of a named external procedure embedded in a module. The procedure declaration must include as part of its specification an SQL status parameter, which can be either SQLCODE or SQLSTATE. SQLCODE returns a zero or negative value to indicate success or failure of a procedure. It can also return 100 to indicate that no data were found. On the other hand, the SQLSTATE indicator can return a five-digit code providing further details about what caused the error. One of these indicators must be included in the routine in order to provide to the calling routine the status of the called routine's execution:

```
<externally-invoked procedure> ::=
    PROCEDURE <procedure name>
        <host parameter declaration setup> <semicolon>
      <SQL procedure statement> <semicolon>

<procedure name> ::= <identifier>
```

An example SQL client module procedure declaration would follow the module declaration, begin with the keyword PROCEDURE, and would be followed by a procedure name, host parameter declarations, and the body of the procedure. If you continue to declare the account_audit module, you could have procedures named balance, credit, and debit to indicate the status, or alter the status, of a customer's account. The procedure declarations are as follows:

```
PROCEDURE balance (SQLCODE,
                    :cust_account_num    INTEGER,
                    :balance        DECIMAL(10,2));
    SELECT balance
    INTO    :balance
    FROM cust_accounts
    WHERE account_num = :cust_account_num;

PROCEDURE debit   (SQLCODE,
                    :cust_account_num    INTEGER,
                    :amount         DECIMAL(10,2));
    UPDATE cust_accounts
    SET balance balance - :amount
    WHERE account_num = :cust_account_num;

PROCEDURE credit   (SQLCODE,
                    :cust_account_num    INTEGER,
                    :amount         DECIMAL(10,2));
    UPDATE cust_accounts
    SET balance balance + :amount
    WHERE account_num = :cust_account_num;
```

The three procedures declared above can be embedded into the module `account_audit` by placing the module declaration before the first procedure's declaration.

The parameters declared in the procedures are specified between parentheses after the procedure name declaration (as was done for the `cust_account_num` and amount and balance in the previous three procedure specifications). The parameter specifications can also have indicators for each parameter, permitting additional SQL status information about the parameter to be passed back to the calling code. An indicator has a return value to indicate a null value (–1) or a valid value (0). The calling program can set the indicator variable to one of these values to tell the called procedure that a null or valid value is found in the associated parameter. The BNF for the procedure parameter declarations is:

```
<host parameter declaration setup> ::=
    <host parameter declaration list>
  | <host parameter declaration>...

<host parameter declaration list> ::=
    <left paren> <host parameter declaration>
        [ { <comma> <host parameter declaration> }... ] <right
paren>

<host parameter declaration> ::=
    <host parameter name> <data type>
  | <status parameter>

<status parameter> ::=
    SQLSTATE
```

The body of the external module's procedure can be any valid SQL statement from the list shown in the BNF below. The procedure statement can be an SQL schema statement, a data statement, a control statement, a transaction statement, a connection statement, a session statement, or a diagnostic statement, as follows:

```
<SQL procedure statement> ::=
      <SQL executable statement>

<SQL executable statement> ::=
      <SQL schema statement>
    | <SQL data statement>
    | <SQL control statement>
    | <SQL transaction statement>
    | <SQL connection statement>
    | <SQL session statement>
    | <SQL diagnostics statement>
```

Valid executable SQL data statements were used in the examples above. In particular, the SQL SELECT and SQL UPDATE statements were used in the three procedures.

SQL client modules, once specified and stored in a client environment, can be called from any external or internal code segment that has the appropriate authority. The module procedures are invoked by a host language call. For example, using the specifications for the balance, debit, and credit from the external module `account_audit`, a calling program would make a call as follows, using C as the foundation language:

```
main ()
  {
  */   variable declarations      */
  long     SQLCODE;
  long     cust_account_num;
  long     balance;
  long     amount;
  */   initialization code access code   */
      .
      .
      .

  balance (&SQLCODE, cust_account_num, &balance);
      .
      .
      .

  credit(&SQLCODE, cust_account_num, amount);
      .
      .
      .
```

```
          debit(&SQLCODE, cust_account_num, amount);
              .
              .
              .

      }
```

The calls indicate which type of parameter is being used. Those parameters containing the ampersand (&) are output parameters. Those without the ampersand are input parameters. In this way, a program can easily interact with an SQL database through a client element. The client module can interface directly with the SQL database using the appropriate rights and access mechanisms.

SQL Server Modules

If there are client modules, you would expect that there should be server modules. Server modules are a bit different from client modules in that they exist in the server instead of the client. Server modules also must adhere to the properties enforced on the server (e.g., the *ACID* properties of transactions). The major difference between the SQL client modules and the SQL server modules is that the server modules exist in the domain of the database and run in this domain under the server's correctness and consistency criteria. SQL server modules exist inside the catalog of the database, at the server. These server modules are therefore schema objects and are known to the database environment. The server modules are database objects, such as tables, views, user-defined types, triggers, objects, assertions, procedures, and functions. SQL server modules contain procedures and functions, and, in addition, these schema objects have the added ability to be altered, dropped, and created. The objects themselves have an additional concept; they can exist in the database as separate unattached objects. That is, procedures and functions do not need to be tightly associated with a module. In the main database modules do not exist; instead, collections of functions and procedures, which perform related or compatible operations, are grouped into larger items, called packages. These packages are referred to, along with unattached procedures and functions, as database persistent stored modules. These are discussed in the following sections.

SQL Persistent Modules

SQL persistent modules are encapsulated collections of routines and declarations, such as cursors, variables, types, tables, views, procedures, and functions. These collections are written in computationally complete SQL, implying that no external host language is needed to perform true computational operations on the database. Variables can be declared in these SQL structures. External status parameters are not needed, since the operations are performed directly on the database objects and and under the control of the resident database system. Nulls do not require indicator variables, as was necessary in the external routines, to detect or operate with nulls. The data impedance mismatch problems that typically existed with host languages no longer exist. The data types of the database are the same as the data types of the support modules. The full power and extent of the SQL typing system is available. Strong typing and subtyping of user-defined abstract data types are supported. The advantage of this system is that many of the problems seen in earlier implementations of SQL in terms of impedance mismatch no longer exist, due to the integrated database and procedural environment. As of this writing, however, an issue is the nonuniform or nonvalidated implementations that have been constructed:

```
CREATE MODULE account_audit
     LANGUAGE SQL
     SCHEMA ORCL.manager

DECLARE ...

PROCEDURE balance (SQLCODE,
                   cust_account_num   INTEGER,
                   balance            DECIMAL(10,2));
     SELECT balance
     INTO    balance
     FROM cust_accounts
     WHERE account_num = cust_account_num;

PROCEDURE debit    (SQLCODE,
                   cust_account_num   INTEGER,
                   amount             DECIMAL(10,2));
     UPDATE cust_accounts
     SET balance balance - amount
     WHERE account_num = cust_account_num;
```

```
PROCEDURE credit  (SQLCODE,
                   cust_account_num   INTEGER,
                   amount             DECIMAL(10,2));
    UPDATE cust_accounts
    SET balance (balance + amount)
    WHERE account_num = cust_account_num;
END MODULE;
```

SQL Routines

Routines in SQL-3 are components of the database server modules. They are therefore "first-class" schema objects. Being a first-class schema object implies that the object is persistently stored and managed in the scope of the database. Its definition and state are available from the database and do not need further exterior interaction to be managed or accessed. The main class of routines supported in SQL's persistent stored module specification is the procedure and function. For example, a simple function to determine if there are customers with the same name can be written as follows:

```
CREATE FUNCTION duplicates
    ( last      CHAR (20),
      first     CHAR (20),
      initial   CHAR (1))
    RETURNS INTEGER;

BEGIN
    DECLARE cnt INTEGER;
    SELECT COUNT (*)
    INTO cnt
    FROM customers c
    WHERE c.last_name = last
        AND c.first_name = first
        AND c.initial = initial;
    RETURN cnt;
END;
```

This function can be created and placed in the database system's schema as a first-class object. This implies that a user could see that this object exists in the database just as a table does and can be described the same way that a table can be described. In addition, as with a table, this function can be called upon to perform its operation as easily as a table is accessed using a SELECT statement. What is so different about these objects as compared with those that traditionally existed in the database? The answer lies in how they are managed and accessed internally in an SQL environment and externally from an SQL client. These and other properties of SQL internal modules will be discussed.

Schema Routines

Schema routines refer to procedures and functions that are stored in the server and are known to the database. That is, they are schema objects known in the server's catalog, the same way a table or view is known to the database. Schema routines are SQL invoked through the use of the CALL statement or a function invocation similar to that of conventional programming languages. The schema routines can be written in SQL, or in an external host programming language. If written in SQL the schema routine is referred to as an SQL routine. If written in an external programming language, it is referred to as an external routine.

Schema routines can have their names reused. That is, they can have their names overloaded. More than one routine with the same name can exist in the schema. Overloaded routines exist in the schema; they each must have a unique signature. The signature of a function or procedure consists of the name with the list of parameters and their types.

Schema routines have parameters and return values. Functions, as with their programming language counterparts, return a value. The parameters for functions can only be in parameters. That is, values get passed into the function through the parameters, but nothing gets passed back through the parameters:

```
fish_name := fname(fish_id)
```

Procedures, on the other hand, can have parameters of type in, out, or in-out, permitting values to pass in both directions to and from a procedure. As with programming language counterparts, procedures do not return a value. Procedures only pass parameters as the means to communicate information back and fourth from the schema procedure to client applications.

Schema routines are written in SQL and can take any number of arguments. The only limits are those put in place by vendor implementations. As with conventional programming languages, SQL routines can

Figure 11.3
SQL routine
structure.

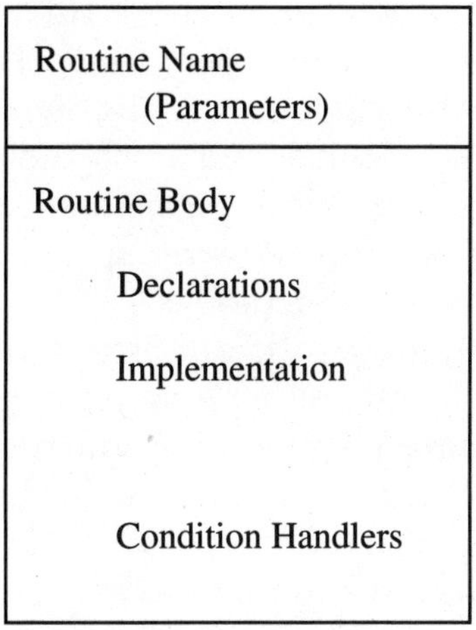

Routine Name
(Parameters)

Routine Body

Declarations

Implementation

Condition Handlers

declare variables of any SQL-supported type. SQL routines do not require the added elements of status parameter and indicator variables (Figure 11.3).

SQL routines, since they are internal database items, do not require transformation between SQL types and any host language types. The SQL routine preserves all the type information and type behavior of the parameters, such as subtyping and abstract data type operations. Since the SQL routines are written in SQL, there is only one language to learn, and therefore it becomes easier to use.

External Routines

External routines exist outside the domain of the database schema. These routines are written in some standard SQL-supported host programming language. At present, SQL supports Ada, C, COBOL, FORTRAN, Mumps, Pascal, and PL/I. External routines, mostly written in external host languages, can have SQL embedded in their boundaries. External routines support embedding of dynamic SQL, embedded SQL, and call-level interface SQL elements. External routines can take any number of arguments as inputs and/or outputs. Routines can be constructed using any construct of the host language. One important difference from traditional programming language routines is that these routines must have an SQL status parameter. These SQL parameters are used to indicate to the database the outcome of the external execution.

For example, they determine if the result of this execution was null or if the execution represents a valid SQL outcome. The parameters passed into or out of external routines must be valid SQL variables of type varchar, date, time, interval, decimal, and so on. You need to be careful, however, to adhere to the specific implementer's variations. Not all SQL types are allowed. They are limited by the specific host language's limitations and implementer's interpretations.

External routines must have their parameters mapped to the internal SQL server interface. Two main mapping styles have been defined in the SQL standard—parameter-style SQL and parameter-style general. Parameter-style SQL has some very specific limitations. First, each parameter must have an associated indicator variable. For example, if the routine is a function, the return value will have an indicator parameter. An indicator variable is a common variable used to allow SQL databases and host programming language structures to pass data between the database and applications. If the routine is a function, the return value will have an indicator parameter. A CHAR(5) output parameter will return the SQLSTATE indicator. A character string is used to pass a variety of parameter styles. A character string can be used as a means to pass the name of the routine to invoke, the specific name of the routine to invoke, or the return message from the called routine (Figure 11.4).

If the parameter style is general, the returns are a bit different. In particular, returns cannot be null, and no additional information can be passed to the external routine. Invocation of the routine in SQL causes the external routine to be executed.

The SQL language constructs allow the return of values from external routines to be cast into some new values. For example, if the following were executed:

```
RETURNS fish CAST FROM sea_cast
```

The external function code returns a value of type sea_cast, which will be cast to a type of fish before such a value is passed back to the SQL engine. Such a facility is used to support external functions on SQL types not supported by the host language (e.g., date, decimal, interval, and so on).

By allowing the use of external routines, SQL can now take advantage of existing libraries and the convenience of what comes with such avail-

SQL external
routine interface.

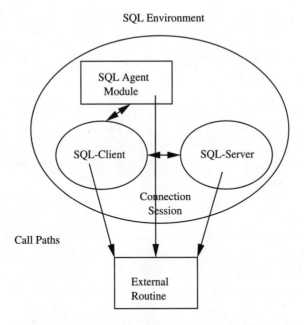

ability. The disadvantage is that the programmer or application user must learn two or more languages, since the external routines can be written in any of the supported languages. Another disadvantage refers to the old issue of impedance of data. The external routine's host language data types must be converted into the database system's supported data types. In addition to the obvious translation problems, there are also issues with loss of type behavior outside of SQL. This implies that the type-checking mechanisms of the database system cannot be used.

Both SQL routines and external routines can specify whether they are deterministic, as well as the kind of SQL access they will perform. Deterministic or nondeterministic indicates whether or not the routine will always return the same result given the same inputs. The designation of deterministic or nondeterministic is important for query optimization.

The designation of SQL access indicates that the routine contains SQL code, reads SQL data, or modifies SQL data. This designation can also aid query optimization. Nondeterministic functions and SQL modification access indications are not allowed in check constraints.

SQL Procedure Language Elements

SQL was not always procedural; historically, SQL was declarative. The use of procedures in SQL application implementations aids programmer efficiency and security. Having procedural constructs is also highly convenient; applications can now be totally written in SQL, requiring no host language to operate. In addition, procedures and functions can allow programmers to create libraries of useful functionality that can later be reused by new applications, decreasing the time it takes to implement applications.

SQL was extended to support the best features of many programming languages. The main elements, procedures, and functions can be embedded in SQL statements and modules. SQL's procedural extensions include items such as variable declaration and compound statements; IF, CASE, LOOP, WHILE, and REPEAT statements; and many more.

Compound Statements

Taking a cue from block structured languages, SQL has adopted a compound statement structure, which permits the grouping of SQL statements into one unit. The grouped statements execute sequentially and are bound together using the BEGIN and END keywords. The syntax for the compound statement is shown in the following BNF:

```
<compound statement> ::=
    [ <beginning label> <colon> ]
    BEGIN [[NOT] ATOMIC]
    [ <local declaration list> ]
    [· <local handler declaration list> ]
    [ <SQL statement list> ]
    END [ <ending label> ]
```

The keywords BEGIN and END are the only required elements of the compound statement. All other elements are optional. As an example, you can specify a compound statement, consisting of a SELECT statement and an UPDATE statement, on the `marine_fish` table:

```
BEGIN
    SELECT common_name FROM marine_fish
    WHERE scientific_name = 'angelichthys ciliaris';
    UPDATE marine_fish SET max_size = 24;
END;
```

To execute this block of code, the user could simply type the block into an SQL interface, and then signal "run" using whatever convention is used in the vendor's implementation. For example, in Oracle's PL/SQL implementation, the slash (/) is used to indicate "execute" and "run." In addition, the user can terminate the block with a semicolon (;) and execute the block of SQL code with a carriage return. Blocks can be embedded into host programs using the EXEC SQL statement to run the block in the code segment:

```
main ()
  {
  EXEC SQL
    BEGIN
      SELECT common_name FROM marine_fish
      WHERE scientific_name = 'angelichthys ciliaris';
      UPDATE marine_fish SET max_size = 24;
    END;
  }
```

This simple code sequence runs in a host language, calls the SQL engine, and executes the block in the SQL engine.

Compound statements can have embedded local variables, local cursors, or condition declarations. The declared items are not persistent. They only persist while the compound statement encasing them is active. When the compound statement terminates, the declared objects are destroyed. The names used in declarations must be unique in the compound statement. This implies that no item in the block can be declared to be of two different types. Only one item with a name is allowed. If blocks are encased in other blocks, an inner block can have a declaration with the same name as one in the outer scope. The inner block definition overrides the outer block definition only in the inner block. SQL objects declared in a block can be defined by their schema name, which is a global declaration, or by their label name for local declarations.

The body of a compound statement can contain most valid SQL statements. Any data manipulation statement, such as SELECT, INSERT, and UPDATE, is allowed. Control statements, such as IF and WHILE, are supported. Transaction control statements, SQL session management statements, diagnostic management statements, dynamic statements, data definition statements, and connect statements are also supported. A compound statement can also be named by using a label:

```
fish_accounts:
   BEGIN
      DECLARE cust_acount     INTEGER;
      DECLARE acount_balance    DECIMAL(10,2);

      SELECT cust_acount_num, balance
         INTO cust_acount, acount_balance
         FROM accounts WHERE balance > 0;
      IF (acount_balance < min ) THEN
         BEGIN
            CALL pay_in_full(cust_acount, account_balance);
            LEAVE fish_accounts;
         END;
      BEGIN ATOMIC
         DECLARE cust_payment DECIMAL(10,2);
         SET cust_payment = fish_accounts.cust_balance * .10;
         CALL min_payment(cust_account, cust_payment);
      END;
   END;
```

The example compound statement above checks the aquarium customer accounts to see if they have a balance. If they do, and it is less than the minimum, they are sent a bill to pay in full. If their balance is above the minimum, they are sent a bill for 10 percent of the balance. Some new features are shown in the example: declarations of block variables, the control structure IF, and the LEAVE statement to exit the block.

Compound statements are used in many SQL persistent stored module elements. They are usually found in the bodies of functions and procedures to encase the code implementing the function or procedures. Compound statements are also used in dynamic SQL environments. The BEGIN keyword signals to the interpreter to compile the following statements into a block to be executed at some later time.

Compound statements can be executed as isolated statements or as an atomic unit. If compound statements are executed as an atomic unit, the failure of any statement in the compound statement causes the failure of all the statements. The failure of a single statement, however, does not always result in the failure of the entire compound statement. An error-handling component can be executed in the compound statement. The default for a block is nonatomic. If you want atomic execution, the keyword ATOMIC must follow the BEGIN statement:

```
BEGIN ATOMIC
   .
   .
   .
   END;
```

Atomic and nonatomic blocks can be included, allowing programmers to tailor the performance of their executions. An atomic block cannot include any commit or rollback statements. A nonatomic block can have as many as the programmer wants.

Local Variables

Functions, procedures, and blocks can have local and/or global variables defined in their structures. The syntax for variable declaration is:

```
<SQL variable declaration> ::=
    <SQL variable name list>
    { <data type> | <domain name> }
    [ <default clause> ]
```

Variables have a name and a type associated with them. They can be created with initial default values and can contain the null value. To define a variable, the keyword DECLARE is used, followed by the name of the variable, the type of the variable, and, optionally, the default clause:

```
DECLARE cust_acount INTEGER;
```

or

```
DECLARE cust_acount INTEGER DEFAULT 0;
```

or

```
DECLARE cust_min_balance FLOAT CONSTANT 15.00;
```

All three of the declarations above are valid variable declarations. The first declares customer accounts as an integer type, the second as an integer with a given initial value, and the third declares the minimum value that a customer account is tested against.

These variables can then be used in the block in which they are declared, or in the higher-order structure in which they are declared. For example, in the previous named block, `fish_acounts`:

```
fish_acounts:
   BEGIN
      DECLARE cust_acount     INTEGER;
      DECLARE account_balance    DECIMAL(10,2);

      SELECT cust_account_num, balance
         INTO cust_account, account_balance
         FROM accounts WHERE balance > 0;
      IF (account_balance < min ) THEN
         BEGIN
            CALL pay_in_full(cust_account, account_balance);
            LEAVE fish_accounts;
         END;
      BEGIN ATOMIC
         DECLARE cust_payment DECIMAL(10,2);
         SET cust_payment = fish_accounts.cust_balance * .10;
         CALL min_payment(cust_account, cust_payment);
      END;
   END;
```

`cust_account` and `account_balance` are declared as variables at the beginning of the block and then are used in the application in the body of the block.

Assignment Statements

Assignment statements are an integral and important portion of any useful programming language. For SQL to reach its goal of being computationally complete, it, too, must have a means to transfer information from one location to another. The way to do this in SQL, as in many other programming languages, is through the assignment statement and its syntax. The assignment statement permits the result of an expression to be assigned to the target variable. The syntax for the assignment statement is:

```
SET variable_name = expression;
```

Some examples of the assignment operator are:

```
DECLARE fish_name  CHAR(30);
SET fish_name = 'lion fish';
```

This statement sets the variable, `fish_name`, to the lionfish:

```
SET fish_name = (SELECT common_name FROM marine_fish
   WHERE scientific_name = 'pterois volitans');
```

The SELECT statement returns the common name of pterois volitans, which is "lionfish." This name is then assigned to the variable fish_name:

```
SET fish_name = NULL;
```

This statement returns the null value, placing this value into the assignment variable fish_name:

```
SET fish_name = :fish INDICATOR :fish_ind;
```

Again, this illustrates the use of an indicator variable. If you had allocated 30 characters for fish_name, and it turned out that the external variable, which was set in some other statement, returned a name with more than 30 characters, the indicator variable would place the first 30 characters in the external variable fish and indicate the size of the entire returned word in the indicator variable fish_ind.

IF Statements

In order for SQL to be elevated to the stature of a computationally complete programming language, it needed to possess statements to conditionally control execution. All modern computationally complete languages possess such statements. One of the most fundamental statements first introduced in SQL-3, was the IF – THEN – ELSE form of a conditional execution statement. The basic form of the statement is as follows:

```
IF conditions true
   THEN SQL-statements
   ELSEIF conditions true
   THEN SQL-statements
      .
      .
      .
   ELSEIF conditions true
   THEN SQL-statements
   ELSE SQL-statements
END IF
```

As an example, you can look at the fish database to examine how to add fish to the inventory as they are depleted. The structure of the IF statement is to look at what has been sold from the aquatic stock. If an item falls below the reorder level, you reorder it by inserting a tuple into the order table. If the item has not fallen below the reorder level, then you simply exit:

```
IF (SELECT qty FROM aquatic_stock
    WHERE stock# = :item) = stock_min
THEN
  BEGIN
    SELECT qty INTO :order_qty FROM aquatic_stock
    WHERE stock# = :item);
    INSERT INTO orders(:item, order_qty+5);
  END;
END IF
```

This example uses no ELSE or ELSEIF clause, since the intention is to test only one condition on the table. If more than one condition is required, then multiple ELSE and ELSEIF clauses can be used. For example, if you add a status column to the customer accounts, you can set up a billing system to add fines for bills past due 30, 60, and 90 days:

```
IF (SELECT acct_type from cust_accounts
    WHERE account_num = account) = '30 past'
THEN
  BEGIN
  DECLARE balance FLOAT(10,2);
  SELECT cust_balance INTO balance FROM cust_accounts
      WHERE
  INSERT INTO payment ('account, '30 days past', balance+20);
  END;
ELSEIF (SELECT acct_type from cust_accounts
    WHERE account_num = account) = '60 past'
THEN
  BEGIN
  DECLARE balance FLOAT(10,2);
  SELECT cust_balance INTO balance FROM cust_accounts
      WHERE
  INSERT INTO payment ('account, '60 days past', balance+40);
  END;
ELSEIF (SELECT acct_type from cust_accounts
    WHERE account_num = account) = '90 past'
THEN
  BEGIN
  DECLARE balance FLOAT(10,2);
  SELECT cust_balance INTO balance FROM cust_accounts
      WHERE
  INSERT INTO payment ('account, '90 days past', balance+60);
  END;
ELSE
  BEGIN
  DECLARE balance FLOAT(10,2);
  SELECT cust_balance INTO balance FROM cust_accounts
      WHERE
  INSERT INTO payment ('account, 'good standing', balance);
  END;
END IF
```

This extended example shows some of the ways in which block structuring and conditional flow of control statements can be used to form more complex operations. Alternatively, you can augment the structures further by providing some error conditions. If, for example, no condition match was found, you may want to raise an exception, which can then be used to handle the condition in some user-defined way. Condition handling is discussed in more detail later in this chapter.

CASE Statements

Many programming languages provide a way to enumerate a list of possible outcomes in one structure. This permits more efficient jumping from a list to the alternative you want. SQL provides such a structure with the CASE statement and its variants. The CASE statement selects an execution path based on the result of an expression's evaluation or, alternatively, on the evaluation of some predicates. The first form of the CASE statement simply evaluates some value-based expression. Based on the outcome of the value expression, one of the paths in the list of alternatives is taken. To make sure that an undefined path doesn't cause the system to terminate, SQL provides an alternative path based on the expression's evaluation. The form of the CASE statement is:

```
<simple case> ::=
    CASE <case operand>
      <simple when clause>...
      [ <else clause> ]
    END
<case operand> ::= <value expression>
<simple when clause> ::= WHEN <when operand> THEN <result>
<when operand> ::= <value expression>
<result> ::= <result expression> | NULL
<result expression> ::= <value expression>
<else clause> ::= ELSE <result>
```

The general form of the CASE statement is illustrated in the following example, which tests what kind of item has been sold from the aquatic stock. The five possible conditions are whether the item is a marine fish, a marine crustacean, a marine mollusk, a marine coelenterate, or a marine echinoderm. You may want to set up an inventory-monitoring table to keep track of the most popular items sold for the home aquarist:

```
CASE (SELECT item_category FROM sales
   WHERE account_num = account)

WHEN 'marine fish' THEN

   UPDATE sale_stats SET count = count +
      (SELECT qty FROM sales
      WHERE item_category = 'marine fish'
      AND account_num = account)
   WHERE item_category = 'marine fish';

WHEN 'marine crustaceans' THEN

   UPDATE sale_stats SET count = count +
      (SELECT qty FROM sales
      WHERE item_category = 'marine crustaceans'
      AND account_num = account)
   WHERE item_category = 'marine crustaceans';

WHEN 'marine mollusks' THEN

   UPDATE sale_stats SET count = count +
      (SELECT qty FROM sales
      WHERE item_category = 'marine mollusks'
      AND account_num = account)
   WHERE item_category = 'marine mollusks';

WHEN 'marine coelenterates' THEN

   UPDATE sale_stats SET count = count +
      (SELECT qty FROM sales
      WHERE item_category = 'marine coelenterates'
      AND account_num = account)
   WHERE item_category = 'marine coelenterates';

WHEN 'marine echinoderms' THEN

   UPDATE sale_stats SET count = count +
      (SELECT qty FROM sales
      WHERE item_category = 'marine echinoderms'
      AND account_num = account)
   WHERE item_category = 'marine echinoderms';
END;
```

You can also find other ways to perform the same set of operations.

An alternative form of CASE is also supported in the SQL-3 language. This form removes the value expression and changes the value items in each alternative for a condition. In this case, the statement looks and acts in a manner similar to the IF – THEN – ELSE combination. The general form of this second alternative is:

```
CASE
   WHEN <condition> THEN <SQL statements>
```

```
        WHEN <condition> THEN <SQL statements>
           .
           .
           .
        ELSE <SQL statements>
END;
```

The more formal BNF for the alternative conditional CASE statement is as follows:

```
<searched case> ::=
    CASE
      <searched when clause>...
      [ <else clause> ]
    END

<searched when clause> ::= WHEN <search condition> THEN <result>

<search condition> ::=
    <boolean value expression>

<boolean value expression> ::=
      <boolean simple expression>
    | <boolean implication>

<boolean simple expression> ::=
      <boolean term>
    | <boolean value expression> OR <boolean term>

<boolean term> ::=
      <boolean factor>
    | <boolean term> AND <boolean factor>

<boolean factor> ::=
    [ NOT ] <boolean primary>

<boolean primary> ::=
      <predicate>
    | <value expression primary>

<predicate> ::=
      <comparison predicate>
    | <between predicate>
    | <in predicate>
    | <like predicate>
    | <null predicate>
    | <quantified comparison predicate>
    | <exists predicate>
    | <unique predicate>
    | <match predicate>
    | <overlaps predicate>
    | <similar predicate>
    | <quantified predicate>
    | <distinct predicate>
    | <boolean predicate>
    | <type predicate>
```

You can see from this extended description that the conditional CASE statement supports any of the valid SQL conditional clauses. You can easily rewrite the above example to this form, as follows:

```
CASE

WHEN (SELECT item_category FROM sales
    WHERE account_num = account) = 'marine fish' THEN

    UPDATE sale_stats SET count = count +
       (SELECT qty FROM sales
        WHERE item_category = 'marine fish'
        AND account_num = account)
    WHERE item_category = 'marine fish';

WHEN (SELECT item_category FROM sales
    WHERE account_num = account) = 'marine crustaceans' THEN

    UPDATE sale_stats SET count = count +
       (SELECT qty FROM sales
        WHERE item_category = 'marine crustaceans'
        AND account_num = account)
    WHERE item_category = 'marine crustaceans';

WHEN (SELECT item_category FROM sales
    WHERE account_num = account) = 'marine mollusks' THEN

    UPDATE sale_stats SET count = count +
       (SELECT qty FROM sales
        WHERE item_category = 'marine mollusks'
        AND account_num = account)
    WHERE item_category = 'marine mollusks';

WHEN (SELECT item_category FROM sales
    WHERE account_num = account) = 'marine coelenterates' THEN

    UPDATE sale_stats SET count = count +
       (SELECT qty FROM sales
        WHERE item_category = 'marine coelenterates'
        AND account_num = account)
    WHERE item_category = 'marine coelenterates';

WHEN (SELECT item_category FROM sales
    WHERE account_num = account) = 'marine echinoderms' THEN

    UPDATE sale_stats SET count = count +
       (SELECT qty FROM sales
        WHERE item_category = 'marine echinoderms'
        AND account_num = account)
    WHERE item_category = 'marine echinoderms';
END;
```

FOR Statements

The FOR statement is not at first what you would expect, particularly if you compare it with the same structure in most programming languages. Typically, you expect the statement to allow iterations over some structure performing operations under the control of FOR loop boundaries. The FOR statement in SQL is an iterative statement. It iterates over elements of a result table for all rows within the table. This is similar to the iteration found in the trigger statement. The main context of the FOR iterator is to execute a group of SQL statements for each row in a table formed as a result of a query expression. This is similar to an implicit cursor definition with subsequent fetches over all the rows.

If a programmer, however, wants to only iterate over some subset of the rows, the LEAVE statement can be used to exit the FOR statement at any time or place in the structure. The FOR statement, as with other statements in SQL, can have labels associated with it, giving programmers a means to directly access the statement from other places in the application. The basic structure of the FOR statement is:

```
FOR variable-name
    AS cursor-specification
    DO SQL-statements
END FOR;
```

As an example of this statement, use the `aquatic_sales` table. You may want to audit the sales for an interval of time, and determine the volume of sales for a particular species or category of fish.

The `aquatic_sales` table is defined as follows:

```
CREATE TABLE aquatic_sales (
    sale_id         INTEGER
        CONSTRAINT   sales_sale_id_pk PRIMARY KEY,
    stock_id        INTEGER,
    sale_item_name  CHAR(30),
    sale_price      DECIMAL(10,2),
    cust_id         INTEGER,
    date            DATE )
CREATE TABLE fish_audit (
    common_surname  CHAR(30),
    count           INTEGER,
    gross_income    DECIMAL(10,2),
)
```

You can form this query above an SQL FOR statement, which acts on this table and the `sales_audit` tables as follows:

```
fish_check:   FOR fish AS SELECT * FROM aquatic_sales
              WHERE date BETWEEN '01-jul-98'
              AND '31-jul-98'
       DO
          IF sale_item_name LIKE '%angelfish' THEN
              UPDATE fish_audit SET count = count + 1,
              gross_income = gross_income + fish.sale_item_price
              WHERE common_surname = angelfish;
          END IF;
       END FOR;
```

LOOP Statements

The LOOP statement is a way for a programmer to construct a control structure, which executes a group of statements continuously. The loop is exited with a LEAVE statement. Without the LEAVE statement, the loop continues infinitely. The structure of the LOOP statement has a label associated with the loop and requires only the LOOP and END LOOP statements to define it. The structure is as follows:

```
Label:   LOOP
       SQL statements
    END LOOP;
```

As an example of the loop, you can apply this as the looping structure to check the sales for each employee. If you assume that employee identifiers begin with 100 and continue until 125, then you can build the exit condition, which detects an employee number that is not part of the employee table. This can also be performed by a test to determine if an employee exists, and whether you have found every employee. This requires a bit more logic. Begin by showing the tables this loop will operate on:

```
CREATE TABLE sales (
    sale_id         INTEGER
        CONSTRAINT sales_sale_id_pk PRIMARY KEY,
    sale_date       DATE,
    stock_id        INTEGER,
    sale_item_name  CHAR(30),
    sale_price      DECIMAL(10,2),
    emp_id          INTEGER,
    cust_id         INTEGER )
```

```
CREATE TABLE aquairium_revenues (
    employee_id     INTEGER,
    present_date    DATE,
    daily_sales     DECIMAL(10,2),
    monthly_sales   DECIMAL(10,2),
    year_to_date    DECIMAL(10,2),
    commissions     DECIMAL(10,2)
)

BEGIN
DECLARE emp_num    INTEGER;
SET emp_num = 100;
emp_vol:    LOOP
    IF emp_num > 125 THEN
        LEAVE emp_vol;
    ELSE
        BEGIN
        SELECT SUM(sale_price) INTO e_sum FROM sales
        WHERE emp_id = emp_num
        AND sale_date = CURRENT_DATE;
        UPDATE aquairium_revenues SET daily_sales = e_sum
        WHERE employee_id = emp_num;
        SET emp_num = emp_num + 1;
    END IF;
    END LOOP;
END;
```

First, the loop adds the sales for each employee for the current day. You could also have continued this process to compute the month-to-date and year-to-date amounts, as well as any commissions due. This loop would execute forever if the LEAVE statement were not included.

Controlling the entrance to and exit from the loop lies fully on the programmer who is designing and coding the LOOP statement. The designer must be careful to include a LEAVE statement, possibly, some error-handling code, and valid testing and initialization conditions to make sure the loop will perform as intended.

REPEAT Statements

Unlike the LOOP structure, the REPEAT statement requires an ending condition in a specific location in the statement so it will terminate. The REPEAT statement is similar to DO WHILE or DO UNTIL structures found in many programming languages. The set of encased statements is repeated until the test at the end of the sequence is met. In addition, this structure will execute the sequence of encased statements at least once, even if the condition to exit is met as soon as the REPEAT is entered. The test is performed at the bottom of the sequence, guaranteeing it will execute at least once. The basic structure of the REPEAT statement is:

```
Label:   REPEAT
      SQL-statements
      SQL-statements
      SQL-statements
   UNTIL <condition>
   END REPEAT;
```

As an example of the REPEAT statement, here is the previous LOOP example, using REPEAT as the structure that permits the execution of the internal statements:

```
BEGIN
DECLARE emp_num    INTEGER;
SET emp_num = 100;

emp_vol:   REPEAT

        BEGIN

        SELECT SUM(sale_price) INTO e_sum FROM sales
        WHERE emp_id = emp_num
        AND sale_date = CURRENT_DATE;
        UPDATE aquairium_revenues SET daily_sales = e_sum
        WHERE employee_id = emp_num;
        SET emp_num = emp_num + 1;

        END;

      UNTIL emp_num > 126

      END REPEAT;

END;
```

Right away, you might have noticed that the number of lines of code to perform the same function has decreased. Much of the overhead associated with controlling the loop has been removed. The explicit LEAVE statement has been removed, though you could still include LEAVE statements anywhere they are valid in the body of the REPEAT statement. In the IF – THEN – ELSE structure in the loop, the test was performed at the beginning. In the REPEAT statement, the test is performed at the end. In addition, note that the boundary being tested was increased by one to make sure that sales for employee 125 were accounted for.

WHILE Statements

The WHILE statement is a converse looping structure available in SQL. The WHILE statement is similar to those in many programming languages. The statement provides repeated execution of an encased group of statements as long as the condition being tested for is true. The test is performed at the beginning of the statement, instead of in the body of the structure, as was done in the LOOP statement, or at the end of the structure, as was done in the REPEAT statement. The WHILE statement has the following basic structure:

```
Label:   WHILE <condition>
       DO
         SQL-statements
         SQL-statements
         SQL-statements
     END WHILE;
```

As an example, using the previous example with the LOOP and REPEAT statements, WHILE is used as the controlling structure, which permits execution of the internal statements:

```
BEGIN

DECLARE emp_num    INTEGER;
SET emp_num = 100;

emp_vol:   WHILE emp_num < 126

         DO

         BEGIN

         SELECT SUM(sale_price) INTO e_sum FROM sales
         WHERE emp_id = emp_num
         AND sale_date = CURRENT_DATE;

         UPDATE aquairium_revenues SET daily_sales = e_sum
         WHERE employee_id = emp_num;
         SET emp_num = emp_num + 1;

         END;

       END WHILE;

END;
```

This example actually resembles the REPEAT statement. The amount of code is about the same, and the internal logic in the execution block has not changed at all. The only changes are the movement of the test from the bottom of the structure to the top and the alteration of the test for the continuation of the repetitive sequence of code until the condition is met. The condition tests for less than instead of greater than. All other conditions and initializations are the same.

Error Handling

No matter how good you think you are as a programmer, errors will creep into your applications in many ways. Some may be actual coding errors; others may be induced by invalid data introduced in your applications. Errors may also be caused by external effects, such as hardware, the operating system, network, and database management system errors. Programmers tend to focus on the task at hand in an application, leaving the handling of these nonproductive elements for a later time. The reality, however, is that errors will be introduced into your applications, and you must write code to defend against these conditions.

Traditional SQL environments had little in the way of error-handling facilities. If errors occurred in the execution of an SQL program, a limited amount of feedback could be given to the host program, which would then have the job of correcting the condition. SQL simply would abort the last sequence of work since the last commit statement, or possibly since the session initiation, if no commits had occurred.

SQL persistent stored modules offer alternatives to these problems of error handling. Since the new SQL has been designed as a computationally complete language, it was necessary to include some form of error detection, signaling, and handling in the new language. SQL calls this form of error management "condition handling." This name was chosen because it can be used for all condition handling, not just handling errors. Condition handling infers both good and bad condition-handling facilities. There is only one facility, but it is general enough to be used for both purposes. The condition-handling mechanisms detect and operate on successful completion of a statement or sequence, a warning, no data return, and unexpected situations.

The basic idea is to allow the stored routines in persistent stored modules to define system behavior, such as UNDO, REDO, CONTINUE, EXIT, and others. The basic form of the mechanisms is illustrated in this simple block:

```
DECLARE

    some declarations

BEGIN

    SQL-statements
    SQL-statements
    SQL-statements

EXCEPTION

    WHEN exception-name OR exception-name

    THEN

        SQL-code to handle condition

END;
```

Raising an exception also affects the diagnostic area. Any previously defined diagnostic information is flushed. Common exceptions that are tested for include NO_DATA_FOUND and so on. The variety of possible exceptions is as great as a vendor can define. The SQL standard specifies a handful of conditions that are tested and passed back in the SQLERROR and SQLCODE variables.

SIGNAL Statements

To construct a condition-handling facility, you first need mechanisms to indicate that a condition has occurred. In SQL, the mechanism is the condition statement, which tests for a condition that may or may not have occurred. There are also blanket conditions that can be tested for, or defaulted to, if none of the designed conditions occur in the code. Once a condition has been verified to have occurred, SQL must do something with it. The mechanism for this is the SIGNAL statement. The SIGNAL statement raises an exception to the tested condition (e.g., SIGNAL bad_data). The raising of the condition that fires the signal passes control to the named exception or condition. In the simple case above control is passed to the bad_data exception.

The basic form of an exception signal is to test a condition and then pass control from the condition to the handler when the condition is found to be true:

```
DECLARE exception_name     EXCEPTION  . . . . ;
          .
          .
          .
IF condition THEN
    SIGNAL exception_name;
```

The declaration defines the exception; the SIGNAL statement causes the named exception to be executed. You also need syntax and semantics for defining the exception and for performing its intended function. In addition, the intended functional limitations of the exception's mechanism must be refined.

If the condition handler cannot handle the signaled condition, an additional form of SIGNAL is available. The RESIGNAL statement allows the condition to be raised again. When this occurs, the condition handler originally signaled can pass the condition to the next-highest handler (Figure 11.5). For example, in the simple description above you can add:

```
DECLARE exception_name     EXCEPTION  . . . . ;
          .
          .
          .
IF condition THEN
    SIGNAL exception_name;
ELSE RESIGNAL exception_name;
END IF;
```

Condition handlers are declared for individual compound statements or blocks. The scope of the condition handling is that of the block's local and contained statements. The handlers in a compound, multileveled block can be overridden by inner declarations. For example, if you have the handler defined above, and on execution it is found that it cannot handle the condition passed to it, two things can occur: The handler will contain a RESIGNAL, which it can use to call a further encased handler, or the handler will release the exception to be handled at a higher-scoped block.

Condition Handling

The signaling or resignaling of a condition does not make the condition and its original effect go away. You need statements, syntax, and semantics, which allow the programmer to handle the condition in a way

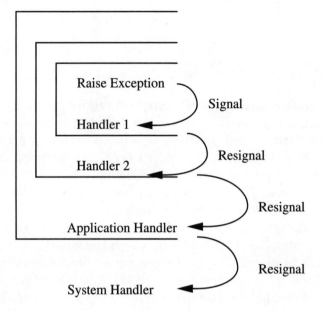

Figure 11.5

Multileveled
condition handling.

amenable to the application and the database's required properties.
These properties must be preserved if the database is to be useful. The
mechanism provided by SQL is called condition handling. At the time
of this writing, there are only a few accepted methods of condition handling in SQL. Hopefully, more will come as vendors and the committees
see the benefits of this mechanism.

SQL condition handlers are found in the context of compound statements. The format of a typical condition handler is as follows:

```
<handler declaration> ::=
        DECLARE <handler type> HANDLER
           FOR <condition value list>
             <handler action>

<handler type> ::=
        CONTINUE
        | EXIT
        | UNDO

<handler action> ::=
        <SQL procedure statement>

<condition value list> ::=
        <condition value> [ { <comma> <condition value> } . . . ]
```

```
<condition value> ::=
        <sqlstate value>
        | <condition name>
        | SQLEXCEPTION
        | SQLWARNING
        | NOT FOUND
```

The sequence of BNF statements above provides a way to declare the method of handling an exception and/or completion condition in SQL persistent stored modules. Condition handling provides syntax to declare a handler, specifying its type, the exception, and/or completion conditions it can handle, and the action the handler can take in response to the raised condition. A condition handler can also explicitly signal exception and/or completion conditions.

The scope of a declared condition handler is the same as the scope of the compound statement in which the handler is defined. This implies that handlers must be written for all blocks of a compound statement as well as an application for full coverage of all possible conditions.

A handler associates one or more conditions with a handler action: an SQL procedure statement. A general handler is one associated with the condition values SQLEXCEPTION, SQLWARNING, and NOT FOUND. All other handlers are specific handlers written to respond to a specific programmer-defined condition.

The current SQL standard provides syntax and semantics for three types of handlers: CONTINUE, EXIT, and UNDO. The CONTINUE handler performs the designed handler operation. On completion, it returns control to the statement following the original firing statement. The EXIT handler performs the handler action. On completion, it passes control out of the block or compound statement where the condition derived. The UNDO handler causes any changes performed by the compound statement to be rolled back. This UNDO includes canceling any triggers that may have been activated by execution of the compound statements. Similar to the EXIT handler, the UNDO handler returns control of execution to the statement outside the compound block that caused the activation of the conditions.

Exceptions and conditions must be explicitly defined. They must have names associated with them and be an SQLSTATE value. Exceptions can be raised explicitly using the SIGNAL and RESIGNAL statements. The handler for a defined exception is associated with the exception through the handler declaration. The name for the handler during the declaration becomes associated with an SQLSTATE value.

The general form of a declaration is:

```
BEGIN
   DECLARE handler_name CONDITION FOR SQLSTATE '00000';
       .
       .
       .
   DECLARE UNDO HANDLER FOR SQLSTATE VALUE '00000'
       Body of handler
END;
```

As an example of condition handling, go back to the example of the aquatic fish stock table. The condition you want to test for is which fish have not been sold since the last audit. If a specific fish has not been sold since the last audit, you want to lower the price to spur sales:

```
DECLARE unsold_species CONDITION FOR SQLSTATE 'xxxxx';
   .
   <sql code>
   .
   test for sales from sale table
   IF no_sale THEN SIGNAL unsold_species;

DECLARE CONTINUE HANDLER FOR xxxxx
   INSERT INTO sale_items VALUES ( . . . );
```

Summary

Persistent stored modules, and the features that comprise this component of the SQL language, represent one of the single most significant improvements to SQL. This element of the language allowed SQL to be removed from its dependency for control context from host languages. The SQL persistent stored modules provide all the elements necessary to make the language computationally complete. The concepts of control structures and block structuring, as well as the module, procedure, function, and package, are all elements that have enhanced the usefulness and reusability of SQL code. Many books are being published that provide more detailed information about the features of SQL/PSM. Refer to "Persistent Stored Modules (SQL/PSM)," in the ISO-ANSI Working Draft (Melton 1998e) for a particularly complete text.

CHAPTER **12**

Miscellaneous Additional SQL-3 Features

Overview of Additional Features

The SQL-3 language added many new features to the basic language introduced in 1986. The new features fall into a handful of major categories. The first category deals with execution extensions, which enhance performance of SQL applications. The second category deals with reliability and recovery. The third category deals with enhancements to constraints and their enforcement. This major category is then followed by enhancements to transactions and cursors. This does not, however, represent an exhaustive list of features. The SQL committee is still refining the language and will continue to even as this version is released. The committee is attempting to initiate a three-year cycle for releasing incremental improvements to the language. Many of the features initially targeted for the all-encompassing SQL-3 language being released in 1999 were deferred and will be seen in increments beginning in 2002 and every three years thereafter. That is the present goal of the SQL-3 database language committee. Time will tell if this schedule can be maintained.

Table Expressions

A table expression is similar to a view in that it is defined over a table and returns some selected subset of the elements of the table. Unlike a view, however, the table expression does not represent a schema-level item. It is not a defined constructed table; it is a selection derived from some constructed dynamic view. A table expression is used in place of a view definition and view reference and is found inside the SQL statement forming the table expression. The BNF for a table expression is:

```
<table expression> ::=
    <from clause>
    [ <where clause> ]
    [ < group by clause> ]
    [ < having clause> ]
```

The result of a table expression execution is a derived table. The row types of the table expression are mapped to the row types of the embedded SELECT statements in the from clause. The difference from a traditional view table is that the table expression does not need to compute and maintain a temporary table. Instead, it simply represents a result table as with any other SELECT statement. The difference from a simple SELECT is that the column names can be changed as part of the table expression execution. An additional benefit of the table expression is that it can embed host variables in the "view" and can enforce groupings on the constructed view.

An example, using the aquarium database, could be to determine the average salary of employees based on the year they were hired. This can be accomplished directly, but, to illustrate the table expression, use the following syntax based on the employee table:

```
CREATE TABLE employees (
    emp_id            INTEGER
       CONSTRAINT employees_emp_id_pk PRIMARY KEY,
    emp_title         VARCHAR(30),
    emp_last_name     VARCHAR(30)
       CONSTRAINT emp_last_name_not_null NOT NULL,
    emp_first_name    VARCHAR(30)
       CONSTRAINT emp_first_name_not_null NOT NULL,
    emp_address       CHARACTER VARYING (30),
    emp_city          CHARACTER VARYING (20),
    emp_state         CHARACTER (2),
    emp_zip           CHARACTER VARYING (9),
    emp_phone         CHARACTER (10),
    emp_start_date    TIMESTAMP,
    emp_pay_rate      DECIMAL (7,2),
    emp_com_rate      DECIMAL (3,2),
    emp_total_sales   DECIMAL(6,2)
)
```

The table expression to perform the action you want is as follows:

```
SELECT position, hire_year, AVG(total_pay)
    FROM (
        SELECT emp_id, YEAR(emp_start_date) AS hire_year,
        emp_title AS position,
        (emp_pay_rate * 2080)+(emp_com_rate*emp_total_sales)
           AS total_pay
        FROM employees
        WHERE emp_start_date > :start_date
        ) AS position_pay
    GROUP BY position, hire_year
```

This example illustrates a few elements of the statement syntax and semantics. First, the table expression is composed of three columns: position, hire_year, and average salary. The table itself is named position_pay and is organized using position and hire_year as sorting keys. In addition, the SELECT statement, which makes up the body of the table expression, uses a computation built on a combination of in-

ternal columns of the employee table. An external variable,
:start_date, was included as one of the restrictions used in constructing the "view."

Common Table Expressions

SQL-3 goes beyond the table expression first introduced in SQL-2. The major change is in the lifetime of the expression. In SQL-2, a table expression can only be used when defined. In SQL-3, table expressions can be defined in a manner similar to views and can be reused at a later time without having to reinstantiate the table expression. The advantage of common table expressions over views is the same as that of general table expressions. The table is defined when needed and does not become part of the database schema.

The advantage of the common table expression over the general table expression is that the programmer can avoid the overhead of reevaluation upon each reference to the table expression. In addition to this benefit, the programmer also can avoid the inevitable errors associated with each reference possibly returning different results. For example, you can generate the same table expression as above, but simply equate it to the table expression name:

```
WITH
   position_pay AS (
      SELECT emp_id, YEAR(emp_start_date) AS hire_year,
      emp_title AS position,
      (emp_pay_rate * 2080)+(emp_com_rate*emp_total_sales)
         AS total_pay
      FROM employees
      WHERE emp_start_date > :start_date
      )
```

You can then write another query on the table expression, just as you can against any general schema-level table. For example, you can write the query to find all the employees who make more than $100,000 per year as follows:

```
SELECT emp_id, position, hire_year FROM position_pay WHERE
total_pay > 100000;
```

This example uses the common table expression in another query, just as if the common table expression had been defined as a base table or a view. These tables give the programmer greater flexibility in defining temporary tables without the need for defining new base tables, which would need to be removed from the database at the end of a program.

Recursive SQL

Another envisioned improvement was to allow self-referencing table expressions and self-referencing views. These are both referred to as recursive queries. The advantage of such queries is to permit the generic network traversal problems and the bill of materials queries to be handled in a more compact query. The major reason for this added feature to SQL was for programmer functionality and for improvements in performance. Classic algorithmic examples, which use such concepts, are the "traveling salesman" problem and the "all pairs shortest path" problem. As an example, you want to examine the fish database for fish distributors. You want to find out how material gets from one place to another and what the cost is to move products from one location to another.

Table 12.1 describes the primary and secondary distributors, the carrier that delivers product, and the average cost to do so.

TABLE 12.1

Fish_distributor
Table

Primary	Secondary	Distributor	Cost
Hawaii	Chicago	UPS	$7
Hawaii	New York	UPS	$6
Hawaii	Boston	FedEx	$8
New York	Detroit	FedEx	$2
Boston	Detroit	FedEx	$6
Chicago	Los Angeles	FedEx	$4
Detroit	Los Angeles	FedEx	$2

By using this table and the concept of a recursive query, you can generate a query to find all cities that can receive stock from Hawaii. The query may look something like this:

```
WITH RECURSIVE deliver_from (Primary, Secondary) AS
   (SELECT Primary, Secondary
    FROM   fish_distributors
    UNION
    SELECT in.Primary, out.Secondary
    FROM deliver_from in, fish_distributors out
    WHERE in.Secondary = out.Primary)
    SELECT * FROM deliver_from WHERE Primary=Hawaii;
```

The result of this query is the following chart:

Primary	Secondary
Hawaii	New York
Hawaii	Chicago
Hawaii	Boston
Hawaii	Detroit
Hawaii	Los Angeles

Recursion is not, however, without some problems. The programmer must be careful regarding when and how to use recursive SQL in a query. For example, negation causes a problem with recursive queries, since negation crosses recursion. Negation can only be applied to relations that are completely known prior to the application of the negation.

Another problem comes with grouping and aggregation. An already adopted element can be changed by newly adopted elements. For example, a new tuple with a matching value may be generated that matches an already existing tuple, causing the existing aggregate value to be modified. The error here is a subtle violation of monotonicity. To rectify this, aggregation can only be applied to those tables that are completely known prior to the operation. One way to work around this side effect is to move the aggregate outside of the recursion.

Recursion can also play havoc with other higher-order SQL operations, such as INTERSECT and EXCEPT. The problem with INTERSECT comes in the form of duplicates left over from the operations. If you use these operations within a recursive statement, the result may possess replica tuples, which must be removed. For EXCEPT, a similar problem occurs with recursion. Some unwanted side effects may occur if the programmer is not careful. The EXCEPT form may leave out some desirable elements, due to the recursive application of EXCEPT.

The recursive OUTER JOIN operation can be used to find items more efficiently than with nonrecursive code. For example, the OUTER JOIN:

```
A LEFT JOIN B ON C
```

is equivalent to:

```
SELECT A.*. B.*
   FROM A,B
   WHERE C
   UNION ALL
   SELECT A.*, NULL, . . . , NULL
   FROM A
   WHERE A.* NOT IN (SELECT A.* FROM A, B WHERE C)
```

This can be restated as a recursive query is as follows:

```
WITH RECURSIVE TABLE-X(...) AS
   (SELECT . . .
   UNION ALL
   SELECT . . .
   FROM (TABLE-X LEFT OUTER JOIN NONTABLE-X . . . ) . . .
```

There are many variations on this query and the semantics may vary slightly from vendor to vendor. As implementations are fielded, and more experience with the semantics occurs, more uses for these features will be discovered.

The FULL OUTER JOIN must not cross recursion. What this implies is that a reference to the recursive table being defined must not be part of the left or right operands of the FULL OUTER JOIN. For example, you cannot use the form of the statement above with the FULL OUTER JOIN in place of the LEFT OUTER JOIN. The following is illegal in SQL-3:

```
WITH RECURSIVE TABLE-X(...) AS
   (SELECT . . .
   UNION ALL
   SELECT . . .
   FROM (TABLE-X FULL OUTER JOIN NONTABLE-X . . . ) . . .
```

There are many other issues that must be taken into account when using recursion in SQL statements. It is often desirable to remove duplicates from the results of a query. This still holds true in recursive queries, although it may be desirable at times to maintain duplicates during the query evaluation at some level, while removing them at another level. In SQL, duplicates can be maintained by "coloring" the duplicate rows. That is, if a duplicate exists, but is derived from a different portion of the query, using appropriate range variables to "mark" the intermediate results can effectively allow the duplicates to exist, while maintaining their derived location information. For example, if you want to find all possible train schedule connections between two cities, you can use the following statements:

```
WITH RECURSIVE TABLE-ALL-PAIRS (Source, Destination) AS
    (SELECT Source, Destination
    FROM Schedules
    UNION ALL
    SELECT in.Source, out.Destination
    FROM TABLE-ALL-PAIRS in, Schedules out
    WHERE in.Destination = out.Source
    )
SELECT * FROM TABLE-ALL-PAIRS;
```

The query uses the range variables over the temporary tables as the means to allow the duplicates to survive during the execution of the query. If the intent of the query is to remove the duplicates, this can be easily achieved by using the UNION, INTERSECT, or DISTINCT operations. For example, if you were to use the same query as specified above, but simply remove the keyword ALL, the UNION would remove duplicates as part of normal operation of the UNION statement:

```
WITH RECURSIVE TABLE-ALL-PAIRS (Source, Destination) AS
    (SELECT Source, Destination
    FROM Schedules
    UNION
    SELECT in.Source, out.Destination
    FROM TABLE-ALL-PAIRS in, Schedules out
    WHERE in.Destination = out.Source
    )
SELECT * FROM TABLE-ALL-PAIRS;
```

The statement can also be altered by the DISTINCT operator to remove duplicates from the intermediate results:

```
WITH RECURSIVE TABLE-ALL-PAIRS (Source, Destination) AS
    (SELECT Source, Destination
    FROM Schedules
```

```
        UNION ALL
        SELECT DISTINCT in.Source, out.Destination
        FROM TABLE-ALL-PAIRS in, Schedules out
        WHERE in.Destination = out.Source
        )
    SELECT * FROM TABLE-ALL-PAIRS;
```

Other facilities of SQL can be further applied to the recursive query to make the statement's operations more clearly understood. For example, the intermediate table results that are being used in the recursive computation can be more clearly delineated if the renaming facilities of SQL are used. Another important aspect of the query operation is to be sure that the operations can be performed on the given sets. In some cases the initial set may be empty, whereas the final set would not be. As long as one of the involved sets has some tuples to process, the final result will have some information to return.

Handling Cycles

A more pressing problem with recursion is to manage the size of the sets that will be examined. If a cycle is encountered in the sets, the size of the sets will become unbounded. To handle this problem, the depth of the searched sets should be bounded to some maximum depth. One way of accomplishing this is to add an additional restriction on the recursive loop. In the example above, the depth of recursion was restricted to three by including a connection count:

```
WITH RECURSIVE TABLE-ALL-PAIRS (Source, Destination, connections) AS
    (SELECT Source, Destination, connections
    FROM Schedules
        UNION ALL
    SELECT in.Source, out.Destination, in.connections + 1
    FROM TABLE-ALL-PAIRS in, Schedules out
    WHERE in.Destination = out.Source
    AND in.connections < 3
    )
SELECT * FROM TABLE-ALL-PAIRS;
```

You can also use other predicates or restrictions to handle cycles and the depth of recursion. The exists and group predicates can be used by operators to further restrict how the data are processed. Exists and not exists predicates can be used to determine if a path of a certain cost exists within the set of paths searched to date. Similarly, the GROUP BY operator can be used to restrict the number of tuples returned for use in the recursion.

An extension to checking for cycles using the above techniques is to use the cycle clause, which is a subpart of the search or cycle clause. The BNF for the cycle clause is:

```
<search or cycle clause> ::=
    <search clause>
   |<cycle clause>
   |<search clause> <cycle clause>

   <cycle clause> ::=
      CYCLE <cycle column list>
      SET <cycle mark column> TO <cycle mark value>
      DEFAULT <non-cycle mark value>
      USING <path column>

   < cycle column list> ::=
      < cycle column > [ { <comma> < cycle column > } . . . ]
   < cycle column > ::= <column name>
   < cycle mark column > ::= <column name>
   < path column > ::= < column name >
   <cycle mark value> ::= <value expression>
   < non-cycle mark value> ::= <value expression>
```

The cycle clause can be used in place of the added column and test condition we set in the previous example, which restricted the depth of a recursive search. The cycle clause uses a column, which records the detection of a cycle; a value, which denotes the cycle detection; a set of navigational columns for detecting the cycle condition; and the name of the column of the resulting table for keeping information to detect a cycle condition:

```
WITH RECURSIVE TABLE_A ( column_a, column_b) AS
    (SELECT column_a, column_b
    FROM TABLE_B
    WHERE column_b = 'value'
       UNION ALL
    SELECT TABLE_A.column_a, TABLE_B.column_b
    FROM TABLE_A, TABLE_B
    WHERE TABLE_A.column_a = TABLE_B.column_b)
CYCLE column_b SET column_c TO '1' DEFAULT '0' USING TABLE_C
SELECT column_a, column_b FROM TABLE_A
```

The query above examines the tables recursively and sets the cycle table values based on what is detected during the operation of the recursive query. The CYCLE statement implements a test similar to what was shown in the previous example, but leaves the actual test implementation up to the implementation, instead of up to the coder of the query.

Figure 12.1

A connected graph.

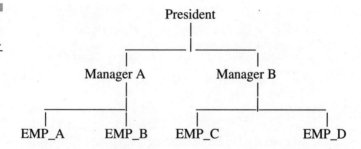

Searching Breadth First and Depth First

The second part of the search or cycle clause is the search condition, whose BNF is as follows:

```
<search or cycle clause> ::=
    <search clause>
    |<cycle clause>
    |<search clause> <cycle clause>

<search clause> ::=
    SEARCH <recursive search order> SET <sequence column>

<recursive search order> ::=
    DEPTH FIRST BY <sort specification list>
  | BREADTH FIRST BY <sort specification order>

<sequence column> ::= <column name>
```

The search of a graph is typically performed in some order. The search clause selects the technique that will be applied in the search of a graph, or connected data items, ordered into some form of connected structure. Given a graph (Figure 12.1) of a family tree or organization, you can represent information as a graph or tree structure. It is desirable to be able to specify how to traverse and search for elements of this structure, giving more control over how data are recovered.

If, for example, you want to retrieve the elements of this structure in breadth-first order, implying that you want to see all elements at each level together, the following code segment suffices:

```
WITH RECURSIVE Table_A (successor, levels) AS
    (SELECT successor, 1
     FROM TABLE_B
```

```
   WHERE predecessor = 'President'
       UNION ALL
   SELECT Table_B.sucessor, levels + 1
   FROM Table_A, Table_B
   WHERE Table_A.sucessor = Table_B.predecessor
   )
SELECT successor from Table_A
ORDER BY levels, successor;
```

In this example, no new features were applied to the solution to output the structure in breadth-first order. The column levels give the distance as node of the graph from the root of the graph. The order by clause on the result of the recursive query returns the items in breadth-first order. Using the new BREADTH FIRST BY operator provides a simpler way to specify the same operations:

```
WITH RECURSIVE Table_A (successor) AS
    (SELECT successor
    FROM TABLE_B
    WHERE predecessor = 'President'
        UNION ALL
    SELECT Table_B.sucessor
    FROM Table_A, Table_B
    WHERE Table_A.sucessor = Table_B.predecessor
    )
    SEARCH BREADTH FIRST BY successor SET levels
SELECT successor from Table_A
ORDER BY levels;
```

In this example, the "system" keeps track of the levels without any coding to specify how this should be done. The effect is the same: The syntax is a bit shorter, but no added functionality is provided.

Similarly, you can perform a depth-first traversal of the graph structure using existing SQL syntax, as follows:

```
WITH RECURSIVE Table_A (successor, visit_list) AS
    (SELECT successor, LIST(predecessor, successor)
    FROM TABLE_B
    WHERE predecessor = 'President'
        UNION ALL
    SELECT Table_B.successor, LIST_append(Table_A.visit_list,
Table_B.successor)
    FROM Table_A, Table_B
    WHERE Table_A.successor = Table_B.predecessor
    )
SELECT successor from Table_A
ORDER BY visit_list;
```

This form requires us to write two functions, LIST and LIST AP-PEND, to add successors to the list. The column, `visit_list`, for each node gives a list of all the keys from the root up to and including the node. The order by clause presents the results of the recursive query in depth-first order. This query can be further cleaned up and made more readable using the syntax provided by the DEPTH FIRST BY operator:

```
WITH RECURSIVE Table_A (successor) AS
    (SELECT successor
    FROM TABLE_B
    WHERE predecessor = 'President'
        UNION ALL
    SELECT Table_B.successor
    FROM Table_A, Table_B
    WHERE Table_A.successor = Table_B.predecessor
    )
    SEARCH DEPTH FIRST BY successor SET visit_list
SELECT successor from Table_A
ORDER BY visit_list;
```

This results in a query where the method of search and the presentation of the result is well known and well defined.

Other forms of recursion are also being considered for the SQL standard. Mutual recursion is a form of recursion where the tables are defined referencing each other. For example, the following query will produce a list of even-counting numbers, which are derived from the odd numbers recursively:

```
WITH RECURSIVE
    EVEN (N) AS
        (Values(0) UNION SELECT M + 1 FROM ODD),
    ODD (M) AS
        (SELECT N + 1 FROM EVEN)
    SELECT * FROM EVEN WHERE N < Max
```

This form of recursion has its place in real applications, such as business management, product construction lists, and many more.

Linear and nonlinear recursion are supported. A recursive query is linear if, in every joined table, the table being defined recursively is referenced once. If the condition is violated, then the recursion is nonlinear. This form of recursion can be used to determine the parts assemblies for products requiring multiple subassemblies.

Extensions to Order By

In SQL, the order by clause is used to specify how the result of a query is to be presented to the user or program. In SQL-92, the order by clause has the following form:

```
<order by clause> ::=
    ORDER BY < sort specification list>

<sort specification list> ::=
    <sort specification> [ { <comma> <sort specification> } . . . ]

<sort specification> ::=
    <sort key> [ <collate clause>] [ <ordering specification> ]

<sort key> ::= <value expression>
<ordering specification> ::= ASC | DESC
```

In the classic use of the order by clause, the returned values from a SELECT statement or cursor are organized in either ascending or descending order based on the type of the column used in the clause. In addition to requiring a column to use in performing the ordering, the column must show up in the list of columns to be provided as output from the query—for example, if you have the marine_fish table, as defined here:

```
CREATE TABLE marine_fish (
    scientific_name    name,
    common_name        name,
    fish_species       name,
    max_size           DECIMAL (5,2)
    food_preference    food,
    geographic_range   region,
    fish_disposition   temperament,
    fish_activity      day_shift
)
```

You can query this table to find the fish that are found in the waters off the Hawaiian Islands and then order them by their common names, as follows:

```
SELECT common_name, scientific_name, max_size
FROM marine_fish
WHERE geographic_range = 'hawaiian islands'
ORDER BY common_name ASC;
```

This results in a list of marine fish in alphabetical order for the species found in the waters off the Hawaiian Islands. What SQL-3 has done is expand on this basic order by clause to allow some added functionality. For example, instead of requiring that the ordering use an element from the list of available columns used in the SELECT statement, the ordering can be done on a column of the same table, not named in the output list:

```
SELECT scientific_name, species, max_size
FROM marine_fish
WHERE geographic_range = 'hawaiian islands'
ORDER BY common_name ASC;
```

This form of the query orders the output by common_name, but the common name does not show up in the list of output data. In addition, the list doesn't appear to be in sorted order, since the common names and the scientific names do not necessarily follow the same order. For example, the lionfish is scientifically known as Pterois volitans; it may not show up in the same location in the final list.

ORDER BY can also include an expression or function performed on the output. For example, if you have an employee table for your database, you can select the employees, their departments, and their hire dates ordered by their salary and commissions as a fraction:

```
SELECT name, dept, hire_date
FROM employees
WHERE manager = 'Jenkins'
ORDER BY salary / (salary + commissions);
```

This query results in a list of employees who work for Jenkins, the departments they work in, and their dates of hire. The list is ordered by the ratio of their salaries divided by the sum of their salaries plus commissions. The order is assumed ascending, since this is the default. The list has employees with the highest commissions versus their salaries listed first followed by those with the smallest commissions.

The SQL standard also provides an additional feature for user-defined data types, a user-defined ordering. This gives the data type specifier the ability to specify an ordering that makes sense for their data type. The BNF for this feature is:

```
<user defined ordering definition> ::=
   <CREATE ORDERING FOR <user-defined type> <ordering form>

<ordering form> ::=
   <equals ordering form>
  |<full ordering form>
```

```
<equals ordering form> ::=
    EQUALS ONLY BY <ordering category>

<full ordering form> ::=
    ORDER FULL BY <ordering category>

<ordering category> ::=
     <relative category>
    |<hash category>
    |<state category>

<relative category> ::=
    RELATIVE WITH <relative function specification>

<hash category> ::=
    HASH WITH <hash function specification>

<state category> ::=
    STATE [ <specification name> ]

<relative function specification> ::= <specific routine designator>
<hash function specification> ::= <specific routine designator>
```

As an example, use the fish table above and create a user-defined type location as an object with functions location_equals, location_near, location_like, and location_within. The functions operate on data of type location to determine if a given region meets the selection criteria:

```
CREATE ORDERING FOR region
    EQUALS ONLY BY RELATIVE WITH FUNCTION locator_order;
```

Then, to use this order by operator, you simply use it in place of the column name in an ORDER BY component of an SQL statement:

```
SELECT common_name, region
FROM marine_fish
ORDER BY region;
```

Roles

SQL-3 adds to the authorization and security concepts available in the SQL-92 language. One particular extension comes from the concept of a role. A role is a named group of related privileges that can be granted to users or other roles. Roles are designed to ease the administration of privileges on user, system, and schema objects. Roles are meant to control access and objects and permit easier management in the database

Figure 12.2

Common user roles.

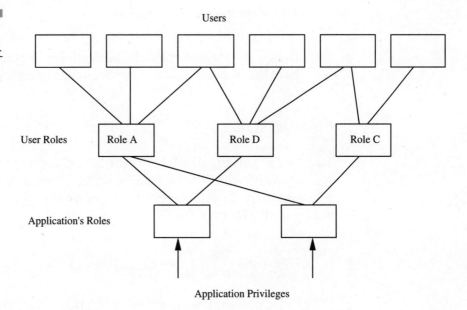

(Figure 12.2). In particular, roles provide for reduced administrative actions, since granting the same set of privileges explicitly to many users can be done with a role once, which can then be granted to many users as a collection of privileges.

Roles can aid in dynamic privilege management by giving the administrator a way to alter the privileges of a group of users instead of altering singular privileges for all users. If an alteration of access for some temporary time is required, roles provide a way to do this in a central place. Roles add other beneficial properties to the database. They can be used for accessing and using security and auditing applications. Roles can be created for application access or for managing privileges for a group.

Application roles give appropriate rights to a group of users to run a given database application. Applications can have several roles; each can have a different set of privileges. User roles are created to group common object privileges to a set of users. Privileges to the objects are then managed by granting the role to specific users.

Database roles have the following properties:

- A role is a collection of privileges on system or schema objects.
- A role can be granted to other roles, but not to itself or circularly.
- A role can be granted to one or more database users or roles.

- A role can be enabled or disabled.
- A role can be revoked from one or more users or roles.
- Indirectly granted roles can be explicitly enabled or disabled based on role relationships (inheritance/ordering).

Create Role

To create a role, the developer must have the privileges from the database administrator. If the CREATE ROLE privilege is granted, then the developer may create roles on developer-owned objects (objects the user has created). The BNF for the create role is:

```
<role definition> ::=
   CREATE ROLE <role name>
   [ WITH ADMIN <grantor>]
```

The role name is used to grant all privileges that have been associated with the role. After creation of the role, there are no privileges associated with the role. These have to be added to the role using the GRANT statements. As an example, create a role, order_fish, to allow members of the sales staff to insert orders into the orders table. The role is created using the following statement:

```
CREATE ROLE order_fish;
```

At this time, the role is not associated with any user; it is not associated with any table, procedure, function, package, user-defined type, object, or any other system or schema object. It is simply a role, which now has a place in the system tables where role information is maintained.

Grant Role

A role can be created by the database administrator or the creator of a database object. This implies that a user who creates a table, view, procedure, function, trigger, object, user data type, or some other schema-level object owned by the user can also grant access to that object to other users or roles.

The GRANT statement is used to grant access to the system and/or user schema objects to users, or roles within the system. The format of the GRANT statement is:

```
<grant statement> ::=
    <grant privilege statement>
   |<grant role statement>

<grant privilege statement> ::=
    GRANT <privileges>
      TO <grantee> [ { <comma> <grantee> } . . . ]
        [ WITH GRANT OPTION ]
        [ FROM <grantor> ]

<grant role statement> ::=
    GRANT <role granted> [ { <comma> <role granted> } . . . ]
        TO <grantee> [ { <comma> <grantee> } . . . ]
        [ WITH GRANT OPTION ]
        [ FROM <grantor> ]

<role granted> ::= <role name>
```

The GRANT statement is used to allow a specific user, the grantee, to use a specific privilege on a specific database object or collection of objects bound into a role. For example, if you want to provide selection privileges to the `marine_fish` table to all the customers who are collected into a role called "customer," the following statement can be used:

```
CREATE ROLE customer;
GRANT SELECT ON marine_fish TO customer;
```

This sequence of statements first creates the role customer, followed by a second statement, which grants the SELECT operation to the role customer. There are a number of variations possible on this statement. For example, instead of using a role, you can grant the SELECT to some specific user. Instead of a SELECT statement, you can authorize the role, or specific user, to perform any of the following operations with a variety of restrictions:

- INSERT a tuple to a table—for example, if you want to give the sales staff the ability to add a new fish to the `marine_fish` table, you can grant the `sales_staff` the INSERT privilege, as follows:

```
GRANT INSERT ON marine_fish TO sales_staff;
```

■ INSERT an attribute or list of attributes in a tuple of a relation—for example, if you want the manager to have the right to insert only the price field in the `marine_stock` table, you can use the following:

```
GRANT INSERT ON marine_fish.price TO manager;
```

■ UPDATE a tuple in a table—for example, if you want to give the same manager the ability to alter the contents of any existing `marine_stock` item, you can use the statement:

```
GRANT UPDATE ON marine_stock to manager;
```

■ UPDATE an attribute or list of attributes in a tuple of a relation—for example, if you want the price to be updated only on existing stock items, you can use the statement:

```
GRANT UPDATE ON marine_fish.price to manager;
```

■ DELETE a tuple from a table—this can be accomplished by granting the DELETE authority to an individual or role. For example, to allow the manager to delete items from the `marine_stock`, you can use the statement:

```
GRANT DELETE ON marine_stock TO manager;
```

■ SELECT a tuple from a table—this can be granted to an individual or role by using the GRANT statement, as follows:

```
GRANT SELECT ON marine_fish TO customer;
```

■ SELECT an attribute or list of attributes from a tuple within a relation—this can be provided by including a list of items from a table. For example, to limit the SELECT to only common names and scientific names, you can write this statement:

```
GRANT SELECT ON (marine_fish.common_name,
marine_fish.scientific_name)
TO customer;
```

- REFERENCES for referencing a table—for example, you can allow the manager to create references to other tables in the schema. REFERENCES can also be used to allow references using an attribute or list of attributes from a relation.

- USAGE of a domain, abstract data type, character set, collation, or translation identified by the privilege. This permits the use of the named object by the named user. For example, to allow a user role called "coder" to use an abstract data type named "address" in defining other tables or abstract data types, write this statement:

```
GRANT USAGE ON address TO coder;
```

- UNDER defines the existence of a privilege on a user-defined type defined by the descriptor. For example, if you have a user-defined data type called "person," and you want to create a new type called "student" using the person type as a basis, you need to possess the UNDER privilege on the person type to create the student type:

```
GRANT UNDER ON person TO coder;
```

- EXECUTE gives the ability to execute packages, procedures, or functions defined by others in the database. EXECUTE defines the privilege to run a routine defined by the descriptor. For example, you have a function `order_fish`. To allow the `sales_staff` role to execute the function requires a statement such as:

```
GRANT EXECUTE ON order_fish TO sales_staff;
```

- Similarly, if you want to allow someone to use a trigger defined on a specific table, you require the specification of a GRANT on the specific table:

```
GRANT TRIGGER ON marine_fish to coder;
```

- In the above statements, if you add the WITH GRANT OPTION, you give the right to the granted user to give others the right to access and use the named object.

Revoke Role/Drop Role

If you have the ability to grant a role or privilege to a user or another role, then you also need the ability to revoke or remove the privilege. The format of the REVOKE role operator is as follows:

```
<revoke statement> ::=
    <revoke privilege statement>
   |<revoke role statement>

< revoke privilege statement> ::=
   REVOKE [ GRANT OPTION FOR ] <privileges>
      FROM <grantee> [ {<comma> <grantee> } . . . ]
         [ FROM <grantor> ]
         <drop behavior>

<revoke role statement> ::=
   REVOKE [ ADMIN OPTION FOR ]
      <role revoked> [ { <comma> <role revoked> } . . . ]
      FROM <grantee> [ {<comma> <grantee> } . . . ]
         [ FROM <grantor> ]
         <drop behavior>
```

As an example, if you want to revoke the ability of the customers to select the scientific names of the marine fish, you can use the following statement:

```
REVOKE SELECT ON marine_fish.scientific_name FROM customer;
```

If you want to revoke all rights granted to the customer role from the user named "timmons," you can use the statement:

```
REVOKE customer FROM timmons;
```

If the role has the administrator option, you can revoke this aspect of the role, leaving all other aspects in place. You add ADMIN OPTION FOR to the above REVOKE statement:

```
REVOKE ADMIN OPTION FOR customer FROM timmons;
```

This results in the revocation of all abilities to grant role privileges given to the customer role from the user "timmons."

If you can grant privileges and roles to users, you should also be able to remove those privileges and roles. You saw how to revoke the privileges granted to users and roles. Now you need to look at how to remove roles completely from the system. The statement to perform this function is the DROP ROLE statement. The format of the DROP ROLE statement is:

```
<drop role statement> ::= DROP ROLE <role name>
```

As an example, to remove the customer role from the database, use this statement:

```
DROP ROLE customer;
```

In general, roles are used for one of two purposes: to manage privileges for a database application or to manage the privileges for a user group. Roles can be granted to local users and to remote users on different database systems or environments. If user applications or tools have access to SQL databases, they can be restricted as to what they can or cannot do to the database and its applications.

Savepoints

A savepoint permits the intermediate marking of the state of a transaction or session execution. Savepoints partition the execution of a long transaction into manageable points in time. A transaction can be rolled back to this point and resume execution (Figure 12.3).

A savepoint can be thought of as an arbitrary marker, which indicates to the underlying database system what the state of the transaction was at some intermediate point in time. This marker can then be used as a means to recover the saved state in a transaction's execution. A good design principle is to use savepoints at points in a transaction where some transitional actions are occurring. For example, create a savepoint before each functional partition of a transaction's work. By using this concept, if at some future point a function fails, the transaction simply returns to the state that existed before the function began. The function executes again. This form of recovery works if the conditions that brought on the rollback to a savepoint are removed from the path of the reexecuted block or subtransactional unit.

Figure 12.3

Savepoints in
transactions.

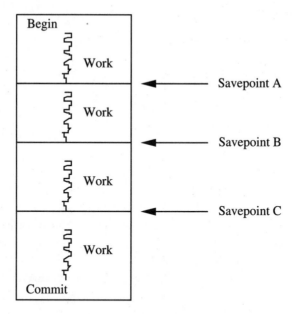

Transaction A

Named Savepoint

Savepoints in SQL-3 are specified using the SAVEPOINT statement, as shown:

```
<savepoint statement> ::= SAVEPOINT <savepoint specifier>

<savepoint specifier> ::=
      <savepoint name>
    | <simple target specification>
```

At the point in a transaction where the SAVEPOINT statement is detected and executed, the database is directed to save the state of all transaction information in the system logs. This command is equivalent to flushing the active log files from volatile storage to nonvolatile storage. The difference is that only information from the transaction that issues the savepoint gets flushed, instead of all system state information.

As an example, the aquarium database contains a table employee, as defined here:

```
CREATE TABLE employees (
    emp_id          INTEGER
        CONSTRAINT employees_emp_id_pk PRIMARY KEY,
    emp_title       VARCHAR(30),
    emp_last_name   VARCHAR(30)
        CONSTRAINT emp_last_name_not_null NOT NULL,
    emp_first_name  VARCHAR(30)
        CONSTRAINT emp_first_name_not_null NOT NULL,
    emp_address     CHARACTER VARYING (30),
    emp_city        CHARACTER VARYING (20),
    emp_state       CHARACTER (2),
    emp_zip         CHARACTER VARYING (9),
    emp_phone       CHARACTER (10),
    emp_start_date  TIMESTAMP,
    emp_pay_rate    DECIMAL (7,2),
    emp_com_rate    DECIMAL (3,2),
    emp_total_sales DECIMAL(6,2)
)
```

A possible transaction would be to increase the salary for all employees who are floor sales clerks. In addition, the database could check to make sure that this is a valid operation in relation to the income brought in by the sales clerks. The increase goes through or the transaction is rolled back:

```
BEGIN
    DECLARE sales_amt DECIMAL(7,2);
    DECLARE temp_salary DECIMAL(10,2);
    . . .
    . . .
    SAVEPOINT clerk_raise;
    . . .
    UPDATE employees
    SET emp_pay_rate = emp_pay_rate +(.1 * emp_pay_rate)
    WHERE emp_title = 'sales clerk';
    . . .
    . . .
```

This code declares the savepoint at some point before the employee table is accessed and the sales clerks are given their raises. In this way, if something should go wrong with the action, the transaction can go back to the point where the clerk_raise savepoint has been set.

Release Savepoint

If a savepoint can be declared, you may also want to release the savepoint. The BNF is:

```
<release savepoint statement> ::=
    RELEASE SAVEPOINT <savepoint specifier>
```

RELEASE SAVEPOINT has the effect of removing the marker from the log, thereby blocking the transaction or session from partially rolling back the effect of some action. For example, in the transaction above, you may want to verify that the action of giving all the employees the raise actually occurred. You can insert the following code segment before the UPDATE statement:

```
SELECT SUM(emp_pay_rate) INTO temp_salary FROM employees
WHERE emp_title = 'sales clerk';
```

Place the following code segment after the UPDATE statement:

```
IF (temp_salary * 1.1) <> (SELECT SUM(emp_pay_rate) FROM
            employees WHERE emp_title = 'sales clerk')
THEN
    do some corrective action
ELSE
    RELEASE SAVEPOINT clerk_raise;
END IF;
```

The effect of these statements is to place a savepoint at the state of the database before the salaries are affected. The operation is performed, and then the database is audited to make sure the action occurred. If the action occurred, the savepoint is removed, making the transaction up to this point undoable. The savepoint is dropped and processing is allowed to continue.

Roll Back to Named Savepoint

More interesting than dropping a savepoint is the recovery of a transaction back to some previous savepoint. The reason for creating a savepoint is to roll back the actions of a transaction to some prior point and to alter the flow in response to database or application state information.

The format of the SAVEPOINT ROLLBACK is located in the framework of the ROLLBACK statement as an optional portion of the syntax. The BNF for ROLLBACK is:

```
<rollback statement> ::=
    ROLLBACK [ WORK ] [ AND { NO ] CHAIN ]
    [ <savepoint clause> ]

<savepoint clause> ::=
    TO SAVEPOINT <savepoint specifier>
```

As an example, you want to give the sales clerks a 10 percent raise in their base pay. In this example, if the sales clerks have not sold more than their new rate, the raise will be taken away. If they have sold enough, the rate becomes permanent:

```
BEGIN
    DECLARE sales_amt DECIMAL(7,2);
    . . .
    . . .
    SAVEPOINT clerk_raise;
    . . .
    UPDATE employees
    SET emp_pay_rate = emp_pay_rate +(.1 * emp_pay_rate)
    WHERE emp_title = 'sales clerk';
    . . .
    . . .
    . . .
    SELECT SUM(sales)
    INTO sales_amt
    FROM orders
    WHERE emp_title = 'sales clerk';
    . . .
    IF (sales_amt < (SELECT SUM (emp_pay_rate) FROM employees
            WHERE emp_title = 'sales clerk')
    THEN ROLLBACK TO SAVEPOINT clerk_raise;
    . . .
END;
```

SAVEPOINTs and ROLLBACKS are significant additional features for code writers, allowing them more freedom in deciding what the correct actions are for the database and which actions are to become permanent and recoverable during application execution.

Additional Predicates

The SQL-3 standard adds some additional predicates to the language to use in restriction clauses in SQL statements. The main classes of additional predicates fall into one of three classes: similar, quantified, and Boolean predicates and their derivatives. These predicates give the programmer additional means to quantify which items from a table, group of tables, or other SQL statements or functions, are being sought.

Character String Matching

SQL-3 has added the similar predicate for finding characters (comparable to the facilities found in most UNIX systems). With this predicate you can specify a string and search for anything similar to this string within some degree of mismatch. The format of the similar predicate is shown in the following BNF:

```
<similar predicate> ::=
   <character match values> [NOT ] SIMILAR TO <similar pattern>
     [ ESCAPE <escape character> ]

<similar pattern> ::= <character value expression>

<regular expression> ::=
   <regular term>
   |<regular expression> <vertical bar> <regular term>

<regular term> ::=
   <regular factor>
   |<regular term> <regular factor>

<regular factor> ::=
   <regular primary>
   |<regular primary> <asterisk>
   |<regular primary> <plus sign>

<regular primary> ::=
   <character specifier>
   |<percent>
   |<regular character set>
   |<left paren> <regular expression> <right paren>

<character specifier> ::= <non-escape character>
   |<escape character>

< non-escape character> ::= !! refer to syntax rules

<escape character> ::= !! refer to syntax rules
```

```
<regular character set> ::=
    <underscore>
    |<left bracket> <character enumeration> . . . <right bracket>
    |<left bracket> <circumflex> <character enumeration> . . .<right
bracket>
    |<left bracket> <colon> <regular character set identifier>
<colon> <right bracket>

<character enumeration> ::=
    <character specifier>
    |<character specifier> < minus sign> <character specifier>

<regular character set identifier> ::= <identifier>
```

The purpose of this form of restriction on a query is to find information when you don't know all the needed components. For example, in the fish database, if you know the general family of a fish, but can't remember the actual name, you can use this predicate to retrieve all fish with the given portion of the name. Then you can pick out the one that you want to extract:

```
SELECT common_name, price
FROM marine_fish, aquatic_stock
WHERE scientific_name SIMILAR TO '%carus%us';
```

This statement searches through the fish database and returns Scarus taeniopterus. It returns this name because it is the first to meet the requirement.

Quantified Predicates

Quantified predicates are a refinement on the predicate search conditions of SQL. For example, if you want to find a few or a portion of some collection of tuples, which meet a specific search condition, you can use the quantified refinements on the predicates—in particular, the FOR ALL or FOR SOME qualifications. These predicates, as with others in SQL, obey the three-valued logic rules. A simple example is to find the lionfish suppliers that do not supply any other fish in quantities greater than 100:

```
SELECT DISTINCT sp.supplier_name
FROM suppliers sp
WHERE sp.scientific_name = 'Pterois volitans'
FOR SOME suppliers spp (spp.supplier_name = sp.supplier_name
AND 100 = spp.quantity);
```

In this query, the quantified predicate FOR SOME looks for suppliers with the same name that do not deliver quantities of any other fish in quantities greater than 100.

Boolean Predicates

SQL-3 also enhances predicates by testing predicate values against Boolean values. For example, you can evaluate a predicate and then compare its results to the Boolean value TRUE for a positive match, against FALSE for a negative match, or against UNKNOWN for an undefined result. In all cases, you can make qualified evaluations instead of simply testing. The Boolean predicate has the following form:

```
<boolean-value> is [NOT] {TRUE | FALSE | UNKNOWN}
```

An example of this statement follows:

```
WHERE (price > 15.99 AND delivery_date > 5) IS FALSE
```

This statement usually tests whether the price is greater than $15.99 and the delivery date is more than five days. However, since the FALSE qualifier was used, you are looking for the opposite result.

Extensions to Cursors

Cursors have been enhanced for additional uses. Cursors are used to point to a tuple in a table and manipulate items in the table, a tuple at a time. This enhances a cursor's flexibility. The scope of a cursor expands beyond the transaction that opened it and permits access to a query result, instead of a copy of the result (as had been the case in prior SQL implementations). The syntax for the cursor is:

```
<declare cursor> ::=
    DECLARE <cursor name> [ <cursor sensitivity> ] [ SCROLL ] CURSOR
    [WITH HOLD]
    [WITH RETURN]
    FOR <cursor specification>
```

```
<cursor sensitivity> ::=
    SENSITIVE
    |INSENSITIVE
    |ASENSITIVE

<cursor specification> ::=
    <query expression> [ <order by clause> []
    [<updatability clause>]

<updateability clause> ::=
    FOR {READ ONLY | UPDATE [ OF <column name list> ] }

<order by clause> ::=
    ORDER BY <sort specification list>

<sort specification list ::=
    <sort specification> [ { <comma> <sort specification> }. . . ]

<sort specification> ::=
    <sort key> [ <collate clause> ] [ <ordering specification> ]

<sort key> ::=
    <value expression>
    <ordering specification> ::= ASC | DESC
```

The two major changes to the clause are the terms HOLD and SENSI-TIVE. These terms involve two additions to cursor semantics. A "hold-able" cursor is kept open after the commit of the transaction that initially opened the cursor, and it retains its position in the cursor table. When a new transaction starts, it uses a new fetch to extract the next piece of information using the cursor. The holdable cursor is kept open, but will be closed if a transaction rollback occurs.

The "sensitive" cursor accesses the actual query result, instead of a copy derived from the query. Updates made in the same transaction with a sensitive cursor are visible for subsequent fetches. This is different from the prior version of the cursor, which was basically a read-only operator and not allowed to affect base table contents.

Extensions to Referential Integrity

Referential integrity defines a rule on columns in one table that guarantees that the values match the values in the columns of a related table (Figure 12.4). The foreign key exemplifies referential integrity in the simplest form. Beyond these simple indicators of referential integrity, rules

Figure 12.4

Referential integrity.

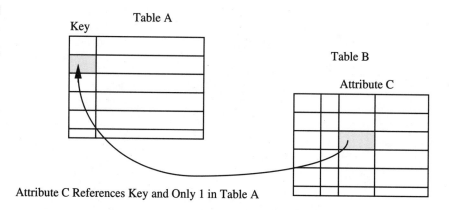

Attribute C References Key and Only 1 in Table A

dictate which types of data manipulation are allowed on referenced values and which effect these actions have on dependent values. The rules associated with referential integrity are: RESTRICT, SET NULL, SET DEFAULT, CASCADE, and NO ACTION.

The format of the referential constraint definition is:

```
<referential constraint definition> ::=
     FOREIGN KEY <left paren> <referencing columns> <right paren>
   <references specification>

<references specification> ::=
     REFERENCES <referenced table and columns>
      [ MATCH <match type> ]
      [ <referential triggered action> ]

<match type> ::=
        FULL
      | PARTIAL
      | SIMPLE

<referencing columns> ::=
       <referencing column list>

<referenced table and columns> ::=
       <table name> [ <left paren> <reference column list> <right
paren> ]

<reference column list> ::= <column name list>

<referential triggered action> ::=
        <update rule> [ <delete rule> ]
      | <delete rule> [ <update rule> ]

<update rule> ::= ON UPDATE <referential action>

<delete rule> ::= ON DELETE < referential action>
```

```
<referential action> ::=
    CASCADE
  | SET NULL
  | SET DEFAULT
  | RESTRICT
  | NO ACTION
```

CASCADE causes all associated dependent information to be updated in the same way when the referenced information is updated. In addition, CASCADE causes the dependent rows to be deleted if the referenced row is deleted.

SET NULL causes all dependent information to be set to null if the referenced information happens to be updated or deleted.

SET DEFAULT causes all dependent information to be set to the pre-defined default if the referenced information is either deleted or updated.

RESTRICT disallows the update or deletion of referenced data. This is similar to the effect that the no action clause has, but the condition is tested on the fly, not at the end of the SQL statement, as is the case with the no action clause.

NO ACTION disallows deletion or update of the referenced information. The referential integrity constraint is checked at the end of the SQL statement execution, before the action is committed to the database.

An example in a sales table is as follows:

```
ALTER TABLE sales
    ADD FOREIGN KEY (last, first)
    REFERENCES customers (c_lname, c_fname) RESTRICT;
```

Extensions to Transactions

A transaction is a logical unit of work for a database system and is where the *ACID* properties are managed. The *ACID* properties guarantee the atomicity, consistency, isolation, and durability of the data in the database. Transactions, as units of work, require initiation statements, intermediate state statements, and ending statements. The syntax for an SQL transaction statement is:

```
<SQL transaction statement> ::=
    <start transaction statement>
  | <set transaction statement>
  | <set constraints mode statement>
```

```
        | <savepoint statement>
        | <release savepoint statement>
        | <commit statement>
        | <rollback statement>

<start transaction statement> ::=
    START TRANSACTION <transaction mode>
        [ { <comma> <transaction mode> }...]

<transaction mode> ::=
        <isolation level>
      | <transaction access mode>
      | <diagnostics size>

<isolation level> ::=
    ISOLATION LEVEL <level of isolation>

<level of isolation> ::=
        READ UNCOMMITTED
      | READ COMMITTED
      | REPEATABLE READ
      | SERIALIZABLE

<transaction access mode> ::=
        READ ONLY
      | READ WRITE

<diagnostics size> ::=
    DIAGNOSTICS SIZE <number of conditions>

<number of conditions> ::= <simple value specification>

<set transaction statement> ::=
    SET [ LOCAL ] <transaction attributes>

<transaction attributes> ::=
    TRANSACTION <transaction mode> [ { <comma> <transaction mode>
}... ]

<set constraints mode statement> ::=
    SET CONSTRAINTS <constraint name list>
        { DEFERRED | IMMEDIATE }

<constraint name list> ::=
        ALL
      | <constraint name> [ { <comma> <constraint name> }... ]

<savepoint statement> ::= SAVEPOINT <savepoint specifier>

<savepoint specifier> ::=
        <savepoint name>
      | <simple target specification>

<savepoint name> ::= <identifier>

<simple target specification> ::=
        <host parameter specification>
      | <SQL parameter reference>
```

```
<release savepoint statement> ::=
    RELEASE SAVEPOINT <savepoint specifier>

<commit statement> ::=
    COMMIT [ WORK ] [ AND [ NO ] CHAIN ]

<rollback statement> ::=
    ROLLBACK [ WORK ] [ AND [ NO ]  CHAIN ]
      [ <savepoint clause> ]

<savepoint clause> ::=
    TO SAVEPOINT <savepoint specifier>
```

START TRANSACTION Statement

Significant changes to the transaction statements in SQL-3 include an explicit START TRANSACTION statement, a SET LOCAL TRANSACTION statement, and the chained transaction subclause. The START TRANSACTION statement permits the explicit beginning of a new transactional context and the chance to reset all transactional attributes that may have been set previously. A missing piece may be the ability to have an explicitly named transaction, which could be called and executed using this statement with the string. A programmer can effectively do this by issuing a START TRANSACTION, or calling a named PSM procedure, package, or function, followed by closing conditions to terminate the transaction:

```
START TRANSACTION READ WRITE ISOLATION SERIALIZABLE
    package.procedure;
COMMIT;
```

SET LOCAL TRANSACTION Statement

The SET LOCAL TRANSACTION statement sets attributes for a "local" branch of a multi-site transaction. For example, if you have a transaction that uses the resources of many servers with their own database management system, this statement allows the local transaction to set its own attributes. Such an operation provides for the optimization of the branches. For example, if you know that the request is read-only, you can set the attributes of the transaction as read-only, permitting higher concurrency at the local site and allowing the remote transaction to continue and possibly receive better service:

```
SET LOCAL TRANSACTION READ ONLY;
```

Chained Transaction Statement

The chained transaction statement is the last addition to the transaction statements for SQL-3. This statement starts a new transactional state at the completion of a previous transaction. It maintains the characteristics of the previous transaction, thereby alleviating the need to reset or initialize a transactional mode. Once this statement has been issued, there is no opportunity to issue a SET TRANSACTION statement until the commit of the new, chained transaction has committed or aborted its execution. As an example, you can begin a new transaction right after the commit, with the same attributes, as follows:

```
START TRANSACTION READ WRITE ISOLATION SERIALIZABLE
   package.procedure;
     COMMIT  WORK AND CHAIN;
```

Similarly, you can tie this into the abort of a transaction using the subclause after the rollback statement:

```
ROLLBACK WORK AND CHAIN;
```

Summary

This chapter attempted to cover some of the enhancements to the SQL language that did not fall into the previous chapters. There are many other features that have not been addressed. As of this writing, the language is close to its international and American release. Several features were deemed immature and were not included in the language. Many of these features met this fate because leading vendors were not able to agree on semantics and syntax. This disagreement is between vendors that already have an implementation of a feature in their prototypes and other vendors that do not want a feature present because their implementations aren't ready. This author, who is not a member of a vendor company, but is an academic, hopes that many of these desirable features find their way back into the language during the next round of deliberations. As the language stands now, it will still take a great deal of time before all the features described in this book are found in all products. In addition, it will also take the validation community a lot of time to establish acceptable tests, which will deem a product as "standard compliant."

CHAPTER **13**

Early SQL-3
Release Vendor
Product Reviews

Contributed by
Vijay Kumar Bommireddipalli
and Rahul Mutha

Introduction

This chapter evaluates the current implementations of Object Relational Database Management Systems (ORDBMSs) by three vendors against the proposed SQL-3 standard. The products evaluated are Oracle Corporation's ORACLE 8.0 Universal Data Server, IBM's DB2 Version 5.0 Universal Database, and Informix's Informix Universal Server. This review will compare the support for complex data types and the flexibility and ease with which each incorporates added data types and added operations supporting advanced data types.

Relational database systems are one of the most time-proven technologies for data management proposed to date. The majority of the world's business data are now stored in the relational form. Relational databases' built-in data types and relational operations defined by the Structured Query Language (SQL) were enough to handle most of the needs of database applications.

In today's enterprise environment, there is a need to store and manipulate data that are complex and no longer just two-dimensional. Multimedia objects such as photographs, maps, audio, video, and so on require data manipulation operations using complex functions, which cannot be predefined because of the diverse nature of these data items. For example, a surveying department might want to store maps in its database and be able to zoom into particular areas, or a video server might want to give out just one-minute clips for a sample instead of the entire file, which could span several gigabytes. Clearly the current relational systems fail to satisfy requirements when it comes to the new generation of multimedia applications. More predefined data types and functions are not needed. The user needs to be able to define new data types and functions and integrate them in the existing database management system. To facilitate incorporation of this functionality, most major RDBMS vendors have migrated toward an Object Relational Database Management System (ORDBMS).

With an ORDBMS, you can incorporate objects and other extended data types into the basic relational tables. The object-relational databases also enable developers to build extensions that support specialized applications, such as advanced text searching, image retrieval, and integrated video management and delivery. The idea behind all of these extensions is to incorporate objects in a controlled manner into the relational system.

ANSI's SQL standards committee has specified a list of object-relational language features and subfeatures as part of the proposed baseline SQL-3 database language. Some of these features are designated as CORE SQL. Products that support the CORE SQL features, but not full SQL, are called entry-level compliant. Most major relational database vendors presently have introduced products that adhere to some subset of the CORE SQL language features. It is anticipated that once the standard is released in 1999, vendors will quickly alter and augment their products to minimally meet these features. Many vendors will provide features from the remaining collection of SQL-3 features based on where the marketplace is going and which segment of this market they are targeting.

It has been our experience that vendors take one of two tracks. With one track, they attempt to provide a solid baseline product, which adheres to all of the baseline features, and then build incrementally upon this baseline toward the full language as the market demands. The second track is to try to provide a superset of the language, along with a variety of tools, to aid the clients in developing products. In each case, something is left out.

This chapter gives an overview of object-relational database products from Oracle, IBM, and Informix and discusses how these products support features developed as SQL-3. Each of the vendors provide user-defined data types, abstract data types, user-defined functions, user-defined procedures, database triggers, and sequences within certain bounds and with slight variations. Nontraditional multimedia data types are supported in many of these products with the help of extensible technology added on top of the DBMS. Oracle refers to these as data cartridges, IBM refers to these as extenders, Informix refers to these as datablades, and Sybase refers to these as plug-ins.

Oracle Support for Complex and User-Defined Data Types

Minimum user-defined data type support (distinct type) is specified as part of CORE SQL-3. All three products support user-defined data types and other complex types, as discussed in the following sections.

ORACLE 8.0 Server

Oracle supports a variety of complex data types in its ORACLE 8.0 server. Oracle's complex data types can be categorized as abstract data types and collection data types.

Abstract Data Types   Abstract data types in Oracle's product consist of one or more subtypes. The subtypes comprising the abstract data types can be base built-in data types or the abstract data types themselves. Abstract data types in this product can be further categorized as either value abstract data types (Value ADTs) or object abstract data types (Object ADTs). For example:

```
CREATE type ADDRESS_TY as OBJECT
(STREET          VARCHAR2(20),
 CITY            VARCHAR2(20),
 STATE           CHAR(2),
 ZIP             NUMBER(8));
```

Value ADTs   In Oracle, Value ADTs are bound to a table and are referred to as column objects; they form attributes of a relational table. They are not system unique; you can have multiple instances of the same object name and values in a database. The items forming the value ADT cannot have user-defined behaviors associated with them. The lone supported behavior is defined by the built-in constructor and destructor functions defined when the object is specified. For example:

```
CREATE TABLE DISTRIB (
 DISTRIBNO       NUMBER(3),
 DISTNAME        VARCHAR2(20),
 ADDRESS         ADDRESS_T,
 PHONE           CHAR (12),
 CONSTRAINT DISTRIB_PRIMARY_KEY PRIMARY KEY (DISTRIBNO));
```

Object ADTs   Object ADTs are referred to as row objects. Row objects appear in object tables (a special kind of table, which provides a relational view of the attributes of those objects). Oracle gives every row object a unique, immutable identifier called an object identifier. Oracle uses these identifiers to construct references to the row objects. No additional attributes, other than the ADT, can be defined in an object table. Object table items are system-unique and are defined with their system-unique identifier. This identifier can be found by querying the object table. It is then used as a pointer to this object in another table using the REF operator. For example:

```
CREATE TYPE ADDRESS AS TABLE OF ADDRESS_TY;
```

The advantages of using objects (as opposed to standalone attributes in flat relations) include application and database type compatibility, code reusability, flexibility, and standardization. The code for both the structure and behavior of an abstract data type can be written once. The code defines an abstract data type and access methods to the ADT and is then reused when the object type is utilized in further type definitions or applications. By defining the type once, instead of multiple times, a standardized specification, in terms of the way logical data are represented and operated upon, is created. The use of abstract data types in building more complex types will result in cleaner table definitions. Abstract data types in Oracle can also be indexed by using CREATE INDEX. This helps the optimizer give improved response to a query based on that abstract data type.

Collection Data Types   ORACLE 8.0 provides two collection types: nested tables and the varying array. These are the only features existing in CORE SQL-3 as collection types. Other collection types, such as the list, bag, and multiset, have been left out of the present standard and may be readdressed during the SQL-4 deliberations.

Nested Tables   Nested tables are tables within tables. Each row could potentially contain a table. This is a way of storing many relationships in one table without having to perform JOINs. Access to these tables is through SQL queries, which require a bit more syntax to construct. For example:

```
CREATE TABLE person (soc_sec NUMBER(9), name VARCHAR2(20),
Projects PROJ_TABLE_TYPE)
NESTED TABLE projects STORE AS nested_proj_table);
```

Varying Arrays   Varying Arrays, or VARRAYS as they are known in ORACLE 8.0, are similar to nested tables but have a limited, specified number of rows, allowing storage of repeating collections of attributes in tables. An array is an ordered set of data elements. The order being specified uses the ordinal location of the item in the table and is not specified as being in sorted order, unless you insert them that way. All elements of a given array are by definition of the same data type. For example:

```
CREATE OR REPLACE TYPE telno_VA AS VARRAY(5) OF VARCHAR2(10);
```

Informix Universal Server Support

Informix categorizes its data types in a hierarchy consisting of the base built-in data types, as defined in the SQL standard, and complex data types, which are further broken down into complex data types and user-defined data types (Figure 13.1).

Complex Data Types

A complex data type in Informix's database product is usually a composite of other existing data types, as was the case with Oracle's product. A complex data type's components can include built-in types, opaque types, distinct types, or other complex types. An important difference between complex types and user-defined types is that you can access and manipulate the individual components of a complex data type with SQL statements. That is, there is no need for user methods defined over these data types. They simply use the constructor and destructor functions, which are automatically defined and generated, along with the specification of the type. This is similar to Oracle's Value ADTs.

Collection Type   A collection type in Informix's product consists of a group of elements of the same data type with some added structure. Collection data types let you store and manipulate collections of similar data in a single row of a table. A collection type has two components: a type constructor and a collection base element type. Type constructors in Informix's implementation include SET, MULTISET, LIST, and ITEM, which were not moved forward into CORE SQL-3 but are desirable to many user communities.

The SET type is a collection data type where elements are not ordered and duplicates are not allowed. The SET collection type is created with the SET constructor. The LIST is a collection data type in which the elements are ordered and duplicates are allowed. The LIST collection data

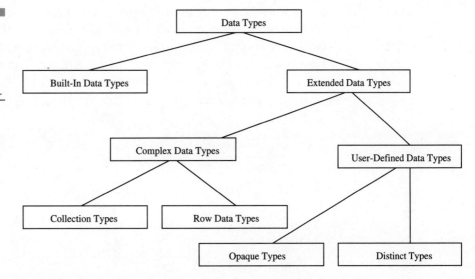

type is created with the LIST constructor. MULTISET is a collection data
type in which elements are not ordered and duplicates are allowed. It is
created with the MULTISET constructor. Element type specifies the
type of data that the collection type can contain. In Informix's implementation, the elements of a collection can be any data type except SE-
RIAL and SERIAL8. SERIAL and SERIAL8 are similar to Oracle's rowid.

For example, to use a SET data type:

```
CREATE TABLE employee (
name          CHAR(30),
address       CHAR (40),
salary        INTEGER,
dependents    SET(ROW(name VARCHAR(30), bdate DATE) NOT NULL)
);
```

If you want to use the LIST and MULTISET data types, the constructor
must be changed to LIST and MULTISET, respectively.

Row Type   A row type is a sequence of one or more elements called
fields. Each field has a name and a data type associated with it. The fields
of a row are comparable to the columns of a table, but there are important differences. There is no default clause on a field. Also, constraints
cannot be defined on a field and fields cannot be used with tables, only
with row types. There are two kinds of row types: named row types and
unnamed row types in the Informix product.

Named Row Types A named row type is a group of bound fields that are defined under a single name. A field refers to a single component of a named row type. Once a named row type is created, the name assigned to it represents a unique type within the database's schema. The fields of a named row type are analogous to the fields of a C-language structure.

For example, to create a named row type:

```
CREATE ROW TYPE address_t (
street VARCHAR(20),
city VARCHAR(20),
state CHAR(2),
zip VARCHAR(9)
);
```

To use a named row type in a table:

```
CREATE TABLE employee (
name            VARCHAR(30),
address         address_t,
salary          INTEGER
);
```

Unnamed Row Types An unnamed row type in the Informix database is a group of fields defined by their composite structure. An unnamed row type can be used to define the type of column or field in the database. Here, only the structure of the field is important, and the database server does not distinguish between unnamed row types having different field names if their field types match. This makes casting relatively easier in unnamed row types compared with named row types. For example:

```
CREATE TABLE student(
s_name      ROW(f_name VARCHAR(20), m_init CHAR(1),
l_name      VARCHAR(20) NOT NULL),
s_address   ROW(street VARCHAR(20), city VARCHAR(20),
state  CHAR(2), zip VARCHAR(9))
);
```

User-Defined Data Types

The user-defined data types for the Informix database product that conform to the SQL-3 database specification include the opaque type and the distinct type.

Opaque Type   An opaque type in Informix Universal Server is a fundamental data type, which stores a single value and cannot be divided into components by the database server. It is implemented as a C data structure and a set of routines written in C that allow the database server to support the data type. C routines that support a new opaque type pass the contents of the external data structure to the database server to store in the database. The database server does not interpret the contents of the structure; it stores the memory contents, byte for byte, in the database. The support routines implement operations, such as comparing two instances of a data type, converting an opaque type to another data type, or displaying an instancing of the opaque data type. The database server calls the support routine supplied for an external operation and passes the C structure or pointer to it in the parameter list. These support routines help the server interact with the internal structure of the opaque type. The opaque type can be further categorized as fixed length and variable length, based on the memory space required to store the elements. An example of a fixed-length opaque data type follows:

```
CREATE OPAQUE TYPE circle (INTERNALLENGTH = 24);
CREATE …functions..
CREATE …casts….
```

This registers the fixed-length opaque data type, supporting routines and casts defined, with the server. Here, the length is specified as 24 bytes using INTERNALLENGTH.

An example of the variable-length opaque data type is:

```
CREATE OPAQUE TYPE var_type (INTERNALLENGTH=VARIABLE,
MAXLEN=4096);
```

The opaque type cannot be used if the type is not "bit-hashable," or the database server cannot use its built-in hash function for the equality comparison. Therefore, the opaque type cannot be used in the GROUP BY clause of a SELECT statement, in hash JOINs, or with the IN operator in a WHERE clause.

Distinct Types   A distinct data type has the same internal structure as some other source data type in the database. The source data type can be either a built-in type or an extended type. What distinguishes a distinct type from the source type are the functions defined on the type. A distinct data type is a database data type based on one of the following source types: a built-in type, an existing opaque type, a distinct type, or a complex type. A distinct type inherits the casts and functions of its source types, as well as the length and alignment on the disk. A distinct type thus makes efficient use of the preexisting functionality of the server. A distinct type and a source type cannot, however, be compared directly. To compare a distinct type and its source type, it must be explicitly cast to the other type. For example:

```
CREATE DISTINCT TYPE dist_type AS NUMERIC;
```

IBM DB2 Universal Database Support

IBM's product is called DB2 and is supported by a set of additional services under the product name Universal Database. This product is mature and exhibits many of the features expected of an SQL-3 implementation, although some items are missing. Again, the assumption is that once the standard is released, and the vendors have time to review the final features, compliant products with extensions will quickly follow.

User-Defined Types

IBM's DB2 supports distinct and structured classes of user-defined types (UDTs). These are similar to Oracle's object tables and row types.

Distinct Types   Distinct types are user-defined types that resemble a source type internally, but differ in terms of the set of operations defined on them. For example:

```
CREATE DISTINCT TYPE audio_d AS BLOB (1M)
```

Although `audio_d` has the same representation as the built-in data type BLOB, it is considered to be a separate type that is not comparable to a BLOB or to any other base type. This allows the creation of functions written specifically for `audio_d`, and assures that these functions will not be applied to any other type (pictures, text, and so on).

Distinct types support strong typing by ensuring that only those functions and operators explicitly defined on a distinct type can be applied to its instances. DB2's distinct type (as opposed to Informix's distinct type) does not automatically acquire the functions and operators of its source type, since these may not be meaningful. For example, the LENGTH function of the audio_d type might return the length of its object in seconds rather than in bytes.

The comparison operators are automatically generated for user-defined distinct types, except those using LONG VARCHAR, LONG VARGRAPHIC, BLOB, CLOB, DBCLOB, or DATALINK as the source type. In addition, functions are generated to support casting from the source type to the distinct type and from the distinct type to the source type. Values with a user-defined type can only be compared with values of exactly the same user-defined type. The user-defined type must be defined using the WITH COMPARISONS clause, which permits comparison.

Structured Types   A structured type is a user-defined data type having a structure that is defined in the database. It contains a sequence of named attributes, each of which has a data type. A structured type may be defined as a subtype of another structured type, called its supertype. A subtype inherits all the attributes of its supertype and may have additional attributes defined. The set of structured types that is related to a common supertype is called a type hierarchy, and the supertype that does not have any supertype is called the root type of the type hierarchy. A structured type may be used as the type of a table or a view. The names and data types of the attributes of the structured type become the names and data types of the columns of this typed table or typed view. Rows of the typed table or typed view can be thought of as a representation of instances of the structured type.

A structured type cannot be used as the data type of a column of a table or a view. There is also no support for retrieving a structured type into a host variable in an application program.

Reference Types   A reference type (REF) in DB2 is a companion type to a structured type. Similar to a distinct type, a reference type is a scalar type that shares a common representation with one of the built-in data types. This same representation is shared for all types in the type hierarchy. The reference type representation is defined when the root type of a type hierarchy is created. When using a reference type, a structured type is specified as a parameter of the type. This parameter is called the target type of the reference.

The target of a reference is always a row in a typed table or view. When a reference type is used, it may have a scope defined. The scope identifies a table (called the target table) or view (the target view) that contains the target row of a reference value. The target table or view must have the same type as the target type of the reference type. An instance of a scoped reference type uniquely identifies a row in a typed table or typed view, called the target row. For example:

```
CREATE TYPE employee_st AS
        (NAME          VARCHAR(40),
         DEPTREF          REF(dept),
         SALARY         DECIMAL(10,2) )
         WITHOUT    COMPARISONS
         NOT FINAL
         MODE DB2SQL

CREATE TYPE president_st UNDER employee_st AS
        (HEADCOUNT INTEGER,
         BUDGET     DECIMAL(10,2) )
         WITHOUT COMPARISONS
         NOT FINAL
         MODE DB2SQL
```

This creates a type hierarchy having a structured type for employee_st and a subtype for president_st. The employee_st has a REF type with its target type as dept. All the REF types in this hierarchy will have the same representation. The WITHOUT COMPARISONS clause specifies that the structured type will not support any comparison operators. The NOT FINAL clause specifies that the structured type may have further subtypes. The MODE clause indicates the mode (the only one supported now).

Product Support for Large Object Data Types

In the following section, we examine what kind of support each of the three products has for the large object (LOB) types of SQL-3. CORE SQL calls out some basic LOB features and subfeatures. These features, however, do not specifically call out the BLOB and CLOB data types. Some of the basic features called out in CORE include scalar functions, such as LENGTH, SUBSTRING support for LOB data types, concatenation of LOB data types, nonholdable locator for LOB data types, and a POSITION function. A discussion of how the three products support these LOB data types follows.

ORACLE 8.0 Server Support for LOBs and Related Data Types

ORACLE 8.0 supports internal LOB data types, BLOB, CLOB, NCLOB, and external data type BFILE. These data types support the storage of large and unstructured data such as text, image, video, and spatial.

When creating a table in ORACLE 8.0 Server, you can optionally specify different table space and storage characteristics for internal LOB columns or internal LOB object attributes from those specified for the table. Internal LOB columns contain LOB locators, which can refer to out-of-line or in-line LOB values. Selecting a LOB from a table actually returns the LOB's locator, not the entire LOB value. The DBMS_LOB package, a vendor-supplied set of built-in operators for LOBs, and the Oracle Call Interface, OCI, provide operations on LOBs that are performed through these returned LOB locators.

To access and populate rows of an internal LOB column, first use the INSERT statement to initialize the internal LOB value to empty (NULL). Once the row is inserted, you can select the empty LOB and populate it using the DBMS_LOB package or the OCI interface commands. For example:

```
CREATE TABLE  personhosrecs_table (
            name CHAR(40),
            medhistory  CLOB,
            picture BLOB)
    LOB (medhistory,picture) STORE AS
        ( TABLESPACE records
          STORAGE (INITIAL 5M NEXT 5M) );
```

This creates a table, `personhosrecs_table`, with LOB columns. The LOB clause indicates that the commands deal with out-of-line data. The STORAGE clause can be used to specify the initial and percent increase, as well as the storage volume this out-of-line data will take.

BLOB, CLOB, and NCLOB Data Types   The BLOB data type stores unstructured binary large objects. BLOBs can be thought of as bit streams with no character set semantics. BLOBs can store up to four gigabytes of binary data.

The CLOB data type stores single-byte character large object data. Variable-width character sets are not supported. CLOBs can store up to four gigabytes of character data.

The NCLOB data type stores fixed-width, multibyte national character set character (NCHAR) data. Variable-width character sets are not supported. NCLOBs can store up to four gigabytes of character text data. You cannot create an object with NCLOB attributes, but you can specify NCLOB parameters in methods.

BLOBs, CLOBs, and NCLOBs have full transactional support; changes made through SQL, the OCI, or the DBMS_LOB package participate fully in the transaction. The LOB value manipulations can be committed or rolled back.

Scalar functions such as READ, SUBSTR, INSTR, GETLENGTH, COMPARE, WRITE, APPEND, ERASE, TRIM, and COPY can be performed on the LOBs using the DBMS_LOB package supplied by the vendor.

Binary File Data Type   The binary file (BFILE) data type enables access to binary file LOBs that are stored in file systems outside the Oracle database. A BFILE column or attribute stores a BFILE locator, which serves as a pointer to a binary file on the server's file system. The locator maintains the directory alias and the file name. Binary file LOBs do not participate in transactions. Rather, the underlying operating system provides file integrity and durability. The maximum file size supported is four gigabytes.

The database administrator must ensure that the file exists and that Oracle processes have operating system read permissions on the file. The BFILE data type allows read-only support of large binary files; you cannot modify a file. Access is provided through APIs to the file data. The primary interfaces that you use to access file data are the DBMS_LOB package and the OCI interface. For example:

```
INSERT INTO lob_table VALUES (22, 'vijay', BFILENAME('IMG',
'image2.gif'));
```

This indicates that the file `image2.gif` stored in directory IMG is a BFILE. When a LOB is deleted, both the locator value and the LOB value are deleted in the case of an internal LOB. If the deleted value is an external LOB, then only the locator value is deleted.

RAW and LONG RAW Data Types   The RAW and LONG RAW data types store data that are not to be interpreted (not explicitly converted when moving data between different systems) by Oracle. These data types are intended for binary data or byte strings. For example, you can use LONG RAW to store graphics, sound, documents, or arrays of binary data; the interpretation is dependent on the data in an application.

The RAW data type is a variable-length data type, similar to the VARCHAR2 character data type, except that Net8 (which connects user sessions to the instance) and the Import and Export utilities do not perform character conversion when transmitting RAW or LONG RAW data. In contrast, Net8 and Import/Export automatically convert CHAR, VARCHAR2, and LONG data from the database character set to the user session character set (set by the NLS_LANGUAGE parameter of the ALTER SESSION command), if the two character sets are different.

LOBs are similar to LONG and LONG RAW types, but differ in several ways. LOBs can be attributes of a user-defined data type (object). The LOB locator is stored in the table column, either with or without the actual LOB value; BLOB, NCLOB, and CLOB values can be stored in separate table spaces. BFILE data are stored in an external file on the server. When you access an LOB column, the locator is returned. LOBs permit efficient, random, piece-wise access to and manipulation of data. More than one LOB column can be defined in a table. With the exception of NCLOB, you can define one or more LOB attributes in an object. LOB bind variables can be declared for applications or persistent stored modules. LOB columns and LOB attributes can be accessed in a SELECT statement. You can insert a new row, or update an existing row that contains one or more LOB columns and/or an object,with one or more LOB attributes. You can set the internal LOB value to NULL or empty. You can replace the entire LOB with data. You can set the BFILE to NULL so that it points to a different file. The product supports updating an LOB row/column intersection or an LOB attribute with another LOB row/column intersection or attribute. You can delete a row containing an LOB column or attribute and thereby also delete the LOB value. For BFILEs, the operating system file is not deleted.

Informix Universal Server Support for LOBs and Related Data Types

Informix categorizes large objects (LOBs) as Simple LOBs and Smart LOBs. Universal Server supports LOBs to handle data that exceed a length of 255 bytes and non-ASCII character data.

Smart LOBs Smart LOBs allow random access to the data and are generally recoverable. Universal Server stores smart large objects in sbspaces. An sbspace is a logical storage area, which contains one or more chunks that only store BLOB and CLOB data. When you access a smart large object column with an SQL statement, the database server does not send the actual BLOB or CLOB data. Instead, it establishes a pointer to these data and returns this pointer. The client application can then use this pointer to perform the open, read, or write operations on the smart large object. The Smart LOB data type in Informix has no maximum size. The LOB column can be up to four terabytes in length. A smart large object allows an application program to randomly access column data. This means you can read or write to any part of a BLOB or CLOB column in any order. For example:

```
CREATE TABLE inmate (
id_num    INT,
picture   BLOB,
felony    CLOB
);
```

This creates a table called `inmate` containing BLOB and CLOB data types.

CLOB The CLOB data type stores a block of text. It is designed to store ASCII text data, including formatted text, such as HTML or PostScript. Although you can store any data in a CLOB object, Informix tools expect a CLOB object to be printable, so they restrict this data type to printable ASCII text. CLOB values are not stored with their rows. They are allocated in whole disk pages, usually areas away from rows. CLOB also supports multibyte characters for GLS functionality

BLOB The BLOB data type in Informix is designed to hold any data that a program can generate—graphic images, satellite images, video clips, audio clips, or formatted documents saved by any word processor or spreadsheet. The database server permits any kind of data of any length in a BLOB column. BLOB data items are stored in whole disk pages in disk areas separate from normal row data. The advantage of the BLOB data type, as opposed to CLOB, is that it accepts any data.

Simple LOBs Simple LOBs refer to columns that are assigned a TEXT or BYTE data type. A simple large object can store and retrieve character data or binary data, but cannot randomly access portions of the column data. In other words, TEXT or BYTE data can be inserted or deleted but cannot be modified. The database server simply stores or retrieves the TEXT or BYTE data in a single SQL statement.

Smart LOBs (BLOBs and CLOBs) have some advantages over Simple LOBs—BYTE and TEXT. An application program can read from or write to any portion of the BLOB or CLOB—(B/C)LOB—object. Access times can be significantly faster, because an application program can access any portion of a (B/C)LOB object. Default characteristics are relatively easy to override. Database administrators can override default characteristics for sbspace at the column level. Application programmers can override some default characteristics for the column when they create a (B/C)LOB object. You can use the equals operator (=) to test whether two (B/C)LOB values are equal. A (B/C)LOB object is recoverable in the event of a system crash and obeys transaction isolation modes (when specified by the DBA or applications programmer). Recovery of (B/C)LOB objects requires buffers that are large enough to handle LOB objects. You can use the (B/C)LOB data type to provide large storage for a user-defined data type. Datablade developers can create indexes on (B/C)LOB data types.

The (B/C)LOB data type also has some disadvantages. The (B/C)LOB data type is allocated in whole disk pages, so a short item wastes space. Restrictions apply as to how you can use a (B/C)LOB column in an SQL statement. It is not available with all Informix database servers. The (B/C)LOB data type cannot be used in arithmetic or Boolean expressions, in a GROUP BY or ORDER BY clause, in a UNIQUE test, or for indexing as part of an Informix B+ tree index. However, Datablade developers can create indexes on CLOB columns.

You can use SQL functions to perform some operations on a LOB column. You can insert data into LOB columns with the dbload or onload utilities, with the LOAD statement (DB-Access), and from BLOB (ifx_lo_t) host variables (INFORMIX-ESQL/C).

Some SQL functions for smart large objects are:

- FILETOBLOB()—Copies a file into a BLOB column.
- FILETOCLOB()—Copies a file into a CLOB column.
- LOCOPY()—Copies BLOB or CLOB data into another BLOB or CLOB column.
- LOTOFILE()—Copies a BLOB or CLOB into a file.

IBM DB2 Universal Database Support for LOBs and Related Data Types

IBM categorizes LOB data types into binary large objects (BLOBs), character large objects (CLOBs), and double-byte character large objects (DBCLOBs). Each of these objects can be up to two gigabytes long. (See Figure 13.2.)

BLOB Strings   A binary large object (BLOB) in IBM's DB2 Universal Database (UDB) is treated as a varying-length string. It is primarily intended to hold nontraditional data, such as pictures, voice, and mixed media. A BLOB holds structured data for exploitation by user-defined types and user-defined functions. BLOB strings are not associated with a character set.

CLOB Strings   A character large object (CLOB) is a varying-length string. A CLOB is used to store large SBCS or mixed SBCS and MBCS character-based data, such as documents written with a single character set. (The CLOB, therefore, has an SBCS or mixed-code page associated with it.) CLOB is a character string.

DBCLOB Strings   A double-byte character large object (DBCLOB) is a varying-length string of double-byte characters. A DBCLOB stores large DBCS character-based data, such as documents written with a single character set. A DBCLOB is a graphic string.

LOB Access and Manipulation

Access to LOBs is via a large object locator (LOB locator). An LOB locator is a host variable with a value that represents a single LOB value in the

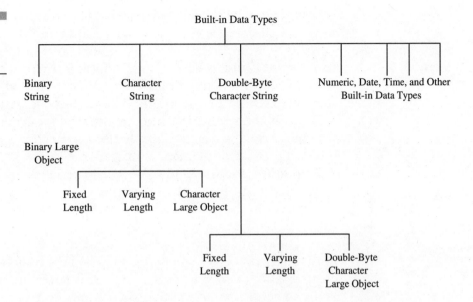

Figure 13.2

IBM DB2 built-in data types.

database server. LOB locators were developed to manipulate very large objects in application programs without having to store the LOB value on a client machine. For example, when selecting a LOB value, an application program could select the entire LOB value and place it into an equally large host variable (which is acceptable if the application program is going to process the entire LOB value at once), or it could select the LOB value into a LOB locator. Then the application program can issue subsequent database operations on the LOB value (such as applying the scalar functions SUBSTR, CONCAT, VALUE, LENGTH; doing an assignment; searching the LOB with LIKE or POSSTR; or applying UDFs against the LOB) by supplying the locator value as input. The resulting output of the locator operation—for example, the amount of data assigned to a client host variable—would then typically be a small subset of the input LOB value.

LOB locators can also represent more than just base values; they can also represent the value associated with a LOB expression. For normal host variables in an application program, when a null value is selected into that host variable, the indicator variable is set to –1, signifying that the value is null. In the case of LOB locators, however, the meaning of indicator variables is slightly different, since a locator host variable itself can never be null. A negative indicator variable value indicates that the LOB value represented by the LOB locator is null. The null information is kept local to the client by virtue of the indicator variable value. The server does not track null values with valid locators.

An LOB locator represents a value, not a row or location in the database. Once a value is selected into a locator, there is no operation that you can perform on the original row or table that will affect the value that is referenced by the locator. The value associated with a locator is valid until the transaction ends or until the locator is explicitly freed, whichever comes first. Locators do not force extra copies of the data in order to provide this function. Instead, the locator mechanism stores a description of the base LOB value. The materialization of the LOB value is deferred until it is actually assigned to some location, either into a user buffer in the form of a host variable or into another record's field value in the database.

A LOB locator is only a mechanism used to refer to a LOB value during a transaction; it does not persist beyond the transaction where it was created. Also, it is not a database type; it is never stored in the database and, as a result, cannot participate in views or check constraints. However, since a locator is a client representation of a LOB type, there are SQL TYPEs for LOB locators so that they can be described in an SQLDA structure used by FETCH, OPEN, and EXECUTE statements.

Restrictions for Using Varying-Length Character Strings and LOBs

Special restrictions apply to an expression resulting in a varying-length string data type, whose maximum length is greater than 254 bytes. The following expressions are not permitted:

- SELECT DISTINCT statement SELECT list
- GROUP BY clause
- ORDER BY clause
- Column function with DISTINCT
- Subselect of a SET operator other than UNION ALL

In addition to the restrictions above, expressions resulting in LONG VARCHAR or CLOB data types are not permitted in the following:

- A Basic, quantified BETWEEN or IN predicate
- A column function
- VARGRAPHIC, TRANSLATE, and date-time scalar functions
- The pattern operand in a LIKE predicate or the search string operand in a POSSTR function
- The string representation of a date-time value

Support for Boolean Data Type

Oracle includes a Boolean data type in its PL/SQL set of data types. The Boolean data type can be used to store the logical values TRUE and FALSE, as well as the nonvalue NULL, which stands for a missing, inapplicable, or unknown value. Only logic operations are allowed on Boolean variables. The Boolean data type takes no parameters. Only the values TRUE and FALSE and the nonvalue NULL can be assigned to a Boolean variable. TRUE and FALSE cannot be inserted into a database column. Also, you cannot select or fetch column values into a Boolean variable.

The Boolean data type stores single-byte, true or false type data. The following chart shows interval and literal representations of the Boolean data type.

Boolean Values	Internal Representation	Literal Representation
TRUE	\0	"T" or "t"
FALSE	\1	"f"
NULL	Internal use only	NULL

You can compare two Boolean values to determine whether they are equal or not. Boolean values can also be compared to the Boolean literals "t" and "f." Boolean values are case-insensitive in Informix; "t" is equivalent to "T" and "f" to "F." Boolean columns can be used to capture the results of an expression.

Summary

The three database products discussed in this chapter support user-defined types as specified in the proposed SQL-3 standard. Oracle does not encapsulate its objects completely, whereas Informix and IBM do. Informix does so in the case of the opaque data type, and IBM does so in distinct types. Encapsulation ensures that the behavior of UDTs is restricted by the functions and operators that can be applied to them. LOB support is also the same, except for the minor differences in terms of the memory size of the elements. Oracle includes Boolean in its PL/SQL set of data types; Informix supports it as a regular data type. There is no support for Boolean data type by IBM.

We anticipate that once the standard is released in 1999, vendors will look at their present implementations and make sure that they adhere to, at the minimum, what is finally represented as CORE SQL. The vendors will also continue to provide value-added extensions to SQL as their business dictates. Each of the vendors has, however, provided some early insight and experience for database application developers as to the power and versatility of the new object-relational version of the SQL database language.

BIBLIOGRAPHY

Abiteboul, S., R. Hull, and V. Vianu. 1995. *Foundations of Databases.* Reading, MA: Addison-Wesley.

Bancilhon, F., C. Delobel, and P. Kanellakis. 1992. *Building an Object-Oriented Database System: The Story of O2.* San Mateo, CA: Morgan Kaufmann.

Barquin, R., and H. Edelstein. 1997. *Building, Using, and Managing the Data Warehouse.* Englewood Cliffs, NJ: Prentice Hall.

Berenson, H., P. Bernstein, J. Gray, J. Melton, E. O'Neil, and P. O'Neil. 1995. "A Critique of ANSI Isolation Levels." *Proceedings of ACM SIGMOD International Conference on Management of Data.*

Bernstein, P. A., V. Hadzilacos, and N. Goodman. 1987. *Concurrency Control and Recovery in Database Systems.* New York: Addison-Wesley.

Bertino, E., and L. Martino. 1993. *Object-Oriented Database Systems: Concepts and Architectures.* Reading, MA: Addison-Wesley.

Blaha, M., and W. Premerlani. 1998. *Object-Oriented Modeling and Design for Database Applications.* Englewood Cliffs, NJ: Prentice Hall.

Bobrowski, S. 1998. *Oracle 8 Architecture.* Berkeley, CA: Osborne/McGraw-Hill.

Bowman, J., S. Emerson, M. Darnovsky. 1996. *The Practical SQL Handbook,* 3d ed. Reading, MA: Addison-Wesley.

Cattell, R. (ed.) 1996. *The Object Database Standard: ODMG-93, Release 1.2.* San Mateo, CA: Morgan Kaufmann.

Celko, J. 1995. *SQL for Smarties.* San Mateo, CA: Morgan Kaufmann.

———. 1995. *Instant SQL Programming.* Chicago, IL: WROX Press.

Chamberlin, D. 1996. *Understanding the New DB2, IBM's Object-relational Database System.* San Mateo, CA: Morgan Kaufmann.

Codd, E. F. 1994. "A Relational Model of Data for Large Shared Data Banks." In *Readings in Database Systems,* 2d ed. San Mateo, CA: Morgan Kaufmann.

———. 1990. *The Relational Model for Database Management,* version 2. Reading, MA: Addison-Wesley.

———. December 1979. "Extending the Database Relational Model to Capture More Meaning." *ACM Transactions on Database Systems.*

Coronel, R. 1997. *Database Systems Design, Implementation, and Management,* 3d ed. Cambridge, MA: International Thompson.

Date, C. 1990, *An Introduction to Database Systems,* 5th ed. Reading, MA: Addison-Wesley.

Date, C., and H. Darwin. 1993. *A Guide to the SQL Standard.* Reading, MA: Addison-Wesley.

Eisenberg, A. February 1995. "A Brief Description of the SQL-3 Data Model." Redwood City, CA: Oracle Corporation.

Elmasri, R., and S. Navathe. 1994. *Fundamentals of Database Systems.* Menlo Park, CA: Benjamin/Cummings.

Feverstein, S., and B. Pribyl. 1997. *Oracle PL/SQL Programming,* 2d ed. Sebastopol, CA: O'Reilly Associates.

Finkelstein, S., N. Mattos, I. Mumick, and H. Pirahesh. March 1996. "Expressing Recursive Queries in SQL." ISO WG3 report X3H2-96-075.

Fortier, P. 1994. "Flexible Real-Time SQL Transactions." In *Proceedings of the Real-Time Systems Symposium* (December 1994).

Fortier, P. (ed.) 1997. *Database Systems Handbook.* New York: McGraw-Hill.

Gallagher, L. 1992. "Object SQL: Language Extentions for Object Data Management." *International Society for Mini and Microcomputers CIKM-92.*

Gray, J., and A. Reuter. 1993. *Transaction Processing: Concepts and Techniques.* San Mateo, CA: Morgan Kaufmann.

Groth, R. 1997. *Hands On SQL.* Englewood Cliffs, NJ: Prentice Hall.

Kim, W. 1994. "UniSQL/X Unified Relational and Object-Oriented Database System." In *Proceedings of the ACM-SIGMOD International Conference on Management of Data, SIGMOD Record,* vol. 23, no. 2 (June).

———. (ed.) 1994. *Modern Database Systems: The Object Model Interoperability and Beyond.* New York: ACM Press.

Koch, G., and K. Loney. 1998. *Oracle8: The Complete Reference.* Berkeley, CA: Osborne/McGraw-Hill.

Kulkarni, K. 1993. "Object-Orientation and the SQL Standard." *Journal of Computer Standards and Interfaces,* vol. 15.

Kulkarni, K., M. Carey, L. DeMichiel, N. Mattos, W. Hong, and M. Ubell. 1995. "Introducing Reference Types and Cleaning Up SQL3's Object Model," ISO WG3 report X3H2-95-456 (November).

Melton, J. (ed.) 1998a. "Call-Level Interface (SQL/CLI)." ISO-ANSI Working Draft, X3H2-98-515, American National Standards Institute, Technical Committee X3H2 Database (September).

———. 1998b. "SQL Global Transactions Interface (SQL/Transaction)." ISO-ANSI Working Draft, X3H2-98-529, American National Standards Institute, Technical Committee X3H2 Database (September).

———. 1998c. "SQL Temporal (SQL/Temporal)." ISO-ANSI Working Draft, X3H2-98-530, American National Standards Institute, Technical Committee X3H2 Database (September).

———. 1998d. "SQL Multimedia (SQL/MM)." ISO-ANSI Working Draft, X3H2-98-535, American National Standards Institute, Technical Committee X3H2 Database (September).

———. 1998e. "Persistent Stored Modules (SQL/PSM)." ISO-ANSI Working Draft, X3H2-98-520, American National Standards Institute, Technical Committee X3H2 Database (September).

———. 1998. "Framework for SQL (SQL/Framework)." ISO-ANSI Working Draft, X3H2-98-518, American National Standards Institute, Technical Committee X3H2 Database (September).

———. 1998. "Database Language SQL—Part 2: Foundation (SQL/Foundation)." ISO-ANSI Working Draft, X3H2-98-519, American National Standards Institute, Technical Committee X3H2 Database (September).

———. 1998. "SQL Host Language Bindings (SQL/Bindings)." ISO-ANSI Working Draft, X3H2-98-521, American National Standards Institute, Technical Committee X3H2 Database (September).

———. 1998. "SQL Object (SQL/MED)." ISO-ANSI Working Draft, X3H2-98-523, American National Standards Institute, Technical Committee X3H2 Database (September).

———. 1998. "SQL Object Language Bindings (SQL/OLB)." ISO-ANSI Working Draft, X3H2-98-522, American National Standards Institute, Technical Committee X3H2 Database (September).

———. 1995. "Accomodating SQL3 and ODMG," X3H2-95-161, American National Standards Institute, Technical Committee X3H2 Database (April 15).

Melton, J., J. Baur, and K. Kulkarni. 1991. "Object ADTs (with Improvements for Value ADTs)." ISO WG3 report X3H2-91-083 (April).

Melton, J., and A. Simon. 1992. *Understanding the New SQL: A Complete Guide.* San Mateo, CA: Morgan Kaufman.

O'Neil. 1995. *Database Principles: Programming and Performance.* San Mateo, CA: Morgan Kaufmann.

Ozsu, T. and P. Valduriez. 1991. *Principles of Distributed Database Systems.* Englewood Cliffs, NJ: Prentice Hall.

Prichard, J. 1995. "Real-Time SQL." Ph.D. Thesis. University of Rhode Island, N. Kingston, RI.

Ramakrishnan, R. 1998. *Database Management Systems.* New York: WCB/McGraw-Hill.

Richey, J. 1995. "Condition Handling in SQL Persistent Stored Modules." *SIGMOD Record,* vol. 24, no. 3 (September).

Sessions, R. 1996. *Object Persistence, Beyond Object-Oriented Databases.* Englewood Cliffs, NJ: Prentice Hall.

Stonebraker, M. (ed.) 1994. *Readings in Database Systems,* 2d ed. San Mateo, CA: Morgan Kaufmann.

Ullman, J., and J. Widom. 1997. *A First Course in Database Systems.* Englewood Cliffs, NJ: Prentice Hall.

Vasta, J. 1985. *Understanding Database Management Systems.* Belmont, CA: Wadsworth.

Widom, J., and S. Ceri. 1996. *Active Database Systems.* San Mateo, CA: Morgan Kaufmann.

Zdonik, S. and D. Maier (eds.) 1990. *Readings in Object-Oriented Database Systems.* San Mateo, CA: Morgan Kaufman.

Online Books

Oracle: *http://technet.oracle.com*

Oracle8 Concepts, Release 8.0

Oracle8 Reference, Release 8.0

Oracle8 SQL Reference, Release 8.0

PL/SQL User's Guide and Reference, Release 8.0

Informix: *http://www.informix.com/answers/oldsite/answers/english/ius91ux.htm*

Informix Guide to SQL: Reference, Version 9.1

Informix Guide to SQL: Syntax, Version 9.1

Informix Guide to SQL: Tutorial, Version 9.1

Extending Informix-Universal Server: Data Types, Version 9.1

IBM: *http://www.software.ibm.com/cgi-bin/db2www/library/*

SQL Getting Started

SQL Reference

Road Map to DB2 Programming

INDEX

ABOUT THE AUTHOR

Paul Fortier is an Associate Professor of Electrical and Computer Engineering at the University of Massachusetts, Dartmouth. He received his D.Sc. in Computer Science from the University of Massachusetts, Lowell in 1993. His research over the last 12 years has focused on the systems and software architecture of very large, distributed, real-time command and control systems. The focus of much of this research is very large, real-time database systems, real-time transaction specification and operations, temporal databases, database language specification, and systems architectural specification.

Dr. Fortier has made important contributions in the areas of real-time and object-relational database language specification as a chairman of government database specification committees and a voting member on the ISO and ANSI database language committees. He has published several books on database systems and database language interfaces and holds a variety of patents dealing with real-time and database systems. He is a member of numerous professional associations and committees. In addition, Dr. Fortier has served on the program committee for the Fifth International Conference on Data and Knowledge Systems for Manufacturing and Engineering (DKSME 96), was the local arrangements chair for the 1997 Real-time Systems Symposium (RTSS 97), and served on the program committee for the NSF Distributed Information, Computation, and Process Management for Scientific and Engineering Environments (DICPM) Workshop in May, 1998.